Introduction to Early Childhood Education

Carteret Community College

Ann Miles Gordon | Kathryn Williams Browne, MA, BA

CENGAGE
Learning·

Australia • Brazil • Japan • Korea • Mexico • Singapore • Spain • United Kingdom • United States

CENGAGE
Learning·

**Introduction to Early Childhood Education:
Carteret Community College**

**Ann Miles Gordon
Kathryn Williams Browne, MA, BA**

Senior Manager, Student Engagement:

Linda deStefano

Janey Moeller

Manager, Student Engagement:

Julie Dierig

Marketing Manager:

Rachael Kloos

Manager, Production Editorial:

Kim Fry

Manager, Intellectual Property Project Manager:

Brian Methe

Senior Manager, Production and Manufacturing:

Donna M. Brown

Manager, Production:

Terri Daley

Beginnings & Beyond: Foundations in Early Childhood Education,
9th Edition
Ann Miles Gordon | Kathryn Williams Browne, MA, BA

> For product information and technology assistance, contact us at
> **Cengage Learning Customer & Sales Support, 1-800-354-9706**
>
> For permission to use material from this text or product,
> submit all requests online at **cengage.com/permissions**
> Further permissions questions can be emailed to
> **permissionrequest@cengage.com**

This book contains select works from existing Cengage Learning resources and
was produced by Cengage Learning Custom Solutions for collegiate use. As such,
those adopting and/or contributing to this work are responsible for editorial
content accuracy, continuity and completeness.

Compilation © 2014 Cengage Learning

ISBN-13: 978-1-305-02445-8
ISBN-10: 1-305-02445-1

WCN: 01-100-101

Cengage Learning

5191 Natorp Boulevard
Mason, Ohio 45040
USA

Cengage Learning is a leading provider of customized learning solutions with
office locations around the globe, including Singapore, the United Kingdom,
Australia, Mexico, Brazil, and Japan. Locate your local office at:
international.cengage.com/region.

Cengage Learning products are represented in Canada by Nelson Education, Ltd.
For your lifelong learning solutions, visit **www.cengage.com/custom.**
Visit our corporate website at **www.cengage.com.**

Printed in the United States of America

Brief Contents

Dedication

To the women who share this regenerative stage
of life with me, with grateful thanks for their abundant
spirits and generous hearts: Puddin Nix, Sally Zimmerman,
and Jan Moore.
— AMG

To the students and colleagues of Skyline
College—a most inspiring mix of professionals
and fellow learners on the path of higher education.
And to Julia and Campbell, once again: my inspiration
as children and now as wonderful adults.
— KWB

Beginnings and Beyond

Foundations in Early Childhood Education

© Cengage Learning

1

Teaching: A Professional Commitment

Learning Objectives

LO1 Understand the roles and responsibilities of today's early childhood teachers with regard to diversity and personal attributes.

LO2 Define the essential attributes of becoming a professional teacher, including professional preparation standards and upholding ethical standards of behavior.

LO3 Demonstrate collaboration skills for team teaching interactions and proficiency in positive team relationships.

LO4 Understand how assessments relate to best teaching practices and professional development.

LO5 Demonstrate knowledge of the importance of field experience and articulate the value of supervised teaching.

naeyc Standards For Professional Development

The following NAEYC Standards for Initial and Advanced Early Childhood Professional Preparation are addressed in this chapter:

Standard 1 Promoting Child Development and Learning

Standard 2 Building Family and Community Relationships

Standard 3 Observing, Documenting, and Assessing to Support Young Children and Families

Standard 4 Using Developmentally Effective Approaches to Connect With Children and Families

Standard 5 Using Content Knowledge to Build Meaningful Curriculum

Standard 6 Becoming a Professional

Field Experience

naeyc Code of Ethical Conduct

These are the sections of the NAEYC Code of Ethical Conduct that apply to the topics of this chapter:

A. Responsibility to coworkers

Ideals:

I-3A.1　To establish and maintain relationships of respect, trust, confidentiality, collaboration, and cooperation with coworkers.

I-3A.2　To share resources with coworkers, collaborating to ensure that the best possible early childhood care and education program is provided.

I-3A.3　To support coworkers in meeting their professional needs and in their professional development.

I-3A.4　To accord coworkers due recognition of professional achievements.

B. Responsibilities to employers

Ideals:

I-3B.1　To assist the program in providing the highest quality of service.

I-3B.2　To do nothing that diminishes the reputation of the program in which we work, unless it is violating laws and regulations designed to protect children or is violating the provisions of this Code.

Principles:

P-3B.1 We shall follow all program policies. When we do not agree with program policies, we shall attempt to effect change through constructive action within the organization.

P-3B.2: We shall speak or act on behalf of an organization only when authorized. We shall take care to acknowledge when we are speaking for the organization and when we are expressing a personal judgment.

P-3B. 4: If we have concerns about a colleague's behavior, and children's well-being is not at risk, we may address the concern with that individual. If children are at risk or the situation does not improve after it has been brought to the colleague's attention, we shall report the colleague's unethical or incompetent behavior to an appropriate authority.

Today's Early Childhood Teachers

Margarita always wanted to be an early childhood teacher, and after high school she went to a community college and earned her Associate in Arts (A.A.) degree. Shortly after her first child was born, she became a licensed family child care provider, and she now cares for infants and toddlers in her own home. It is important to Margarita that she feels she is making a contribution to the family's well-being, as well as enjoying a satisfying career. She hopes to pursue a bachelor's degree in the future.

Paul has a bachelor's degree in special education and spent several years teaching in a school for children with severe developmental delays. He is now a lead teacher for 4-year-olds at the child care center, where he is gaining experience with children whose developmental patterns are typical. Paul wants to remain a teacher but is concerned about the salary levels. He has given himself one more year before he makes a decision to stay or leave the field.

Ginger, a former kindergarten teacher, participated in a parent cooperative nursery school with her three children. She is now the director of a parent co-op where children range from ages 2 to 5. She particularly enjoys leading weekly parent discussion groups.

Elva was the most sought-after parent aide in the city's preschool program. This success stimulated her to get an A.A. degree in early childhood education, then a bachelor's degree in child development. She is now a certified second grade teacher in a bilingual program and is working on her Master's degree.

These teachers had different motivations, yet they all were drawn to the early childhood classroom. They teach in different settings and have different interests. What they share is a commitment to teaching young children and knowing that the work they do is important.

Meeting together helps teachers maintain quality in their programs and reinforces their professional roles and responsibilities.

Comparison with Teaching in Other Educational Settings

The nature of teaching in the early years is unlike that of other age groups. At first glance, the differences in teaching preschool and older children may outweigh any similarities. Common elements, however, link the two:

- Early childhood teachers teach what other teachers teach. The curriculum in the early years is rich in math, science, social studies, history, language, art, and geography, as it is in any other grade.
- Early childhood teachers and their elementary and high school counterparts share many of the frustrations of the teaching profession—long hours, low pay, and a people-intensive workplace.
- They also share the joy of teaching—the opportunity to influence children's lives and the satisfaction of meeting the daily challenges that teaching children provides.

Figure 5-1 highlights the similarities and differences between early childhood teachers and others.

 **DIVERSITY**

Teacher Diversity

According to the U.S. Bureau of Labor Statistics (2010), the following percentages represent the racial and ethnic diversity among early childhood teachers.

Teaching Level	White	Black	Asian	Hispanic/Latino
Child Care Worker	78.3	16.0	3.4	19.1
Preschool and Kindergarten	82.7	13.4	2.7	9.6
Elementary and Middle School	86.7	9.3	2.4	7.3
Special Education Teachers	89.4	6.8	2.0	6.2
Teacher Assistants	81.5	12.7	2.9	15.1
Racial Diversity of Children in the United States (ChildStats, 2011)	54.0	14.0	4.0	23.0

On the surface it appears that most ethnic groups are equitably represented between the teaching and student populations. The one obvious exception is among the Hispanic/Latino teachers and children, particularly in preschools, kindergarten, elementary and middle schools, special education, and teaching assistants. A less obvious exception is among the Asian teaching population. The percentage of Asians teachers is in close alignment with the racial diversity of Asian children, however, a longitudinal study in three California communities from 1994 to 2000 (Whitebrook, et al., 2001) noted that while 50 percent of the classrooms in the study had Chinese-speaking children, only 7 percent had a staff member who spoke Cantonese or Mandarin. Forty-four percent of the classrooms had Spanish-speaking children, yet only half were staffed by Spanish-speaking teachers or caregivers. Parents in these programs reported difficulty in communicating with the staff because of language barriers. This raises the question of how the early childhood field is upholding the Code of Ethical Conduct in their approach to diversity in hiring practices and employment opportunities. The ability of the teaching staff to communicate with the full spectrum of ethnic, cultural, and linguistic backgrounds is a serious issue for today's teachers.

The Early Childhood Teacher's Roles: Professionalism in Action

The variety of roles early childhood teachers perform has been described in many ways:

Storyteller	Traffic director	Conflict mediator
Custodian	File clerk	Mediator
Carpenter	Poet	Plumber
Adult educator	Parent	Musician
Purchasing agent	Resource	Faculty member
Staff supervisor	Nurse	Program planner
Personnel	Business manager	Treasurer
Director	Employee	Employer
Psychologist	Sociologist	Scientist

This diversity is what makes teaching in the early years so appealing. The multiple roles a teacher plays add challenge to the job and underscore the importance of teachers who are well grounded in developmental and learning theory. Knowledge and experience enhances the teacher's ability to think on their feet as they collaborate and interact with children during the intense activity of the classroom. Collaboration reinforces the notion underlying many definitions that teachers are, first and foremost, lifelong learners. The teacher as collaborator is a significant part of the definition of the teacher's role in the schools of Reggio Emilia, Italy (see Chapter 10).

Let's look at the larger role of the early childhood teacher in and out of the classroom.

Interacting with Children

Teacher–child interactions, the spur-of-the-moment crises, the on-the-spot decisions, the caring and nurturing bring both satisfaction and challenges. Helping Rhonda separate from her grandmother, soothing Josh and Benno after they bump heads, and talking with Alexa about her science project are examples of what is at the heart of teaching young children. These encounters help to establish good relationships with the children. It is during these spontaneous, anything-can-happen-and-probably-will times that teachers display their craftsmanship and professionalism.

Early Childhood Teachers: Differences and Similarities

Elements of Teaching and Learning	Early Childhood Settings	Elementary and High School Settings
How teaching and learning occur	Through teacher–child interactions and concrete use of materials	Through lectures and demonstrations that are often teacher dominated
	Guides children toward discovery	Teaches subject matter
Play opportunities	Primary learning medium is play	Usually just at recess
Opportunity for child to make choices	Many choices throughout the day both inside and outside	Few options—all students do same activity most of the day
Classroom environment	Abundant floor space, many activity centers, variety of materials for play	Rows of desks and tables
Daily schedule	Large blocks of time for unlimited exploration of materials and for play	45-minute to 1-hour periods on subject matter
Small group interactions	Majority of teaching	Much less frequent
Large group interactions	Few times a day	Majority of teaching
Outdoor activity	Teachers involved as intensively as they are in the classroom	Others usually supervise play yard—little direct teacher interaction
Parent relationships	Frequent, if not daily, contact	May see them once a year as child grows older
Working with other adults	Often works with aide, assistant teachers, and parents	Usually teaches alone or with part-time aide
Educational materials	Toys, games, natural materials, blocks	Textbooks and worksheets
Evaluating students	Observational and anecdotal assessments, portfolios	Grades, tests, and report cards
	Emphasis on growth of whole child	Standardized academic assessment
Age range of students	May have two- to two-and-a-half-year age span or greater	Usually same age
Art, music, and physical education	Available throughout the day as an ongoing part of curriculum	Restricted to a special class, time, or teacher
Teacher training	Strong child development foundation	Emphasis on subject matter

FIGURE 1-1 The nature of teaching in the early years is unlike that of other age groups.

The art of teaching comes alive on the floor of the classroom. Teachers intuitively use their knowledge base, experience, and proven techniques as they reach back in their minds for all those things they know about children. Throughout the school day they apply that combination of knowledge and know-how. Good classroom management is dependent on how teachers spend their time away from the children and give added depth and strength to the program after children leave.

Managing the Classroom

Being a classroom manager is a little like being a juggler. Both require the ability to think about and react to more than three things at once. With a simple gesture, a significant look, or merely moving nearby, the teacher maintains the ongoing activity.

Anticipating a clash between Nathan and Julie, the teacher, Miriam, intervenes, redirects them, and moves away. At the same time, she has kept a watchful eye on Bobby at the bathroom sink. Passing close to Francie, she touches the child's shoulder in brief acknowledgment, smiling down as Francie struggles with her story writing. Miguel and Lea run up to her, grab her by the skirt and hand, and pull her toward the science display. They need to ask her something about the snake . . . now! Jake, the handyman, has come into the classroom wanting to know exactly which of the climbers needs repair. Sarah, the parent volunteer, waves to Miriam: It's time to check on the corn bread baking in the kitchen. Miriam files a mental note of the names of the children who accompany Sarah to the kitchen. As she reaches for a copy of *Ranger Rick* (the book with the great snake pictures in it), she

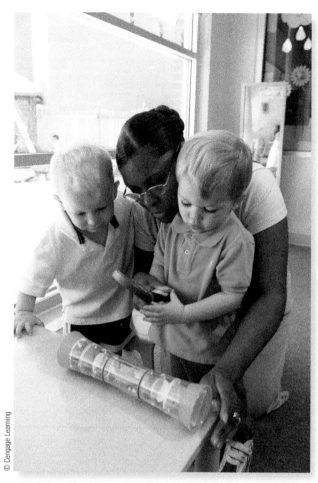

© Cengage Learning

Teachers model learning, listening, and loving.

observes Angie and her father entering the room. They both look upset. Telling Miguel and Lea she will return, Miriam walks over to greet the latecomers. As she moves past Doug, the student teacher, she comments on how well his language game is going and suggests he continue for another five minutes. Glancing at the clock, she realizes it is almost cleanup time. Assistant teacher Cheryl watches Miriam and a nonverbal signal passes between them. Without a word, they both understand that snacks will be a little late today. Angie's father begins to explain their delay as Miriam bends down to invite the child to come and look at the new snake cage with her.

In this setting, the teacher's role is to supervise a number of people, all of whom add to the richness of a program. But it is Miriam who coordinates and supervises their various functions. Her role as a supervisor and manager includes:

- Caretaker for a safe environment
- Observer of and listener to children
- On-the-spot teacher trainer for students, aides, and volunteers
- On-site supervisor for student teachers
- Liaison and communicator with parents

Setting the Tone

From the moment the teacher steps into the classroom, she sets the emotional framework. The use of body language, tone of voice, facial expressions, and verbal and nonverbal communication set the tone for teaching and learning.

Children are sensitive to adult moods and attitudes. When you exude calm and confidence, strength and support, the result is a more relaxed, comfortable atmosphere. When the mood is tense, the tone of the classroom is as well. When you believe that children deserve respect and are intelligent, capable human beings, the learning atmosphere is lively and supportive.

Tantrums, crying, resistance, curiosity, impatience, emotional swings, noise, and self-centeredness are typical behaviors in the early years as children strive to achieve a sense of their separate self. The atmosphere that a teacher creates in the classroom is a key element in helping them through that process.

Planning and Evaluating Curriculum

As teachers move through the school day interacting with children, managing the classroom, and sensing the tone, they consciously or unconsciously evaluate what is happening:

- The relay race outdoors produced more tears than cheers; most of the children were interested in participating when the game started but drifted away. Why?
- The clay was not used today. How can we make this a more inviting activity?
- The toddlers are beginning to participate fully in the "Eensy Weensy Spider" finger play. What might they like to learn next?
- Several children have asked about Sasha's accent. When would be a good time to have him teach the class a few words in Russian?

The teacher notes where and how children played, the quality of their interactions, and possible "next steps" in curriculum. These observations are discussed with other staff members at the end of the day or in weekly planning sessions. This process has its roots in constructivist theory: teachers watching and observing children to give meaning and support to their learning. Early childhood teachers use their observation skills, collect data as they work with children, and build emergent curriculum around their knowledge of actual classroom practice and behavior. Effective ways to develop curriculum planning are further discussed in Chapter 10.

Staying the Course/Shaping Young Minds

Developmentally appropriate practices (DAP) are the basis for high quality early education programs. We know that children are active learners who enjoy hands-on experiences and who learn best in environments that provide opportunities, choices, and challenges for growth. We base our teaching on sound child developmental theory and principles. We recognize that play is fundamental to children's learning. But are our basic tenets compatible with brain research findings?

Several researchers have linked some of the defining elements of DAP with neuroscience in a way that demonstrates the compatibility of what we believe to be best practices and what brain research tells us about how learning takes place. What follows is NAEYC's position statements on DAP and brain research principles (Rushton et al., 2010), with our added applications for classroom use.

1. DAP: Development in one domain influences and is influenced by development in other domains.

   Brain-Based Research: Each region of the brain consists of a highly sophisticated neurological network that interconnects one portion of the brain to another.

   Classroom Applications: Use integrated curriculum to allow for individual differences; make use of the five senses and Gardner's multiple intelligences as much as possible.

2. DAP: Development proceeds at varying rates in each child as well as unevenly within different areas of each child's functioning.

   Brain-Based Research: Each brain is unique; learning new skills and knowledge changes the brain's structure; a spread in differences up to 2 or 3 years is normal in a developing brain.

   Classroom Applications: Give children choices that meet their developmental needs; make time for discussion, movement, and active learning; encourage mixed-age groups or looping.

3. DAP: Optimal periods exist for certain types of development and learning.

   Brain-Based Research: "Windows of opportunity" exist in the brain and the brain's plasticity allows for greater information to be processed and stored.

   Classroom Applications: Repeated experiences in various activity centers help develop problem-solving skills and long-term memory: large blocks of time give children time to absorb both new and familiar information; class and group discussions allow children to interact with each other on a regular basis.

4. DAP: Children are active learners, drawing on direct physical and social experience as well as culturally transmitted knowledge to construct their understanding of the world.

   Brain-Based Research: Learning does not take place as separate and isolated events in the brain.

   Classroom Applications: Learning environments must include opportunities for children to interact with diverse people of all ages and cultures; field trips, guest speakers, and multicultural curriculum help children better understand society and themselves.

Questions

1. What other elements of DAP reflect what you know about brain research?
2. How important do you think brain-based research is? Why?
3. How does this information linking DAP with brain research help you respond to those who promote a more academic structure to young children's learning?

Record Keeping

The type and variety of records vary from program to program. Report writing and record keeping are essential to any good early childhood program. Record keeping is based on a number of factors:

- *The purpose for which the records are used.* In programs that rely on government funding, record keeping is not optional. Children's progress, teacher's performance, and the program itself must be evaluated on a regular basis to ensure continued funding.
- *The philosophy of the school.* In many programs, but especially in laboratory schools and teacher-training centers, teachers write periodical progress reports on the children to guide them in planning and to share with families.
- *As part of a teacher-training process.* Documentation is necessary in some early childhood training programs. Child Development Associates (CDA) candidates submit a written portfolio of their experiences in the classroom as supporting evidence of their competency as teachers of young children.
- *As part of an accreditation process.* NAEYC's accreditation procedures require documentation of the school's operation, ranging from governance and management issues to teacher effectiveness, space usage, parent involvement, school philosophy, and curriculum.

As a commitment to quality and developmentally appropriate practices. A brief note taken on the run, a thoughtful anecdote written after class, or a checklist of the child's playmates for one day give teachers information and insights for a greater understanding of the children's needs and development.

As a means of family information and education. Recorded observations, notes, and similar data may show that Abraham is not participating in any strenuous physical activity and avoids activities that involve balancing and climbing. This information, when shared with parents, could lead to a medical evaluation and diagnosis of possible perceptual problems.

As a means of developing curriculum. Emergent curriculum plans and learning activities sprout from such reports and records. It was not until such data were collected for entry into first grade that the kindergarten teacher realized most of the children in the class were not sufficiently proficient with scissors. A project approach remedied the need and the class learned a necessary skill.

Attending Meetings

Teachers need to communicate with the other people who are involved in the lives of the children as well as attend professional meetings. Figure 1-2 lists the most common types of meetings.

Organizing and Collecting Materials

Some of a teacher's after-hours activities fortify and vitalize the classroom by adding additional materials such as photos for the bulletin board, replenishing curriculum materials, new books from the library, and researching a field trip to the organic farm. In some programs teachers serve on committees and assist with ordering supplies and materials. All of these responsibilities fall to the family child care provider.

Making Contacts

Teachers may call or e-mail families to check on children who are sick or absent, return calls from parents and colleagues, or update a parent about a child's progress. For children with special needs, teachers may need to contact doctors, therapists, and other specialists. The popularity of e-mail has made some communications with families much faster and easier.

Working with Families

Working with families may include working on multicultural events and curriculum or organizing class fairs or school fund-raising events. These duties are a part of the job of teaching young children, but many will be shared with staff. Though time-consuming, these responsibilities add to the creativity and care that teachers express for the children and their families. Chapter 8 discusses the teacher–family relationship in depth.

Common Types of Meetings

Staff Meetings

Held usually once a week for individual teaching teams. Purpose is to plan curriculum, set goals, and discuss children's progress. Faculty meetings for all school personnel may be held less frequently.

Parent–Teacher Conferences

May be offered on a scheduled basis or they may be called by either parents or teachers as needed. Each school defines its own policy as to the number and frequency of parent contacts.

Parent Education Meetings

Many schools offer evening programs for parents. Teacher attendance may or may not be required.

Professional Meetings

Attendance at workshops, seminars, in-service training. Local, state, and national conferences are sponsored by the National Association for the Education of Young Children, Association for Childhood Education International, and Child Care Coordinating Council.

Student–Teacher Conferences

In schools used as training sites, teachers arrange time with individual students assigned to their classes.

Home Visits[1]

May or may not be optional. Some schools schedule them before opening day. Otherwise teachers must arrange them on their own time.

[1] Many parents welcome teacher's visits. Others may fear criticism or judgement about their home environment or family practices.

FIGURE 1-2 Teachers attend many different types of meetings, which help them create better programs, learn more about children, and learn how to become better teachers.

Sharing insights with colleagues helps the early childhood professional become more self-aware.

Personal Attributes of Early Childhood Educators

All good teachers have dedication, compassion, insight, a sense of humor, flexibility, patience, energy, and self-confidence. Other hallmarks of a true professional are physical and mental well-being, a sense of ethical responsibility, and reliability. Well-rounded teachers also know that their interest in the world at large transmits itself to children. The following are some other essential characteristics.

Self-Awareness

How do I make a difference in the lives of the children I teach? Asking that, you have taken the first step toward self-awareness. Reflective and critical thinking about your teaching experiences gives you insights that foster your growth and learning. Implicit in the NAEYC's standards (see Figure 1-2) is that early childhood professionals are lifelong learners, pursuing the skills and knowledge they need through coursework, professional development, degree programs, training, and licensing. You have a greater appreciation of learning when you have a sense of it in your own life. You affect children's lives when you know the answers to these questions:

Do I see myself as a learner? Where does my learning take place? How?
Do I learn from other adults?

Do I learn from children?
What happens to me when something is difficult or when I make a mistake?

Opening yourself up to the possibility of learning from students stretches your capacity to grow into relationships with children based on mutual respect and trust. This is especially important when teachers do not share the same cultural background or have no experience with a particular disability. Opening yourself to learning from other teachers creates a foundation for mutual support, collegiality, professional development, and deepening of friendships.

Self-knowledge—examining values and personal qualities—takes courage and a willingness to take risks. Accepting oneself is where to begin in accepting children.

Attitudes and Biases

Values and attitudes weave their way into every relationship and reflect the ethical framework by which we live and teach. This can be both positive and negative. Personal beliefs concerning race, culture, gender, abilities, and economic status may negatively affect our teaching in ways we are not aware. Facing prejudices about children and families based on long-held beliefs may be one of the most difficult things for a teacher to do. Most teachers will not have lived through the significant expe-

In addition to working with children, teachers support parents when they keep in touch. A brief, friendly phone call can make a family feel included in their child's education process.

rience of adapting to a new culture, learning a new language, surviving on food stamps, or living in a wheelchair. They may be uncomfortable with people who have faced these challenges.

Personal histories are filled with biases. We have opinions of what is "good" or "naughty" behavior, about children who are messy, who have odors, whose clothes are too big or too small, who eat strange food, who don't do what girls or boys are supposed to do. Some of these biases can be resolved, but only if a teacher takes the time to examine personal beliefs and biases.

The anti-bias approach to teaching young children (Derman-Sparks & Edwards, 2010) is an important teaching method. Widespread racial and ethnic prejudice is still prevalent in this country and causes concern about the harm they do to children's self-identity and self-esteem.

The anti-bias movement promotes the concept that all children are worthy of our respect and challenges teachers to examine beliefs, attitudes, and actions that might deny any child that unconditional respect. (See sections in Chapters 9, 11, and 15 for further discussion.)

The anti-bias approach affords teachers an opportunity to confront their own anxieties and biases through questions that promotes greater self-awareness:

- Am I aware of my identity and its influences on my beliefs and behaviors?
- Do I have ethical beliefs that I follow? Is there a system of ethical behaviors related to working with children and families that I could learn?
- Do I foster respect for the value of those who are different from me? How?
- Do I examine my biases and look at ways I can change my own attitudes? When? How?
- Do I show preference for children who most closely fit my own ethnic, cultural, and religious background? When? How?
- Do I somehow pass along my biases to the children I teach? When? How? With whom?
- Do I truly enjoy differences in human beings? When? With whom?

As you reflect on your answers and gain more insights into your teaching, you are enhancing children's culture and family by learning to understand your own.

Teacher Burnout

Teacher burnout results when teachers are faced with a demanding workload, uncertain or inadequate rewards, and other pressures that prevent work effectiveness. Low morale, stress, and disillusionment occur too often in a profession in which staff quality is the most important single factor in program quality. At its most extreme, teacher burnout can drive a good professional out of the field altogether, a common situation in early childhood settings and one that creates *one of the highest occupational turnover rates in the nation.* Between 25 percent to

Teachers' values and attitudes are reflected in the way they work with children.

40 percent of child care workers leave the field each year (National Association for Child Care Resources & Referral, 2011).

Bloom (2005) cites 10 characteristics that produce a healthy and positive school climate that, in turn, promote high morale among the teaching staff:

- Friendly, supportive, and trusting staff relationships
- Emphasis on personal and professional growth
- Leadership with clear expectations who encourage and support staff
- Clearly defined roles and policies
- Fairness and equity regarding promotions, raises, and other rewards
- Staff involvement in decision-making
- Agreement among staff on philosophy, goals, and objectives
- Emphasis on efficiency and good planning
- A physical environment that promotes responsible teaching and learning
- The ability to adapt to change and solve problems

Directors and staff must take the responsibility to work together to create the kind of climate that enhances success and satisfaction in the workplace. These issues are further explored in Chapter 15.

Becoming a Professional: What You Need to Know

Becoming a professional teacher takes time and the integration of knowledge, training, and experience. The strengths and convictions one has as a person blend with those values one holds for working with children and their families. Professional standards and well-defined teaching attributes form the basis for the beginnings of professionalism.

Professional Standards for Teacher Preparation

NAEYC has developed standards for the field of early childhood education to ensure that teachers receive the best possible professional preparation available. Highly trained teachers define the quality in early education and the programs, not the curriculum, assessments, or environmental setting that have the greatest effect on children's learning and development. These standards for professional preparation identify common expectations of what today's teachers should know and do as they pursue education, specialized training, and ongoing professional development. The standards parallel the professional values found in the Code of Ethical Conduct, including the diversity of age ranges and programs in the early childhood field and emphasizing a multidiscipline approach to educating teachers. On the inside covers of this text is a handy chart that shows where to find the standards in each chapter. Figure 1-3 outlines the aspects of NAEYC's professional standards.

Essential Attributes of a Professional Teacher

There are essential attributes that shape the professional formation of a teacher. Each characteristic is echoed in the Standards for Professional Preparation and the Code of Ethical Conduct.

1. Possess the knowledge and skills
2. Abide by a code of ethics
3. Participate in continuing education; professional development and professional affiliations
4. Have knowledge of career options
5. Engage in reflective teaching
6. Become culturally competent
7. Advocate for children and their families
8. Practice intentional teaching

Possess the Knowledge and Skills

There is a body of knowledge and educational foundation that is assumed of anyone entering the early childhood profession, as noted in Figure 1-3: the NAEYC's Standards. Some basic teaching skills are also necessary. These include methods and techniques appropriate for teaching the very young child, your ability to relate to other adults, the quality of your interactions with children, and skills in program planning.

The NAEYC Standards for Early Childhood Professional Preparation outline other key elements that begin with having a common background with others that comes from studying child development and human behavior, family relations, parent education and development, and curriculum planning.

Teaching experience under the guidance of a master teacher is expected, as is familiarity with observation and recording techniques. Standard 3 provide the framework for professional development as teachers acquire further skills on the job, and Standard 5 encourages lifelong learning that advances teaching practices.

Becoming a professional teacher involves progressing along a continuum of development. The state you

NAEYC's Standards for Initial and Advanced Early Childhood Professional Preparation

What Today's Teachers Should Know and Do

1. Promote Child Development and Learning.
   - Know and understand young children's characteristics and needs
   - Know and understand the multiple influences on development and learning
   - Use developmental knowledge to create healthy, respectful, supportive, and challenging learning environments
2. Build Family and Community Relationships.
   - Know and understand diverse family and community characteristics
   - Support and engage families and community through respectful, reciprocal relationships
   - Involve families and communities in their children's development and learning
3. Observe, Document, and Assess to Support Young Children and Families
   - Understand the goals, benefits, and uses of assessment
   - Know about and use observation, documentation, and other appropriate assessment tools and approaches
   - Understand and practice responsible assessment to promote positive outcomes for each child
   - Know about assessment partnerships with families and professional colleagues
4. Use Developmentally Effective Approaches to Connect with Children and Families
   - Understand positive relationships and supportive interactions as the foundations of working with children
   - Know and understand effective strategies and tools for early education
   - Use a broad repertoire of developmentally appropriate teaching/learning
   - Reflect on your own practice to promote positive outcomes for each child
5. Use Content Knowledge to Build Meaningful Curriculum
   - Understand content knowledge and resources in academic disciplines
   - Know and use the central concepts, inquiry tools, and structures of content areas or academic disciplines
   - Use your own knowledge, appropriate early learning standards, and other resources to design, implement, and evaluate meaningful, challenging curricula for each child
6. Becoming a Professional
   - Identify and involve oneself with the early childhood field
   - Know about and uphold ethical standards and other professional standards
   - Engage in continuous, collaborative learning to inform practice
   - Integrate knowledgeable, reflective, and critical perspectives of early education
   - Engage in informed advocacy for children and the profession

FIGURE 1-3 What today's teachers should know and do. (The Standards and Key Elements are from NAEYC, "NAEYC Standards for Early Childhood Professional Preparation." Position Statement. Washington, DC: NAEYC. Reprinted with permission from the National Association for the Education of Young Children [NAEYC]. Copyright © 2009 by NAEYC. Full text of all NAEYC position statements is available at www.naeyc.org/positionstatements. These correlations are suggested by the authors.)

live in may or may not have regulations for early childhood teachers; some states offer a specialized certification for those in the early childhood field. Professional expectations mandated by the states provide some degree of professionalization of early childhood teachers.

Figure 1-4 is an example of the California statewide certification program. This *career matrix* has a number of levels, each with alternative qualifications for meeting the requirements. Within each level, there are a variety of teaching roles. Each state defines its own certification standards. Information is available through the state's department of education.

Look back to the teachers you met at the beginning of the chapter. Margarita is making plans to move from being a licensed home caregiver to pursuing a bachelor's degree. Match her plans with Figure 1-3 to see what other options she will have.

Experience and education work together to refine the skills and knowledge of the early childhood professional as shown in Figure 1-4. In addition, Figure 1-5 has some useful descriptions of the various roles teachers have in early childhood programs. This chart also shows how the progression from teacher aide to master teacher is matched to increasing responsibilities and education.

A Career Lattice: Child Development Permit Matrix

Level	Education Requirement	Experience Requirement
Assistant	6 units of ECE or CD	None
Associate teacher	12 units ECE/CD, including core courses	50 days of 3+ hours/day within 2 years
Teacher	24 units ECE/CD, including core courses + 16 general education (GE) units	175 days of 3+ hours/day within 4 years
Master teacher	24 units ECE/CD, including 16 GE units + 6 specialization units + 2 units adult supervision	350 days of 3+ hours/day within 4 years
Site supervisor	A.A. (or 60 units) with 24 ECE/CD units, including core + 6 units administration + 2 units adult supervision	350 days of 4+ hours/day including at least 100 days of supervising adults
Program director	B.A. with 24 ECE/CD units, including core + 6 units administration + 2 units adult supervision	Site supervisor status and one program year of site supervisor experience

© Cengage Learning 2011

FIGURE 1-4 A combination of education and experience work together to form a career ladder for early childhood professionals in California who want a child development permit.

General Role Definitions for the Early Childhood Teacher

Title	Description	Minimum Qualifications
Apprentice/ Teacher Aide	Is responsible to teacher for implementing program	Entry level, no previous formal training but enrolled in early childhood education classes
Assistant or Associate Teacher	Is part of the teaching team under the direction of teacher; may implement curriculum, supervise children, and communicate with parents.	Child Development Associate (CDA) credential
Teacher	Is coleader who plans and implements curriculum, works with parents, and evaluates children's progress	Associate's degree in early childhood education or related field
Lead Teacher	Creates a model classroom, applies good early childhood education practices, supervises other team members, develops new curriculum, provides leadership to team	Bachelor's degree in early childhood education or related field; supervised teaching experience; additional coursework work in family life, assessment, supervision, etc.

FIGURE 1-5 There are many ways to reach the top of a career ladder. Each role has its own job description that varies with the type of early childhood education setting. The qualifications are based on individual programs and their needs. (Adapted from *Blueprint for Action: Achieving Center-Based Change through Staff Development*, by P. J. Bloom, © 2005 New Horizons.)

Abide by a Code of Ethical Conduct

Every day, situations arise with parents, children, other teachers, and administrators that cause genuine conflict about behavior. Some cases are clearly ethical dilemmas: suspected child abuse by a parent or teacher, talking about children and their families outside of school, or the firing of a staff member without due cause. Others may not seem as obvious. Some examples are:

When parents:

- Ask you to advance their child into the next class against your advice.

- Want you to use discipline practices common to their family and culture but at odds with your own sense of what children need.
- Attempt to gossip with you about another child, staff member, or family.

When another teacher:

- Suggests a private staff meeting outside of school with a select group of teachers.
- Refuses to take a turn cleaning out the animal cages.
- Regularly misses staff meetings.
- Disagrees with the school's educational philosophy and continues to teach in ways that differ from the approved methods in that setting.
- Goes to the school administrator with a complaint about a staff team member.

When the administrator:

- Insists on adding one more child to an already over-enrolled class.
- Makes personnel decisions based on friendship, not performance.
- Backs a parent who complains about a teacher without hearing the teacher's side of the story.

Doing what is right becomes difficult at times; knowing what is right may be elusive. Even identifying what is right—an ethical conflict—may not be obvious. The NAEYC Standard 5 points out that professionals are guided by an ethical code, such as the NAEYC Code of Ethical Conduct (see Appendix A and the beginning of each chapter).

Ethics are the moral guidelines by which we govern our own behavior and that of society. We can strictly define ethics as *the system* that suggests that a personal code of ethics can be supported by a professional code of ethics. A code of ethics is a set of statements that helps us deal with the temptations inherent in our occupations. A code of ethics provides collective wisdom and advice from a broad base in the profession. It states the principles by which each individual can measure and govern professional behavior. It says that a group or association has recognized the moral dimensions of its work. It provides teachers with a known, defined core of professional values—those basic commitments that any early childhood educator should consider inviolate. This protects teachers and administrators from having to make hard ethical decisions on the spur of the moment, possibly on the basis of personal bias. An established professional code supports the teacher's choice by saying, "It isn't that I won't act this way: No early childhood educator should act this way" (Kipnis, 1987).

NAEYC's Code of Ethical Conduct and Statement of Commitment includes four sections: 1) ethical responsibilities to children; 2) ethical responsibilities to families; 3) ethical responsibilities to colleagues; and 4) ethical responsibilities to community and society. The Code of Ethical Conduct and Statement of Commitment may be found in Appendix A at the back of this text. Figure 1-6 shows a basic list of core values that has emerged from this work.

Participate in Continuing Education, Professional Development, and Affiliations

Creative and stimulating classrooms are the product of teachers who continue to learn more about how to teach. After the initial stage of teaching, many teachers begin to seek new challenges and new ways to improve the quality of their teaching. Usually this search leads to some form of continuing education, such as participation in workshops, courses, or seminars. Standard 5 reinforces the concept of teachers as lifelong learners.

A classic work by Katz (1999) describes four distinct stages of teacher development, ranging from Survival to Maturity. The beginning teacher often feels inadequate and ill-prepared during the first year of teaching (survival) but soon begins to focus on individual children and specific behavior problems (consolidation). By the third or fourth year (renewal) the teacher is ready to explore new ideas and resources and, within another year or two, has come to terms with teaching

---

Core Values of NAEYC's Code of Ethical Conduct

- -

- Appreciating childhood as a unique and valuable stage of the human life cycle.
- Basing our work with children on knowledge of child development.
- Appreciating and supporting the bond between the child and family.
- Recognizing that children are best understood and supported in the context of family, culture, community, and society.
- Respecting the dignity, worth, and uniqueness of each individual (child, family member, and colleague).
- Respecting diversity in children, families, and colleagues.
- Recognizing that children and adults achieve their full potential in the context of relationships that are based on trust and respect.

© Cengage Learning 2014

FIGURE 1-6 These core values form the basis of agreement in the profession about standards of ethical behavior. See Appendix A for a full version.

The Code of Ethical Conduct is shared with all members of the center or school staff.

and searches for insights and perspectives (maturity). At each stage, teachers need differing degrees of on-site support (mentoring), with increased exposure to professional conferences and organizations.

There are many ways to pursue continuing education:

- In-service training programs in the school setting. Special resource personnel who provide specific information about relevant topics and lead the staff in discussions about children's behavior, family relationships, assessment charts, science curricula, and creating multicultural classrooms.
- The teaching staff develops a program of their own, offering their expertise to fellow faculty at an in-service meeting.
- A computer specialist, art resource teacher, or multicultural expert visits the classrooms, instructing children and providing staff with some useful ideas and plans.
- A family therapist speaks at a staff meeting about strategies for supporting families in crisis.
- A library for teachers, stocked with professional books, journals (such as *Young Children*), newspapers (such as *Education Week*), and e-letters such as *Exchange Every Day*, provides the staff with the means to keep up with current trends and practices.
- Parents who are professionals in a variety of fields can be utilized whenever possible to enrich the knowledge and skills of the staff.

Look back at the career matrix (Figure 1-4) and see how many opportunities there are for advancement with the right education and experience. As you achieve each

level, there are challenges to be met. A course in group dynamics, cultural sensitivity, or adult assessment portfolios enhances your chances to move into more satisfying work and enlarge your contributions to those you work with and to the profession as a whole.

Standard 6 of the NAEYC Standards for Initial and Advanced Early Childhood Professional Preparation encourages professional development by joining one of the organizations related to the early childhood field. One of the largest, the National Association for the Education of Young Children (NAEYC), has local and state affiliate groups through which one can become a member. NAEYC offers a range of services to its members, including conferences and publications such as the journal *Young Children*. The Association for Childhood Education International (ACEI) has a similar function, whereas the Society for Research in Child Development (SRCD) focuses on child psychology, research, and development. Abundant resources are available from these groups, and their websites are at the end of this chapter and on the textbook website.

Have Knowledge of Career Options

The need for quality programs for young children has never been greater, and the demand for early childhood specialists will continue, fostered by national attention to the issues of children and families. If you are considering a career in early childhood education (ECE), the options are many and varied. Several of the Standards point to specific early childhood careers. For instance, Standard 1 suggests a teaching and/or consulting job, or Standard 2 may lead toward a calling as a family–child therapist or community organizer. Figure 1-7 lists some of the possibilities that exist in this profession.

TeachSource Video

Watch the TeachSource Video Case entitled "Teaching as a Profession: An Early Childhood Teacher's Responsibilities and Development." After you study the video clip, view the artifacts, and read the teacher interviews and text, reflect on the following questions:

1. One of the primary values in the NAEYC Code of Ethical Conduct is that children are best understood in the context of their family, culture, and society. Where and how does teacher Samantha Brade weave this into the interview?

2. In the case, Samantha defines many roles and responsibilities that challenge her as a professional. Comment on her ability to be self-reflective as she talks about teaching.

Career Options in Early Childhood Education

Direct Services to Children and Families

Teacher in early childhood program
Director of child care facility nursery school,
    Montessori program
Family day-care provider
Nanny or au pair
Foster parent
Social worker/adoption agent
Pediatric nurse/school nurse
Family therapist/parent educator
Pediatrician
Parent educator
Early intervention specialist
Recreation leader
Play group leader
Home visitor

Community Involvement

State/local licensing worker
Legislative advocate
Child care law specialist
ECE environmental consultant
Interior designer for children's spaces
Government planning agent on children's issues
Consultant in bilingual education, multiculturalism
Nutrition specialist for children
Child care referral counselor

Indirect Services to Children and Families

Curriculum specialist
Instructional specialist—computers
Child development researcher
ECE specialist
Program consultant
Consumer advocate
Teacher trainer, two- and four-year colleges
Consultant
Resource and referral programs
State and national departments of education and/or
    human services

Other Options

Communications consultant
Script writer/editor
Freelance writer
Children's book author
Children's photographer
Microcomputer specialist/program consultant

FIGURE 1-7 There are many challenges in a variety of careers awaiting the early childhood professional. (Adapted from "Career Options in Early Childhood Education" by Dianne Widmeyer Eyer. In *Beginnings & Beyond: Foundations in Early Childhood Education*, 3rd Ed., Clifton Park, NY: Thomson Delmar Learning.)

Engage in Reflective Teaching

A reflective teacher stops, looks, and listens. **Reflective teaching** is the process of thinking seriously and thoughtfully about your teaching and how children learn and how these are expressed in what and how you teach. A reflective teacher ponders each experience, probing more deeply for a greater understanding of what was taught and what was learned and how this informs the teaching process. Reflective teaching is the result of insightful examination, self-awareness, and self-assessment. Reflective dialogue with fellow students, colleagues and coworkers, supervisors, and mentors provides the opportunity to challenge yourself and strengthen your professional knowledge and understanding of the meaning of teaching.

Become Culturally Competent

Throughout this text, you will be exposed to cultural awareness and sensitivity in many contexts: in Chapter 1—diversity, immigrant children, class differences; in Chapter 3—cultural sensitivity and family cultural influences; in Chapter 7—culturally appropriate guidance; in Chapter 8—the changing American family; in Chapter 10—culturally appropriate curriculum, inclusive curriculum, multicultural curriculum, and culturally responsive teachers; and in Chapter 15—multicultural education, bilingual education, the challenges for immigrants, class differences, equal play and gender issues, and sexuality.

The culturally competent early childhood professional must be aware of the issues addressed in those chapters. The population trends within the United States have changed dramatically over the past few decades and the ability to adapt to a diversified group of families is the challenge for the teachers of the 21st century. Today's teachers need to build strong family and community relationships (Standards 2, 4, 5) across all types of cultural diversity.

Practice Intentional Teaching

Intentional teaching means that everything you do as teacher has specific goals and a purpose; that you have given your actions a great deal of thought; and that if anyone asks you why you have done something, you have a sound explanation (Epstein, 2007). Just as the teacher is deliberate in choosing furniture placement and specific guidance strategies, so too does intentionality play a part in what makes for the best kind of learning experience. We know that children can and should learn by choosing to work and play in an area of interest to them. We also know that there are concepts and content that is best learned through teacher-directed learning experiences. Both experiences are important to the growing child. Through intentional teaching, a teacher sets goals, plans the lesson, selects teaching strategies, and focuses on the most effective way to help children learn. As children react and get involved, the teacher maintains the focus and control on the experience.

Intentional teaching can and should be fun. It allows for creative thinking on the part of the teacher and the class. Jim wants his kindergarten class to focus on creating and extending patterns as part of the math curriculum, to learn that math can be fun, and to involve the class in creating the next steps. He begins by laying out pattern cards and colored blocks to match, which is an activity most of the children have mastered. Next, he adds textured squares to the activity and suggests the children make up their own patterns. Several days later, Jim adds a box of shells. Lena and Tony have been intrigued with each addition to the activity and ask Jim "What else can we add?"

At group time, Jim poses the question to the class: "What else would you like to add to the pattern table?" Jody wants feathers, Jesus wants bigger blocks, Mike wants string, and Paola wants spaghetti. As the children called out further suggestions, Jim added them to the list he was making, and said that he wanted some beans. The children became more animated and made more suggestions of food. "Okay," said Jim. "Those are great suggestions but some of them seem more like lunch than math! Let's vote on four that you like the most." The class voted and the four items were added to the math table. "My pattern is so pretty I want to keep it," said Carly. The next day Jim added construction paper and glue to the table. At group time the children shared their patterns by describing them to the class. Ryan went first: "I've got a brown shell, a red bean, a yellow spaghetti, and green string, and then I have it all over again." As they finished group time, Jim asked them to think about what they would do if one of the choices for their pattern ran out. The next day, he found out.

As Jim explained to one of his colleagues, part of his plan was to assess which children were grasping the concept of patterning and were ready for more challenges and to see what experiences other children might need to further understand patterns. This is intentional teaching at its best.

In each chapter of this text you will find a "Teaching With Intention" box that expands the definition of intentional teaching.

Think About This

1. How does "teaching with intention" alter your teaching strategies?
2. What is the most comfortable style for you right now: child-guided learning or teacher-guided learning? Why?
3. Describe your own definition of "teaching with intention."

Advocate for Children and Their Families

Children need advocates to speak for them and their families on issues ranging from health care to education to poverty to professional quality, staff, and wages. It is up to the early childhood professional to give voice to the issues concerning our young children and to educate the public about those issues. Public policy makers on the local, state, and national level need to hear from those who can speak out for those who cannot. Part of the role of a professional early childhood educator is to join the voices that support educational and teaching reforms as specifically stated in Standard 5. Volunteer with a local organization and make a difference in the lives of teachers and caregivers. Local NAEYC affiliates need volunteers to support *The Week of the Young Child* campaign each year and to monitor public policy at the local and state levels. Some early childhood professionals find it useful to sit on the boards of child care and health organizations.

Team Teaching: Professional Collaboration

Numerous adults are included in the early childhood setting. Some of these people may be:

- Other teachers, aides, and student teachers
- Volunteers
- Program directors and administrators

- School support personnel: clerical and janitorial staffs, food-service workers, bus drivers
- Families
- Consultants and specialists

That list defines the broader meaning of team teaching. The majority of classroom interactions, however, are with other teachers, and these relationships are among the most important a teacher can have. The beginning teacher may join a team of teachers or may teach in a small class alone. This depends on:

- The age level of the children
- Licensing or accrediting requirements
- The size of the classroom
- The school's philosophy and practices

Team teaching is defined as two or more adults working together in one classroom with one group of children (Browne & Gordon, 2009). The team approach is common in many nursery schools and child care centers where larger groups of children attend. Kindergarten and first- and second-grade teachers generally teach alone in self-contained classrooms, sometimes with an aide. In extended-day and after-school programs, high school and college students may make up the rest of the team.

Team Composition

Most teams are composed of people with varying skills, experience, and training. A typical group has a lead or head teacher—someone who is trained in child development or early childhood education. Assistants with less experience and training add support. Student teachers, interns, and volunteers may round out the group. A resource teacher—someone who specializes in art, music, or physical development, for instance—may also be available on a part-time basis.

Many state regulations mandate a minimum number of adults in the early childhood setting, and this minimum varies with the ages of the children. In infant programs, for instance, there is a higher ratio of adults per child (NAEYC suggests an optimal a ratio of 1:4), so it is more likely there are several teachers in one classroom. Together the teachers shape, direct, and participate in that program as a team of teachers.

The prescribed ratio of adult to children changes as the children mature and become able to function in more independent ways. (See Chapter 2 for more examples.)

Role Definition and Satisfaction

In order to function successfully, each person on the team must have a satisfying role to play and to be appreciated for the special something he or she brings to the team. All teachers want to know how their special talents and experiences contribute to the success of this program.

A written job description helps teachers understand the scope of their own position, as well as those of other staff members. Clearly defined roles also serve as a guard against legal and ethical problems, especially if children are injured at school. A clear understanding of the roles and responsibilities a teacher has is essential for the teacher's own sense of well-being and for the smooth functioning of the program.

Flexibility

It is important to adapt to the varying needs of children and equally important to respond to the needs of other staff members. Flexibility involves a willingness to offer and accept negotiation and compromise to preserve the effectiveness of the whole staff's effort. A professional teacher has a willingness to change with the changing needs of coworkers, to be open to new ideas proposed by others, and to help children become comfortable with flexibility and change.

Open and Frequent Communication

The ability to communicate thoughts, concerns, and feelings to others honestly and openly is perhaps the most important factor in promoting good team relationships. Good teachers work at becoming better teachers by developing skills in interpersonal relationships with other adults, just as they promote good social relationships among the young children they teach.

Communication problems and conflicts arise in every teaching situation. The Code of Ethical Conduct provides a road map for navigating some of the issues that create conflicts. The Code outlines clear expectations for professional and collegial behavior among staff members and employers. Review them in Appendix A. Communication takes many forms: verbal and nonverbal, written and spoken, and body language.

The three basic reasons for developing successful communication links with others on the teaching staff are:

1. *To share information*—about children and their families ("Sheila's grandmother died yesterday"), about changes in the schedule ("The dentist is unable to visit today; who wants to conduct group time?"), and about child development strategies ("Remember, we are all going to observe Leah's gross motor skills this week").
2. *To contribute new ideas*—teachers encourage one another to keep teaching fresh and alive when they

share a recent article of interest, reports from a conference they attended, or a successful art activity.

3. *To solve problems*—accepting differences in opinions, approaches, personality, and style among people is part of the challenge of working closely with others. Open communication is an ongoing process in which people have honest and frequent discussions of their differences, respecting each other's feelings and integrity and working together for mutually agreeable solutions. If the problem relates to another staff person, Section P-3A.1 of the Code of Ethical Conduct states that when we have concerns about the professional behavior of a coworker, we let that person know of our concerns and attempt to resolve the problem in a collegial manner.

Who Am I?

As noted earlier, self-awareness is a prerequisite to becoming a professional teacher. The kind of self-knowledge that contributes to success as a member of a teaching team is your knowledge of how your strengths and weakness complement or conflict with other team members. How you perceive yourself as a leader and your ability to follow others can affect team relationships. Be aware of what you have done lately that caused you to learn more about yourself, especially as a member of a teaching team.

Mutual Respect and Acceptance

Appreciating and accepting the individuality of other team members are as important to the success of the program as are appreciating and accepting the individuality of each child. The climate of trust created through mutual respect allows each staff member to contribute openly and

Professional attitudes and behaviors enhance team teaching.

innovatively to the program. It helps to know what you have in common with your coworkers, whether or not their teaching philosophies differ from you and from one another, and what values they hold dear. You want to be clear about what you want them to respect and accept about you as well. Section P-3B.1 of the Code of Ethical Conduct makes it clear that when we do not agree with program policies, we first work within the organizational structure to effect change.

Collegiality

A sense of being a team does not happen by accident, but by conscious effort. Every member of the staff must be committed to working together on a daily basis, as well as to the long-term goals of the program. Jorde-Bloom (2005) defines collegiality as the extent to which a team is friendly, supportive, and trusting of one another. Teachers can find support from one another as they share planning problems and achievements and grow in admiration and respect for one another.

Sharing the Spotlight

Tension among staff members can arise from a sense of competition. Teams function best when members learn how to share their strengths in ways that support the team without creating a competitive atmosphere. There must be a feeling of shared success when things work well, just as there is a shared responsibility when problems arise. One of the challenges of working on a team is to deal with feelings that may come from judging another teacher's abilities and/or successes. It helps to know how you feel and react when a parent praises another teacher in front of you or a child prefers another teacher to you. Section P-3A.2 of the Code of Ethical Conduct reminds us to base our views regarding the personal attributes or professional conduct of others on firsthand knowledge and its relevancy to the children and the program.

Evaluations

Evaluations are part of the privilege of claiming membership in the teaching profession. No teacher can become truly successful unless provisions are made for ongoing evaluations that provide a clear picture that confirms strengths and pinpoints areas for growth. The evaluation process is discussed in depth later in this chapter.

Why Team Teaching Works

There are many reasons why teaching in teams is such an integral part of so many early childhood programs. The advantages are numerous:

- *Variety of adult role models.* Teachers who are male, female, disabled, young, middle-aged,

TeachSource Video ▶❚❚

Watch the TeachSource Video Case entitled, "Teaching as a Profession: Collaboration with Colleagues." After you study the clip, view the artifacts, and read the teacher interviews and text, reflect on the following questions:

1. What is your "safe teacher box," and what would you do to move out of it?

2. What did the math work group show you about the benefits of collaboration?

3. How would you support greater collaboration in your school setting?

older, and varying in ethnic backgrounds bring equally diverse attitudes, approaches to children, interests, skills, and knowledge to share. This teaches children to accept differences in people as they watch adults interact with others on the teaching team.

- *Support for children.* The absence of one teacher is not as disruptive when the children can count on other familiar faces. This enables children to learn to trust the teaching environment because someone they know is always there.
- *Lightened workload.* There is a sharing of all the teaching tasks, from curriculum planning and cleanup to parent conferencing and record keeping.
- *Enriched program.* Talents and resources of the team are used to best advantage so that team members teach to their strengths, adding richness to the program.

Performance Assessment: Key to Improved Teaching Practices

Teachers are the single most important factor in determining program quality, and annual performance assessments promote continual professional improvement and growth. Timely and objective feedback guides teachers toward more effective teaching in their work with children, coworkers, parents, and administrators.

Purposes for an Annual Performance Review

Many programs require an annual assessment of the teaching staff. An evaluation is a professional expectation and reflects the NAEYC's Standards for a well-prepared early childhood professional. Personal performance reviews lend support to self-awareness, lifelong learning, and reflective teaching. There are a number of purposes for a performance review.

To Define and Clarify Job Responsibilities

A clearly defined job description outlines a teacher's duties and responsibilities and forms the basis for the evaluation. Assessing specific job responsibilities is a part of one's professional self-definition, as well as a clarification of actual duties. Studying ourselves helps us know who we are and what we do. Assessing job responsibilities aids in this process and holds us accountable for our work.

To Monitor Teacher Effectiveness

Once clear guidelines are set for teaching expectations, a method is needed to monitor teacher effectiveness. This process may vary from school to school. In some schools, teaching effectiveness is measured, in part, by child achievement, such as how children score on tests. Other centers may solicit the opinions of parents and coworkers. Direct observations while teachers are working with children form a significant part of the assessment.

To Identify Strengths and Challenges

Timely feedback about teaching practices and other job responsibilities is helpful to all teachers, whether beginners or experienced personnel. An assessment that offers teachers information about how to perform their job better

Evaluations are a professional responsibility that help to clarify job performance, professional growth, and challenges.

contributes to job competence and satisfaction. By recognizing strengths, teachers receive positive feedback for high-quality work. By identifying areas of concern, they can begin to set realistic goals for improvement.

To Create a Plan for Professional Development

One function of teacher evaluation is to foster professional development. Teachers do not become "good" and then stay that way for life. Regardless of their stage of development, teachers need to establish annual goals to continually improve. To be effective, goal setting must be embedded in an ongoing system of professional development. Reflect back on Figure 1-3, which shows how education and experience work together to form a career ladder that can be used for goal setting purposes. Figure 1-6 outlines many career options as well.

To Determine Employment

An evaluation can also be used to decide whether teachers should be retained, promoted, or released. Assessment procedures are an administrator's most valuable tools in making that decision. A clear and effective evaluation tool enables the administrator to monitor performance and target specific areas for improvement. The administrator then has a fair and equitable way to determine the promotional status of each employee.

To Meet Accreditation Requirements

Many programs seek accreditation by organizations whose standards they embrace. NAEYC is the leading accrediting body for early childhood programs through its National Academy of Early Childhood Programs. The self-study aspect of the accreditation process includes a teacher's self-assessment, the director's assessment of the teaching staff, and the teacher's assessment of the director. The criteria in the self-study provide the standards by which these evaluations are made, providing concrete ways to measure quality.

Components of an Effective Assessment

An effective evaluation process helps to challenge methods and assumptions and to identify ways to provide support for growth and change. Certain elements are common to all evaluations, such as those found in Chapter 6 for child assessments and in Chapter 2 for program assessments. In the assessment of teachers, the important components are: purpose (as described earlier), evaluators, type of assessment, follow-through, and cultural sensitivity.

Who Are the Evaluators?

Several models have been developed around the issue of who assesses teacher performance.

Self-Evaluation

Self-assessment encourages reflective thinking and self-awareness and can be an important step in the evaluation process. Your insights and perspectives and self-identified strengths and challenges help you to define your goals and objectives for the coming year.

Goals are the learning outcomes you want to achieve, such as improving your ability to help children resolve conflicts. Goals are broad-based challenges that improve your teaching practices.

Objectives are observable and define how you will achieve your goals. Action might include practicing observation skills to become more aware of a potential crisis before it erupts and intervening earlier in children's interactions. Objectives provide the detail for achieving your goals.

Figure 1-8 is an example of a staff evaluation form, which can also be used as a self-assessment tool.

Supervisor Evaluation

Job performance is an administrator's responsibility; therefore, teachers can expect their supervisor, director, or head teacher to be involved in their evaluation. Supervisors often use a single form combining a teacher's self-assessment and the supervisor's evaluation, such as Figure 1-8. This kind of form assures the teacher and supervisor that both are using the same criteria for evaluation and includes appropriate categories for assessment, as noted in Figure 1-8. In some programs, videotapes and portfolios add to the assessment process.

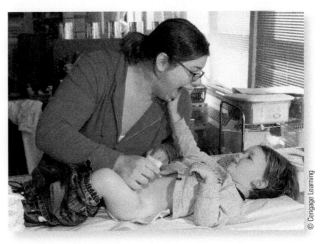

A teacher's self-evaluation provides an opportunity to improve his or her effectiveness with children.

Staff Evaluation

Employee _____

Evaluation Period _____

	C (90–100%)	F (60–89%)	O (30–59%)	N (0–29%)
General Work Habits				
1. Arrives on time				
2. Reliable in attendance; gives ample notice for absences				
3. Responsible in job duties				
4. Alert in health and safety matters				
5. Follows the center's philosophy				
6. Open to new ideas				
7. Flexible with assignments and schedule				
8. Comes to work with a positive attitude				
9. Looks for ways to improve the program				
10. Remains calm in a tense situation				
11. Completes required written communication on time				
Professional Development, Attitude, and Efforts				
1. Takes job seriously and seeks to improve skills				
2. Participates in workshops, classes, groups				
3. Reads and discusses distributed handouts				
4. Is self-reflective with goals for ongoing development				
Attitude and Skills with Children				
1. Friendly, warm, and affectionate				
2. Bends low for child level interactions				
3. Uses a modulated, appropriate voice				
4. Knows and shows respect for individuals				
5. Is aware of development levels/changes				
6. Encourages independence/self-help				
7. Promotes self-esteem in communication				
8. Limits interventions in problem solving				
9. Avoids stereotyping and labeling				
10. Reinforces positive behavior				
11. Minimal use of time out				
12. Regularly records observations of children				
Attitude and Skills with Parents				
1. Available to parents and approachable				
2. Listens and responds well to parents				
3. Is tactful with negative information				
4. Maintains confidentiality				
5. Seeks a partnership with parents				
6. Regularly communicates with parents				
7. Conducts parent conferences on schedule				
Attitude and Skills with Class				
1. Creates an inviting learning environment				
2. Provides developmentally appropriate activities				
3. Develops plans from observation and portfolio entries				
4. Provides materials for all curriculum components				
5. Provides an appropriate role model				
6. Anticipates problems and redirects				
7. Is flexible and responsive to child's interests				
8. Is prepared for day's activities				
9. Handles transitions well				
Attitude and Skills with Co-Workers				
1. Is friendly and respectful with others				
2. Strives to assume a fair share of work				
3. Offers and shares ideas and materials				
4. Communicates directly and avoids gossip				
5. Approaches criticism with learning attitude				
6. Looks for ways to be helpful				

Comments:

FIGURE 1-8 The quality and effectiveness of teaching is affected by the quality and effectiveness of the evaluation process. This form is useful for a self-evaluation and supervisory evaluation and can be downloaded from the Education CourseMate website. (From *The Visionary Director: A Handbook for Dreaming, Organizing, and Improving Your Center,* by Margie Carter and Deb Curtis, pp. 266–277. Copyright © 1998 by Margie Carter and Deb Curtis. Reprinted with permission from Redleaf Press, St. Paul, Minnesota, www.redleafpress.org.)

Types of Assessments

Many evaluations are based on observable, specific information about a teacher's activities and responsibilities. This is known as a performance-based assessment. Figure 1-9 is an example of performance-based assessment in regard to a teacher's work with children. When paired with specific goals and expectations, this system is known as competency-based assessment.

Competency-based assessments outline exactly what teachers must do to demonstrate their competency, or skill, in their job responsibilities. Criteria are set and areas are targeted that pinpoint what knowledge, skills, and behaviors the teacher must acquire.

The evaluation tools or format determine the validity of the gathered information. Informal techniques may result in unreliable conclusions. A process that is formalized and systematic, related to goal setting and professional development, has a greater chance of success. Although it is important to select an appropriate method and assessment tool, keep in mind that it is the process through which the evaluation is conducted that matters most.

Creating a portfolio is a developmentally appropriate practice that reflects your professional growth and your insights about the nature of teaching young children.

The Classroom Assessment Scoring System (CLASS) (Pianta et al., 2008) is an observation tool that evaluates teachers on two critical aspects of performance. CLASS measures the emotional climate, and as noted earlier in this chapter, setting the tone, or the emotional climate, is the teacher's responsibility. A supportive and positive climate fosters children's learning. CLASS also focuses on a variety of teaching strategies and how they set the stage for optimum learning.

Follow-Through

What follows an evaluation is critical to the overall success of an evaluation process. The important thing to remember is that assessment should be a continuous process because without follow-through, long-lasting improvement in unlikely to occur. Figure 5-10 shows how the circular process works in a feedback loop. Data are collected on teacher behavior and given to the teacher in person. Goals are set to improve teaching. A follow-up check is done periodically to see how—and if—goals are being met. Teaching improves as recommendations are put into practice.

Follow-through makes the feedback loop complete as information about improvement is communicated.

Evaluations take hard work, time, and dedication to a higher quality of teaching. It is also a shared responsibility. The supervisor must be explicit about a teacher's performance and be able to identify for the teacher what is effective and what is problematic. Teachers themselves must value the process and understand its implications for their professional growth.

Cultural Sensitivity

Cultural sensitivity affects how a teacher interacts with others, and this needs to be taken into consideration when assessing a teacher's performance. Insight about a

Performance-Based Assessment

Teacher Goal	Example
To help each child develop a positive self-concept	I greet each child with a smile and a personal comment.
To help each child develop socially, emotionally, cognitively, and physically	I have goals for each child in each developmental area, fall and spring.
To help provide many opportunities for each child to be successful	My parent conference sheets have examples; for instance, Charlie didn't want to come to group time, so I had him pick the story and help me read it—he comes every day now!
To encourage creativity, questioning, and problem solving	This is my weak point. I tend to talk too much and tell them what to do.
To foster enjoyment for learning in each child	I do great group times and give everyone turns.
To facilitate children's development of a healthy identity and inclusive social skills	I participated in our center's self-study and am taking an anti-bias curriculum class.

© Cengage Learning 2011

FIGURE 1-9 Performance-based assessment ties the goals of the program to the teacher's work. This example asks the teacher to do a self-assessment; a director, parent, or peer could observe and make a second assessment.

Portfolio-based assessments are a popular tool for helping teachers consolidate the experiences that help them become better teachers. A **portfolio** is not an assessment tool in and of itself. It is the display or collection system used to demonstrate evidence of professional growth. Folders, boxes, files, and binders are all used to house the collection of data. It is an intentional compilation of materials and resources collected over a period of time that provides evidence of your professional growth.

Documentation is an important part of creating a portfolio because it provides concrete evidence of how you understand and implement developmentally appropriate practices and how you translate theory into action.

Your portfolio is ever changing and reflects your individuality by virtue of what it contains. As an assessment tool, a portfolio is useful in many ways. It helps you clarify your values, keeps you focused on the goals you have set, provides an avenue for self-reflection, and demonstrates

growth. By what is included and what is omitted, a portfolio shows an evaluator tangible evidence of your abilities, provides a framework for setting new goals, and gives a more personal sense of your commitment and professionalism. A portfolio may include but is not limited to the following:

Materials developed by you for use in the classroom
A videotape of your teaching performance
Lesson plans with an evaluation of a specific activity
Samples of conference hand-outs and programs, notes from
    in-service training, articles, and other materials you use
    as professional growth
Articles written for newsletters and for families and
    colleagues
A journal of teaching experiences
Photos of field trips or projects
Self-reflective notes on your teaching
Professional articles

---

teacher's social and cultural background is particularly useful if the evaluator is a member of the majority population and the teacher is not.

There are five specific cultural factors that can affect communication, particularly where supervisors and staff

FIGURE 1-10 A feedback loop is a continuous cycle in which teacher behavior is observed for a performance evaluation. The evaluation is offered through growth goals, which are set in order to affect teacher behavior. Thus, the circle is continuous, with each part helping the next.

members are concerned (Caruso and Fawcett, 2006). They are:

1. *Time sense.* Being on time and doing tasks in a timely fashion are high priorities for many people raised in mainstream American culture. Each culture has its own concept of time, and the teacher who is always late for meetings may be reflecting the cultural context in which he or she was raised.

2. *Space.* How close you get to someone while talking is also a function of cultural context. In some cultures, invading another's personal space (the "comfort zone") is considered rude. If a teacher backs away, she may be considered cold and unfriendly. If the teacher is the one getting too close, he may be seen as forward and aggressive. These perceptions may be innocent reactions based on their cultural sensibilities and should be considered in that light.

3. *Verbal and nonverbal communication.* Eye contact is seen in some cultures to be disrespectful if prolonged; to others it may be a sign of interest and attentiveness. Other facial expressions, such as smiling (or not), gestures, and body language, communicate different things from culture to culture. Silence, too, is used in different cultures in a variety of ways with an assortment of meanings. Speaking loudly may be a cultural norm or it may communicate anger and accusations. Teachers and their supervisors need to learn each other's communication styles and be particularly aware of those that are culture-bound.

4. *Values.* Our values drive our behavior and responses. If a teacher comes from a background that emphasizes dependency in the early years and the school philosophy is one that encourages early independence, a cultural conflict can erupt and affect a teacher's evaluation adversely. Supervisors and teachers must understand each other's value system and what causes each of them to make certain decisions.

5. *Concepts of authority.* The way people deal with authority is also culture-specific. Early childhood professionals who supervise and evaluate staff members from cultures different than their own need to be aware of what cultural expectations surround the issue of authority. In some instances, authority figures are often male, and females are raised not to question authority. A correct answer may be more culturally appropriate than expressing one's true feelings or ideas. The supervisor can avoid misunderstandings if he or she is aware that the teacher is used to an authoritarian style of leadership from supervisors and thus gear the conversation accordingly.

Evaluators have a rare opportunity to create bridges of understanding between and among many cultures. Within their school community, they can create a two-way interchange about culturally relevant issues.

Field Experience: Practice What You Teach

Professional preparation standards either require or recommend at least one practicum or field experience of supervised work with young children in a group setting. For some students, a practicum may be the first hands-on opportunity to work with children.

Learning Through the Practicum Experience

The student practicum experience provides opportunities to test yourself out as a teacher. Through this professional preparation, you learn to:

- Connect knowledge and theory with classroom experience: Children's behavior exemplifies the child development principles learned in textbooks. Theory becomes alive as you observe children play and learn.
- Discover how children function in groups and with other children and adults: The range of children's social skills is apparent as they interact with peers and teachers. You notice how differently children behave as they work alone, in small groups, or participate in a large group time experience.

© Cengage Learning

Through experience, teachers learn how to handle large groups of children. Learning to develop story time and reading skills is an ongoing process.

- Collaboration techniques for working as a team member: Learning to be part of a team takes patience and practice. You learn to work with a variety of adults who have different skills and who model diverse teaching strategies.
- Intensive self-searching through self-assessment and reflective dialogue: You come to understand more about yourself and your abilities as you explore the broader meaning of teaching. You gain new insights as you take time to think about your role, attitude, behavior, and responses to the children you teach.
- Work with an on-site supervisor or mentor teacher: You and your supervising teacher will forge a working relationship based on the goals the two of you set for your practicum experience. Your supervisor observes, guides, and evaluates your experience, as well as encourages and supports your progress.
- Conduct group times and plan curriculum: Your first opportunity to plan curriculum is both exciting and challenging. Your knowledge of child development helps you create activities that are meaningful learning experiences. As you evaluate the activity with your supervising teacher, you gain greater understanding of the children you teach and your own skills as a teacher.
- Gain insights into yourself through ongoing feedback: Throughout your practicum you receive feedback from your supervising teacher that helps you identify the strengths you bring to the teaching experience and the areas in which you need to improve. Evaluations and feedback promote reflective teaching, increase your skills, and tell you what progress you are making in meeting your goals. Feedback increases your confidence and promotes the standards of the early childhood profession.

- Approaches and strategies for developing relationships with children: The teachers you work with model highly polished skills as they relate to children. As you observe them and gain experience you learn to help children solve conflicts, lead them in group discussions, and soothe their hurts. You also learn to ask a lot of questions of the teaching staff to find out why this approach didn't work and that strategy was successful.
- Engage in developmentally appropriate practices: Your practicum experience should lead you to a greater understanding of DAP. You see how teachers plan reasonable goals for each child, based on the individual's developmental levels. You come to see that DAP is more than a definition of what to do; it is a way to meet children where they are.
- Appreciate the role of families in their children's development and learning: Through the family we gain greater knowledge and understanding of the individual child. You learn how teachers build strong relationships with families in order to strengthen the bond between home and school. You also find a broad definition of "family" as it pertains to the diversity of the children in the classroom.

(Based on Browne and Gordon. (2012). *Early childhood field experience: Learning to teach well.* New York: Pearson.)

A field experience can be a productive and valuable asset to your professional growth. Theory evolves into practice, knowledge and skills are polished, and the living laboratory provides rich opportunities to focus on professional preparation.

Summary

LO1 Today's early childhood teachers have much in common with other teachers. The format may differ but the curriculum is similar and includes math, science, language, social studies, geography, and literacy. Early childhood teachers have multiple roles. They supervise and manage the classroom, interact with children and adults, and set the emotional tone. There are meetings to attend, reports to write, parent conferences to hold, and materials to purchase. These after-hours duties add to the depth of classroom experiences the teacher provides for the children. Personal attributes of the early

childhood professional should include a high degree of self-awareness, including attitudes and biases that would inhibit good teaching practices.

LO2 Becoming a professional teacher means that there are professional guidelines and standards to follow. NAEYC's Standards for Professional Preparation serve as a challenge for what today and tomorrow's teachers should know and be able to do. The Code of Ethical Conduct fosters professionalism as teachers apply its ideals and principles to everyday situations. A professional code of ethics sets standards of behavior based on core values and commitments all early childhood professionals share. It can support decisions individuals have to make in the best interests of children. Professionalism is enhanced by a teacher's knowledge and skills, professional development, reflective teaching, and the practice of intentional teaching.

LO3 Team teaching is common in many early childhood programs. Creating a successful team effort is based on collaborative skills, which include role definition and satisfaction, flexibility, open and frequent communications, self-awareness, mutual respect and acceptance, and evaluations of the team.

LO4 An annual assessment that is linked to professional growth is a key to maintaining quality programs for children. Some purposes of annual performance reviews are to clarify roles and responsibilities, monitor teacher effectiveness, identify teacher strengths and challenges, plan for professional development, determine employment, and meet accreditation requirements.

The process should include a self-evaluation by the teacher who, with a supervisor, sets appropriate professional goals that relate to the program's philosophy and mission. Continuing growth within the professional field includes understanding the cultural context from which teachers relate to the children, families, other staff members, and supervisors.

LO5 Through a field experience, students gain valuable practice working directly with children under the supervision of a mature teacher. The student practicum helps beginning teachers connect knowledge and theory to the classroom reality of how children learn and behave, find approaches and strategies for relating to young children, and plan developmentally appropriate group times and curriculum. Working with a supervising teacher, students learn collaboration techniques for working on a team and gain insights as they become more aware of who they are in the lives of children.

Key Terms

emotional framework	core values	competency-based assessment
self-awareness	continuing education	feedback loop
anti-bias	reflective teaching	portfolio-based assessments
professional standards	intentional teaching	portfolio
entry level	team teaching	
ethics	performance-based assessment	

Review Questions

1. What are the most important characteristics that today's early childhood professional should possess?
2. How do the professional standards for teaching preparation and the NAEYC Code of Ethical Conduct foster a sense of professionalism?
3. What are the most important collaboration skills that help build positive relationships for team teaching?
4. How does an annual performance assessment guide and inform best teaching practices?
5. What is the value of field experience?

Observe and Apply

1. Survey a classroom where you teach or observe. How many different cultures are represented? How does the teacher respond to the cultural diversity?
2. Read the ethical situations posed in the section, "Abiding by a Code of Ethical Conduct." Think about how you would solve them. Discuss your answers with a member of your class, a teacher, and a parent.
3. Observe a teacher working in a team situation and one who works alone in a classroom. What seem to be the advantages of each? Disadvantages? Which would you prefer for your first year of teaching? Why? Your third year? Your seventh year?
4. In small groups, discuss the popular images of teachers as reflected in current movies and literature. Is there a consensus of the portrait of teachers today? Where do early childhood professionals fit into the picture? Are issues raised about teachers being addressed anywhere? Where? How? By whom? What would you conclude about your role as a member of the teaching profession?

Helpful Websites

Center for Child Care Workforce **www.ccw.org**

Council for Professional Recognition (CDA)
  www.cdacouncil.org

National Association for the Education of Young
  Children **www.naeyc.org**

Association for Childhood Education International
  www.acei.org

Child Care Information Exchange **www.ccie.com**

ERIC Clearinghouse on Elementary and Early
  Childhood Education **www.eric.ed.gov**

National Black Child Development Institute
  www.nbcdi.org

🔲 The Education CourseMate website for this text offers many helpful resources and interactive study tools. Go to CengageBrain.com to access the TeachSource Videos, flashcards, tutorial quizzes, direct links to all of the websites mentioned in the chapter, downloadable forms, and more.

References

Bloom, P. J. (2005). *Blueprint for action: Achieving center-based change through staff development.* Lake Forest, IL: New Horizons.

Browne, K. W., & Gordon, A. M. (2009). *To teach well: An early childhood practicum guide.* Upper Saddle River, NJ: Prentice.

Caruso, J. J., & Fawcett, M. T. (2006). *Supervision in early childhood education: A developmental perspective.* New York: Teachers College Press.

Derman-Sparks, L., & Edwards, J. O. (2010). *Antibias education for young children and ourselves.* Washington, D.C.: National Association for Education of Young Children.

Epstein, A. S. (2007). *The intentional teacher: Choosing the best strategies for young children's learning.* Washington, D.C.: National Association for the Education of Young Children.

Eyer, D. (1989). Career options in early childhood education. In A. Gordon & K. W. Browne (Eds.), *Beginnings and beyond: Foundations in early childhood education.* Clifton Park, NY: Thomson Delmar Learning.

Katz, L. G. (1999). *Talks with teachers of young children.* Norwood, NJ: Ablex.

Kipnis, K. (1987, May). How to discuss professional ethics. *Young Children,* pp. 26–30.

National Association for the Education of Young Children. (2011). *Code of ethical conduct and statement of commitment.* Washington, D.C.: National Association for the Education of Young Children.

National Association for the Education of Young Children. (2010). NAEYC Standards for Early Childhood Professional Preparation Programs. http://www.naeyc.org/files/ncate/file/NAEYC%20 Initial%20and%20Advanced%20Standards%20 3_2011.pdf. National Association for the Education of Young Children. (2005). *Core values.*

National Association of Child Care Resource & Referrals Agency. (2011). *Child care workforce.* http://www.naccrra.org, Retrieved November 2011.

Pianta, R. C., La Paro, K. M., & Hamre, B. K. (2008). *Classroom assessment scoring system (CLASS).* Baltimore: Paul H. Brookes.

Rushton, S., Juola-Rushton, A., & Larkin, A. (2010). Neuroscience, play and early childhood educations: Connections, implications, and assessment. *Early Childhood Education Journal,* 37, pp. 351–361.

U.S. Bureau of Labor Statistics. (2010). *Labor force characteristics by race & ethnicity, 2007.* Report # 1032 Washington, D.C.: U.S. Government Printing Office.

Whitebrook, M., Sakai, L., Gerber, E., & Howes, C. (2001). *Then and now: Changes in child care staffing, 1994–2000.* Washington, D.C.: Center for the Child Care Workforce.

2

Developmental and Learning Theories

Learning Objectives

LO1 Compare and contrast the eight major theoretical perspectives that relate to child development.

LO2 Examine central developmental topics of cultural diversity, attachment, play, gender, moral development, and brain-based research as vehicles for creating developmentally appropriate practices.

LO3 Articulate how developmental and learning theories explain children's growth and development.

naeyc Standards For Professional Development

The following NAEYC Standards for early childhood professional development are addressed in this chapter:

Standard 1 Promoting Child Development and Learning
Standard 2 Building Family and Community Relationships
Standard 5 Using Content Knowledge to Build Meaningful Curriculum
Standard 6 Becoming a Professional

naeyc Code of Ethical Conduct

These are the sections of the NAEYC Code of Ethical Conduct that apply to the topics of this chapter:

Section I. We are committeed to supporting children's development and learning.

Ideals:

I-1.1   To be familiar with the knowledge base of early childhood care and education and to stay informed through continuing education and training.

I-1.2   To base program practices upon current knowledge and research in the field of early childhood education, child development and related disciplines, as well as on particular knowledge of each child.

Introduction

While taking a routine report at an elementary school, a police officer was interrupted by a girl of about 6 years old. Looking the officer up and down, she asked, "Are you a cop?" "Yes," said the woman, and continued writing the report. "My mother said if I ever needed help I should ask the police. Is that right?" "Yes, again," replied the officer. "Well, then," she said as she extended her foot forward, "would you please tie my shoe?"

What was this child thinking? Can you see how she took in information from her mother and then applied it to her own life? How do children do that? What is the process of listening, thinking, and then doing?

While working for an organization that delivers lunches to elderly shut-ins, a mother used to take her preschool son on the afternoon rounds. He was always intrigued by the various appliances there, particularly the canes, walkers, and wheelchairs. One day, she saw him staring at a pair of false teeth soaking in a glass. He turned to her and whispered, "The tooth fairy will never believe this!"

Look how this child applied his fantasy world to what he encountered. During the years from birth to middle childhood, how do young children come to understand the world? How do they make sense of what they see, touch, and experience?

The father of 6-month-old Michiko puts one end of a toy monkey in his mouth and dangles it in front of her. Michiko gazes intently, getting still and wide-eyed, finally reaching up tentatively to touch the doll. Yet, when Keith's nanny tries the same thing with him, the 9-month-old smiles and laughs as he grabs it and tries to shove it back into her mouth.

How is it that two children can respond so differently? Is this simply a few months' age difference? Is it because of their gender or ethnic differences? Or has one child played this game before and not the other?

Major Theories

So many remarkable transformations take place in the early years. Development, the orderly set of changes in the life span, occurs as individuals move from conception to death. Those of us curious about children want to know the nature of these changes and the reasons why things happen.

A developmental theory is a "systematic statement of principles and generalizations that provides a coherent framework for understanding how and why people change as they grow older" (Berger, 2012). A learning theory attempts to explain how learning takes place. By observing children, theorists try to make sense out of what they see, looking for patterns and variations to make a kind of story that explains the reasons or causes of the details. Research allows us to look at many children or a group of children over time, even one child with intense scrutiny, to seek these explanations.

Early childhood education draws from several fields of study. Much of what we know about children today comes from child development and child psychology research that tries to answer these questions:

- How do children develop?
- What do they learn and in what order?
- What do children need to be ready to learn?
- What affects learning?
- Do all children develop in the same ways?
- What are the similarities and differences in growth and development?

To begin to answer these questions, we need some way to look for information and then choose and organize the facts so that we can understand what we see. In other words, we need a theory. Theories are especially useful in providing a broad and consistent view of the complexity of human development (Berger, 2012).

- Theories produce hypotheses. They allow us to make an educated guess (called a hypothesis) about children's behavior and development.
- Theories generate discoveries. Because these theories are based on experience, teachers can check their validity as they observe children every day.
- Theories offer practical guidance. The theories you read form the foundation of developmentally appropriate practice (DAP) that is a guide for teachers at all levels of early education.

The basic quest for sound theories about development and knowledge and for systematic statements about behavior and development has given educators much to consider in forming their own ideas about children.

Early childhood teachers should know how children develop and how they learn. Knowing how children develop is critical in making the daily decisions about curriculum, the classroom setting, and children. To be effective with children, teachers need a thoughtful philosophy and approach that is based on what we know about how children develop and what works to help them learn and understand. The teacher who is well-versed in theory has invaluable tools to work with parents, advise the family of the range of typical behavior, and talk to parents about concerns that are beyond the norms. Therefore, it is important to have a background in both developmental psychology and learning theories.

The Nature of Development

A child is a blend of many parts that interrelate in different ways and change with growth over time. Such complexity and dynamic change call for ways to organize our thinking through identifying developmental domains and posing major questions.

Developmental Domains

The study of human development requires insight and information from many disciplines because each person develops simultaneously in body, mind, and spirit; thus, we usually divide development into three domains to make it easier to study. We try to consider separately the three aspects that make up the whole of development (Figure 2-1). We can then better understand the major processes of development that parallel these developmental areas:

- Biological processes describe changes in the body.
- Cognitive processes are those changes in one's thought, intelligence, and language.
- Socio-emotional processes reflect changes in an individual's relationships with other people, emotions, and personality.

Questions about Development

Major issues are raised in the study of development. The science of development seeks to understand why and how people change or remain the same over time; as a science, it depends on theories, research methods, and critical analyses to understand the what, how, and why of development. Because of this, all kinds of children—younger and older, rich and poor, of various ethnicities, backgrounds, culture and experience—must be studied. Three major questions drive research and practice:

1. *Is children's development due more to maturation or experience?* The changes we see in children over time may be due to internal or external influences. Some theories claim children change because of innate, biologic, or genetic patterns built into the human being; others claim that they are shaped by the environment and experiences (such as parents, materials, TV, school, and so on) of life. This argument is often referred to as the nature/nurture controversy, also known as the problem of heredity versus environment. As you remember from Chapter 1, this issue has been discussed for centuries. On the "nature" side, Rousseau argued that the child is born with natural, or innate, goodness. Locke, however, asserted that it

© Cengage Learning 2014

FIGURE 2-1 The various domains of child growth and development are interrelated and interdependent.

was "nurture" that mattered. He contended that children entered the world with a *tabula rasa*, or clean slate, on which all experience and learning was then written. Today, most psychologists and educators agree that the patterns of development and learning are complex and not so simply explained. The eight theories discussed here focus on variations that emphasize one or the other (Figure 2-2).

2. *Is growth smooth and continuous or more stage-like?* Some theories emphasize a gradual, cumulative kind of growth, more like "from an acorn, a giant oak will grow." The seedling becomes more oak-like gradually over time. This continuity of development is usually the viewpoint of theories that emphasize experience (nurture). Other theories depict children's growth as a sequence of stages that are clearly marked by distinct changes, more like "caterpillar into butterfly." In the cocoon, the chrysalis does not become more caterpillar-like, but, instead, becomes

a different kind of organism. This viewpoint emphasizes the innate conditions of development (nature).

3. *What can theory and research do for early childhood educators?* Science has opened our eyes to the amazing complexity of the mind and the wondrous path of growth in the body. This was not always so.

In previous generations, little scientific information was available by which parents (and teachers) could assess the validity of theories. Many beliefs were espoused by adults about children, such as "You'll spoil the baby if you respond to his demands too quickly," or "Children who suffer early neglect and deprivation will not realize their normal potential." These statements can be powerful, particularly as they are passed on to you by your family and culture. However, some ideas are rooted in myth rather than reality.

The study of child development was mostly confined to the study of trends and descriptions of age

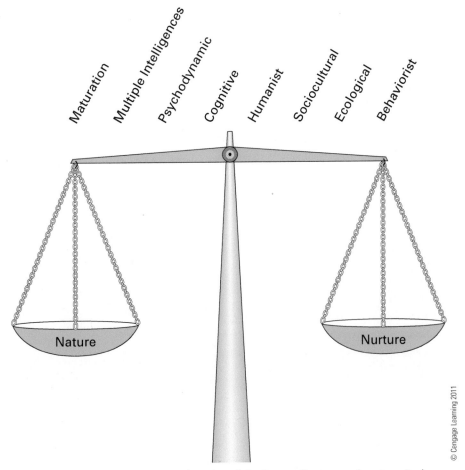

© Cengage Learning 2011

FIGURE 2-2 Development is a combination of the forces of nature and nurture. Each theory offers its own emphasis on heredity/prenatal conditions and environmental/life experiences.

changes. As the 20th century progressed, the scope and definition of child development changed radically. Developmental psychologists studied how psychological processes begin, change, and develop. Child development focused on language acquisition, various early effects on later intellectual development, and the process of attachment to others. Now, developmentalists are taking a life-span approach to development, taking into considerations the many directions and contexts of development, understanding the power of culture and the resilience and plasticity of individual growth, and using new tools of technology to unlock the secrets of the brain.

Child development researchers and theorists have accumulated a rich store of knowledge, based on scientific hypothesis that is then tested with evidence. They can help sort fact from fiction.

The Most Excellent Eight

No one set of principles encompasses all developmental and learning theories. We have chosen eight theories. Some are grand theories that describe either universal processes or the entire span of development (psychodynamic, behaviorist, cognitive). Others are mini-theories that explain just a part of development (multiple intelligences, maturation, humanistic). A few are emergent theories (sociocultural, ecological) that are relatively new. They are commonly known as 1) psychodynamic theory, 2) behaviorist theory, 3) cognitive theory, 4) sociocultural theory, 5) ecological theory, 6) multiple intelligences theory, 7) maturation theory, and 8) humanistic theory.

While writing this chapter, we were reminded of this children's incident:

> While playing "school" in the dramatic play area, Noemi insisted on wearing pretend glasses, as her favorite teacher did. "No!" cried Venecia. "They will make you mad and crabby!" (In fact, her teacher only wore the glasses when she was too tired to wear contact lenses.) "Yes, I will," replied Noemi. "She wears them cuz they makes her smarty-pants." (This is another viewpoint and a kind of myth about intelligence and eyewear.) "You're both wrong," called out Charly. "Everybody knows you have to wear glasses and hoop earrings to be a teacher." (As a matter of fact, the teacher did look like this.) Everyone looked puzzled, and then the play resumed.

Just like these children, not all the experts agree or even think alike. Because the field of child development is broad, encompassing a wide variety of opinion and fact, there is no one theory that describes everything.

Moreover, these theories arose at different time periods, in various countries. Each theory describes children and their processes in different ways. It is up to you, the educator, to decide which ones best describe children and their growth. Read carefully, and then compare your experiences with the theories and concepts you read here. As a teacher, you have a diversity of theories from which to establish a professional philosophy.

Psychodynamic Theory

Psychodynamic theory is about personality development and emotional problems. Psychodynamic theories look at development in terms of internal drives that are often unconscious, or hidden from our awareness. These motives are the underlying forces that influence human thinking and behavior and provide the foundation for universal stages of development. In psychoanalytic terms, children's behavior can be interpreted by knowing the various stages and tasks within those stages.

Sigmund Freud

Sigmund Freud began his career as a medical doctor and became interested in the irrational side of human behavior as he treated "hysterics." His technique, asking people to recline on a couch and talk about everything, was ridiculed by the medical establishment as the "talking cure." Then, as patients revealed their thoughts, fantasies, and problems, he began to see patterns.

Psychoanalytic Theory

According to Freud, people possess three basic drives: the sexual drive, survival instincts, and a drive for destructiveness. Of the first, childhood sexuality, Freud outlined development in terms of psychosexual stages, each characterized by a particular part of the body (Figure 2-3). In each stage, the sensual satisfaction associated with each body part is linked to major challenges of that age. For instance, the toddler issues of biting and thumb sucking, the preschool interest in "doctor play," and the school-age focus on gender identification can be seen in a psychosexual context. Each stage also has its own conflicts between child and parent, and how the child experiences those conflicts determines basic personality and behavior patterns.

Freud (1920) put forth this theory, and his ideas were expanded on by Anna Freud (his daughter), Carl Jung, Karen Horney, and others. Although Freud's interest was abnormal adult behavior and its causes, his conclusions have had a major effect on our conception of childhood and its place in the life span.

Freudian Stages of Childhood Psychosexual Development

Stage	Age	Description/Major Area
Oral	Birth to 2	Mouth (sucking, biting) source of pleasure
		Eating and teething
Anal	2–3	Bowel movements source of pleasure
		Toilet learning
Phallic	3–6	Genitals source of pleasure
		Sex role identification and conscience development
Latency	6–12	Sexual forces dormant
		Energy put into schoolwork and sports
Genital	12–18	Genitals source of pleasure

© Cengage Learning 2011

FIGURE 2-3 Freud's psychoanalytic theory of childhood development. Psychoanalytic theory contends that each stage has its own area of pleasure and crisis between the child and parent of society.

To Freud, the personality was the most important aspect of development, more central to human growth than language, perception, or cognition. Personality was defined by three structures:

1. Id—the instinctive part that drives a person to seek satisfaction
2. Ego—the rational structure that forms a person's sense of self
3. Superego—the moral side that informs the person of right and wrong

He thought that the personality developed in a fixed pattern of stages that emerged as the body matured naturally. How children were treated while going through those stages determined whether they developed healthy or abnormal personalities. In particular, the mother–child relationship was important in each stage. Thus, the interaction between the child's wishes and needs and how these were treated (by the mother or other adults) was a focal point for proper development.

All psychoanalytic explanations of human development emphasize the critical importance of relationships with people and the sequence, or stages, of personality development. The psychoanalyst Erik Erikson expanded and refined Freud's theory of development. It is Erikson whose ideas have most affected early childhood education.

Erik Erikson

Erik Homberg Erikson is perhaps the most influential psychoanalyst of the modern era and certainly a key figure in the study of children and development. His interests in children and education included a teaching background in progressive and Montessori schools in Europe.

After clinical training in psychoanalysis, he remained interested in the connections between psychotherapy and education. His books, *Childhood and Society* (1950) about his version of Freud's theory, and Pulitzer Prize–winning *Gandhi's Truth* (1969), helped him become well known in the United States. Erikson became the first child analyst in the Boston area and worked for both University of California at Berkeley and Stanford University.

Psychosocial Theory

Erikson's theory of human development, like those of Freud and Piaget, states that life is a series of stages through which each person passes, with each stage growing from the previous ones. He proposes eight stages of psychosocial development, each representing a critical period for the development of an important strength. Positive growth allows the individual to integrate his or her physical and biologic development with the challenges that the social institutions and culture present. Each stage is characterized by an emotional challenge.

A key point of Erikson's theory is how the stages build from previous experience. A stage is a period during which certain changes occur. What one achieves in each stage is based on the developments of the previous stages, and each stage presents the child with certain kinds of problems to be solved. When children succeed, they go on to attack new problems and grow through solving them. Erikson gave us the term identity crisis to describe how people struggle with a pair of competing urges at each stage as they try to answer, "Who am I?" (Figure 2-4).

A second key point of Erikson's theory is balance. In Erikson's framework, balancing a child's wishes and the demands of the environment with a mentally healthy dose of each emotion is essential for personality strength. Everyone

© Cengage Learning 2011

FIGURE 2-4 Eriksonian crisis in a young child's life. Psychosocial theory claims that conflicts are opportunities to balance competing urges. The child who takes initiative (grabbing a toy) can also feel guilt (returning it).

has certain biologic, social, and psychological needs that must be satisfied to grow in a healthy manner. Medicine and neuroscience have learned much about physical needs—diet, rest, and exercise. Basic intellectual, social, and emotional needs also must be met for an organism to be healthy. Eriksonian theory speaks to these needs. Whether these needs are met or left unfulfilled affects development.

Erikson differed from Freud in some fundamental ways. First, he emphasized the drive for identity and meaning in a social context rather than the Freudian notion of sexual and aggressive drives. Second, development occurs throughout the life span, in contrast with the notion that personality is shaped only in childhood. Finally, the developmental struggles that occur during one's life can be overcome later. You can go back; while it is true that the first four stages play a key role in developing ego identity, problems of childhood can be dealt with in later stages so that the adult can achieve vitality.

The following text elaborates on the first four stages in the early childhood period because of their importance to the field of early childhood education. (See Figure 2-5 for all eight stages.)

Stage 1: Trust versus Mistrust (Birth to 1 Year)

Erikson's first stage is roughly the first year of life and parallels Freud's oral-sensory stage. Attitudes important to development are the capacity to trust—or mistrust—inner and outer experiences. By providing consistent care, parents help an infant develop a basic sense of trust in self and an ability to trust other people. They give affection and emotional security as well as provide for physical needs. Inconsistent or inadequate care creates mistrust. In extreme cases, as shown by Spitz's classic studies on infant deprivation, lack of care actually led to infant death (Spitz & Wolf, 1946). A less extreme case might form isolation or distrust of others. Given a solid base in early trust, though, the typical infant develops the virtue, or strength, of hope.

Babies must learn trust at two levels: first, a belief that significant adults will be present to meet their needs, and, second, a belief in their own power to make changes and cope. As adults engage with infants, they encourage attachment by holding babies close when feeding them and responding right away to their distress when they cry. When working with infants and toddlers, teachers must take special care to provide a predictable environment and consistent caregiving. Babies are totally dependent on adults to meet their needs; they are particularly vulnerable to difficulties because they have few skills for coping with discomfort and stress. Therefore, it is critical that they be cared for by warm, positive adults who are sensitive and respond affectionately to an infant's needs as soon as they arise. The topic of attachment discussed in this chapter and Chapter 8 reinforces the critical role of collaboration

Psychosocial Stages of Erikson's Theory

Stage	Description	Challenge	Strength
Stage One	Newborns	Trust vs. Mistrust	Hope
Stage Two	Toddlers	Autonomy vs. Shame and Doubt	Willpower
Stage Three	Childhood	Initiative vs. Guilt	Purpose
Stage Four	School	Competence (or industry) vs. Inferiority	Competence
Stage Five	Adolescence	Search for identity vs. Role confusion	Fidelity
Stage Six	Young adulthood	Intimacy (love and friendship) vs. Isolation (loneliness)	Love
Stage Seven	Grown-ups	Generativity (caring for the next generation) vs. Stagnation	Care
Stage Eight	Old age	Integrity vs. Despair	Wisdom

© Cengage Learning 2011

FIGURE 2-5 Erikson's theory of psychosocial development. Centering on basic crises at each stage of development, the theory proposes that these conflicts are part of the life process and that successful handling of these issues can give a person the "ego strength" to face life positively.

with families and teachers. In this way, the very young develop the key strength of trust.

Stage 2: Autonomy versus Doubt (2 to 3 Years)

The second stage, corresponding to the second and third years of life, parallels the muscular-anal period in Freudian theory. The child learns to manage and control impulses and to use both motor and mental skills. To help a child develop a healthy balance between **autonomy** and doubt, parents should consider how to handle their toddlers' toilet learning and growing curiosity to explore. Restrictive or compulsive parents may give the child a feeling of shame and doubt, causing a sense of insecurity. Successful growth in this stage gives children strength of will. "This stage, therefore, becomes decisive for the ratio of love and hate, cooperation and willfulness, freedom of self-expression and its suppression. From a sense of self-control without loss of self-esteem comes a lasting sense of good will and pride; from a sense of loss of self-control and of foreign over-control comes a lasting propensity for doubt and shame" (Erikson, 1963).

Encouraging a sense of autonomy while teaching limits without shaming is a delicate balance. Budding curiosity means high energy, so the daily schedule should include plenty of time for active movement and flexibility to deal with fluctuating energy and mood. Toileting is a learned behavior just as dressing, painting, and singing are; a relaxed attitude about this area helps the child gain mastery without shame. The key strength of positive identity can be developed. Chapter 7 elaborates on how to help guide children using positive discipline.

Stage 3: Initiative versus Guilt (3 to 5 or 6 Years)

The third stage of Eriksonian theory corresponds to the preschool and kindergarten years and parallels Freud's phallic stage of development. The developmental task is to develop a sense of purpose. Out of autonomy comes initiative, and from healthy doubt can come a conscience. For example, a preschooler grabs another's toy; he may run and hide when the crying begins. The teacher gently leads the child to give it back and allows the regret to be expressed through making amends. A group of kindergarten girls have a great idea to put on a play but are disorganized about planning, so the teacher guides them to choose a title, name the various roles, and make a "to do" list so that they can execute in constructive and cooperative ways. Adult interaction matters: An overly restrictive adult may end up with a child who is easily discouraged and inhibited. On the other hand, parents or teachers signaling no restraints give the

child no clear idea of what is socially acceptable and what is not.

Teaching children of this age is both exhilarating and exasperating. Many find this stage easier physically than the previous two but more challenging socially. It is a time when children move in two opposing directions: accomplishment or destruction. To support children's development of initiative with reasonable expectations, teachers can:

- Encourage children to be as independent as possible.
- Focus on gains and attempts rather than on mistakes.
- Set expectations aligned with a child's individual abilities.
- Focus curriculum on real things and on doing instead of simply listening.

The key strength that grows out of this stage is purpose. Chapters 9 and 10 concentrate on environmental and curricular issues.

Stage 4: Industry versus Inferiority (6 to 12 Years)

Erikson's fourth stage, beginning with the primary school years and ending with puberty, parallels Freud's latency period. The major theme in this stage is mastery of life, primarily by adapting to laws of society (people, laws and rules, relationships) and objects (tools, machines, the physical world). This is the child's most enthusiastic time for learning. The stage is "the end of early childhood's period of expansive imagination. The danger in the elementary school years is the development of a sense of inferiority—of feeling incompetent and unproductive" (Santrock, 2009). It is also a time of great adventure. Children begin to think of being big and to identify with people whose work or whose personality they can understand and admire.

- *Find a place in my own school:* Be the line leader on the way to the cafeteria, the goalie on the soccer field, scribe at a scout meeting.
- *Applying myself to something new:* Try organizing and serving snacks at the after-school center.
- *Handling the "tools of the tribe":* Learn to use colored pencils, to read aloud, to fill out forms, to check out balls and bats.

Problems arise if the child feels inadequate and inferior to such tasks. A parent or teacher who overemphasizes children's mistakes could make them despair of ever learning, for instance, the multiplication tables or cursive handwriting. This is particularly sensitive for the child with special needs and for those who are learning a second language. Adults should "mildly but firmly coerce children into the adventure of finding out that one can learn to accomplish things which one would never have thought possible by oneself" (Erikson, 1963). Parents must not let their children restrict their own horizons by doing only what they already know. Particularly in social situations, it is essential for children to learn to do things with others, as difficult and unfair as this may sometimes be. The key strength that can develop is mastery. Chapters 11 to 14 address curriculum for all domains.

Applying Psychosocial Theory to Work with Children

First, Erikson has a clear message about the importance of play. Second, the theory offers guidelines for the role of adults in children's lives.

Play is a critical part of children's total development. Most schools for children younger than age 6 have periods of time allotted for play called "choice time" or "free play." Erikson supports these ideas explicitly by stating that the senses of autonomy and of initiative are developed mainly through social and fantasy play. He suggests that child's play is "the infantile form of the human ability to deal with experiences by creating model situations and to master reality by experiment and planning.... To 'play it out' in play is the most natural self-healing measure childhood affords" (Erikson, 1964). (See the Developmental Topic on "Play" later in this chapter.)

The adult is primarily an emotional base and a social mediator for the child. Teachers become interpreters of feelings, actions, reasons, and solutions. We help children understand situations and motives so that they can solve their own problems. Look at each child's emotional makeup and monitor his or her progress through developmental crises; each crisis is a turning point of increased vulnerability and also enhanced potential. Allow the child, in Erikson's words:

> ... to experience over and over again that he is a person who is permitted to make choices. He has to have the right to choose, for example, whether to sit or whether to stand, whether to approach a visitor or to lean against his mother's knee ... whether to use the toilet or to wet his pants. At the same time he must learn some of the boundaries of self-determination. He inevitably finds that there are some walls he cannot climb, that there are objects out of reach, that above all, there are innumerable commands enforced by powerful adults (1969).

In infant/toddler programs, adults foster independence in toddlers by giving children simple choices ("Juice or milk?") and not false ones ("Do you want your diaper changed?"). In preschool and kindergarten, a teacher allows

In Erikson's theory, the adult serves as a social mediator for the child.

children to take initiative and does not interfere with the results of those actions. Still, adults help children learn reasonable limits and results. The third-graders at a birthday party are laughing and shouting in the bedroom, when suddenly the birthday girl emerges in tears with several others in tow trying to tell what happened. The adult who helps them lets them take turns in the telling and declares how scary it was when someone fell off the bouncing bed and bumped her head helps the children acknowledge real feelings and learn to interact around social challenges.

The issues of early childhood, from Erikson's theory, are really human issues. The remnants of these stages stay with us all our lives, and teachers who are aware of their own processes can fully appreciate the struggles of children.

Behaviorist Theory

Behaviorism is the most pragmatic and functional of the modern psychological ideologies. Behaviorist theories describe both development and learning. Initiated during the 1920s and continually modified today, behaviorism is considered the most distinctly American theory because 20th century psychology in the United States expanded its concepts in research and application so widely. To summarize the behaviorist theory, we have chosen five theorists: Ivan Pavlov, John Watson, Edward Thorndike, B.F. Skinner, and Albert Bandura.

The Behaviorists

What is known today as "behaviorism" begins with the notion that a child is born with a "clean slate," a *tabula rasa* in Locke's words, on which events are written throughout life. The conditions of those events cause all important human behavior. Behaviorists often insist that only what can actually be observed is accepted as fact. Only behavior can be treated, they say, not feelings or internal states. This contrasts to the psychodynamic approach, which insists that behavior is just an indirect clue to the "real" self, that of inner feelings and thoughts.

Ivan Pavlov, a Russian physiologist, was working in a laboratory, studying how animals digest food. He noticed that the dogs in his laboratory would anticipate their meals when they heard or saw their attendants making preparations. Instead of starting to salivate just when food was set in front of them, the dogs would salivate to a number of stimuli associated with food. He identified this simple form of learning as respondent conditioning. The association of involuntary reflexes with other environmental conditions became known as classical conditioning, a cornerstone of behaviorist theory.

John B. Watson was an American theorist who studied Pavlov's experiments, then translated those ideas of conditioning into human terms. In the first quarter of the 20th century, Watson made sweeping claims about the powers of this classical conditioning. He declared that he could shape a person's entire life by controlling exactly the events of an infant's first year. One of his ideas was to discourage emotional ties between parents and children because they interfered with the child's direct learning from the environment (though he later modified this). Nonetheless, he gave scientific validity to the idea that teachers should set conditions for learning and reward proper responses.

Edward L. Thorndike also studied the conditions of learning. Known as the "godfather of standardized testing," Thorndike helped develop scales to measure student achievement and usher in the era of standardized educational testing (see Chapter 6). He set forth the famous stimulus–response technique. A stimulus recalls a response in a person; this forms learned habits. Therefore, it is wise to pay close attention to the consequences of behavior and to the various kinds of reinforcement.

B.F. Skinner took the idea of *tabula rasa* one step further to create the doctrine of the "empty organism." That is, a person is like a vessel to be filled by carefully designed experiences. All behavior is under the control of one or more aspects of the environment. Furthermore,

Skinner maintained that there is no behavior that cannot be modified. Some people argue that Skinnerian concepts tend to depersonalize the learning process and treat people as puppets. Others say that behaviorist psychology has made us develop new ways to help people learn and cope effectively with the world.

Albert Bandura refined behaviorism beyond conditioning into a social learning theory. Socialization is the process of learning to conform to social rules. Social learning theorists watch how children learn these rules and use them in groups. They study the patterns of reinforcement and reward in socially appropriate and unacceptable behavior and how children learn. Children acquire most of their social concepts—the rules by which they live—from models. They observe parents, teachers, and peers in the course of daily life. Social learning theory implies that the models children are most likely to imitate are those who are warm, rewarding, and affectionate. Attachment is also part of the process. The most significant models are people to whom the child is emotionally tied.

From this arose a new concept known as modeling. This is what used to be known as learning and teaching by example. For instance, children who see their parents smoking will likely smoke themselves, and those who witness kindness to others are likely to imitate it. In fact, Bandura's studies provided "strong evidence that exposure to filmed aggression heightens aggressive reactions in children. Subjects who viewed the aggressive human and cartoon models on film exhibited nearly twice as much aggression than did subjects in the control group who were not exposed to the aggressive film content" (Bandura, 1963). This work suggests that pictorial mass media—television, video games, and computer activities—serve as important sources of social behavior. Any behavior can be learned by watching it, from language (listening to others talk) to fighting (watching violence on television).

Bandura's theory (2001) has expanded into a cognitive model of self-efficacy, theorizing that children think hard about what they see and feel. Children learn from observing and modeling others, but also from understanding and acting on their own behavior. This leads to self-regulated learning. As early as the preschool years, children are developing internal standards and reflective thinking that influences a child's behavior "from the inside out." Thus, personal and cognitive factors influence behavior, as does the environment, and, in turn, children's behavior can affect the environment around them. Adding the factors of modeling and reflective thinking to behaviorist theory links it to Erikson's psychosocial theory and to Piaget's cognitive theory (discussed next in this chapter).

Theory of Behaviorism and Social Learning

What is behavior, or learning, theory all about? Learning occurs when an organism interacts with the environment. Through experience, behavior is modified or changed. In the behaviorist's eyes, three types of learning occur: 1) classical conditioning; 2) operant conditioning; and 3) observational learning or modeling. The first two are based on the idea that learning is mostly the development of habit. What people learn is a series of associations, forming a connection between a stimulus and response that did not exist before. The third is based on a social approach. Figure 2-6 summarizes these three types of behaviorist learning processes.

Classical Conditioning

Classical conditioning can be explained by reviewing Pavlov's original experiments. A dog normally salivates at the sight of food but not when he hears a bell. When the sound of a bell is paired with the sight of food, the dog "learns" to salivate when he hears the bell, whether or not food is nearby. Thus, the dog has been conditioned to salivate (give the response) for both the food (unconditioned stimulus) and the bell (conditioned stimulus). Similarly, when the school bell rings in the afternoon, children begin to gather their papers into backpacks to go home. They have been conditioned to the sound of the bell; ask any teacher who has had to deal with a broken bell system how strong this conditioning is. Classical conditioning can also account for the development of phobias. Watson used a young boy in a laboratory to test this theory. He showed the boy a white rat, then sounded a loud noise. After only seven pairings, the boy would cringe at the sight of the rat without the bell sounding at all. Only a few painful visits to a childhood dentist can teach a lifetime fear of dental health professionals.

Operant Conditioning

Operant conditioning is slightly different from classical conditioning in that it focuses on the response rather than the stimulus. In operant conditioning, the process that makes it more likely that a behavior recurs is called reinforcement. A stimulus that increases the likelihood of repeated behavior is called a reinforcer. Most people are likely to increase what gives them pleasure (be it food or attention) and decrease what gives them displeasure (such as punishment, pain, or the withdrawal of food or attention). The behaviorist tries to influence the organism by controlling these kinds of reinforcement.

A positive reinforcer is something that the learner views as desirable:

"social reinforcers"	attention, praise, smiles, or hugs
"nonsocial reinforcers"	tokens, toys, food, stickers

For example, you would like Claire to begin to use a spoon instead of her hands to eat. Before conditioning, you talk to her whenever she eats. During the conditioning period, you can give attention each time she picks up a spoon during feeding times and ignore her when she uses her hands. Afterward, she is more likely to use a spoon and less often her hands. This is an example of a positive reinforcer, something that increases the likelihood of the desired response.

The reinforcers can be negative as well. A negative reinforcer is removal of an unpleasant stimulus as a result of some particular behavior. Circle time is Jimmy's favorite activity at school. Yet he has difficulty controlling his behavior and consistently disrupts the group. Before conditioning, he is told that if he talks to his neighbors and shouts responses at the teacher, he will be asked to leave the circle. During the conditioning period, Jimmy is praised whenever he pays attention, sings songs, and does not bother those around him (positive reinforcement). When he begins to shout, he is told to leave and return when he can sing without shouting (negative reinforcement). A negative reinforcer is used to stop children from behaving in a particular way by arranging for them to end a mildly aversive situation

Behaviorist Learning Processes

	Classical Conditioning	Operant Conditioning	Modeling
Kind of behavior	Reflexive	Voluntary	Voluntary
Type of learning	Learning through association	Learning through reinforcement	Learning through observation and intimation
Role of learner	Passive	Active or passive	Active

FIGURE 2-6 Behaviorist learning processes. Classical conditioning, operant conditioning, and modeling are three ways of learning, describing how behavior is learned and the role of the learner in each process.

immediately (in this case, the boy has to leave the group) by improving their behavior. Jimmy, by controlling his own behavior, could end his isolation from the group.

Punishment is different from negative reinforcement. Punishment is an unpleasant event that makes the behavior less likely to be repeated; that is, if Jimmy were spanked every time he shouted, then his shouting would be the punished behavior, and it is likely he would begin to shout less. However, when leaving the group is the reinforcer for shouting, he tries to stop shouting to increase the likelihood of being able to stay and not be taken away from the group. Negative reinforcement thus increases the likelihood that the desired behavior is repeated (staying in the group) and removes attention from the less desirable behavior (the shouting). The "time-out" chair, for instance, could be viewed as either a punishment or a negative reinforcer. If used as exclusion from the group or a withdrawal of playing privileges, a child would find the time out as a punishment. On the other hand, if a child could leave the time out more quickly by exhibiting certain behaviors (instead of the "bad" behavior), it might be seen as a negative reinforcer.

Reinforcement, both positive and negative, is a powerful tool. It is important for adults to realize that it can be misused. It is wise to be careful, particularly in the case of negative reinforcement. An adult may not be gentle with a negative reinforcer when angry with a child's inappropriate behavior. Educators and parents should be aware of the possibilities and check their own responses.

Modeling

Modeling is the third kind of conditioning and is also known as observational learning. Social behavior is particularly noteworthy to early childhood professionals, as most work with children in groups and thus witness social behavior constantly. Any behavior that involves more than one person can be considered social. One of the most negative social behaviors is aggression. It is this type that Albert Bandura researched, finding that much of it is learned by watching others.

Aggression is a complex issue, involving various definitions and behaviors. To illustrate social learning theory, Bandura defines aggression as behavior intended to inflict harm or discomfort to another person or object. Bandura showed a short film of aggressive behavior to young children. The original mid-1960s studies are summarized next.

Each child in Bandura's experiment viewed one of three films. In all three films, an adult hit, kicked, and verbally abused an inflated Bobo doll in ways that young children are unlikely to do spontaneously. The films differed in what happened to the model after the aggressive sequence. In one film, the model was lavishly rewarded with praise and foods that appealed to preschoolers, such as candy and caramel popcorn. In another film, the model

© Cengage Learning

Social reinforcers include attention and smiles as well as praise.

was punished in a dramatic way, including severe scolding and a spanking. The third film simply ended after the model's aggressive behavior, with no consequences following the aggression. After viewing one film, each child in the experiment was allowed to play in a room with a Bobo doll, all the toys used in the aggression film, and a variety of other toys.

The results are most impressive, especially to those working with young children. The level of aggression expressed by each child was directly related to what the children saw as the consequences in the film. When offered prizes, they imitated almost exactly what their model had done. Also, children appeared more likely to attack one another after viewing the attacks on the Bobo doll in film. Further studies have shown that children's levels of aggression are higher right after viewing the film but less so when shown it again six months later (Berger, 2011). Regardless of the controversy that may surround any study of children's aggression or the effects of watching filmed violence on youngsters, the social learning theory deserves serious consideration. The effect of television and media viewing on children is discussed in Chapter 15.

Can Rewards Actually Punish?

Alfie Kohn, a nationally known educator and author, is a strong critic of behaviorism. He cites research showing that rewards decrease motivation; in fact, the more rewards are used, the more they seem to be needed. Furthermore, punishment and negative reinforcement produce short-term compliance only and often disregard feelings, needs, and intentions. "Skinnerian thinking—caring only about behaviors— has narrowed our understanding of children and warped the way we deal with them…. In a nutshell, it's the child who engages in the behavior, not the behavior itself, who matters" (Kohn, 2006).

Teachers intentionally shape children's behavior, deliberately reinforcing what the want children to do, and attempting through behavior modification techniques to get children to move away and stop behavior that adults find unacceptable. These intentions must be implemented carefully, however, or unintended consequences may occur.

Think About This
1. Do you think children end up being "punished by rewards"?
2. How do you shape children's behavior?
3. How much of what we do with children can be explained by behaviorism?

Applying Behaviorist Theory to Work with Children

Behaviorist theories make a strong case for how the environment influences our behavior:

- *Physical environment:* A teacher arranges the room so that positive learning is enhanced.
- *Daily schedule:* Routines and sequence of events are planned to encourage habits.
- *Teacher/child interaction:* Teachers respond carefully to children to shape their behavior.

Adults are powerful reinforcers and models for children. A learning situation comprises many cues; it is up to adults to know what those cues are and how to control them. Teachers who use behavior modification techniques know both what children are to do and how they are reinforced for their behavior.

Each teacher and program must consider the impact of this theory and how to apply it to classroom and client.

What children learn is shaped by the circumstances surrounding the learning. Experiences that are enjoyable are reinforcing. From the peek-a-boo game with an infant to a 7-year-old's first ride on a skateboard, an experience is more likely to be repeated and learned if it is pleasant. Social learning is particularly powerful in the lives of young children. Adults must be mindful of their own behavior; watching children as young as 2 years old play "family" or "school" convinces the most skeptical critic that any behavior is learnable and can become part of children's behavioral repertoire.

Cognitive Theory

Adult: What does it mean to be alive?
Child: It means you can move about, play—that you can do all kinds of things.
Adult: Is a mountain alive?
Child: Yes, because it has grown by itself.
Adult: Is a cloud alive?
Child: Yes, because it sends water.
Adult: Is wind alive?
Child: Yes, because it pushes things.

How do children learn to think, and what do they think about? Cognitive theory describes the structure and development of human thought processes and how those processes affect the way a person understands and perceives the world. Piaget's theory of cognition forms a cornerstone of early childhood educational concepts about children; others have developed this theory further into a constructivist theory of learning.

Jean Piaget

Jean Piaget was one of the most exciting research theorists in child development. A major force in child psychology, he studied both thought processes and how they change with age. Piaget's ideas serve as our guide to cognitive theory because of the thoroughness of his work. He had great influence on child psychology, theories of learning, intellectual development, and even philosophy. He became the foremost expert on the development of knowledge from birth to adulthood.

How did Piaget find out about such matters? A short review of his life and ideas reveals a staggering volume of work and a wide scope of interests. Born at the turn of the century, Piaget built on his childhood curiosity in science and philosophy by working with Dr. Simon at the Binet Laboratory (Simon and Binet devised the first intelligence test). While recording children's abilities to answer questions correctly, he became fascinated with children's incorrect responses. He noticed that children tended to give similar kinds of wrong answers at certain ages.

Thus, Piaget launched into a lifelong study of intelligence. He believed that children think in fundamentally different ways from adults. He also developed a new method for studying thought processes. Rather than using a standardized test, he adapted the psychiatric method of question and response. Called the *methode clinique*, it is a technique in which adults ask questions and then adapt their teaching and further inquiries based on children's answers (see Chapter 6).

Piaget then began studying children's thought processes. With his wife, one of his former students, he observed his own children. He also began to look closely at how actively children engage in their development. Prolific his entire life, Piaget gave us a complex theory of intelligence and child development. He recorded, in a systematic way, how children learn, when they learn, and what they learn.

Theory of Cognitive Development

While others thought that the development of thinking was either intrinsic (nature) or extrinsic (nurture), Piaget thought that neither position offered a full explanation for a child's amazing and complex behaviors.

His theory relies on both maturational and environmental factors. It is called maturational because it sets out a sequence of cognitive (thinking) stages that is governed by heredity—how the body is structured biologically, with automatic (instinctive) behaviors such as an infant sucking at birth. It is called an environmental theory because the experiences children have directly influence how they develop and build their own knowledge rather than simply absorbing instruction (Piaget & Inhelder, 1972).

Theory Basics

The basic premise of cognitive theory is that thinking and learning are processes of interaction between a person and the environment. Piaget also believed that all species inherit a basic tendency to organize their lives and adapt to the world around them. This is known as a constructivist theory (see next section); that is, children actively construct knowledge on an ongoing basis. They are developing and constantly revising their own knowledge. All people use three basic processes to think: the adaptive processes of assimilation and accommodation and the balancing process of equilibration (see Figure 2-7).

As they experience the world, they take in new information and either absorb it into what they already know assimilation or create a new place for it accommodation, thus returning to a sense of balance equilibration. In doing so, children figure out what the world is all about and then work toward surviving in that world. Piaget believed children learn best when they are actually doing the work (or play) themselves, rather than being told, shown, or explained to, which were the dominant teaching methods of the day. Having studied Montessori methods, Piaget concluded that teachers could prepare a stimulating environment and also interact with the children to enhance their thinking.

Regardless of their age, all people develop schemas, or mental concepts, as a general way of thinking about, or interacting with, ideas and objects in the environment. Very young children learn perceptual schemas as they taste and feel; preschool children use language and pretend play to create their understanding; school-age children develop more abstract ideas, such as morality schemas, which help them determine how to act.

Piaget theorized that thinking develops in a certain general pattern in all human beings. These stages of thinking are the psychological structures that go along with adapting to the environment. Piaget identified four major stages of cognitive development:

Sensorimotor stage	0 to 2 years
Preoperational stage	2 to 6 or 7 years
Concrete operational stage	6 to 12 years
Formal operational stage	12 years to adulthood

TeachSource Video

Watch the three TeachSource Videos on "Piaget's Sensorimotor, Preoperational, and Concrete Operational Stages." After you study the video clips, reflect on the following questions:

1. How does children's thinking change over the early years, and how does this affect what is planned in early childhood education classrooms for the three age groups?

2. Why should teachers know developmental or learning theories before they create programs for young children?

Piaget's Three Processes of Cognitive Adaptation

Assimilation:
Taking new information and organizing it in such a way that it fits with what the person already knows.

Example: Juanita sees an airplane while walking outside with her father. She knows that birds fly. So, never having seen this flying thing before, she calls it a "bird (pájaro)." This is what we call *assimilation*. She is taking in this new information and making it fit into what she already knows. Children assimilate what they are taught into their own worlds when they play "school" by taking turns and "house" with their dolls and toys or other people.

Accommodation:
Taking new information and changing what is already thought to fit the new information.

Example: Aaron is at the grocery store with his mother and newborn baby. He calls the woman in the line ahead of them "pregnant" although she is simply overweight. After being corrected, he asks the next person he sees, "Are you pregnant or just fat?" This is what we call *accommodation*. Having learned that not all people with large bellies are pregnant, he changes his knowledge base to include new information. Children accommodate to the world as they are taught to use a spoon, the toilet, or a computer.

Equilibration:
A mental process to achieve a mental balance, whereby a person takes new information and continually attempts to make sense of the experiences and perceptions.

Example: Colby, age 7, gets two glasses from the cupboard for his friend Ajit and himself. After putting apple juice into his short, wide glass he decides he'd rather have milk, so he pours it into Ajit's tall, thin glass. "Look, now I have more than you!" says his friend. This puzzles Colby, who is distressed (in "disequilibrium"): How could it be more when he just poured it out of his glass? He thinks about the inconsistency (and pours the juice several times back and forth) and begins to get the notion that pouring liquid into different containers does not change the amount (the conservation of liquids). "No, it isn't," he says, "it's just a different shape!" Thus, Colby learns to make sense of it in a new way and achieve equilibrium in his thinking. Children do this whenever they get new information that asks them to change the actual schemas, making new ones to fit new experiences.

© Cengage Learning 2014

FIGURE 2-7 In Piagetian theory, the processes of assimilation, accommodation, and equilibration are basic to how people think (cognition) and learn.

Each person of normal intelligence goes through these stages in this order, although the rate depends on the individual and experience. Each stage of development has critical lessons for the child to learn in order to think and make sense of the world (Figure 2-8).

Piaget's theories revolutionized our thinking about children's thinking and challenged psychologists and educators to focus less on *what* children know than the *ways* they come to know. But was Piaget right? Researchers have been exploring and debating the ideas of cognitive theory for many years, often engaging in what Piaget himself called "the American question": Can you speed up the rate in which children pass through these intellectual stages of development?

There are two main criticisms of Piaget's theory: the age and the stage.

1. *The Age:* He seems to have been wrong about just how early many cognitive skills develop. For example, virtually all the achievements of the concrete operational period are present in at least rudimentary or fragmentary form in the preschool years.

This might simply mean that Piaget just had the ages wrong—that the concrete operations stage really begins at age 3 or 4.

2. *The Stage:* Research on expertise now shows that specific knowledge makes a huge difference. Children and adults who know a lot about some subject or some set of materials (dinosaurs, baseball cards, mathematics, etc.) not only categorize information in that topic area in more complex and hierarchical ways; they are also better at remembering new information on that topic and better at applying more advanced forms of logic to material in that area.

Developmental psychologists now believe that Piaget's theory of distinct stages is not correct, but the idea of a sequence in thinking is. Furthermore, neuroscience research has discovered that brain maturation seems to follow a sequence that parallels the various thinking stages of development (see later in this chapter). Children progress from one stage to the next, changing their thinking depending on their level of maturation and experience with the environment.

Stages of Early Childhood Cognitive Development

As a baby

Sensorimotor Period

Key concept

Object permanence

Definition

—the understanding that objects continue to exist even when they are out of sight

—essential to understanding the physical world

Explanation

—Birth to four months, infants respond to objects but stop tracking them if they are covered.

—Four to eight months, infants will reach for an object if it is partially covered.

—By eight to twelve months, infants will search for hidden objects randomly, anywhere.

—By 12 to 18 months, toddlers will search for an object where they last saw it.

—By—18 to 24 months, toddlers will search for hidden objects in systematic way.

As a preschooler

Preoperational

Key concept

Symbolic play and language

Definition

—the use of ideas, images, sounds, or symbols to stand for objects and events = symbolic play

—the use of an abstract, rule- governed system of symbols that can be combined to communicate information = language

—essential to developing the capacity to think

Explanation

—From 14 to 19 months, representational ability emerges.

—By 24 months, most can use substitute objects in pretend play.

—Nine to twelve months, infants begin to use conventional social gestures.

—Around one year, first words emerge.

—18 to 24 months, first sentences appear.

As a primary child

Concrete Operational

Key concept

Reasoning

Definition

—Actions can be carried out mentally.

—Logical reasoning replaces intuitive thinking in concrete situations.

—Classification skills develop.

—Essential to ability to think logically.

Explanation

—can coordinate several characteristics rather than a single property

—reversibility emerges; can see the same problem from several perspectives

—can divide things into sets and reason about their relationships

—Conservation skills emerge; an amount of liquid remains the same, no matter the container.

FIGURE 2-8 During each stage of cognitive development, children learn a key concept that enhances their thinking and reasoning.

Certain innate physical skills, such as fine motor coordination, determine how much a child is capable of doing. Certain environmental factors, such as the kinds of experiences the world and adults provide, influence the rate of growth. Throughout the process, as new information comes in, the child learns and grows (Ginsburg & Opper, 1987).

Applying Cognitive Theory to Work with Children

What can teachers learn from the complicated cognitive theory? Piaget's writings do not apply directly to classroom methods or subject matter per se, and therefore, careful interpretation is required. In fact, he never claimed to be an educator. However, Piaget's theories provide a framework, or philosophy, about children's thinking. A constructivist theory of education has arisen. Additionally, Piagetian theory has three implications for both environment and interactions.

Constructivist Theory

The constructivist theory of education changed the century-old transmission model of teaching, in which the teacher possesses the knowledge and transmits it directly to the children. In contrast, a new method based on Piaget's theory emerged. Constructivism is a theory of learning that states that individuals learn through adaptation. What they adapt to is directly influenced by the people, materials, and situations with which they come into contact.

This theory holds that people build on pre-existing knowledge, be it intellectual, social, or moral. One of its basic tenets is that children learn by creating their own knowledge by giving subjective meaning to what they experience. Another fundamental idea is that children learn by taking new ideas and integrating them into their existing knowledge base. This is exactly in line with Piaget's processes of assimilation and accommodation.

Based on ideas from Dewey and Piaget and supported by sociocultural theory, this transactional model of teaching actively engages a child in tasks designed to create personal meaning. Learning is an active process, based on the belief that knowledge is constructed by the learner rather than transferred from the teacher to the child. Although there may still be some direct instruction and demonstrations as there are in classes based on behaviorist views, a constructivist program promotes children's social, cognitive, and moral development more than do most teacher-centered programs. It is a theory used extensively in the emergent curriculum model (see Chapter 10).

Materials

Materials are used in a special way in applying Piaget's theory to early education. Children need many objects to explore so that they can later incorporate these into their symbolic thinking. Such materials need to be balanced among open-ended ones (such as sand and water activities, basic art and construction materials), guided ones (cooking with recipes, conducting experiments, classification and seriated materials), and self-correcting ones (puzzles, matching games, such as some of the Montessori materials). It is important to remember that young children need to be involved with concrete objects and to explore and use them in their own ways, which include both sensorimotor and beginning symbolic play.

Scheduling

Scheduling is giving children plenty of time to explore their reality, especially through the use of play. A Piagetian classroom is likely be noisy, with periods of time for children to "act out" their own ideas. Also, time is scheduled for imitation of adult-given ideas (songs, finger plays, and stories). Constructivist classrooms look diverse because the style and cultures of the teacher and children prevail. Children have choices and make decisions on significant parts of their learning. The teacher is a facilitator and co-constructor of the curriculum, does less talking while the learners do more, and provides more guidance and written observations rather than enforcing rules or giving tests.

Teachers

Teachers must have a particular developmental point of view. The teacher who knows the stages and levels of thinking of the children is one who can guide that class into new and challenging opportunities to learn and grow.

In working with children younger than the age 5, we must remember that, because they do not understand mental representations very well, they have trouble recognizing that another person may view or interpret things differently than they do. This egocentric viewpoint is both natural and normal but must be factored into teachers' thoughts as they work with children. For instance:

- You may be able to ask a 6- or 7-year-old: "How would you feel if you were in that situation?" For a younger child, the question is incomprehensible.
- The preschool child is likely to have trouble distinguishing how things seem or appear from how they really are (see Figure 2-9). If something *seems* dangerous (the scary-looking shadow in their bedroom), it *is* dangerous, and the friendly-acting strangers are safe because they look non-dangerous. Young children are gullible and trusting, in part because of their inadequate understanding that things may not be as they appear.

The teacher's role is to build an environment that is stimulating and conducive to the process of constructing meaning and knowledge. The preprimary schools of Reggio Emilia (see Chapters 9 and 10) encourage children to create their own material representations of their understanding by using many types of media (drawing, sculpture, stories, puppets, paper). At kindergarten and school-age levels, learning literacy and mathematics is considered a developmental process that the teacher facilitates by providing modeling, authentic experiences, mini-lessons on specific topics, and frequent opportunities for students to consult with and learn from each other. Many constructivist classrooms work on creating

FIGURE 2-9 Children's ideas, or mental representations, change with age. The older child recognizes that, although the contents of the box are only one thing out in the world, they can be represented in people's heads in more than one way—a possibility that escapes the younger child. (Special thanks to John Flavell for the example and the research. Reprinted by permission of John Flavell.)

community through rule-creating; in fact, teachers in those classrooms would tell us that "The only way to help students become ethical people, as opposed to people who merely do what they are told, is to have them construct moral meaning" (Kohn, 2005).

To encourage thinking and learning, teachers should refrain from telling children exactly how to solve a problem. Rather, the teacher should ask questions that encourage children to observe and pay attention to their own ideas. Teachers should:

- Use or create situations that are personally meaningful to children.
- Provide opportunities for them to make decisions.
- Provide opportunities for them to exchange viewpoints with their peers.

Perhaps more important is the awareness that all children have the capability to reason and be thinkers at their particular stage of development.

Teachers must remember that young children:

1. Think differently from adults.
2. Need many materials to explore and describe.
3. Think in a concrete manner and often cannot think out things in their heads.
4. Come to conclusions and decisions based on what they see, rather than on what is sensible and logical to an adult.

5. Need challenging questions and the time to make their own decisions and find their own answers.

The thoughts and ideas of Piaget are impressive, both in quantity and quality. The collective works of this man are extremely complex and often difficult to understand. Yet they have given us a valuable blueprint.

It is Piaget's genius for empathy with children, together with true intellectual genius, that has made him the outstanding child psychologist in the world today and one destined to stand beside Freud with respect to his contributions to psychology, education, and related disciplines. Just as Freud's discoveries of unconscious motivation, infantile sexuality, and the stages of psychosexual growth changed our ways of thinking about human personality, so Piaget's discoveries of children's implicit philosophies, the construction of reality by the infant, and the stages of mental development have altered our ways of thinking about human intelligence (Elkind, 1977).

Sociocultural Theory

An awareness of culture and family influences on development and an interest in the programs at Reggio Emilia, Italy, have led to a closer look at the works of Vygotsky. His sociocultural theory focuses on the child as a whole and incorporates ideas of culture and values

DAP Take Piaget with You

Piaget's stages of cognitive development can be used to implement the first "umbrella handle" (see Figure 2-1) of developmentally appropriate practices. Read these examples, then answer the questions.

Age in years	Stage	Description	Activity
0–2	Sensorimotor	Thinking with their hands and feet, eyes and ears	Have toys near the crib so that young infants can bat and create movement (mastery of hands); cover an interesting toy with a blanket so that an older infant can look for it (object permanence); offer toddlers blocks to stack (coordination of schemes)
2–7	Preoperational	Exploring with activity & curiosity	Create water play with containers and play dough with rollers (centration); when in conflict, help children to articulate their wishes and views first, then listen to another's differing view; point out differences then find a common solution (egocentrism)
7–11	Concrete operational	Reasoning with beginning logic	Using water and clay, ask children to explain their reasons and see if they can follow transformation from beginning to end (reversibility); with chapter books, ask them to explain a character's reasoning for their actions, then to contrast it with their own (de-center)

into child development, particularly the areas of language and self-identity. In his view, children's development was more than just a response to personal experience. Rather, children are influenced in fundamental ways by their family, community, and socioeconomic status. Studies on cognitive and language patterns among young children in selected populations (Fouad & Arredondo, 2007) have confirmed the deep role of culture in learning.

Lev Vygotsky

Born in 1896 in Byelorussia, Lev Vygotsky graduated from Moscow University with a degree in literature in 1917. For the next six years, he taught literature and psychology and directed adult theater as well as founding a literary journal. In 1924, he began work at the Institute of Psychology in Moscow, where he focused on the problems of educational practice, particularly those of handicapped children. Toward that end, he gathered a group of young scientists during the late 1920s and early 1930s to look more closely at psychology and mental abnormality, including medical connections. Unfortunately, his career was cut short by tuberculosis; he died in 1934 at age 38. Yet in that short time, he studied the works of Freud, Piaget, and Montessori. His theory is also rooted in experimental psychology, the American philosopher William James, and contemporaries Pavlov and Watson (see the behaviorist theory section of this chapter).

Sociocultural Theory

Vygotsky's work is called sociocultural because it focuses on how values, beliefs, skills, and traditions are transmitted to the next generation (Vygotsky, 1978). There are similarities to several other theories:

- Like Erikson, Vygotsky believed in the connection between culture and development, particularly the interpersonal connection between the child and other important people.
- Like Maslow (see later in this chapter), he considered the child as a whole, taking a humanistic, more qualitative approach to studying children.

Like Piaget, Vygotsky asserted that much of children's learning takes place during play. This is because language and development build on each other, and the best way to develop competency is through interaction with others in a special way.

At the same time, sociocultural theory has unique perspectives that differ from other theories:

- *Behaviorist.* Though he understood the primary behaviorists of his day, he differed from them in that he emphasized family, social interaction, and play as primary influences in children's lives, rather than the stimulus-response and schedules of reinforcement that were becoming so popular in his day.
- *Piagetian.* Rather than moving through certain stages or sequences (as Piaget proposed), children's

mastery and interaction differ from culture to culture. Adults, Vygotsky noted, teach socially valued skills at a very early age; children's learning is, therefore, quite influenced by what is valued in their social world. Piaget insisted that, although children needed to interact with people and objects to learn, the stages of thinking were still bound by maturation. Vygotsky claimed that interaction and direct teaching were critical aspects of a child's cognitive development and that a child's level of thinking could be advanced by just such interaction.

Vygotsky believed that the child is embedded in the family and culture of his community and that much of a child's development is culturally specific. There are three ways culture is passed on: The first is imitative learning (like Bandura); the second by instructed learning (such as following directions); and the third by collaborative learning (working together with guided help or in play). Children learn through guided participation with others, especially in a kind of apprenticeship in which a tutor supports the novice not only by instruction but also by doing. Social interactions lead to continuous step-by-step changes in children's thoughts and behavior, so relationships between a teacher and a learner both impart skills and provide the context and cultural values of that skill, as well as teaching how to build relationships and use language: Engaging together matters (Berk, 2000).

Three concepts are key to understanding sociocultural theory.

1. *Zone of proximal development.* When a mentor senses that the learner is ready for a new challenge—or simply wants the learner to come along—he or she draws the novice into a zone of proximal development (ZPD), which is the range of learning that would be beyond what the novice could learn alone but could grasp with help. For example, Sergio can ride a tricycle alone and has hopped onto his sister's two-wheeler. Surely he will fall. But if his uncle runs alongside and helps him get balanced, he can do more. Of course, it takes many attempts, but with assistance, Sergio can increase his ZPD and eventually ride on his own.

   Who can help a child's ZPD? Initially, of course, it is the family. For instance, a young girl is carried even as a toddler to the open market with her mother. There, she watches and is guided toward learning how to touch cloth, smell herbs, taste food, and weigh and compare amounts. Is it any wonder she learns advanced math skills and the language of bargaining early? Second, the teacher is involved. For example, assisting a child complete a puzzle, put on mittens, or

resolve a conflict helps children learn problem solving skills. Third, other children—older ones who have more expertise or peers who may have superior skills or simply offer help—can help a child's learning. Cooperative learning, in which small groups of peers at varying levels of competence work toward a shared goal is common in a Vygotskian classroom.

2. *Scaffolding.* This concept describes the kind of scaffolding, or helpful structure, created to support the child in learning. Although not originally used by Vygotsky, the term helps define the most important components of tutoring. Just as a physical scaffold surrounds a building so that it might be worked on, so does the child get hints, advice, and structure in order to master a skill or an activity. This can be seen in children's developing speech, in guidance, and in ordinary tasks, as learning to ride a bike. Adults can arouse interest in a task, simplify it—scaffold it—so that it is within the child's ability and teach enthusiasm by helping the task get accomplished.

3. *Private speech.* Vygotsky believed that language, even in its earliest forms, was socially based and critical to how children internalize and learn. Rather than egocentric or immature, children's speech and language development during the ages of 3 to 7 years is merged with and tied to what children are thinking. During these transitional years, the child talks aloud to herself; after a while, this self-talk becomes internalized so that the child can act without talking aloud. Vygotsky contended that children speak to themselves for self-guidance and self-direction and that this private speech helps children think about their behavior and plan for action. With age, private (inner) speech (once called "egocentric speech"), which goes from out loud to whispers to lip movement, is critical to a child's self-regulation.

Applying Sociocultural Theory to Work with Children

Sociocultural theory has five implications for the classroom teacher.

1. Family and culture. *A child's family and culture need to be incorporated into a child's schooling.* Teachers must genuinely embrace (rather than give lip service) to the concept that the child's first teacher is the family. Each family may emphasize certain skills—vocabulary development, cooperation with siblings, self-care, and independence—that serve as the sociocultural context for learning. For instance, children of color in American society are socialized

© Belinda Images/SuperStock

In Vygotsky's sociocultural theory, children learn as other people create a kind of scaffolding to support the children.

to operate in two worlds and thus must achieve a kind of bicognitive development (along with bicultural and perhaps bilingual skills). Such work has led to a focus on "learning styles" (see Chapter 10). Research done with different cultural groups has reinforced the importance of looking at culture as part of the context in which the child lives and learns (Rogoff, 1990; York, 2005).

2. Teacher/child relationship. Teacher/child relationships are vital to learning. The teacher and learner adjust to one another; teachers use what they know about children to guide their teaching and plan their curriculum. Sociocultural theory supports both emergent curriculum (see Chapter 10) and spontaneous, teachable moments of the anti-bias curriculum (see Chapter 9). Of course, young children need adults to help create curriculum and set an environmental stage for learning. But they also need teachers to mediate social relationships and conflicts, to ask questions and know where a child is headed. Adults help children learn by seeing the challenge, giving assistance when needed, and noticing when the task is mastered and the child is ready for a new challenge.

3. Tools for learning. Pay close attention to the psychological and cultural "tools" used to teach. For example, some American children are taught to tie a string around their fingers as a memory device, whereas in Russia they tie a knot in their handkerchief. Tunes can aid learning (like the alphabet song); the higher mental functions need the help of a person who knows the tools of the society to learn.

4. Value of play. *Play is crucial for learning.* It is in play that the child practices operating the symbols and tools of the culture. Vygotsky (1978) puts it this way:

> Action in the imaginative sphere, in an imaginary situation, the creation of voluntary intentions, the formation of real-life plans and volitional motives— all appear in play and make it the highest level of preschool development. The child moves forward essentially through play activity. Only in this sense can play be considered a leading activity that determines the child's development.

> For instance, children might build a structure with blocks; the teacher encourages them to draw the building and then map the entire block corner as a village or neighborhood. The adult serves an important role as an intellectual mediator, continually shifting to another set of symbols to give children a different way of looking at the same thing.

5. Individual differences. *Individual differences still matter.* In a Vygotskian classroom activities are planned to encourage both assisted and cooperative learning. Teachers observe for opportunities to increase an individual's ZPD by planning experiences for extending the upper limit. Classrooms work best with multi-aged grouping, or at least with plenty of opportunity for older "buddies" to lead and younger ones to help.

Ecological Theory

The ecological theory is based on the premise that development is greatly influenced by forces outside the child. "No person can be understood in isolation, at just one moment in time. Urie Bronfenbrenner deserves credit for recognizing this fact" (Berger, 2011). Bronfenbrenner applied a general systems theory to human development in the 1970s, as the ecology movement began in America and Europe. Development is "a joint function of person and environment and human ecosystems include both physical factors—climate, space, home, and school—and the social environment—family, culture, and the larger society" (Bronfenbrenner, 2000).

Urie Bronfenbrenner

Born in the former Soviet Union, Bronfenbrenner immigrated to the United States at age 6, settling in New York. After studying psychology and music at Cornell University, he did graduate work in developmental psychology. He served as a clinical psychologist in the United States Army during World War II. When he returned to civilian life, he worked on the faculties of the University of Michigan and Cornell University, where he crafted this well-known theory (Bronfenbrenner, 1979).

Ecological Systems Theory

Bronfenbrenner's model describes four systems that influence human development, nested within each other like a circle of rings. With the child at the center, these four are the settings in which a child spends a significant period of time, the relationships of those settings, the societal structures, and then the larger contexts in which these systems operate (see Figure 2-10). The influences among these systems are critical to acknowledge: Just as in nature, activity in one part affects all the other parts. For example, a sudden income drop affects the family in many ways: The parents may be preoccupied and unavailable to the child, who may then need more attention from the caregivers at school, who in turn may ask for more resources from the community for the family.

Applying Ecological Theory to Work with Children

The usefulness of this theory is in its combining of many methods—multidisciplinary, multicultural, and multidirectional—to understand the developing child. The values of the community (the exosystem) can influence social conditions (the macrosystem) and, in turn, be influenced by the individual family or program (microsystem). For example, think of an area where several families with young children move into the neighborhood. The community priorities shift to incorporate more family interests; parents get everyone involved in creating a neighborhood playground. In doing so, the city council lobbies the state legislature to adopt more "family-friendly" political policies. Many systems thus have a profound effect, both directly and indirectly, on children's development.

Imagine if the situation were reversed. Parents with very little voice in their community might have had a city council that was unresponsive to their needs. The playground would never have been built, the children would have little visibility in the neighborhood except to be

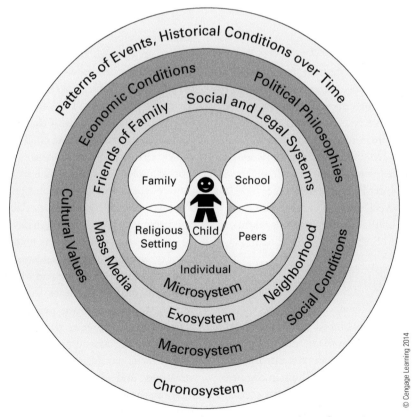

© Cengage Learning 2014

FIGURE 2-10 Ecological theory shows the various systems that influence in a child's development.

troublesome, and the families would feel like outsiders in the community. Thus, the dynamic nature of many systems is described well in ecological theory.

The ecological theory underscores the need for working partnerships between early childhood programs, the families they serve, and the societal structures children need to grow. The mesosytem, for instance, involves all the connections between the microsystems. Put the young child in the center (see Figure 2-10), and it includes all the communication processes between the child's family and teachers. Therefore, letters home, parent–teacher conferences, chats on arrival and departure, and phone calls would all contribute to the child's mesosystem. In this regard, the ecological theory possibly best encompasses most of the questions about the nature of development posed at the beginning of the chapter.

Multiple Intelligences Theory

There is a century-old argument about whether intelligence is a single, broad ability (as measured by an IQ test) or a set of specific abilities (more than one intelligence). Gardner's theory promotes the idea of many, or multiple, intelligences.

Howard Gardner

Howard Gardner, a professor of human development at the Harvard Graduate School of Education, has been very influential in the ongoing debate about the nature of intelligence. Born in Pennsylvania, he earned both bachelor and doctorate degrees at Harvard University and was fortunate to have Erikson as a tutor. Influenced by the works of Piaget and working with Jerome Bruner, Gardner became part of the Harvard's Project Zero research center for education where he wrote several seminal books on this theory (Gardner, 1983, 1993, 2000). Gardner currently teaches at Harvard in education and Boston University in neurology.

Theory of Multiple Intelligences

The theory of multiple intelligences asserts that there is strong evidence, both from the brain-based research (see discussion in this chapter) and from the study of genius, that there are at least nine basic different intelligences. Gardner's view of the mind claims that "human cognitive competence is better described in terms of sets of abilities, talents, or mental skills, which we call 'intelligences.' All normal individuals possess each of these skills to some extent; individuals differ in the degree of skill and the nature of their combination" (1993). Multiple intelligences theory thus pluralizes the traditional concept of intelligence, which becomes the ability to solve a problem or to create a product (see Figure 2-11). First conceived as seven intelligences, Gardner revised his work to add naturalistic and then existential intelligences as useful constructs to describe the expanded definition.

Solving a problem includes the ability to do so in a particular cultural setting or community. The skill needed and developed depends very much on the context in which the child lives. For example, we know now that certain parts of the brain are designated for perception, bodily movement, language, or spatial processing. Everyone who has a functional brain is able to demonstrate some skill in these areas. But the child who has special "musical intelligence," for instance, hears a concert and insists on a violin (as did Yehudi Menuhin). Or the child whose culture depends on running for its daily living (as do some people of Kenya) is more likely to have children well developed in that area of intelligence. Gardner writes of Anne Sullivan, teacher of blind and deaf Helen Keller, as an example of interpersonal intelligence, for she could understand what Helen needed in a way no one else could.

Applying Multiple Intelligences Theory to Work with Children

Gardner's theory of multiple intelligences has had a big impact on schools, transforming curricula and teaching methods from preschool to high school (Gardner, 2000). Even *Sesame Street* has taken to applying the theory to developing its programs. Teachers in early childhood use the theory daily as they individualize their environments, curricula, and approaches. The child whose facility with puzzles exceeds that of his classmates is given a chance to try more complex ones. The children who thrive in dramatic play are offered a time to put on a puppet show for the class. The one whose mind works especially musically, logically, or interpersonally is encouraged to develop those special gifts.

At the same time, there is no one right way to implement multiple intelligences. Project Zero was founded to study and improve the design of performance-based assessments and to promote the use of multiple intelligences to achieve more personalized curriculum and instruction (Gardner et al., 1998). In a similar way to a constructivist classroom, a class with a multiple intelligences focus would have teachers developing their own strategies and developing curricula and assessment methods based on both their own and their children's culture and priorities and on the individual children's intelligences (see Chapters 10 and 12).

How Are You Smart?

Area	Definition	Example
Musical Intelligence	The capacity to think in music, to be able to hear patterns, recognize them, and then remember them.	Gardner cites the importance of music in cultures worldwide, as well as its role in Stone Age societies, as evidence of this.
Bodily-Kinesthetic Intelligence 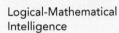	The capacity to use parts or all of your body to solve a problem or make something.	We can see this in a person's ability in sport (to play a game), in dance (to express a feeling, music or rhythm), in acting, or in making a product.
Logical-Mathematical Intelligence 	The capacity to think in a logical, often linear, pattern and to understand principles of a system; most common intelligence tested with standard "IQ" tests.	Problem solving is often remarkably rapid (as in gifted children), and this thinking is often nonverbal (the familiar "Aha!" phenomenon).
Linguistic Intelligence	The capacity to use language to express thoughts, ideas, and feelings and the ability to understand other people and their words.	The gift of language is universal; spoken language is constant across cultures, and the development of graphic language is one of the hallmarks of human activity.
Spatial Intelligence	The capacity to represent the world internally in spatial terms, as in problem navigation, in the use of maps, and in relying on drawings to build something.	Playing games such as chess and all the visual arts—painting, sculpting, drawing—use spatial intelligence, as do the sciences such as anatomy, architecture, and engineering.
Interpersonal Intelligence	The capacity to understand other people and focus on contrasts in moods, temperaments, motivations, and intentions.	Master players in school notice how others are playing before entering; some children seem to be born leaders; teachers, therapists, religious or political leaders, and many parents seem to have the capacity to notice distinctions among others.
Intrapersonal Intelligence 	The capacity to understand yourself, knowing who you are, how you react, and the internal aspects of one's self.	Often having access to their own feeling life, they draw on a range of emotions as a means of understanding and guiding their own behavior. Children with an innate sense of what they can and cannot do and often know when they need help.
Naturalist Intelligence	The capacity to discriminate among living things (plants, animals), as well as a sensitivity to other features of the natural world (clouds, rock configurations).	This intelligence is valuable for hunters, gatherers, and farmers and is important to those who are botanists or chefs.
Existential Intelligence	The ability to contemplate questions beyond sensory input, such as considering the infinite or unexplained phenomena.	Individuals who are drawn to issues of life and death and questions of morality, and ponder the meaning of existence and other matters of the spirit, such as clergy, shaman, and spiritual leaders.

FIGURE 2-11 Gardner's multiple intelligences theory describes a new way of looking at intelligence.

Maturation Theory

In the 1940s and 1950s, Dr. Arnold Gesell established norms for several areas of growth and the behaviors that accompany such development. His theory of maturation underscores these norms (Gesell, 1940).

Arnold Gesell

As noted in Chapter 1, Arnold Gesell was a physician intrigued with the notion that children's internal clock seemed to govern their growth and behavior. The Gesell Institute, which fosters the work of Dr. Louise Bates Ames (1979) and others, continues to provide guidelines for how children mature from birth to puberty. The Word Pictures discussed in Chapter 3 are excellent examples of the information maturational theory and research have provided.

Theory of Maturation

Maturation, by definition, is the process of physical and mental growth that is determined by heredity. The maturation sequence occurs in relatively stable and orderly ways. Maturation theory holds that much growth is genetically determined from conception. This theory differs from behaviorism, which asserts that growth is determined by environmental conditions and experiences, and from cognitive theory, which states that growth and behavior are a reflection of both maturation and learning.

Maturation and growth are interrelated and occur together. Maturation describes the quality of growth; that is, while a child grows in inches and pounds, the nature (or quality) of that growth changes. Maturation is qualitative, describing the way a baby moves into walking, rather than simply the age at which the baby took the first step. Growth is *what* happens; maturation is *how* it happens.

Studies have established that the maturation sequence is the same for all children, regardless of culture, country of origin, or learning environment. But there are two vital points to remember:

- Although maturation determines the sequence of development, the precise age is *approximate*. The sequence of developmental stages may be universal, but the rate at which a child moves through the stages varies tremendously.
- Growth is *uneven*. Children grow in spurts. Motor development may be slow in some stages, fast in others. For instance, a baby may gain an ounce a day for two months, then only half a pound in an entire month. Usually there is a growth spurt at puberty, with some children at age 13 nearly their adult

height, others not yet five feet tall. This unpredictability brings, again, much individual variation.

Applying Maturation Theory to Work with Children

Maturation theory is most useful in describing children's growth and typical behavior. In Chapter 3, these normative data were used to develop Word Pictures that describe common characteristics of children at different ages. Such charts help adults understand behavior better and keep them from expecting too much or too little.

At the same time, be cautious not to overgeneralize from the normative charts. Remember that there is great individual variation and uneven growth. Gesell's initial data were focused on a narrow portion of the population and were derived from American children only. Further work in the past three decades has adjusted the ranges with succeeding generations of children and an ever larger and more diverse population. Maturation theory has inspired developmental norms that help parents, teachers, and physicians alike determine whether a child's growth is *within* the normal range.

Humanistic Theory

As the field of psychology began to develop, various schools of thought emerged. The humanist theory has a place in early childhood education because it attempts to explain how people are motivated.

The Humanists

By the middle of the 20th century, two "camps" dominated the American psychological circles. The first (psychodynamic) included the Freudians and Eriksonians. The second (behaviorism) began with Watson and Thorndike and expanded with Skinner and Bandura. Abraham Maslow articulated another set of ideas. He called it the "third force" (or humanistic psychology), which focused on what motivated people to be well, successful, and mentally healthy (Goble, 1970).

Humanistic theory is centered on people's needs, goals, and successes. This was a change from the study of mental illness, as in psychotherapy, or the study of animal behavior, in the case of much behaviorist research. Instead, Dr. Maslow studied exceptionally mature and successful people. Others (Rogers, Perls, Watts, and Fromm) added to what was known about healthy personalities.

The humanists developed a comprehensive theory of human behavior based on mental health. Maslow's theory of human needs is clearly a "Western" philosophy, although it is often presented as a universal set of ideas. In fact, other cultures would see life differently. For instance, an African worldview might see the good of the community as the essential goal of being fully human. Scandinavian cultures with more of a "collective" orientation, rather than an emphasis on the individual or self, would see serving the family or group as the ultimate goal of humanity. Humanistic psychology can also be seen as being at odds with cultures and religions that seek ultimate reliance on a supreme deity, putting "God" rather than "self" at the top of the hierarchy. One must always question the underlying values of a theory, and humanist theory is no exception.

Theory of Human Needs

Maslow's theory of self-actualization is a set of ideas about what people need to become and stay healthy. He asserts that every human being is motivated by a number of basic needs, regardless of age, gender, race, culture, or geographic location. According to Maslow (1954), a basic need is something:

- Whose absence breeds illness.
- Whose presence prevents illness.
- Whose restoration cures illness.
- Preferred by the deprived person over other satisfactions, under certain conditions (such as very complex, free-choice instances).
- Found to be inactive, at low ebb, or functionally absent in the healthy person.

These needs, not to be denied, form a theory of human motivation. It is a hierarchy, or pyramid, because

The maturational sequence is the same for all children, although the precise age is approximate, so there is tremendous individual variation in children of a particular age.

there is a certain way these needs are interrelated, and because the most critical needs form the foundation from which the other needs can be met (see Figure 2-12).

Applying Humanistic Theory to Work with Children

The basic needs are sometimes called deficiency needs because they are critical for a person's survival, and a deficiency can cause a person to die. Until those are met, no other significant growth can take place. How well a teacher knows that a hungry child ignores a lesson or is simply unable to concentrate. A tired child often pushes aside learning materials and experiences until rested. The child who is deprived of basic physiologic needs may

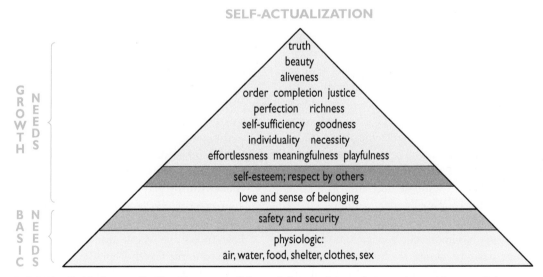

FIGURE 2-12 Maslow studied healthy personalities and theorized that what people need for growth is a hierarchy of basic and growth needs. (Adapted from Maslow, 1954.)

be able to think of those needs only; in fact, "such a man can fairly be said to live by bread alone" (Maslow, 1954). The humanists would strongly advocate a school breakfast or lunch program and would support regular rest and nap times in programs with long hours.

Once the physiologic needs are satisfied, the need for safety and security emerges. Maslow points at insecure and neurotic people as examples of what happens when these needs are left unfulfilled. These people act as if a disaster is about to occur, as if a spanking is on the way. Given an unpredictable home or school, a child cannot find any sense of consistency and so is preoccupied with worrying and anxiety. Maslow would advise teachers to give freedom within limits, rather than either total neglect or permissiveness.

The growth needs can emerge when the basic needs have been met. Higher needs are dependent on those primary ones. They are what we strive for to become more satisfied and healthy people.

The *need for love and belonging* is often expressed directly and clearly by the young children in our care. A lack of love and sense of belonging stifles growth. To learn to give love later in life, one has to learn about love by receiving it as a child. This means learning early about the responsibilities of giving as well as receiving love.

The *need for esteem* can be divided into two categories: self-respect and esteem from others. Self-esteem includes such needs as a desire for mastery, for adequacy, for a sense of confidence that comes with competence and achievement, and feelings of independence and freedom. When one gets recognition and appreciation, one gets respect from others and feels a sense of status and reputation.

Self-actualization is what gives a person satisfaction in life. From the desire to know and understand the world and people around us comes a renewal of self-knowledge. For the early childhood educator, these needs are expressed in the enthusiasm, curiosity, and natural drive to learn and try. In meeting these needs, a person finds meaning for life, an eagerness to live, and a willingness to do so.

Children must have their basic physical and emotional needs met before higher cognitive learning can be fulfilled. Moreover, the child who seems stuck in a particular "needs area" likely stays there until that basic need is satisfied. A hungry, insecure, or hurt child is a poor learner. Teachers must continually advocate better physical and social conditions for all children.

Maslow's theory has important implications for child care. Children's basic needs are teachers' first concern: Teachers must ensure that children are properly clothed, fed, and rested as well as safe and secure. Only then are they ready to address curriculum and skill development.

Developmental Topics

There are several special issues that apply developmental and learning theories to work with children. Five topics most relevant to early childhood education are 1) cultural diversity, 2) attachment, 3) play, 4) gender, 5) moral development, and 6) brain-based research. The teacher well versed in these developmental topics is able to make better decisions concerning classrooms and curricula. Moreover, they are able to connect with families around those points and those people most important to them: the children.

Cultural Diversity

"Human nature is a cultural process. As a biological species, humans are defined in terms of our cultural participation. We are prepared by both our cultural and biological heritage to use language and other cultural tools and to learn from each other" (Rogoff, 2003). Development can be fully understood only when it is viewed in the larger cultural context. We can readily see the importance of culture in child rearing and family interaction, yet we often overlook its effect on education. We must know about children in their own setting, their own context, to understand them well enough to teach them. The ecology of a child's life must be acknowledged and brought into our work.

Global Examples

A quick international scan shows the influence of cultural orientation:

- England. The primary curricular emphasis is on children's social development until age 3, after which academic competence is emphasized.
- Norway and Sweden. Educators focus on developmental issues, particularly socio-emotional development, and families are encouraged to wait on formal academic teaching until primary school at age 6.
- Japan. In Asian countries where children's physical well-being and primary health care have improved to the point where they are no longer issues, the focus is on academic achievement and excellence.
- China. Model kindergartens in China include choices during playtime as well as structured outdoor exercises and whole-group instruction that includes child participation and questions.
- Eastern Europe. While academic achievement is not stressed in the Czech Republic or Hungary, young children are taught the importance of work and art, and they participate in cultural programs by the time they are 3.

Let us turn to the United States. "[I]nterpersonal episodes [are] absolutely saturated with cultural assumptions about the right way to think, feel, and behave. There are some real cultural differences about how to be a good parent and how to be a good child," states Stanford University's Hazel Markus (2005). For example:

- A mom leaned over a stroller, handed a silent 3-year-old a juice drink and announced, "It's hot. You must be thirsty."
- A 7-year-old ran up to his mother and grandmother and tried to get the younger woman's attention. She said, "I don't care how excited you are—don't interrupt your grandmother when she's speaking."
- A dad, sounding exasperated, told his 18-month-son, "Okay, now, you have a choice: either you wear this hat or we put on sunscreen. Which do you want?" The child replied, "I want juice."

These conversations reflect values—middle-class Euro-American, Latino, or East Asian. Ethnicity and cultural identity clearly play an important role in child development.

Three Key Issues

Teachers are challenged to work from an understanding of different patterns in culture and parenting and practices. Three issues are helpful to keep in mind.

1. *Watch for a culture gap.* Large numbers of children are members of a cultural group but are being taught by members of other cultural groups. Although this need not be catastrophic, research shows that four problems tend to develop (Lawrence-Lightfoot, 2004):

   There are problems when the *language* that is spoken by the child is not understood by caregivers from another culture.

   There are problems when caregivers have low *expectations* for children based largely on the children's membership in a low-status cultural group, rather than on the actual abilities of the children.

   There are problems when caregivers are unprepared to deal with children whose general behavioral *style* is different from that of the caregivers.

   There are problems when standard *testing* and *assessment* techniques are applied to certain cultural groups with insufficient recognition of, or respect for, the cultural patterns of the group.

2. *Update your theory.* Most early theories were based on observations of male or white subjects. This risks a skewed view of development. We encourage you to read studies of development that include other ethnic populations (Phinney, 2006). Ethnic minority

children have been ignored in past research or viewed as variations from the norm. Often the group studied is given an ethnic label (such as Latino) that assumes the group is homogeneous and glosses over critical differences among the people in the group.

Moreover, when ethnic groups are studied, often the focus is on children's problems. The range of existing differences makes more research—and also more teacher interest in individual family cultures—essential. Without such knowledge, teachers may misunderstand children with cultural patterns that are different from the mainstream and children and their families, in turn, may misunderstand the larger society or a school's practices and a teacher's behaviors.

3. *Theories have their limits.* Theories can foster a broad outlook about children in general, but these theories must be viewed in light of both cultural diversity and a respect for individuality.

If we wish to have more inclusive educational policies and practices—those that embrace the full variety of children and families residing on our communities—it is essential to have a theoretical interpretation of our common experiences as humans that can also help us to understand those ways in which we diverge from one another. While the field of psychology has done much to help us understand the individual mechanisms of behavior and development, . . . cultural psychology, . . . makes clear that what is highly valued and nurtured in one cultural setting may be considered improbable, if not inappropriate, from a cross-cultural perspective. (New & Beneke, in Feeney et al., 2009).

While children are forming their identity and self-worth, they often struggle with conflicting messages from home, media, school, and peers about who they are and what they are worth.

Knowing what child development information to use across cultures and what varies among cultures helps teachers apply theories (see Figure 2-13). Chapter 3 helps you identify these universals. While reading all these theories, try to look beyond any one model, and define a set of principles that are fundamental to good practice and that can information.

Attachment

Attachment is a term used particularly in the works of John Bowlby and Mary Ainsworth and a concept used in Burton White's descriptive work and Magda Gerber's Resources for Infant Educarers (RIE) programs for infants and toddlers. Attachment is the emotional connection, an "affectional tie that one person or animal forms

Children: All, Some, One

All children are alike . . .
- have the same needs and rights
- go through the same developmental stages
- have the same developmental goals

Some children are alike . . .
- similar cultural and social expectations will create commonalities
- rate of vocabulary increase is similar within groups with priority of language expression
- children show similar helping behaviors from families who value harmony

Each child is unique . . .
- genetic makeup
- temperament
- sensory sensitivity
- interests
- motivation

FIGURE 2-13 Make child development theories useful without overgeneralizing (patterned after Caldwell, 1983).

between himself and another specific one—a tie that binds them together in space and endures over time" (Ainsworth, 1979).

Expression and Types of Attachment

The child or adult who is attached to another uses that person as a "safe base" from which to venture out into the world, a source of comfort when distressed or stressed, and a support for encouragement. Attachment behaviors are anything that allows a person to get and stay attached, such as smiling, eye contact, talking, touching, and even clinging and crying.

"It is an essential part of the ground plan of the human species—as well as that of many other species—for an infant to become attached to a mother figure. This figure need not be the natural mother but can be anyone who plays the role of the principal caregiver" (Ainsworth, 1979).

Freud believed infants became attached to those who fed them. Erikson asserted that the first year of life was critical for attachment, in the stage of trust versus mistrust.

Research does show that human and animal babies do indeed send signals to their mothers very early. Infants begin the social smile at 6 weeks and positive reactions to familiar people by 3 months. The human infant's early signals include crying and gazing, both of which are powerful to adults, and a kind of rhythmic sucking that appears to keep the mother engaged. Soon after appears the synchrony, a coordinated interaction between an infant and caring adult that connects the two. Becoming more frequent and elaborate as time goes on, it helps the infant express feelings and the sensitive adult to respond.

Developmentally, children develop an initial bond and then proceed to develop real mutuality—that is, to learn and practice almost a "dance" between themselves and their favored loved one. Bowlby (1969, 1973) found that, although virtually all infants develop attachments, including to multiple caregivers, they differ in how secure they are in those attachments. Furthermore, attachment can be measured in the infant and toddler, as seen in children's response to a stranger both in and out of the parent's presence (see Figure 2-14).

An Alternative View

Not everyone believes that attachment is so important to later competence and identity. Infants are resilient, and children can grow positively within wide variations of parenting. Researchers have found cultural variations in attachment. German babies are more likely than American babies to be categorized as avoidant, but this might be because the culture encourages early independence. Japanese babies are more likely to be seen as avoidant, but this could also be a factor of the method used to record it, which calls for children to be left in a room without the mother, a situation that rarely occurs for most Japanese infants.

Some developmentalists claim the theory ignores the context and diversity of how children are socialized, and by whom. "I believe that European Americans are obsessed with attachment because we hold our babies less than almost any other cultural group in the world," writes a colleague (Saxton, 2001). "Attachment does not seem to be an issue, much less a concept, in cultures in which children are carried, held, or sleep with their parents for the better part of the first three years." Most children get attached to a primary caregiver. While in most cases it is the mother, it is who is part of the daily life that counts—it might be the father, grandparents, or other adults.

Researchers have found that most infants tested in the stranger situation demonstrated secure attachment. Still, when attachment fails, children are placed at

Patterns of Attachment

	Exploratory Behavior Before Separation	Behavior During Separation	Reunion Behavior	Behavior with Stranger
Secure	Separates to explore toys; shares play with mother; friendly toward stranger when mother is present, touches "home base" periodically.	May cry; play is subdued for a while; usually recovers and is able to play.	If distressed during separation, contact ends distress; if not distressed, greets mother warmly; initiates interaction.	Somewhat friendly; may play with stranger after initial distress reaction.
Anxious/ambivalent (resistant)	Has difficulty separating to explore toys even when mother is present; wary of novel situations and people; stays close to mother and away from stranger.	Very distressed; hysterical crying does not quickly diminish.	Seeks comfort and rejects it, continues to cry or fuss; may be passive—no greeting made.	Wary of stranger; rejects stranger's offers to play.
Anxious/avoidant	Readily separates to explore toys; does not share play with parent; shows little preference for parent versus stranger.	Does not show distress; continues to play; interacts with the stranger.	Ignores mother— turns or moves away; avoidance is more extreme at the second reunion.	No avoidance of stranger.

FIGURE 2-14 Patterns of attachment. (From Ainsworth, M. D. S., & Wittig, B. A., 1969. "Attachment and Exploratory Behavior of One-Year-Olds in a Strange Situation." In B. M. Foss, Ed. *Determinants of Infant Behavior* [Vol. 4] London: Methuen. From Understanding Children, by Judith Schickendanz, © 1993 by Mayfield Publishing Company. Reprinted with permission of McGraw-Hill Companies.)

tremendous risk (White, 1995). Failure of attachment can come from:

- Parents who did not have secure attachments as children
- Neglectful conditions, such as depression, abject poverty
- Abusive parents that discourage bonding
- Premature infants with underdeveloped systems
- Blind infants who cannot engage in gazing

Intervention can help unattached persons learn the skills to connect, teaching specific interactive techniques with ongoing supports such as crisis hotlines and personal counseling.

Careful questions should be asked about full-day care, particularly for infants, to ensure that children's attachment to their families is not undermined. We can conclude that children are not at any higher risk in high-quality child care. This highlights the need for such programs, as is addressed further in Chapter 15.

Play

Play! What a wonderful word! It calls up images from the past, those childhood years when playing was the focus of our waking hours. "Will you play with me?" is one of the most expressive, expectant questions known. It carries with it hope and anticipation about a world of fun and make-believe, a world of adventure and exploration, a world of the young child.

City streets, parks and fields, tenements, huts, empty rooms, and backyards are all settings for play. Play is a way of life for children; it is their natural response. It is what children do and it is serious business to them. Any activity children choose to engage in is play; it is never ending.

Play is the essence of creativity in children throughout the world. Play is universal and knows no national or cultural boundaries. Educators and psychologists have called play a reflection of the child's growth, the essence of the child's life, a window into the child's world (Frost, Wortham, & Reifel, 2011). It is a self-satisfying activity through which children gain control and come to understand life. Play teaches children about themselves; they learn how tall—or short—they are, what words to use to get a turn on the swing, and where to put their hands when climbing a ladder. Through play, children learn about the world: what the color purple is, how to make matzo balls, and how to be a friend. Play helps children define who they are.

Types of Play

Play takes many forms. Children play when they sing, dig in the mud, build a block tower, or dress up. Play can be purely physical (running, climbing, ball throwing) or highly intellectual (solving an intricate puzzle, remembering the words to a song). Play is creative when crayons and paint are used. Its emotional form is expressed when children pretend to be mommies, daddies, or babies. Skipping rope with a friend, playing tag, and sharing a book are examples of the social side of play.

There is a general sequence to the development of play (see Figure 2-15). Babies and toddlers have a clearly defined social self. Infant play begins with patterns established at birth: babies gaze, smile, and make sociable sounds in response to the quality and frequency of attention from a parent or caregiver. Socialization of infants occurs through interaction. By the end of their first year, infants smile at and touch one another and vocalize in a sociable effort. Toddlers play well on their own (*solitary play*) or with adults. They begin solitary pretend play around 1 year of age. They still watch others (*onlooker*). During the toddler years, as children become more aware of one another, they begin to play side by side, without interacting (*parallel play*). They are aware of and pleased about but not directly involved with the other person. It is during this year that toddlers begin some form of coordinated play, doing something with another child. The preschool years bring many changes for

children in relation to social development. The number and quality of relationships increase as does the ability to play with other children. At first, this is accomplished just by a child's presence in a group: playing at the water table with four other children or joining a circle for finger plays (*associative play*). When children join forces with one another in an active way, when they verbalize, plan, and carry out play, group play is established. It can be characterized as "Let's do it together," whether building a house for the farm animals or engaging in rough-and-tumble wrestling. *Cooperative play* is the most common type of peer interaction during the preschool years and into the school-age period.

Keep in mind that children's play always portrays their own social values and family ethnic practices. Developmentally and culturally appropriate practice would remind us that our understanding and knowledge about play have been based on Euro-American cultural patterns (Parten, 1932). Wise early childhood practitioners incorporate this perspective into their work with children.

Most play is unstructured and happens naturally when the curriculum is designed for play. Spontaneous play is the unplanned, self-selected activity in which children freely participate. Children's natural inclinations are toward play materials and experiences that are developmentally appropriate. Therefore, when they are allowed to make choices in a free play situation, children choose activities that express their individual interests, needs, and readiness levels.

Dramatic play—or imaginative or pretend play—is a common form of spontaneous play. Three- and four-year-olds are at the peak of their interest in this type of activity. In dramatic play, children assume the roles of different characters, both animate and inanimate. Children identify themselves with another person or thing, playing out situations that interest or frighten them. Dramatic play reveals children's attitudes and concepts toward people and things in their environment. Much of the play is wishful thinking, pretending great strength and deeds. This is the way children cope with their smallness or lack of strength and is considered important in psychodynamic theory.

Two types of dramatic play are noteworthy:

1. Superhero play is appealing to children because it so readily addresses their sense of helplessness and inferiority. Pretending to be Wonder Woman makes it easier to understand and accept the limitations of the real world. It helps children learn about power and friendship, allows them a way to test their physical limits and explore feelings, and answer the "big questions about the world, such as 'what is right and wrong, what is good and bad, what is fair and unfair,

TeachSource Video

Watch the TeachSource Video Case entitled, "Young Children's Stages of Play." After you study the video clip, view the artifacts, and read the teacher interviews and text, reflect on the following questions:

1. How can teachers plan curriculum for each stage of play?

2. What can a teacher do during parallel play to enhance development?

3. Watch the bonus video about Dramatic Play and list examples of vocabulary learned, plus how teachers can use this play situation to build oral and literacy skills.

Play Categories

Unoccupied Play

- May stand in one spot
- Looks around the area
- Performs random movements that have no apparent goal

Solitary Play

- Plays alone
- Plays independently of others

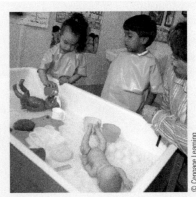

Onlooker Play

- May watch while others play
- May talk but does not enter play
- Shows active interest in the play

Parallel Play

- Plays alongside others
- Plays separately from others but with toys or actions that are similar to the others

Associative Play

- Play involves social interaction but little or no organization
- Interested in each other without an agreed-upon plan

Cooperative Play

- Socially interacts in a group with a sense of group identity
- Joins an organized activity, a prototype for games

FIGURE 2-15 Parten's play categories, developed by observing free play patterns in nursery school settings.

what is life and death, what is a boy and a girl, and what is real and fantasy'" (Hoffman, 2004).

At the same time, this kind of play makes many adults uncomfortable because the children's play is often loud, disruptive, filled with conflict and problems, and solved with violence. Children sometimes end up in stereotypical, repetitive play that seems to ignore other learning. (See Chapter 14 for strategies.)

2. Sociodramatic play happens when at least two children cooperate in dramatic play. Dramatic play provides the means for children to work out their difficulties by themselves. By doing so, they become free to pursue other tasks and more formal learning.

Both types of play involve two basic elements: imitation and make-believe.

Pretending to be a firefighter, Sherry grabs a piece of rope and runs toward the playhouse, saying "shhshhsh-shshshsh" while pretending to squirt water on the fire. She shouts to her playmates, "Over here! Come over here! The fire is on this side."

Sherry's make-believe scenario and her ability to follow the rules of behavior common to firefighters (grabbing hoses, calling for help) are the two critical factors from Vygotsky's point of view: That firefighting scene supports his theory that cognitive skills develop through social interactions. Sherry exemplifies a child moving from concrete to abstract thought because she did not require realistic objects (a hose and water) but imagined them with a rope and her ability to create the sound of water. This ability to separate thoughts from actions and objects will stand Sherry in good stead when she studies math concepts. Rules that children follow in make-believe play teach them to make choices, to think and plan about what they will do, and to show willingness toward self-restraint, as children learn to follow the social rules of pretend play. This is important preparation for real-life situations.

Value of Play

For the first half of the 20th century, interest in children's play focused on emotional causes and effects. The main theme was the emotional releases that play provided children. Psychodynamic theory recommended play as a suitable outlet for expressing negative feelings, hostility, and aggression. Clay can be pounded, balls can be kicked and thrown, and dolls can be spanked. Young children give free expression to a wide range of emotions, playing them out and releasing tension.

But play is more than an avenue for emotional release. Play is universal to childhood experiences because it is intrinsically motivated; that is, it is naturally satisfying to children. In addition,

- Play is relatively free of rules except for those children impose on themselves.
- Play is controlled and dominated by the children.
- Play is carried out as if the activity were real life.
- Play focuses on the activity—the doing—rather than on the end result or product.
- Play requires the interaction and involvement of the children.

Play promotes learning for the whole child, providing benefits for all developmental domains (American Academy of Pediatrics, 2007; Elkind in Washington & Andrews, 2010).

Play as the Cornerstone of Learning

Outside of child development circles, there has been little appreciation in the United States culture for the value and importance of play for young children. In times of rising expectations and academic standards, educators and families feel pressured to focus on activities related to school readiness. If children are just playing, how will they learn? Play is viewed by some as the opposite of work, not as a cornerstone of learning. Play is often trivialized by sayings like "That is mere child's play."

A growing body of research shows that every school success indicator is enhanced by play (Elkind, 2010).

Learning through play takes many forms and happens naturally in unplanned, self-selected activities.

Moreover, young children learn by doing because they live in the world of action and feelings more than words. To reclaim play as a special activity crucial to children's development, we should look at play as the foundation from which children venture forth to investigate, to test out. Curriculum takes on expression through play; teachers plan curriculum that uses play as the medium for learning. As they mature, children integrate and assimilate their play experiences. What started out as play—the sheer fun of it—is transformed into learning experiences. Curiosity about magnets at age 5 nourishes a scientific attitude for the later years, as well as a foundation for studying gravity, planetary movements, and the like. Feeling free to sing out at group time at age 3 can prepare a child to be an active participant in the kindergarten classroom at age 6.

Teachers want children to learn about themselves, to learn about the world around them, and to learn how to solve problems. A childhood filled with play opportunities should culminate in these three types of learning:

1. *Learning about themselves* includes developing a positive self-image and a sense of competence. Children should know and feel good about themselves as learners. They should develop a sense of independence, a measure of self-discipline, and knowledge based on full use of their sensory skills.

Play is the cornerstone for learning.

2. *To learn about others and the world around them* means developing an awareness of other people. Teachers want children to perfect their communication and social skills so that they are more sensitive participants in the world in which they live. This means that children learn and appreciate the values of their parents, the community, and society at large. When children become aware of the demands of living in today's society, that awareness can help them become more responsible citizens. The emphasis on social interaction and group relationships in the early childhood setting underscores this goal.

3. *To learn to solve problems*, children need to be accomplished in observation and investigation. When exploring a puzzle, for example, children need to know how to manipulate it, take it apart, and put it back together, to see how other people solve puzzles, and to know how to get help when the pieces just do not seem to fit together. They should know how to predict and experiment. What will happen, wonders a kindergartner, when a glass is placed over a glowing candle? How will that change if the glass is large or small? What is the effect if the glass is left over the candle for a long time or for a second? Young children also need to learn how to negotiate, discuss, compromise, and stand their ground, particularly when they encounter and solve problems socially. "I want the red cart and someone already has it," thinks the preschooler. "Now what? How can I get it? What if the other person says no? Will the plan that works with my best friend work with someone else? When do I ask for help? Will crying make a difference?" To be effective problem solvers, children must know and experience themselves and others.

Play in the early years is a key to school success and solid development.

Gender

Are girls and boys different in terms of development and learning? What are these differences, and how do they occur? What differences are caused by "nature" and which ones by "nurture"? Should we treat our girls and boys the same or differently? The realities and the myths surrounding sex differences and their effect on behavior from infancy to adulthood is the subject of interest, controversy, and research.

Definitions

Sex differences are the biological differences between males and females; gender differences are culturally imposed distinctions in the roles and behaviors. While boys and girls are about the same size and shape in childhood, gender differences and adult distinctions are more significant.

There are two aspects of gender development that are particularly important in the early years: gender identity (the sense of being female or male, which most children acquire by age 3), and gender role (the set of expectations that define how a male or female should behave, think, and feel). Gender is important to some developmental and learning theories.

Theories and Research

Freud asserted that behavior was directly related to reproductive processes. His stages of psychosexual development reflect the belief that gender and sexual behavior are instinctual. Erikson also claimed that anatomy was destiny: Males were more intrusive because of genital structure, and females were more inclusive. He later modified his view, saying that women were overcoming their biological heritage. Erikson's identification theory came from the view that the preschool child finds the opposite-sex parent attractive but steers away from this by identifying with the same-sex parent.

Piaget and Bandura both emphasized that children learn through observation and imitation, and that through reinforcement, children learn gender-appropriate behavior. Proponents of this view point to how parents encourage girls and boys to engage in certain activities and types of play. Certainly the media communicates sexist messages; this theory would claim that such stereotyping influences the development of gender roles.

The works of Eleanor Maccoby (1974, 1998) have provided both hard data and an open forum for discussions about how people grow and the complex interaction

 **DIVERSITY**

Male/Female Concepts in Girls and Boys

For all the current talk about gender differences, research about gender differences lagged at the end of the 1900s in favor of other topics. Some contemporary developmentalists have a new interpretation, known as gender-schema theory. Children develop mental ideas, or schema (a Piagetian concept) about gender on the basis of the behavior patterns they see (a behaviorist model). Gender-schema, then, is a cluster of concepts about male and female physical characteristics, behaviors, and personality traits. As soon as children understand labels of "girl" and "boy," they seek out information about each and then try to imitate those that match their identity. Thus children use sex as one way to organize their perceptions (schema) about the world. Boys show better memory for "masculine" toys, and girls for "feminine" ones (Martin & Ruble, 2006).

For instance, the "strength-weakness" dimension may be taught and shown to children such that strength is linked to maleness and weakness to female stereotype. Because children work toward gender-appropriate behavior, it is likely that most boys fight when in a conflict, in part because that is expected, and girls attempt gentleness or helplessness to build an identity in line with that gender-schema (Ruble et al., 2006).

---

between heredity and environment that makes child development so fascinating. These findings help teachers understand gender identity and its implications for education:

- By age 2, children name themselves as girl or boy and can identify adult strangers as daddies or mommies.
- By age 4, children label toys (dolls, trucks) and some roles (soldier, nurse) appropriate for one gender and not the other.
- Children develop gender stability (the understanding of staying the same sex throughout life) by age 4 and gender constancy (a person keeps the same gender regardless of appearance) by about 5 or 6.
- Sex-typed behavior begins to appear at age 2 or 3, when children tend to choose same-sex playmates and sex-typed toy preferences, and children become more selective and exclusive as they mature.
- By elementary school, the playground is like a "gender school," with children showing a clear preference for same-sex peers.

Developmental Differences

What are the real differences between girls and boys? Physically, males grow to be 10 percent taller than females, and girls are less likely to develop physical or mental disorders than are boys. Boys are also more active than girls and physically more aggressive overall. However, there are fewer differences in verbal aggression, although males do show less self-regulation than females (Eisenberg, Martin, & Fabes, 1996). There are no significant differences between girls and boys in intelligence or reasoning behavior. Some cognitive functioning and personality differences do exist, but overall the differences are small and there is no overall pattern.

Teachers and parents, as well as researchers, have observed that boys and girls seem to show distinct differences in their play choices, play behavior, and toy selection from an early age. Although biology certainly plays a part, it would seem that parents and society exert powerful influences. The toys parents and teachers choose (dolls for girls, trucks for boys), the predominance of females in early childhood settings, television shows and advertising, and toy store displays combine to communicate a very strong reinforcement of traditional sex-role expectations.

Gender Stereotyping

To break through the restrictiveness of gender stereotyping, teachers need to pay careful attention to the messages they give children. One challenge we face is the female culture of early childhood programs. Women dominate the early childhood education workforce, so children are often only exposed to women's interaction styles (Wardle, 2004). If boys struggle in our programs, we must be alert to the activities and schedules we establish, behaviors we may reward or punish, the "goodness of fit" for both boys and girls in our programs. In the environments we prepare for them, the materials they use, and the examples we model, children create their own ideas and learn behavior that works for them in the world.

Moral Development

People used to assume that young children needed to be taught exactly what was "right" and "wrong" and that was enough. In the past 30 years, research has shown that moral development is a more complex process with both a cognitive and an emotional side to it. Several theorists and researchers have proposed how to think about children's moral development. The theories of Jean Piaget, Lawrence Kohlberg, Nancy Eisenberg, and Carol Gilligan are discussed here.

Cognitive-Developmental Base

Piaget (1965) investigated children's moral reasoning by presenting children with pairs of stories and asking them which child was "naughtier." From this, he discovered that children younger than age 6 base their judgment on the amount of damage done, not the child's intentions. By middle childhood, children are beginning to take intent into account so that one can begin to see a shift in moral reasoning toward the end of the early childhood period from objective judgments based on physical results and concrete amounts to more subjective considerations (such as the purpose of the perpetrator or psychological factors). The connections to children's cognitive stage of development is interesting, and adults might consider that a child's protests over wrongdoing ("I didn't mean to do it!") may very well signal a new level of reasoning, with the realization that one's intentions do matter.

Kohlberg (1981) is best known as a theorist in social development, addressing educational practice and gender constancy as well. Building on Piagetian dimensions, Kohlberg's theory of moral development involves both social growth and intellectual reasoning. People move from stage to stage as a result of their own reasoning power, and they see for themselves the contradictions in their own beliefs. As with Erikson and Piaget, Kohlberg's stages are hierarchical—a person moves forward one by one, and no stage can be skipped. On the basis of children's responses to moral dilemmas similar to those of Piaget, Kohlberg identified three levels of moral development (Figure 2-16). For early childhood educators, research shows that preconventional reasoning (stages 1 and 2) is dominant into elementary school.

Kohlberg's theory has been criticized for placing too much emphasis on moral thought and not enough of moral behavior. Most of the stories, or dilemmas, that Piaget and Kohlberg used were about stealing, lying, disobeying rules, and the like. Further, many point out that his view is culturally biased and the stories asked are not applicable to all children. Western moral doctrine emphasizes individual rights; other cultures focus on a greater respect for traditional codes and practices.

Modern Revisions

Researcher and theorist Nancy Eisenberg (1983, 1992) has explored the kinds of reasoning children use to justify good (prosocial) behavior. She asks children what they would do in situations with a moral dilemma. One

---

Kohlberg's Stages of Moral Development

I. Preconventional Morality

Stage 1: Punishment and obedience orientation
Might makes right; obey authority and avoid punishment.

Stage 2: Individualism and relativist orientation
Look out for number one; be nice to others so they will be nice to you.

II. Conventional Morality

Stage 3: Mutual interpersonal expectations
"Good girl, nice boy"; approval more important than any reward.

Stage 4: Social system and conscience
"Law and order"; contributing to society's good is important.

III. Postconventional Morality

Stage 5: Social contract
Rules are to benefit all, by mutual agreement; may be changed same way; the greatest good for the greatest number.

Stage 6: Universal ethical principles
Values established by individual reflection, may contradict other laws.

© Cengage Learning 2011

FIGURE 2-16 Kohlberg's Stages of Moral Development. Cross-cultural data and extensive American research indicate a persuasive universality and a strong sequence of stage development in children's moral development.

of her stories involves a child on the way to a friend's birthday party. The child encounters someone who has fallen and is hurt. What should the child do: help the hurt child and miss cake and ice cream, or leave the child and go on to the party?

Such questions brought to light several levels of prosocial reasoning. In the early childhood years, children seem to be engaged in level one (*hedonistic reasoning*), in which the individual's own needs are put first. In the case mentioned earlier, the child would leave the hurt person and go to the party ("I won't help because I have to go to the party"). As children move through middle childhood, they tend to move to level two, in which the needs of another begin to be considered and to increase in importance. Answers to the story would begin to shift toward including others ("I'd help because they'd help me next time"). Eisenberg's stages roughly parallel Kohlberg's and help broaden these concepts without contradicting the fundamental arguments.

Carol Gilligan (1982, 2011) challenges Kohlberg's strong emphasis on justice and fairness and his omission of caring for others. Gilligan notes that because girls and boys are socialized differently, their moral judgments will be quite different. For instance, boys may be raised with the idea that justice and fairness are the key moral bases, whereas girls may be taught that caring and responsibility to others are central. Buzzelli (2002) has also worked extensively on young children's moral understanding and has applied recent research to children's development of peer relationships. Although this claim of different moral ideas based on gender differences has yet to be fully researched, it is an important thought to keep in mind, particularly when teaching and raising young children.

Moral development is often deleted from the curriculum in American schools. Further, one aspect of moral development that has been studied very little is that of children's spirituality and faith. Because of the separation of church and state in American public schools, many educators shy away from discussions of anything that might be considered "religious." In doing so, educational programs also find themselves staying out of anything that helps children understand who they are and the greater questions of life and its meaning. Yet even John Dewey called moral education the "hidden curriculum," conveyed through the atmosphere of every program. Elementary schools occasionally have some kind of teaching for "character education," or a values clarification class. In addition, most caregivers will tell you what children notice about life and death issues and about caring for others is part of everyday experiences.

Brain Development

We are aware of the importance of the first 5 years in the physical, social, and cognitive-language development of the child (Copple & Bredekamp, 2009). These same five years are the most critical with respect to the developing brain. Neuroscience research has developed sophisticated technologies, such as ultrasound; magnetic resonance imaging (MRI); positron emission tomography (PET); and effective, noninvasive ways to study brain chemistry (such as the steroid hormone cortisol). Brain scans and other technologies have made it possible to investigate the intricate circuitry of the brain. We now know the number of dendrite connections are estimated to be more than 100 billion (Miller & Cummings, 2007), and the implications are equally staggering.

Forming language, identifying cultural and social norms, and learning to distinguish right from wrong requires this intensive neurological growth to take place, thus strengthening the connections between neurons. This rapid growth in the minds of young children inspires them to explore, to discover, to play, and to make the natural connections between self, others, and their surrounding world.

No aspect of biological growth is more critical than the rapid growth of the brain. A newborn's skull is disproportionately large, because it must be big enough to hold the brain, which at birth is 25 percent of its adult weight. In contrast, the neonate's body is typically only 5 percent of adult weight. By age 2, the brain is almost 75 percent of adult brain weight; the child's body is only about 20 percent as big as it will be. During the prenatal and early childhood period, the brain develops faster than any other part of the body so that by age 7 it is almost fully grown (Berger, 2012).

We once believed that brains were entirely formed by genes and prenatal influences only. Certainly, by the sixth prenatal month, nearly all of the billions of neurons (nerve cells) that populate the mature brain have been created, with new neurons generated at an average rate of more than 25,000 per minute (Thompson, 2001). Today, neuroscientists believe in plasticity, the concept that growth changes throughout life for a variety of reasons. The timetable for brain development varies by region, and it is likely that brain development continues into adulthood. Still, early childhood is a critical time for brain development. The timing and quality of early experiences combine to shape brain architecture (Shonkoff et al., 2008; Galinsky, 2010).

What We Have Learned

At least three important conclusions can be made at this time:

1. *The brain operates on a "use it or lose it" principle.* Brain development begins at one month in utero

and proliferates the nerve cells. "Once neurons are formed, they quickly migrate to the brain region where they will function. Neurons become differentiated to assume specialized roles, and they form connections (synapses) with other neurons that enable them to communicate and store information" (Thompson, 2001).

Using a dual process of blooming and pruning, neurons first create more synapses than the brain retains, and then prunes back those that are not used. At birth, one has about 100 billion brain cells and 50 trillion connections among them. With use, these cells grow bases (axons) and branches (dendrites) that reach out to make connections with other cells. The brain thus adapts to the stimulation and experience the child receives. Newborns respond to universal sounds, but their speech perception over time becomes limited to that of the family (and child care) languages. The typical experiences of hearing and responding to language, for instance, contribute to brain growth.

2. *The brain is vulnerable in early childhood.* Chronic maternal stress during pregnancy and after birth can threaten healthy brain growth. As children move from infancy through preschool, their brain functions are developing according to what is received. "Neural development, stress hormones, and brain specialization are three areas of brain research that inform and support developmentally appropriate practices (DAP) in early childhood education" (Gallagher, 2005). When the brain perceives a threat or stress, the body reacts. Stress can trigger a flood of hormones, particularly cortisol, that may create an overreaction. Continuous overproduction of cortisol can create other problems with the endocrine system. In contrast, satisfying and responsive circumstances soothe and avoid such flooding. Teachers contribute to brain growth as they provide DAP educational experiences. Important, too, are prenatal and postnatal health care, and efforts to avoid malnourishment and keep stresses manageable at home.

3. *The quality of the environment is crucial.* The biological environment takes a huge role in brain development, so the level of nutrition and health care and protection from drugs and environmental toxins must be monitored. By age 2, most pruning of dendrites has already occurred. By age 7, the brain has grown to its adult size, and the basic areas of sensory and motor cortexes are functioning. Myelination, the fatty coating of dendrites and axons, speeds transmission of nerve impulses between neurons and enables children to think and

react faster. Fast and complex communication can now occur.

The core of the environment is interpersonal: People matter. Positive adult–child interaction promotes brain development.

Most of the significant ways that caregivers promote healthy development occur quite naturally during the course of sensitive adult–child interactions. For instance, the "parent-ese" that facilitates early language, the caregiving routines that promote predictability and memory skills, the patient structuring of an activity to make it manageable for a child, and the protective nurturance that manages a baby's emotions show that when sensitive adults do what comes naturally, their behavior is optimally suited to promoting early cognitive, socio-emotional, and neurobiological growth (Thompson, 2001).

With impoverishments, you may lose the dendrites. Stressed, depressed, or absent parents or caregivers do not give children the environmental experiences they need for neurobiological growth. Established patterns of behavior are increasingly difficult to change as individuals get older; it is more effective and efficient to get things right the first time than to try and fix them later.

"One theme from the research on children and learning is that babies' brains appear to be wired to help them understand and know about the world in specific ways, and that this learning begins long before babies can be taught this kind of knowledge" (Galinsky, 2010). Moreover, after the sensory and motor areas of the brain develop, the prefrontal cortex development begins. This is the part of the brain that controls the executive functions of managing attention, emotions, and behavior; it begins in the preschool years and doesn't mature until young adulthood. It is this area of the brain that is needed for the person to acquire essential life skills: focus and self-control; perspective taking; communicating; making connections; critical thinking; taking on challenges; and self-directed, engaged learning (Galinsky, 2010).

Applications to Early Education

Applying brain research to early education programs is a challenge. It is easy to become overwhelmed with unfamiliar vocabulary and complex neurological processes. By becoming knowledgeable about the brain and well-versed in DAP, early childhood professionals can create healthy environments and engaging, meaningful experiences (see Figure 2-17). The study of the brain assists educators in understanding how children learn best and provides them with evidence for how to build optimal educational experiences.

How Brain-based Research Aligns with Developmentally Appropriate Practices

Brain-based Research (BBR) Suggests . . .	Developmentally Appropriate Practice (DAP) Asserts . . .	Early Childhood Education (ECE) in Action . . .
The human brain is constantly seeking information from outside stimuli and uses all senses.	Learning occurs in a setting that provides choices and variety in the environment.	A sensory table, a block corner, dress-up clothes, and painting are offered during activity time.
No intelligence or ability unfolds until or unless it is offered and/or modeled.	Development advances when children have opportunities to practice newly acquired skills both at and just beyond their present level of mastery.	Children have access to ongoing, familiar materials (play dough, sand, trikes) and challenging lessons (sink/float experiment, story dictation, obstacle course)
The brain processes on many paths, can deal with many inputs at once, and prefers multiprocessing	Development proceeds toward greater complexity and organization as children internalize experience.	Multisensory activities are offered and organized for both low and high order thinking, and connections are shown when introducing new information
A number of areas of the brain are simultaneously activated during a learning experience	Children are active learners, drawing on direct physical and social experience as well as culturally transmitted knowledge.	Field trips, activities, presentations from families, technology, and multicultural units are offered.
The brain changes physiologically as a result of experience, with new dendrites forming that hook new experiences to old ones.	Development occurs in a relatively orderly sequence, with later abilities and skills building on those already acquired.	Hands-on activities provide strong associations, and curriculum by theme or project aid in connected learning.
Each region of the brain is a sophisticated network of cells that interconnect one part of the brain to another.	Domains of children's development are closely related, with growth in one area influencing other domains.	Integrated curriculum allows for learning in many ways, and activities are presented using Gardner's multiple intelligences.
Each brain is unique, with differences from 2 to 3 year age span, and learning new knowledge or skills changes the gain structure.	Development proceeds at varying rates from child to child as well as unevenly within each child.	Choices allow children to select activities appropriate to their developmental level, mixed age groupings are encouraged, and individualized education plans are created.

FIGURE 2-17 Discoveries in neuroscience parallel the work described in developmentally appropriate practices and have clear application to early education activities. (Based on Rushton et al., 2009.)

Using Developmental and Learning Theories

As a teacher, you must think about what you believe about children, development, and learning. Theories, research, and key developmental topics are part of educational philosophy. Two critical questions arise: 1) How do I reconcile contradictions among the theories? and 2) How can I decide which is "right"?

To answer the first question, remember that each theory addresses a particular aspect of development. Psychodynamic theory focuses on the development of personality, behaviorist on the conditions of learning, cognitive on how children think and learn, maturation on how development progresses, and humanist on the

Connect the Dots: How Neuroscience Supports Theory and DAP

Neuroscience research is intertwined with basic principles of learning and appropriate practices of early childhood education. Rushton (2011) provides these four principles; we connect the dots to classroom practice, then ask you to do the same.

Principle #1: "Every brain is uniquely organized." . . . *Provide materials that match child skills at several levels.* For instance, alphabet awareness would call for writing materials in the art area, sandpaper letters in the library, sand trays with an alphabet chart in the sensory corner, and alphabet blocks in the block corner.

Principle #2: "The brain is continually growing, changing, and adapting to the environment." . . . *Provide a* *people-friendly environment.* Children are welcomed with a smiling greeting, have familiar places for their belongings, are invited to help create classroom space, and have teachers who are responsive to their changing mood and energy.

Principle #3: "A brain-compatible classroom enables connection of learning to positive emotions." . . . *Give children reasonable choices.* Allowing children to make some decisions ("Do you want to brush you teeth first or set up your nap space?") and some choices ("What game shall we play at outside circle today?") leads to feelings of positive power and competence.

Principle #4: "Children's brains need to be immersed in real life, hands-on, and meaningful learning experiences that are intertwined with a commonality and require some form of problem-solving." . . . *Set up time for small groups to get immersed in a topic without interruption.* If a child walks in with an interesting item, facilitate exploration and sharing instead of sending it to the cubby. Encourage children to elaborate—to you, to visitors, or anyone else who will listen—their explanations and critical thinking.

Questions
1. What play experiences encourage brain growth?
2. What hazards in a school day might be inappropriate to brain development?

conditions for overall health. Moreover, each topic has its avid proponents with a body of research that supports it. Because every theory and topic has its own focus and advocates, they are all rather subjective and somewhat narrow. In other words, no *one* theory tells us everything.

To address the second question, thoughtful teachers develop their own viewpoints. Begin to decide what you believe about children, learning, and education. Try to avoid the pitfall of taking sides. Instead, integrate theory into your teaching practices by comparing the major developmental and learning theories with your own daily experiences with young children.

Most early childhood educators are eclectic in their theoretical biases. That is, they have developed their own philosophies of education based on a little of each theory. Each teacher has an obligation to develop a clear set of ideas of how children grow and learn. We are fortunate to have choices (see Figure 2-18).

Basic Tenets

Most educators agree on some basic tenets based, in part, on theories of development and learning:

1. *Basic needs.* Children's basic physiologic needs and their needs for physical and psychological safety must be met satisfactorily before they can experience and respond to "growth motives." [Humanist, Brain Development]

2. *Factors in development.* Children develop unevenly and not in a linear fashion as they grow toward psychosocial maturity and psychological well-being. A wide variety of factors in children's lives, as well as the manner in which they interpret their own experiences, has a bearing on the pattern and rate of progress toward greater social and emotional maturity. [Psychosocial, Behaviorist, Maturation, Ethnicity/Culture]

3. *Crises in Childhood.* Developmental crises that occur in the normal process of growing up may offer maximum opportunities for psychological growth, but these crises are also full of possibilities for regression or even negative adaptation. [Psychosocial, Cognitive, Ecological, Play, Moral Development]

4. *Striving for Mastery.* Children strive for mastery over their own private inner worlds as well as for mastery of the world outside of them. [Psychosocial, Cognitive, Multiple Intelligences, Play]

5. *Relationships and Interactions.* The child's interactions with significant persons in his life play a major part in his development. [Psychosocial, Behaviorist, Sociocultural, Humanist, Attachment, Gender Identity, Brain Development]

Summary of Major Theories

Theory	Major Theorists	Important Facts
Psychoanalytic	Sigmund Freud	Basic instinctual drives of sex, aggression, and destructiveness Stages of psychosexual development Personality structures of id, ego, and superego
Psychosocial	Erik Erikson	Maturational emphasis Stage theory of social and emotional development Crises at each level Teacher: Emotional base, social mediator
Behaviorist	John Watson Edward Thorndike B. F. Skinner Albert Bandura	Environmental emphasis Stimulus–response Conditioning (classical and operant) Reinforcement (positive and negative) Modeling Teacher: Arranger of environment and reinforcer of behavior
Cognitive	Jean Piaget	Maturational and environmental emphasis Assimilation and accommodation Stage theory of cognitive development Teacher: Provider of materials and time and supporter of children's unique ways of thinking
Sociocultural	Lev Vygotsky	Zone of proximal development Private speech Collaborative/assisted learning
Multiple intelligences	Howard Gardner	Many kinds of intelligence Problem-solving and product-creating
Maturation	Arnold Gesell	Emphasis on heredity Normative data Teacher: Guider of behavior based on what is typical and normal
Humanist	Abraham Maslow	Environmental emphasis Mental health model Hierarchy of human needs Teacher: Provider of basic and growth needs
Developmental topics	Mary Ainsworth John Bowlby Nancy Eisenberg Carol Gilligan Lawrence Kohlberg Eleanor Maccoby	Attachment and categories research Attachment theory Expands moral development to prosocial Questions categories of moral development Moral, cognitive, and sex-role development Sex differences research
Brain development	Bruce Perry Daniel Siegel Stephen Rushton Ellen Galinsky Ross Thompson	New insights into early development "Use it or lose it" principle DAP and brain-based research connections Life skills and brain development Parallels between all domains and brain growth

© Cengage Learning 2011

FIGURE 2-18 Major theories include the "most excellent eight" and several key developmental topics, including brain development.

Developmental Research Conclusions

Research, and the information it yields, must serve the needs of the practitioner to be useful. Teachers can combine researchers' systematic data with personal observations and experiences, including the significance of relationships, language and thinking, biologic factors, and special needs (see Chapter 6). To keep in mind the real child underneath all these theories, teachers apply developmental research to their own classroom settings. "Theories of child development can serve as guides for assessing the developmental levels of any children. They can help us know what children's

One of the conclusions of research and theory is that children's interactions with significant people in their lives play a major role in development.

competencies are and where we should begin instruction. Theories of development can serve as guides for planning instruction for individuals and for groups" (Charlesworth, 2011). Figure 2-19 consolidates what developmental research has found and how it can be put into practical use with young children.

There is so much information now about children and their development. It is easy to feel overwhelmed, and easier still to believe what we read. Santrock (2009) advises us:

- Be cautious about what is reported in the popular media.
- Do not assume that group research applies to an individual.
- Do not generalize about a small or clinical sample.
- Do not take a single study as the defining word.
- Do not accept causal conclusions from correlational studies.
- Always consider the source of the information and evaluate its credibility.

Conditions for Learning

Caring for children means providing for total growth, creating optimal conditions for learning in the best possible environment. Developmental theory helps define conditions that enhance learning and from which positive learning environments are created. Research on all theories extends the knowledge of children and learning. Coupled with practical application, both theory and research have helped all to recognize that:

1. *Learning must be real.* We teach about the children's bodies, their families, their neighborhoods, and their school. We start with who children are and expand this to include the world, in their terms. We give them the words, the ideas, and the ways to question and figure things out for themselves.
2. *Learning must be rewarding.* Practice makes better, but only if it is all right to practice and to stumble and try again. We include the time to do all this by providing an atmosphere of acceptance and of immediate feedback as to what was accomplished (even what boundary was just overstepped). Also, practice can make a good experience even better, as it reminds children in their terms of what they can do.
3. *Learning must build on children's lives.* We help connect the family to the child and the teacher. We realize that children learn about culture from family and knowledgeable members of the community, such as teachers, librarians, grocers, and the like. We know important family events and help the family support happenings at school. For children, learning goes on wherever they may be, awake and asleep. Parents can learn to value learning and help it happen for their child.
4. *Learning needs a good stage.* Healthy bodies make for alert minds, so good education means caring for children's health. This includes physical, emotional, and mental health. Psychological safety and well-being are theoretical terms for the insight, availability, and awareness teachers bring to their classrooms. On the lookout for each child's successes, we prevent distractions in the way furniture is arranged, how noisy it is, and how many strangers are around. Mental health is both emotional and intellectual. We try to have a variety of materials and experiences, and a flexible schedule when someone is pursuing an idea, building a project, or finishing a disagreement.

As long as we care for children, we will have our hands full. With the theoretical underpinnings presented here, we have the tools with which to make our own way into the world of children and of early childhood education.

Developmental Research Tells Us	Teachers Can
1. Growth occurs in a sequence.	Think about the steps children will take when planning projects. Know the sequence of growth in their children's age group.
2. Children in any age group will behave similarly in certain ways.	Plan for activities in relation to age range of children. Know the characteristics of their children's age group.
3. Children grow through certain stages.	Know the stages of growth in their class. Let family know of any behavior that is inconsistent with general stages of development.
4. Growth occurs in four interrelated areas.	Understand that work in one area can help in another.
5. Intellectual growth:	
Children learn through their senses.	Have activities in looking, smelling, tasting, hearing, and touching.
Children learn by doing and need concrete experiences.	Realize that talking is abstract; have children touch.
Cognitive growth happens in four areas: Perception (visual, auditory, etc.)	Provide materials and activities in matching, finding same/different, putting a picture with a sound, taste, or with a symbol. Provide opportunities to find and label things, talk with grown-ups, friends, tell what it "looks like," smells like, etc.
Language Memory	Know that memory is helped by seeing, holding objects, and people. Recognize that reasoning ability is just beginning, so children judge on what they see rather than what you may want them to realize.
Reasoning	Be sure adult explanations aid in understanding reasons. Practice finding "answers" to open-ended questions such as "How can you tell when you are tired?"
6. Social growth:	
The world is only from the child's viewpoint.	Expect that children will think of only their own ideas at first. Be aware that the rights of others are minimal to them.
Seeing is believing.	Remember that if they cannot see the situation, they may not be able to talk about it.
Group play is developing.	Provide free-play sessions, with places to play socially. Understand that group play in structured situations is difficult because of "self" orientation.
Independence increases as competence grows.	Know that children test to see how far they can go. Realize that children will vary from independent to dependent (both among the group and within one child).
People are born not knowing when it is safe to go on.	Understand that children will need to learn by trial and error.
Adult attention is very important.	Know the children individually.
Young children are not born with an internal mechanism that says "slow down."	Move into a situation before children lose control.
7. Emotional growth:	
Self-image is developing.	Be alert for each child's self-image that may be developing. Give praise to enhance good feelings about oneself. Know that giving children responsibilities helps self-image. Talk to children at eye level. Children learn by example. Model appropriate behavior by doing yourself what you want the children to do.
8. Physical growth:	
Muscle development is not complete.	Do not expect perfection, in either small- or large-muscle activity.
Muscles cannot stay still for long.	Plan short times for children to sit.
Large muscles are better developed than small ones.	Give lots of chances to move about; be gentle with expectations for hand work.
Hand preference is being established.	Watch to see how children decide their handedness. Let children trade hands in their play.
A skill must be done several times before it is internalized.	Have materials available to be used often. Plan projects to use the same skill over and over.
Bowel and bladder control is not completely internalized.	Be understanding of "accidents." If possible, have toilet facilities available always, and keep them attractive.

FIGURE 2-19 Developmental research tests theories of growth and learning to find out about children and childhood.

Teaching With INTENTION

Put Those Theories to Work!

Decision making in teaching can be difficult. Can theory help us?

It is 10 AM at the infant-toddler center. Fifteen-month-olds Kenya and Peter are crying and fussy this morning. Neither has eaten since breakfast. They have been indoors all morning.
Theory: *Maturation theory.* Children's physical developmental needs affect their emotional states.
Plan: Schedule regular times for active movement. Be sure to offer food and watch for signs of hunger.

Mario and Therese, both in wheelchairs, joined the first grade last month, but their parents report that neither wants to come to school. Their academic work is at grade level, but they participate very little. They seem familiar with their teacher.
Theory: *Sociocultural theory.* Children need to feel part of the class culture in order to learn well.

Theory: *Psychosocial theory.* The children can identify with the teacher and become successful but may feel incompetent with unfriendly or indifferent classmates.
Theory: *Cognitive theory.* They can understand other points of view as long as it is in real situations.
Plan: Put each child in a small group to design and build wheel toys for pets. Building on the newcomers' expertise in a cooperative activity gives all the children the scaffolding needed to be successful and helps the new children become accepted into the class.

Preschoolers Jared and Panya have been arguing about who has brought the "best" toy to child care. Others have heard the ruckus and have stopped to watch the two start a fight.
Theory: *Cognitive theory.* Their egocentric thinking prevents them from seeing any view other than their own.

Also, they are unable to hold two ideas at the same time, so they cannot see that both toys are "good."
Theory: *Behaviorist theory.* The children can learn from watching others and applying other's example to their own behavior.
Plan: The teacher engages the children in a conflict resolution method that gets all children to express their own ideas, both about the problem and for some solutions, so they can practice hearing another's ideas while still holding their own. The teacher models praising each child's positive characteristics in the other's presence, showing other ways to behave appropriately and how the children and their toys can play together.

Think About This
1. How can theory illuminate what is going on with a child or in a center?
2. Which theories make the most sense to you—and why?

Summary

LO1 Developmental and learning theories form the cornerstone of our knowledge about children. The eight major theoretical perspectives that relate to child development and learning are psychodynamic, behaviorist, cognitive, sociocultural, ecological, multiple intelligences, maturation, and humanist.

LO2 The central developmental topics of ethnicity and culture, attachment, play, gender, moral development, and brain development are vehicles for creating developmentally appropriate practices. Each offers new vistas of possibility and better teaching and learning.

LO3 Developmental and learning theories explain much of children's growth and development. There are several basic tenets in early childhood education that connect with the theories and topics. Developmental research offers useful conclusions that outline conditions for learning. By consistently applying the insights from research and theory, we show our willingness to make a commitment to children.

Key Terms

theory
hypothesis
nature/nurture controversy
psychodynamic theory
unconscious
psychosocial
identity crisis
autonomy
behaviorist theory
stimulus–response
reinforcement
socialization
social learning theory
modeling
self-efficacy
observational learning
classical conditioning
phobia
operant conditioning
reinforcers

positive reinforcement
negative reinforcement
punishment
cognitive theory
assimilation
accommodation
equilibration
schemas
sensorimotor
transmission model
constructivism
transactional model
egocentric
sociocultural
zone of proximal development
   (ZPD)
scaffolding
private (inner) speech
bicognitive development
multiple intelligences

maturation
maturation theory
humanist theory
self-actualization
basic needs (deficiency needs)
growth needs
attachment
spontaneous play
superhero
sociodramatic play
sex differences
gender differences
gender identity
gender role
prosocial
synapses
dendrites
cortisol
myelination
eclectic

Review Questions

1. Match the theorist with the appropriate description:

   B.F. Skinner   Ecological theory
   Abraham Maslow   Multiple intelligences
   Jean Piaget   Sex differences
   Albert Bandura   Attachment
   Mary Ainsworth   Social learning
   Eleanor Maccoby   Zone of proximal
         development

   Erik Erikson   Psychosocial development
   Arnold Gesell   Behaviorism
   Lev Vygotsky   Developmental norms
   Howard Gardner   Cognitive theory
   Uric Bronfenbrenner   Self-actualization

2. Describe in a sentence each of the major developmental topics and its connection to early childhood education.

   Ethnicity and culture
   Attachment
   Play
   Gender
   Moral development
   Brain development

3. "Using developmental and learning theories, teachers create developmentally appropriate practice in their programs." Explain this concept and give three specific examples.

Observe and Apply

1. You are a teacher in a large urban child care center. Your preschool children arrive by 7:00 AM and usually stay until after 5:00 PM each day. What would you do first thing in the morning? Use Maslow's hierarchy of needs to justify your answer. What do you know about your group's development? Use Piaget's cognitive stages to build your answer. What assumptions, if any, can you make about their cultural background? How do you find out about what each child is ready to learn?

2. What do you think of the influence of television on children's behavior? Consider the typical cartoons that the children you know are watching. From a behaviorist perspective, what are they learning? With sociocultural theory in mind, what else would you have them watch or do?

3. Observe children in a center as they say good-bye and then start their day. What can your observations tell you about their attachment levels? What can teachers do to support attachment and also help children separate? What is the difference in play when 1) a teacher interacts with children in their play and 2) a teacher is not involved? What are your conclusions?

Helpful Websites

Alliance for Childhood
www.allianceforchildhood.org

American Educational Research Association
www.area.net

ERIC (Educational Resources Information Center)
www.eric.ed.gov

Early Childhood Research Quarterly
www.naeyc.org/publications/ecrq

Gesell Institute   **www.gesellinstitute.org**

National Association for the Education of Young Children   **www.naeyc.org**

National Institute for Early Education Research
www.nieer.org

Society for Research in Child Development
www.srcd.org

⊕ The Education CourseMate website for this text offers many helpful resources and interactive study tools. Go to CengageBrain.com to access the TeachSource Videos, flashcards, tutorial quizzes, direct links to all of the websites mentioned in the chapter, downloadable forms, and more.

References

General Texts

Berger, K. S. (2012). *The developing person* (9th Ed). New York: Worth.

Berk, L. (2011). *Infants and children* (7th Ed). Boston: Allyn & Bacon.

Charlesworth, R. (2011). Developmental theory: The foundation of developmentally appropriate practice. In A. M. Gordon & K. M. Browne, *Beginnings & Beyond* (8th Ed). Belmont, CA: Wadsworth/Cengage.

Santrock, J. W. (2009). *Children* (11th Ed). Boston, MA: McGraw Hill.

Psychodynamic Theory

Erikson, E. H. (1963). *Childhood and society* (2nd Ed). New York: Norton.

Erikson, E. H. (1964). Toys and reasons. In M. R. Haworth (Ed.), *Child psychotherapy: Practice and theory*. New York: Basic Books.

Erikson, E. H. (1969). A healthy personality for every child. In P. H. Mussen, J. J. Conger, & J. Kagan (Eds.), *Child development and personality* (3rd Ed). New York: Harper & Row.

Erikson, E. H. (1969). *Gandhi's truth*. New York: W.W. Norton & Company.

Freud, S., & Hall, G. Stanley. (1920). *A general introduction to psychoanalysis*. New York: Boni & Liveright.

Spitz, R. A., & Wolf, K. M. (1946). Analytic depression: An inquiry into the genesis of psychiatric conditions in early childhood, II. In A. Freud, et al. (Eds.), *The psychoanalytic study of the child (Vol. II)*. New York: International Universities Press.

Behaviorist Theory

Bandura, A. (1963). Imitation of film-mediated aggressive models. *Journal of Abnormal and Social Psychology*.

Bandura, A., Barbaranelli, C., Vittorio Caprara, G., & Pastorelli, C. (2001). Self-efficacy beliefs as shapers of children's aspirations and career trajectories. *Child Development*, 72(1), pp. 187–206.

Kohn, A. (2006). *Unconditional Parenting: Moving from Rewards & Punishments to Love & Reason*. New York: Atria Books/Simon & Schuster.

Skinner, B. F. (1953). *Science and human behavior*. New York, NY: MacMillan Co.

Cognitive Theory

Elkind, D. (1977). Giant in the nursery school—Jean Piaget. In E. M. Hetherington & R. D. Parke (Eds.), *Contemporary readings in psychology*. New York: McGraw-Hill.

Elkind, D., & Flavell, J. (Eds.). (1996). *Essays in honor of Jean Piaget*. New York: Oxford University Press.

Ginsburg, H. & Opper, S. (1987). *Piaget's theory of intellectual development*. New York: Prentice Hall.

Kohn, A. (2006). *Unconditional parenting*. New York: Atria Books/Simon & Schuster.

Piaget, J., & Inhelder, B. (1972). *The psychology of the child* (2nd Ed). New York: Basic Books.

Sociocultural Theory

Berk, L. (2000). Vygotsky's sociocultural theory. In A. Gordon & K. W. Browne, *Beginnings and beyond* (5th Ed). Clifton Park, NY: Thomson Delmar Learning.

Fouad, N. A., & Arredondo, P. (Eds). (2007). *Becoming culturally oriented: Practical advice for psychologists and educators*. Washington, D.C.: American Psychological Association.

Rogoff, B. (1990). *Apprenticeship in thinking: Cognitive development in a social context*. New York: Oxford University Press.

Vygotsky, L. S. (1978). *Mind in society: The development of higher psychological processes*. Cambridge, MA: Harvard University Press.

York, S. (2005). *Roots and wings: Affirming culture in early childhood programs*. St. Paul, MN: Redleaf Press.

Ecological Theory

Berger, K. S. (2011). *The developing person* (9th Ed). New York: Worth.

Bronfenbrenner, U. (2000). Ecological system theory. In A. Kazdin (Ed.), *Encyclopedia of Psychology*. Washington, D.C.: American Psychological Association and Oxford Press.

Bronfenbrenner, U. (1979). *The ecology of human development: Experiments by nature and design*. Cambridge, MA: Harvard University Press.

Multiple Intelligences Theory

Gardner, H. (1983). *Frames of mind*. New York: Basic Books.

Gardner, H. (1993). *Multiple intelligences*. New York: Basic Books.

Gardner, H., Gridman, D. H., Krechevsky, M., & Chen J-Q. (1998). *Project Zero frameworks for early childhood education* (Vol. 1–3). New York: Teachers College Press.

Gardner, H. (2000). *Intelligence reframed: Multiple intelligences for the 21st century*. New York: Basic Books.

Maturation Theory

Ames, L. B., & Ilg, F. (1979). *The Gesell Institute's child from one to six; The Gesell Institute's child from five to ten; The infant in today's culture*. New York: Harper & Row.

Gesell, A. (1940). *The first five years of life*. New York: Harper & Row.

Humanist Theory

Goble, F. G. (1970). *The third force: The psychology of Abraham Maslow*. New York: Grossman.

Maslow, A. H. (1954). *Motivation and personality*. New York: Harper & Row.

Developmental Topics

Ethnicity and Cultural Diversity

Caldwell, B. (1983). *Child development and cultural diversity*. Geneva, Switzerland: OMEP World Assembly.

Lawrence-Lightfoot, S. (2004). *The essential connection: What parents and teachers can learn from each other*. New York: Ballantine Books.

Markus, H., in Vaughan, L. J. Culture as sculptor: Markus explores 'Models of Self'. Stanford University, *The Bing Times*, November, 2005.

New, R. R., & Beneke, M. (2009). Negotiating diversity in early childhood education: Rethinking notions of expertise. In Fenney, S., Galper, A., & Seefeldt, C. (Eds.) *Continuing issues in early childhood education* (3rd Ed). Columbus, OH: Merrill/Pearson.

Phinney, J. S. & Alipuria, L. I. (2006). Multiple social categorization and identity among multiracial, multiethnic, and multicultural individuals. In R. J. Crisp & M. Hewstone (Eds.), *Multiple social categorization: Process, models, and applications*. New York: Psychology Press.

Rogoff, B. (2003). *The cultural nature of human development*. New York: Oxford University Press.

Attachment

Ainsworth, M. (1979, October). Infant-mother attachment. *American Psychologist*, pp. 131–142.

Bowlby, J. (1969, 1973). *Attachment and loss* (Vols. I and II). New York: Basic Books.

Saxton, R. (2001). *Personal communication*.

White, Burton L. (1995). *The new first three years, revised*. NY: Fireside Publications.

Play

American Academy of Pediatrics: Ginsberg, K.R., Committee on Communications, and Committee on Psychosocial Aspects of Child & Family Health. (2007). Clinical report: The importance of play in promoting healthy child development. http://www.aap.org/pressroom/playFINAL.pdf.

Elkind, D. (2010). Play. In V. Washington & J. D. Andrews (Eds.). *Children of 2020: Creating a better tomorrow*. Washington, D.C: Council for Professional Recognition.

Frost, J. L., Wortham, S. C., & Reifel, S. (2011). *Play and child development* (4th Ed). Upper Saddle River, NJ: Prentice Hall.

Hoffman, E. (2004). *Magic capes, amazing powers: Transforming play in the classroom*. St. Paul, MN: Redleaf Press.

Parten, M. B. (1932). Social participation among preschool children. *Journal of Abnormal and Social Psychology*, 27, pp. 243–269.

Gender

Eisenberg, N., Martin, C. L., & Fabes, R. A. (1996). Gender development and gender effects. In D.C. Berliner & R.C. Calfee (Eds.), *Handbook of educational psychology*. New York: Macmillan.

Maccoby, E. E. (1998). *The two sexes*. Cambridge, MA: Harvard University Press.

Maccoby, E. E. & Jacklin, C. N. (1974). *The psychology of sex differences*. Stanford, CA: Stanford University Press.

Martin, C. L. & Ruble, D. (2006). Children's search for gender cues: Cognitive perspectives on gender development. *Current Directions in Psychological Science*, 13(2), pp. 67–70.

Ruble, D. N., Martin, C. I., & Berenbaum, S. A. (2006). Gender development. In N. Eisenberg, W. Damon, & R. M. Lerner (Eds.) *Handbook of child psychology, Vol 3. Social, emotional, and personality development*. Hoboken, NJ: Wiley.

Wardle, F. (2004). The challenge of boys in our early childhood programs. *Early Childhood News* (January-February, 2004).

Moral Development

Buzzelli, C. & Johnston, B. (2002). *The moral dimensions of teaching: Language, power, and culture in classroom interaction*. London: Routledge.

Eisenberg, N., Lenon, R., & Roth, K. (1983). Prosocial development in middle childhood: A longitudinal study. *Developmental Psychology*, 23, pp. 712–718.

Eisenberg, N. (1992). *The caring child*. Boston, MA: Harvard University Press.

Gilligan, C. (1982). *In a different voice*. Cambridge, MA: Harvard University Press.

Gilligan, C. (2011). *Joining the resistance*. Boston: Polity/Wiley & Sons.

Kohlberg, L. (1981). *The philosophy of moral development*. New York: Harper & Row.

Piaget, J. (1965). *The moral judgment of the child*. NY: Free Press.

Brain-Based Research

Copple, C., & Bredekamp, S. (Eds.) (2009). *Developmentally appropriate practice in early childhood programs serving children from birth through age 8* (3rd Ed). Washington, D.C.: National Association for the Education of Young Children.

Galinsky, E. (2010). *Mind in the making*. Washington, D.C.: National Association for the Education of Young Children.

Gallagher, K. (2005). Brain research and early childhood development: A primer for developmentally appropriate practices. *Young Children*, 60(4), pp. 12–20.

Miller, B. & Cummings, J. (Eds.) (2007). *The human frontal lobes*. New York: Guilford Press.

Rushton, S. (2011). Neuroscience, early childhood education and play: We are doing it right! *Early Childhood Education Journal*, 39, pp. 89–94.

Rushton, S., Joula-Rushton, A., & Larkin, E. (2010). Neuroscience, play and early childhood education: Connections, implications and assessment. *Early Childhood Education Journal*, 37, pp. 351–361.

Shonkoff, J. P., et al. (2008). The timing and quality of early experiences combine to shape brain architecture: working paper 5. Cambridge, MA: Harvard University Center on the Developing Child.

Thompson, R. A. (Spring-Summer 2001). Development in the first years of life. *The Future of Children, Vol. 11, No. 1, Caring for Infants and Toddlers*, pp. 20–33.

Types of Programs

naeyc Standards For Professional Development

The following NAEYC standards for initial and advanced early childhood professional preparation are addressed in this chapter:

Standard 1 Promoting child development and learning

Standard 2 Building family and community relationships

Standard 3 Observing, documenting, and assessing to support young children and families

Standard 4 Using developmentally effective approaches to connect with children and families

Standard 5 Using content knowledge to build meaningful curriculum

Standard 6 Becoming a professional

Field Experience

naeyc Code of Ethical Conduct

These are the sections of the NAEYC Code of Ethical Conduct that apply to the topics of this chapter:

Section I:

I-1.2 To base program practices upon current knowledge and research in the field of early childhood education, child development and related disciplines as well as on particular knowledge of each child.

P-1.7 We shall strive to build individual relationships with each child: make individual adaptations in teaching strategies, learning environment, and curricula; and consult with the family so that each child benefits from the program.

Section II:

I-2.8 To help family members enhance their understanding of their children, as staff are enhancing their understanding of each child through communications with families, and support family members in the continuing development of their skills as parents.

P-2.2 We shall inform families of program philosophy, policies, curriculum, assessment system, cultural practices, and personnel qualifications, and explain why we teach as we do—which should be in accordance with our ethical responsibilities to children.

Section IV:

I.4.1 To provide the community with high quality early childhood care and education programs and services.

P.4-6 We shall be familiar with laws and regulations that serve to protect the children in our programs and be vigilant in ensuring that these laws and regulations are followed.

Learning Objectives

LO1 Examine the underlying theoretical principles of developmentally appropriate practices applied to a variety of early childhood programs.

LO2 Describe the core programs of early childhood education, program types, and their differing philosophies.

LO3 Identify the variation of program options and range of delivery systems that impact the lives of children and their families.

LO4 Assess early childhood programs utilizing indicators of quality early childhood practices that support all children including those with diverse characteristics.

Developmentally Appropriate Practice in Early Childhood Programs

Throughout this text and whenever NAEYC principles are discussed, we use the term *developmentally appropriate practice*. What exactly is developmentally appropriate practice, or DAP, as it is more familiarly known?

More than 20 years ago, NAEYC published a position paper, which articulated standards for high quality care and education for young children. The guidelines were a response to the need for a set of unified standards for accreditation through NAEYC's newly established National Academy of Early Childhood, and gave a necessary antidote to the more teacher-directed, academic preparation and skills-teaching methods that were encroaching on many early childhood programs.

The DAP approach stressed the need for activity-based learning environments based on what we know about children through years of child development research and what we observe of their interests, abilities, and needs. The position paper was revised over the years to be more inclusive by moving from an "either/or" point of view to that of "both/and." In other words, there are many right ways to apply DAP principles.

Three Core Components of DAP

The position statement of "Developmentally Appropriate Practice in Early Childhood Programs Serving Children from Birth through Age 8" (NAEYC, 2009) cites three core considerations on which teachers and caregivers should base their decisions about young children's growth and development:

1. *What is known about child development and learning*—knowledge of age-related characteristics that permit general predictions about what experiences are likely to best promote children's learning and development. This is the core around which the idea of *developmentally appropriate* is built.
2. *What is known about each child as an individual*—what practitioners learn about each child that has implications for how best to adapt and be responsive to individual variations.
3. *What is known about the social and cultural contexts in which children live*—the values, expectations, and behavioral and linguistic conventions that shape children's lives at home and in their communities that practitioners must strive to understand in order to ensure that learning experiences in the program

or school are meaningful, relevant, and respectful for each child and family. Figure 3-1 shows how these three core principles work together.

The following scenario shows how these core considerations are applied when planning a developmentally appropriate program for toddlers:

1. *What does child development tell us about toddlers?* We know that toddlers express their need to do everything by themselves, usually more than they can actually achieve. They like to feel independent and learn quickly if given a little help and then encouraged to do what they can for themselves (see Chapters 3 and 4 for more detail).
2. *What do we know about each child as an individual?* Many of these toddlers rely on their parents to help them put on their clothes, feed them, or put their toys away. Others are being taught these tasks at home. Most of the children come to the teachers for assistance and a few ask for help. One toddler will persist at a dressing task for nearly five minutes while another will throw shoes across the floor if they do not fit the first time.
3. *What do we know about the social and cultural context in each child's life?* Most of the children in this group come from homes in which help is readily available from siblings and extended family members. The group's dominant cultural values and child-rearing practices reinforce dependence and community, although there is a smaller group of families that want their children to become independent as soon as possible.

By looking at all three core considerations together, we have some decisions to make about setting goals toward greater independence for the toddlers. Respecting cultural and social contexts means we begin by talking to families,

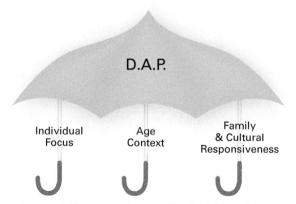

FIGURE 3-1 There are a variety of early childhood programs to fit the needs of children and their families.

Courtesy of the author

A developmentally appropriate program takes into consideration this child's age, individual abilities, and the culture of her home and family.

perhaps at a parent meeting, in which families are invited to share their child-rearing practices from their cultural viewpoint. Once we have an understanding of what families expect and want, we have an opportunity to work together to negotiate a solution that will be beneficial both for the toddlers and for the families. When developmentally appropriate elements are taken into consideration, the bonds between families and teachers are strengthened and the best interests of the children prevail.

Guidelines for DAP

DAP provides the context for learning environments in which children's abilities are matched to the developmental tasks they need to learn. DAP is based on what we know about how children learn and what we know about individual children and their families. This collective knowledge is applied to each decision that is made about the program. Copple and Bredekamp (2009) suggest five key areas of practice that guide the decision-making process.

1. *Creating a Caring Community of Learners* begins with programs that support and value all children, regardless of age, ability, gender, or racial and ethnic background and where respectful, cooperative, and positive relationships create optimum learning conditions. The learning environment has a positive emotional climate that supports the enjoyment of learning and fosters each member's well-being.

2. *Teaching to Enhance Development and Learning* includes a balance of teacher-directed and child-initiated learning, time for in-depth exploration, integrated curriculum, and scaffolded learning.

3. *Planning Curriculum to Achieve Important Goals* reflects the knowledge of how children learn, what they learn, and when they learn it. Articulated goals include standards to be met. Curriculum relates to children's interests and needs and includes all developmental domains.

4. *Assessing Children's Development and Learning* is ongoing and monitors each child's progress in meeting program goals. Assessment methods include observations and work samples and the results are used to plan curriculum that further the effectiveness of classroom experiences.

5. *Establishing Reciprocal Relationships with Families* means developing collaborative relationships with families that promote a sense of partnership based on mutual need, understanding, and negotiation.

Each chapter of this text, individually and collectively, supports and demonstrates these five guidelines for developmentally appropriate practices in developmentally appropriate programs.

DAP in Action

Developmentally appropriate principles reflect the many intentional decisions teachers make based on their knowledge of how children learn and grow. Developmentally appropriate principles benefit children in many ways:

1. In constructing their own understanding of concepts and from instruction by more competent peers and adults.

2. Through opportunities to see connections across disciplines through integration of curriculum and engaging in in-depth study.

3. With a predictable structure and routine in the learning environment and from the teacher's flexibility and spontaneity in responding to children's emerging ideas, needs, and interests.

4. By making meaningful choices about what children will do.

5. From situations that challenge children to work at the edge of their capacities and from ample opportunities to practice newly acquired skills.

What DAP Looks Like

- Programs and curriculum respond to the children's interests as well as their needs.

  While digging in the sand pit, four children uncover water. Others rush to see it. The teacher sees their interest and asks them about the bridges and tunnels they are starting to build.

- Children are actively involved in their own learning, choosing from a variety of materials and equipment.

  Some children search the yard for materials that will bridge the water. Others go inside to find the big book on bridges. Still others dig in other areas of the sandpit to find more water and to try building tunnels for the water. One child finds a walnut shell and floats it on the water. The teacher encourages and supports each child's involvement.

- Play is the primary context in which young children learn and grow.

  Each day, the children rush outside to see their bridges and tunnels. The teacher has helped them find materials that will act as a cover over the bridge. Inside, several children are making dolls from twigs and fabric scraps to use in the project.

- Teachers apply what they know about each child and use a variety of strategies, materials, and learning experiences to be responsive to individual children.

  Josephina is drawing a picture of the bridge and is having trouble with the arches. Knowing that Josephina is somewhat shy and uneasy in large groups, the teacher asks Aldo (who is easygoing and loves to draw) to look at Josephina's picture to see if he might help her. The two children focus on the drawing, each making observations that help Josephina take the next step in her artwork.

- Teachers consider widely held expectations about each age group and temper that with challenging yet achievable learning goals.

  In preparation for a field trip to see two bridges that are near the school, the teacher sets out her expectations (walk with a buddy, stay together, stay on the sidewalk, do not run, etc.). Because this is their first field trip of the school year, the teacher rehearses the children for several days prior to the trip. Music and rhythm accompany them as they practice walking with a friend and play number games of "two-by-two" during group times.

- Teachers understand that any activity has the potential for different children to realize different learning from the same experience.

After the field trip, Josephina draws a different type of arch for her bridges. Selena, Gracie, and Sam take over the block corner to build bridges and tunnels; three others join them. Maddie finds a book on flowers; they look like some of the flowers she saw on the way to the bridges. Reilly wants to play London Bridge at group time.

- All aspects of development—physical, social-emotional, cognitive, and language—are integrated in the activities and opportunities of the program.

  The bridge project promotes physical (walking, digging), cognitive (learning how bridges and tunnels are built, researching in books), language (construction terms, such as piers, spans, suspension), social-emotional (pairing up two-by-two), and creative (drawing a bridge, adding flowers, trying tunnels).

Each of these examples shows how to meet the needs of all children, no matter their abilities and background. Keep in mind that while each principle defines one particular factor, all of the principles are interrelated and that cultural and social differences, for instance, are a factor in all of the principles.

Early Childhood Core Programs

From the types available, to the numbers of children who attend these schools, the name of the game in early childhood programs is diversity. The range can encompass a morning nursery school for toddlers, a primary school classroom, an infant-parent stimulation program, or a full child care service for 3- to 6-year-olds. Some programs

---

TeachSource Video

Watch the TeachSource Video Case entitled "Curriculum Planning: Implementing Developmentally Appropriate Practice in an Early Childhood Program." After you study the video clip, view the artifacts, and read the teacher interviews and text, reflect on the following questions:

1. What examples of developmentally appropriate practices did you see or hear mentioned by preschool teacher Ke Nguyen and her colleagues? Compare and contrast your observations with the text.

2. How would you judge the quality of this program? What are some of the criteria you would use?

Developmentally and Culturally Appropriate Practice (DCAP)

"One of the most profound aspects of education in the United States today is its cultural complexity" (Hyun, 2007). The need for consistency between a child's home culture and school, what Hyun calls "culturally congruent learning," challenges today's teachers to be culturally responsive in all areas of teaching. Culturally appropriate practice is the ability to go beyond one's own sociocultural background to ensure equal and fair teaching and learning experiences for all. This concept, developed by Hyun (1998, 2007), expands DAP to address cultural complexities that emphasize the adult's ability to reflect more than a single perspective or knowledge. Preparing teachers and caregivers for multiculturalism is not just about becoming sensitive to race, gender, ethnicity,

religion, socioeconomic status, or sexual orientation, according to Hyun. It is also related to an understanding of the way individual histories, families of origin, and ethnic family cultures make us similar to and yet different from others. Through such insights, teachers are able to help all children develop a sense of their own self-identity as they respond to the emerging identities of others.

Teachers support a more culturally congruent atmosphere when they address the social and cultural context in which children live by asking themselves:

1. Do the activities and materials help children see the relationship between what happens in school and the lives of their home and community?

2. Does their learning create new possibilities for multicultural understandings?
3. Is the inclusion of cultural knowledge and materials done without demeaning or devaluing a child's heritage?
4. Do the activities and materials support one culture's domination over others?

There are many ways to meet the third core component of DAP that highlight the importance of connecting a child's sense of cultural continuity between home, school, and community. Interview a teacher of an early childhood program about how their program promotes cultural congruity. Would you add any questions to the previous list?

run for only a half-day; others are open from 6:00 AM until 7:00 PM. Still other centers, such as hospitals, accept children on a drop-in basis or for 24-hour care. Child care arrangements can range from informal home-based care to more formal school or center settings. Religious institutions, school districts, community-action groups, parents, governments, private social agencies, and businesses may run schools.

Factors That Determine Types of Programs

Programs in early childhood settings are defined by many factors, and each is an integral part of the mission of the program. Any given program is a combination of these factors and each has an impact on the quality and type of learning that takes place. Some of the factors that influence programs are:

1. Ages of the children who are being served
2. Philosophical, theoretical, or theological ideals
3. Goals of the program
4. Purpose for which the program was established
5. Requirements of sponsoring agency
6. Quality and training of teaching staff

Individual attention and warm relationships are essential components of every program.

7. Shape, size, and location of physical environment
8. Cultural, ethnic, economic, and social make-up of the community
9. Financial stability

Programs for young children also exist to serve a number of needs, which impact programs goals and mission. Some of these are:

- Caring for children while parents work (e.g., family child care homes or child care centers)
- Enrichment programs for children (e.g., half-day nursery school or laboratory school)
- Educational programs for parent and child (e.g., parent cooperatives, parent–child public school programs, or high school parent classes)
- An activity arena for children (e.g., most early childhood programs)
- Academic or readiness instruction (e.g., primary grades and many pre-kindergarten programs)
- Culturally or religiously specific programs (e.g., a school setting with a definitive ethnic focus or a church-related school that teaches religious dogma)

These programs generally reflect the needs of society as a whole. Millions of mothers of children younger than age 6 are in the labor force. Early childhood programs provide a wide range of services for children to meet the demands of working parents. In 2008, 78 percent of mothers with children from ages 6 to 17 were in the labor force, compared with 64 percent of mothers with children younger than the age of 6 (U.S. Bureau of Labor Statistics, 2011).

Special Program Features

A program usually has any number of goals or missions. One mission may be to encourage children to learn from one another. This philosophy has two important features that are reflected in many early childhood programs. The following two sections describe how mixed-age groupings and looping contribute to the goals of the program.

Mixed-Age Groupings

Placing children of several age levels into the same classroom is called mixed-age grouping. In these classes, younger children learn from older children and older children learn by teaching younger children. This practice is often referred to as family, heterogeneous, vertical, or ungraded grouping and has been around for many years. The one-room schoolhouse, the schools of Reggio Emilia, Waldorf schools, and Montessori programs reflect mixed-age groupings. The age range among children in mixed-age groups varies, and there is usually a difference from 2 to 4 years.

There are many advantages to mixed-age groups:

- The program is geared toward the needs of each child's developmental level and pace, allowing children to advance as they are ready.
- A sense of family and community is fostered through caring and a sense of responsibility toward one another. Siblings may be in the same class.
- Social skills are enhanced as children learn from and model interactions with children of different ages.
- A wide range of behaviors, learning styles, and temperaments are valued and accepted. Older children learn patience as they help younger children problem solve. Younger children are challenged by older peers who teach them more complex activities.
- Cooperative learning is encouraged.
- Teachers come to know and understand children in greater depth that allows them to build programs and curriculum well-suited to each child's strengths and challenges.

There are challenges associated with mixed-age groupings. The potential for older children to take over and/or overwhelm the younger ones is real, as is the possibility that younger children will pester the older children. This requires monitoring by the teaching staff, and the Reggio Emilia schools offer a good model of this process. In these Italian programs, older children have the responsibility to work with the younger children, explaining things and helping them find appropriate roles to take in their projects.

The academic and social advantages of mixed-age grouping cannot occur without a variety of activities from which children may freely choose and the opportunity for small groups of children to work together. Teachers must be intentional about encouraging children to work with others who have skills and knowledge they do not yet possess, and teachers need adequate preparation to succeed with a mixed-age group.

It is easy to see how mixed-age groupings reflect the principles of Dewey, Piaget, Gardner, and Vygotsky, whose "zone of proximal development" is made more available through the interactions of peers as well as adults. The practice of mixed-age grouping has much to commend it and must be seriously addressed as an issue in programs for young children.

Looping: Continuity of Care

The practice of keeping a teacher and the same group of children together in the same class for at least two years is called looping. As with mixed-aged grouping, it is an old idea revisited to provide greater continuity of care and education. Today, looping is customary in the Waldorf schools, Reggio Emilia programs, and Montessori, and it has emerged in other programs for a number of reasons. Proponents of looping suggest that it:

- Offers stability and emotional security to children and allows them to grow at their own rate.
- Gives teachers a greater opportunity to get to know children and therefore be able to individualize the program for them.
- Fosters better social interactions among children and strong relationships between teachers and families.
- Allows children to experience being both the youngest and the oldest in the class as students move on and new students join the group.
- Enhances a sense of family and community within the classroom.

In the schools in Reggio Emilia, infants and toddlers are kept in the same class with the same teachers for three years to provide a family-like environment. Looping is often paired with multi-aged classrooms, which further extends the natural, family-like atmosphere.

Critics of looping cite the need for experienced teachers who enjoy teaching across the age levels and who can work with the same children over an extended period of time. Looping does not fit all teachers and all children, and it could be offered as an option for parents and teachers to meet the needs of those who believe its advantages are worthwhile.

Any of the following early childhood programs may include mixed-age groups and looping. The educational and philosophical goals of the program determine what features to include.

The Core of Programs of Early Childhood Education

The following sections explore the different types of programs available to families. Each has unique characteristics, emphases, and challenges.

Traditional Nursery School/Preschool

The **traditional nursery school**/preschool exemplifies a developmental approach to learning in which children actively explore materials and in which activity or learning centers are organized to meet the developing skills and interests of the child. Most of these programs serve children from 2½ to 5 years of age.

The philosophy of these schools is best described by Katherine Read Baker in her now classic book *The Nursery School: A Human Relationships Laboratory* (1950). First published more than sixty years ago, this book serves as an encyclopedia of the traditional nursery school, its methods, and its philosophy, reflecting the influence of Comenius, Locke, Rousseau, Pestalozzi, Froebel, and Montessori.

The idea of a school as a place of human activity mirrors the thoughts of Dewey, Piaget, Erikson, and others. Baker develops this philosophy fully with an educational model that emphasizes the human needs, growth patterns, and relationships in a young child's life.

Developmentally, a traditional nursery school focuses on social competence and emotional well-being. The curriculum encourages self-expression through language, creativity, intellectual skill, and physical activity. The basic underlying belief is the importance of interpersonal connections children make with themselves, each other, and adults.

The daily schedule (see Figure 3-2) reflects these beliefs. Large blocks of time are devoted to free play, a time when children are free to initiate their own activities and become deeply involved without interruptions, emphasizing the importance of play. In this way, children learn to make choices, select playmates, and work on their interests and issues at their own rate. A dominant belief is that children learn best in an atmosphere free from excessive restraint and direction.

Typically, there is a balance of activities (indoors and out, free choice, and teacher-directed times) and a wide variety of activities (large- and small-muscle games, intellectual choices, creative arts, and social play opportunities).

A nursery school is often a half-day program, but many offer extended hours.

The Role of the Teacher The role of the teacher and methods of teaching are important factors in a traditional nursery school. They assume that young children need individual attention and should have personal, warm relationships with important adults. Therefore, the groups of children are generally small, often fewer than 20 in a class.

Half-Day Schedule	
9:00	Children arrive at school
9:00–9:45	Free play (indoors)
9:45	Cleanup
10:00	Singing time (large group)
10:15–10:30	Toileting/snack time (small group)
10:30–11:30	Free play (outdoors)
11:30	Cleanup
11:45	Story time
12:00	Children leave for home

FIGURE 3-2 A sample schedule for traditional half-day nursery schools is the core of early education programs.

The teacher–child ratio is low, as few as 6 to 10 children for each teacher. Teachers learn about children's development and needs by observation and direct interaction, rather than from formalized testing. They work with children individually and in small groups and often teach through conversation and materials. Teachers encourage children to express themselves, their feelings, and their thinking. Such rapport between teacher and pupil fosters self-confidence, security, and belonging. Proponents of the traditional nursery school believe that these feelings promote positive self-image, healthy relationships, and an encouraging learning environment.

Universal Preschools Increasing numbers of school districts offer pre-kindergarten programs for 4-year-olds, although some include 3-year-olds as well. Depending on their goal, these programs fall somewhere between traditional nursery schools and not quite full-day care. For some, the focus is to promote school readiness; others give priority to children at risk for school failure, children who come from families in which English is not spoken, or low-income families. Universal preschools for 3- and 4-year-olds could meet the growing demand for child care in families where both parents work outside the home. In states in which early education has achieved a level of support, all 4-year-olds are eligible for enrollment, regardless of income. The concept for universal preschools is and will be a continuing issue (see Chapter 15 for further discussion).

Child Care Centers

By definition, a child care center is a place for children who need care for a greater portion of the day than what the traditional nursery school offers. The school schedule is extended to fit the hours of working parents. A longer day means that ordinary routines such as meals and naps are woven into the program. These full-day options are also educational settings, echoing but extending the curriculum of a half-day program.

Child care needs are met in many ways, from center-based care to family settings. Child care centers can include preschools, employer-sponsored care, Head Start, for-profit and nonprofit institutions, religious institutions, colleges, YMCAs, public schools, social service agencies, and family child care.

Full-day child care is not a modern phenomenon. Some of the first nursery schools in England operated from 8:00 AM until 4:00 or 5:00 PM. (as noted in Chapter 1). Child care centers often serve infants and toddlers, as well as 2½- to 5-year-olds. Many offer kindergarten, before- and after-school options, and summer programs.

Routines, such as eating, provide a balance to an active and busy day at the child care center.

Scheduling Compare the nursery school schedule (Figure 3-2) with the child care schedule (Figure 3-3). The morning starts slowly. Children arrive early because their parents must go to work or school. The center may supply breakfast, midmorning and midafternoon snacks, and a noon lunch. A nap period for one to two hours for all the children gives a needed rest and balances their active, social day with quiet, solitary time. The program also includes extended experiences outside the school—field trips, library story hour, or swimming lessons—because children spend the major portion of their waking hours on-site. As the day draws to a close, children gather together quietly, with less energy and activity.

Full-Day Schedule

7:00–8:30	Arrival/breakfast; limited indoor play
8:30	Large group meeting
8:45–9:45	Free play (inside)
9:45	Cleanup/toileting
10:00	Snack time (small groups)
10:15–11:30	Free play (outside)
11:30	Cleanup/hand-washing
12:00	Lunch
12:30	Toothbrushing/toileting
1:00–2:00	Nap time
2:00–3:00	Free play (outside)
3:00	Group time
3:15	Snack time (small groups)
3:30–5:00	Inside and outside free play/library hour
5:00	Cleanup
5:15–5:30	Departure

FIGURE 3-3 A typical full-day care schedule. Most child care programs combine education and caring for basic needs.

Licensing Licensing is the process of fulfilling the legal requirements, standards, and regulations for operating child care facilities. There are no national standards or policies regarding licensing of child care facilities in the United States. Many local and state governments require licensing of child care centers and family child care homes, but there is no central licensing agency in every state. Depending on the state, a license may be issued by the Department of Health, Department of Education, or Department of Social Welfare.

Children spend long hours in child care, and many programs are sponsored by a variety of agencies such as churches, public schools, and private for-profit firms. With this diverse mix, a universal set of standards for licensing is imperative to ensure the best possible care for all children who need these services.

Staffing The staff in a full-day setting is often called on to deal with the parenting side of teaching. Children in full-day care may need more nurturing and clearer consistency in behavioral limits. At the same time, they need individual flexibility, understanding, and regular private time with caring adults.

Parents' needs also may be greater and require more of the teachers' time. Child care parents may require extra effort; they have full-time jobs as well as child-rearing responsibilities draining their energies. It takes a strong team effort on the part of the teacher and the parent to make sure the lines of communication stay open and that families and schools are mutually supported.

The teaching staff has staggered schedules, a morning and an afternoon shift. Administration of this type of program is therefore more complex. An effort must be made to ensure that all teachers get together on a regular basis to share the information and details about the children in their care. Both shifts must be aware of what happens when they are not on-site to run the program consistently. (See Chapter 15 for further discussion on child care issues.)

Family Child Care

In **family child care**, the provider takes care of a small number of children in a family residence. The group size can range from two to twelve, but most homes keep a low adult–child ratio, enrolling fewer than six children. It is reminiscent of an extended family grouping.

More than 1.7 million children are in family child care arrangements (NACCRRA, 2010). The home setting, sometimes right within the child's own neighborhood, offers an intimate, flexible, and convenient service for working parents. Children in a family child care home can range from infants to school-age children who are cared for after regular school hours.

The developmental ranges that family child care providers must meet may range from infancy up to 12 years, which poses a challenge to develop experiences and activities for a mixed-age group of children. Family child care providers work and live in the same environment posing logistical problems of storage, space definition, and activity space. Often, family child care providers care for their own children within their programs, leading to problems with separation and autonomy of their children and providing enough time to the child as a parent. Family child care providers are administrators and managers, as well as teachers and caregivers, faced with budgets and fee collections.

Advantages Family child care is good for children who do well in small groups or whose parents prefer to place them in a family-style setting. This is especially true for infants and toddlers. Family child care homes often schedule flexible hours to meet the needs of parents who work. The wide age range can be advantageous as well. Consistency and stability from a single caregiver throughout the child's early years and a family grouping of children provide a homelike atmosphere that is especially appropriate for infants and toddlers.

Family child care providers own and operate a small business in their homes. Providing child care is a way for women who want to remain at home with their children to contribute to the family income. Meeting the requirements for licensing; fulfilling all the administrative tasks of a business and an educational program; and keeping current with the local, state, and federal tax requirements are part of the professionalism required for this type of child care arrangement.

Challenges Many homes are unregulated; that is, they are not under any sponsorship or agency that enforces quality care, and many are exempt from state licensing. Family child care providers often lack knowledge of child development and early education and are not required to take courses. The National Association for Family Child Care has established an accreditation system and promotes high-quality family child care through professional development, public education, and policy initiatives (NAFCC, 2011).

Family child care providers can feel isolated from others in the child care field. A hopeful sign, however, is that more articles on family child care are being included in professional publications, and early childhood conferences and workshops are now including issues related to the family child care provider. This type of care could be a star in the galaxy of child care options. Small and personalized, it offers parents an appealing choice of home-based care. It

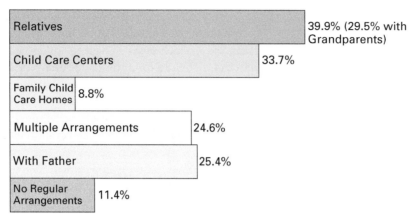

FIGURE 3-4 Child care options. (Data from: U.S. Bureau of Census. *"Who's Minding the Kids?"* Childcare Arrangements, Spring, 2005. Survey of Income and Program Participation. Retrieved August 2011.)

is obvious, though, that further regulation of standards, availability of training for providers, and an awareness of the advantages of family child care need to be addressed. For those who need child care, this should be a viable alternative; for those who want to work at home, this type of career should be given serious consideration.

The options for child care are many. In Figure 3-4 the choices that parents make when looking for child care are addressed.

Variations of Core Programs

There are many variations of the core programs that provide care and education for young children. These programs differ primarily due to the sponsoring agencies, the children they serve, their underlying mission, and whether or not they are nonprofit or for-profit organizations.

Head Start: An Early Intervention Model

In 1965, the federal government created the largest publicly funded education program for young children ever. Head Start began as part of this country's social action in the "war on poverty," and the implications of the program were clear: If at-risk poverty-stricken children could be exposed to a program that enhanced their schooling, their intellectual functions might increase, and these gains would help break the poverty cycle.

Over the past 40-plus-year history, Head Start has served more than 27 million children and their families

(Head Start, 2011). The success of Head Start can be attributed to its guiding objectives and principles, most expressed through:

- *Its comprehensive nature.* The child is seen as a whole, requiring medical, dental, and nutritional assessment, as well as intellectual growth. Extensive health, education, and social services are offered to children and their families.
- *Parent participation and involvement.* Head Start expects parents to serve as active participants and get involved in the program at all levels: in the classroom as teacher aides, on governing boards making decisions about the program, and as bus drivers and cooks.
- *Services to families.* Many of the comprehensive services offered to children are extended to parents as well to assist them in their fight against poverty. Paid jobs in the program, continuing education, job training, and health care are some of the support services families received.
- *Community collaboration.* Interest and support from the local community help Head Start respond to the needs of the children and families it serves. Public schools, religious institutions, libraries, service clubs, and local industry and businesses help to foster responsible attitudes toward society and provide opportunities for the poor to work with members of the community in solving problems.
- *Multicultural/multiracial education.* Since its inception, Head Start has sought to provide a curriculum that reflects the culture, language, and values of the children in the program. Head Start efforts in this regard have been the models for other early childhood programs.

• *Inclusion of children with special needs.* Since 1972, Head Start has pioneered the inclusion of children with disabilities in its classrooms. By 2009, 11.5 percent of Head Start enrollment consisted of children with disabilities (Head Start, 2010).

• *Ecology of the family.* Head Start programs look at children within the context of the family in which they live and view the family in the context of the neighborhood and community. This concept of taking the many forces that work against low-income families and viewing them as interrelated is a key factor in Head Start's success (see also Chapters 1 and 15).

The success of Head Start led to the creation of three specific programs that furthered the goals of Head Start: Parent & Child Centers, which serve infants and toddlers and their families; the Child and Family Resource Programs, which provide family support services; and the Child Development Associate credential, which provides early childhood training and education for Head Start teachers.

It should be noted that, at the beginning, one aim of Head Start was to change the language and behavior patterns of the low-income children served, many of whom came from minority groups, and to resocialize them into cultural patterns and values of the mainstream, middle class. Head Start was a "compensatory" program, and the implications were that children from poor or minority families were unprepared for the demands of school in terms of language and cognitive skills, achievement, and motivation. This widely held perspective of the 1960s was known as the "cultural disadvantage" model, which suggests that any language, cognitive, or relational style that differs from the Anglo, mainstream, middle-class style is necessarily detrimental to rather than supportive of the educational process.

Contrast this view with the more recent, pluralistic perspective, called the "cultural difference" model, which affirms that no one way of "behaving and believing" should be required for successful participation in school or society. Figure 3-5 summarizes today's Head Start programs.

Early Head Start

Early Head Start was established in 1994 as part of the Head Start Reauthorization Act. This program serves low-income families with infants and toddlers and pregnant women and is based on Head Start's four cornerstones: child development, family development, staff development, and community building.

Nine principles guide the efforts of Early Head Start: 1) high quality; 2) prevention of developmental concerns and promotion of healthy child development; 3) positive relationships and continuity in care-giving; 4) parent involvement; 5) inclusion; 6) culture; 7) comprehensiveness, flexibility, responsiveness and intensity to respond to families needs; 8) smooth transitions into Head Start programs; and 9) collaboration with local communities to maximize resources available to families.

Evaluating Early Intervention Effectiveness

The High/Scope Perry Preschool Project was not a Head Start program but had an enormous impact on policy makers and government officials and affected Head Start funding in significant ways.

There are similarities among all programs, but the relationship among parents, children, and caregiver is the universal consideration.

A Picture of Head Start

Enrollment	
904,153 children	
Ages Enrolled	
5-year-olds:	3%
4-year-olds:	51%
3-year-olds:	36%
Under 3:	10%
Race/Ethnic Population	
Native American/Alaskan Native:	4%
Hispanic/Latino:	35.9%
Black/African American:	30%
White:	39.9%
Asian/Pacific Islander:	2.3%
Biracial/Multiracial:	7.8%
Other:	16.7%

FIGURE 3-5 Head Start continues to be a vital program that serves the needs of a diverse population. This information is for the fiscal year 2010. (U.S. Department of Health and Human Services, the Office of Head Start, 2011.)

The High/Scope Perry Preschool Study. This project presented the most convincing evidence to date of the effectiveness of early intervention programs for low-income children. Started in the 1960s, it is the first longitudinal study to measure the effects of preschool education and to track the children from preschool years through age 27.

Children from one randomly assigned group were placed in high quality early childhood programs at age 3; the other group did not attend preschool. The results showed great differences between the children who had the advantage of a high quality program and those who did not. Low-income children who had attended preschool significantly outperformed those who had not.

The children attending the preschool program were better educated, spent fewer than half as many years in special education programs, had higher earnings, were less likely to receive welfare, and were five times less likely to be arrested. Gender differences were also noted. Preschool program girls had a significantly higher rate of graduation than did the girls who did not attend preschool, whereas, in comparison, preschool program boys completed slightly less schooling than nonpreschool boys (Weikart, n.d.).

Not only did this study underscore the need for high quality preschool programs for children who live in poverty, but it also demonstrated the potential impact that Head Start had on the country's future. It is the first study of its kind to suggest the economic impact of early intervention. Because most of the children in the high quality early childhood program required less remedial education, had better earning prospects, and were less costly to the welfare and justice systems, early intervention in education was shown to be cost-effective.

Head Start Today

Head Start has had a rocky history, its contributions notwithstanding. Struggling against budget cuts and controversy over its effectiveness, Head Start has undergone program improvements and expansions.

The original vision of Head Start was improved and expanded for the 1990s as a model that challenges the effects of poverty and promotes physically and mentally healthy families. Head Start has a formidable challenge ahead as it protects the high quality of its original charter while expanding and increasing services. As the early childhood field has become more professionalized, so has Head Start. By 2013, all Head Start head teachers will be required to have a bachelors' degree, continuing its efforts as a model of effective early intervention, child care, and education.

Variety of Early Childhood Program Options

Early childhood programs take many forms and allow families to choose the best option to meet their needs. Variations of the core programs are outlined in Figure 3-6.

Infant/Toddler Programs

The inclusion of infants and toddlers in group care is the result of more mothers in the workforce. Infant/toddler programs may be full-day centers or they may be part-time. Most are a combination of physical care coupled with intellectual stimulation and development.

Parent relationships are an especially important part of any program for babies and toddlers. The general intention of these centers is to provide care that is supplemental to family life and that supports the child's family structure. To do that, the caregiver at an infant/toddler center:

- involves the parents in the everyday decisions about the care of their child,
- provides them with information about the child's day, and
- strengthens the child's sense of belonging to that particular family.

Philosophy of Infant/Toddler Care

Through the insights of Piaget and Erikson (see Chapter 4) and continuing research in brain development, we have come to view the infant as an involved person, one who experiences a wide range of intellectual and emotional abilities. Although they may appear to be helpless beings, babies are in fact persons with feelings, rights, and an individual nature.

Caregiving routines are at the heart of the infant/toddler program and are the curriculum foundation for this age group. The challenge is to find ways to use these daily routines to interact, develop trust and security, and provide educational opportunities. In many cases, the caregiver's role extends to helping parents use these same common occurrences to promote the optimal development of their child. Magda Gerber, a pioneer in infant care, coined the term *educaring* to describe the relationship between an infant and an adult. Observing, listening, and reading babies' cues are key elements in educaring.

Gerber's philosophy is based on the use of responsive and reciprocal interactions in which baby and caregiver learn about each other. Communicating through care giving routines (diapering, feeding) in one-to-one intense and focused interactions is a foundation of Gerber's approach to caring for infants and toddlers (Gerber, 1979).

More recently, The Program for Infant/Toddler Care (PITC) has gained attention for its philosophy of a

Chart of Variations of Early Childhood Programs

Type	Sponsor	Ages	Schedule	Key Characteristics	Settings
Parent cooperative	School districts, private owners	Preschoolers; often mixed-age groups	Full-day and/or half-day	Parents commit to teaching in the classroom on a regular basis; regular parent education meetings; time-consuming; lower costs	Community centers, privately owned buildings, churches, synagogues
Laboratory schools	College or university	Preschool, infant/toddlers	Full-day and/or half-day	Students and teachers often participate in teacher training and research activities; offer model programs	Located on or near campus
Employer sponsored	Individual business or corporation	Infant/toddlers, preschooler, school age	Full-day and/or half-day	Is an employee benefit option for parents; may be available as a voucher for any child care arrangement	Often on or near job site; hospitals, factories, and government agencies, as well as child care centers and family child care homes
For profit (proprietary)	Corporations and individuals	Infant/toddler, preschool, kindergarten, before-school and after-school ages	Full-day and/or half-day	May be part of a national/regional chain or individually owned; great variety of services and programs offered year-round; major purpose is to make a profit	Individual centers owned by franchise or corporation
Nonprofit centers	Community, churches, synagogues, government agencies	Infant/toddlers, preschool, school age	Full-day and/or half-day	Subsidized by sponsoring organization or government agency, which often provides low or free rent	Community buildings, government office buildings, churches, synagogues
Programs in religious institutions	Religious organization	Infant/toddler, preschool, school age	Full-day and/or half-day	May be a community outreach program where no religious dogma is taught or may be part of the ministry of the sponsor and include religious dogma in the curriculum; tends to be one of the largest providers of child care in the United States; tax exempt as a nonprofit; sharing space with congregational programs may be difficult	Churches, synagogues
Before-school and after-school care	Public schools, community organizations, YMCAs, YWCAs, churches, synagogues	Preschool and elementary school ages	Before and after school hours	Safe place for children during parent's working hours; may provide holiday, vacations, and summer programs	Schools, community centers, YMCAs, YWCAs, child care centers

FIGURE 3-6 There is a diverse array of programs that are considered variations on the core of early childhood education.

relationship-based curriculum. Caregivers get "in tune" with each infant and learn from the child what he or she needs, thinks, and feels. They design environments that offer appropriate developmental challenges and strengthen the child's family and cultural identity. Caregivers study the infants and reflect on and record what they observe for future learning encounters (The Program for Infant/Toddler Care, 2011).

Unique Characteristics

Infant and toddler programs differ from preschool programs in a number of ways. There is a greater need for security, exploration, and social-emotional growth. Infant and toddler programs reflect these needs by:

- Creating a stable environment with low staff turnover and low caregiver–child ratios.

- Providing more one-to-one physical care.
- Ensuring immediate response from adults.
- Following up with parents and families on a daily basis.
- Using ordinary routines as learning opportunities.
- Developing skills that go beyond teaching: mothering, being a playmate.
- Promoting intentional rather than discovery learning.
- Developing finely tuned interpretation skills to recognize need and distress signals in young children.
- Understanding the significance of cultural sensitivity as children gain a sense of their own identity.

An important consideration in infant care is the daily separation of parent and child. As you will learn in Chapter 4, attachment is the deep bond and personal relationship that connects infants to the important people in their lives, such as parents and caregivers. The more secure the attachment, the more positive effects it has on the child. Research on the influence of daily separation suggests that it is the *quality* of care that impacts attachment security. When the caregiver–infant ratio is low and the caregiver's interactions are warm, positive, and knowledgeable about child development, children's cognitive, social, and emotional development thrive (McCartney et al., 2007).

The distinction between programs for infants and those for toddlers is also important. Just as a scaled-down version of preschool is not a toddler program, neither is a scaled-down version of a good day for toddlers an appropriate model for infants. The mobility of the toddler, for instance, requires different amounts of space and time in the schedule than those required for infants. Routines are also the focus of the toddler's day but in a different way. Mealtimes and toileting provide daily opportunities for toddlers to explore and to express their emerging sense of self. Hand-washing—even eating—becomes a time to fill, to taste, to dump, and to pick up. Again, the curriculum emerges from a developmental need toddlers have of "Me! Mine!" To foster that independence, that wanting to "do it myself," routines that allow for experimentation, mistakes, and messes make a good toddler curriculum. Good programs for infants and toddlers, then, are distinctly arranged for their developmental needs and are not simply modified versions of what works well in a program for 3-year-olds.

Kindergarten

The kindergarten year is one of transition from early childhood programs into a more formal school setting and is considered the first year of formal teaching. Kindergarten programs abound throughout the United States. They are found in elementary public and private

Active involvement with people and objects helps infants and toddlers develop feelings of self-identity, curiosity, and creativity.

schools, religious institutions, and as part of preschool child care centers.

Length of Day

The length of kindergarten programs is under debate in many states and schools districts. A few states require a full-day kindergarten and nearly all states offer only half-day kindergarten. Some states do not offer kindergarten at all. Kindergarten may be mandatory for 5-year-olds in some states and not in others.

Too often the arguments regarding the costs of such programs overshadow a more basic question: What are the best and most appropriate kindergarten programs, teaching methods, and curricula, regardless of the length of day? The following should be considered in response to this question:

- *The purpose of the kindergarten program.* How will the kindergarten program foster the goals in appropriate curricula and adapt to the needs of children? The goal should begin with the child and build the program to fit the child's needs, skills, and developing abilities.
- *The effects of a full day on children.* Many children have already been in a child care setting for up to 10 hours a day and have shown they thrive in programs that are suited to their ages, development styles, and needs. There is no question that most children can handle a full-day kindergarten program, providing it is adapted to their age, interests, and abilities.
- *The needs and concerns of families.* Some families may want a full-day program because they work and need a safe and nurturing place for their children. Others who do not work outside the home may want to keep their children with them a while

longer. Families need to have a choice about the type of program that best suits their family.

- *The effect on teachers.* A full-day kindergarten means that class is extended for a longer period of time, providing opportunities to improve the quality of the program by individualizing the curriculum. Teachers in half-day kindergartens often teach one class in the morning and one in the afternoon. The negative effects on planning, continuity, parent relationships, and individualizing curriculum are obvious, not to mention the risk of teacher burnout.
- *The concerns of the administration.* The cost-effectiveness of extending a kindergarten program all day undoubtedly requires more staff, more supplies and equipment, and greater food-service costs. The policy makers in any school setting must take these into account along with the other issues, but one would hope they are not limited by them.
- *The nature and quality of the extended-day program.* Often, in programs in which children are in half-day kindergarten, the quality of the extended-care part of their day is not equal to their school experience. In many extended-day programs, the staff is untrained, has a high turnover rate, and does not reflect the same program goals for the kindergartener.

School Entry Age

Most states establish an arbitrary date (e.g., September 1) by which children must be a certain age to enter kindergarten. Lowering and raising the age for beginning kindergarten is debated frequently. Some parents hold children out of kindergarten for one year and enroll them when they are age 6, a practice called "redshirting" (Katz, 2000). Teachers retain many children each year in kindergarten; and administrators have created an array of kindergarten-substitute programs such as "developmental," "extra-year," or "transitional" kindergartens. By the time they finally reach kindergarten, children are now in class with late 4-year-olds and 5- and 6-year-olds—a vast developmental span under one roof. Research shows mixed results for these practices.

Some of the methods used to create more homogeneous kindergarten classrooms or to raise expectations for kindergarten admittance are:

- Inappropriate uses of screening and readiness tests.
- Discouragement and/or denial of entrance for eligible children.
- Creation of transitional classes for those who are considered not ready for kindergarten.
- An increasing use of retention (NAECS/ NAEYC, 2001).

The issue of school readiness has been a hot topic for years. Early childhood professionals agree that children should be able to enter kindergarten when they are of legal age and that schools should be prepared to meet the needs of children where they are in their development. Instead schools have developed a variety of methods noted earlier to create more homogeneous classes rather than address the variety of developmental stages of children of kindergarten age. There are many reasons children enter school without the resources and tools to succeed, such as poverty, language and cultural differences, access to high-quality early education programs, and lack of effective early intervention that includes comprehensive services. These are the necessary tools children need to be ready for school.

Curriculum: Developmental or Academic?

Critical issues such as school-entry age and length of school day are related to kindergarten curriculum issues. Kindergarten programs range from relatively traditional classes to highly structured, academically oriented classes. Over the past 20 years, the push to teach separate skills, such as reading, writing, and math, has created more and more academically focused kindergartens in which worksheets and teacher-directed lessons are the norm. As kindergartens have changed, there is greater pressure on teachers to accelerate children's learning. Hatch (2005) cites three specific changes that have altered the course of kindergarten programs:

1. Children today experience very different childhoods than even a decade ago.
2. Knowledge of how children learn and develop has expanded.
3. The standards-based reform movement has changed expectations for kindergarteners by imposing arbitrary standards of performance. This increases the academic expectations on them and the pressure on teachers to comply with regulations.

It is clear that Froebel's "children's garden" has wandered far from its child development roots. Curricula in which play is not respected as a vehicle for learning, reading is taught as a separate skill, and attempts are made to accelerate children's learning are at odds with kindergarten history. Revisit Chapter 1 and read again about Froebel, Dewey, Piaget, Patty Smith Hill, Susan Isaacs, and other pioneers and their approach to learning. Educating the whole child is very much in evidence in their work as is their basic connection to child development theory and research. (For further discussion on the negative effects of early academics, see Chapter 3 for developmental ranges and Word Pictures for appropriate expectations. In Chapter 6, the related questions of standardized

Redshirting and Readiness

Neuroscience has established the fact that the brain is constantly changing. This *plasticity* means that the brain is always adapting and reorganizing on a daily basis. New connections are being created by everyday experiences and learning is taking place. Brain plasticity persists into adulthood but is especially pronounced in the early stages of life. At the same time the brain is growing, it is *pruning* itself, getting rid of unused synapses in a "use it or lose it" function. If the brain is rewiring itself so extensively in the preschool and early elementary years, and requires meaningful, positive experiences to grow, it begs the question: "Why is redshirting, or keeping children back one year, still being practiced?" It would appear that redshirting is actually counterproductive because it deprives the child of a challenging and stimulating school environment. The best way to give children the greatest opportunity to learn is to put them in their age-appropriate classroom setting as soon as possible where their brains are immersed in growing, learning, and changing.

The issue of school readiness has been a hot topic for years. Early childhood professionals agree that children should be able to enter kindergarten when they are of legal age and that schools should be prepared to meet the needs of children where they are in their development. This is supported by recent brain development research that stresses stimulation and challenges as a way to foster brain growth and learning. Instead, schools have developed a variety of methods noted earlier to create more homogeneous classes rather than address the variety of developmental stages of children of kindergarten age. (See further discussion of school readiness in Chapter 15.)

There are many reasons children enter school without the resources and tools to succeed, such as poverty, language and cultural differences, access to high-quality early education programs, and lack of effective early intervention that includes comprehensive services.

Readiness has been defined as ready children, ready families, ready communities, ready early care and education, and ready schools (Rhode Island KIDS COUNT, 2005). All of these are necessary if we want all children to be ready for successful school experiences that use their brain potential to greatest advantage.

Questions
1. When might it be appropriate to delay a child's entry into school?
2. Why do disadvantaged children have the most to lose from delayed entry into school?

---

testing and screening are discussed. In Chapters 10 and 15, related issues are explored.)

Kagan and Kauerz (Gullo, 2006) provide four reflections on what kindergartens can and should be in the future. They integrate concerns about the developmentally appropriate integrity of kindergartens and the domination of imposed standards and testing:

1. Kindergarten must remain "special," that unique year in which play is a legitimate medium for establishing children's learning patterns, and in which curriculum, standards, and assessments are in sync with preschool and first grade.
2. Kindergarten must keep the child front and center, even with the new emphasis on content. Curriculum must address the full range of developmental domains (social, emotional, cognitive, and physical) to prepare children for more formally taught content. Children's curiosity, enthusiasm, initiative, and willingness to learn must be nurtured to enhance their overall ability to learn.
3. Kindergarten must acknowledge and support differences in the needs of children and their families.

Different learning styles in children must be addressed as well as family needs for flexibility in the structure, such as full- or half-day sessions.
4. Kindergarten must foster positive relationships between the children and their teachers, between families and the school, and between the school and the community. The success of these relationships can help establish trust and respect that last throughout the child's school years.

Kindergarten is a significant transition in the lives of children and families and a critical year in a child's growth and development. It should be made available and accessible to all children in the United States.

Early Elementary/Primary Grades

Early childhood is defined as children from birth through age 8. Often overlooked as part of a comprehensive view of young children are first through third grades, serving children from ages 6- to 8-years-old. These grades focus on the basic academic skills of reading, writing, math, science, social studies, art and drama, health and safety, and physical

Kindergarteners are able to enjoy close friendships.

education. Although these subjects are usually taught separately, the curriculum should be integrated so that children learn subject matter through a variety of activities.

Unique Characteristics

Dramatic changes are taking place in the primary-age child. Children this age are eager to learn and are developing logic and reasoning skills as they move from Piaget's preoperational stage to one of concrete operations (see Chapter 4). Their learning tasks are more difficult than in kindergarten and require greater persistence and effort. Starting at about age 6, children begin to plan out and think through their actions and take others' views into consideration. As they grow more independent in their learning, primary-age children like choosing their own tasks, working cooperatively in small groups with their classmates, and participating in planning each day's work. Group discussions and planning projects address the child's needs to be part of the planning process. Enhancing the child's enthusiasm for learning is a primary task for the teachers of this age group.

Play for the primary-age child now revolves around rules that accompany organized games, board games, and cards. Learning still takes place through independent exploration and manipulation of materials, so classroom centers are an important part of the environment. The classroom itself may be more structured but it is important that developmentally appropriate early childhood principles, practices, and environments are applied through third grade.

The Challenge of Academic Standards

Teaching in the primary grades presents challenges due to the pressure of local, state, or national standards that dictate what children need to learn at this age and grade level. All states now have these standards for each grade level and each subject matter. As a result, teachers may have little or no control over what they teach and the unfortunate result may be a curriculum that "teaches to the test"; that is, one that stresses only the subject matter on which the child is tested. The best curriculum for the primary-age child is one that is in alignment with the standards so that the subject matter matches what the standards say children should know and do at this grade and subject level. Accountability through learning standards continues to have a strong impact on the early elementary years. (Further discussion of early learning standards and their effect on teaching and learning is discussed in many of the following chapters.

School-Age Child Care

Before-school and after-school programs are designed for children before they start or after they finish their regular academic day. This type of care is usually available for children from ages 5 to 12. There are 8.4 million children participating in after-school programs, and that number continues to grow (America After 3PM, 2011).

Staff for after-school programs comes from a variety of backgrounds, most of which include some experience with children, such as teachers, recreation specialists, or specialists within the arts. As with most child care programs, however, high turnover and low wages affect the quality of the service. Finding qualified staff is the major challenge facing school-age providers, along with finding space and funding (Neugebauer, 2007).

Two national organizations, the National School-Age Care Alliance and the National Institute on Out-of-School Time created an accreditation system for after-school care. Their goals are to set professional standards, accredit high quality programs, and support program improvement.

There is a critical need for safe, recreational programs for after-school care. *America After 3 PM* reports that more than 25 percent of America's school children are on their own in the afternoons. These self-care children are a young and vulnerable population. Children need the safety, the creative opportunity, and the emotionally supportive relationships that out-of-school care can provide. These programs are natural extensions of responsible child care and are essential services to children and their families.

Homeschooling

The homeschool movement began in the 1950s as an alternative to public education. Today, approximately 1.5 million students are homeschooled, nearly 3 percent of the school age population. The majority (84 percent) of homeschooled children receive all of their education

A Thoughtful Beginning

As a beginning kindergarten teacher Shawndra wants to establish appropriate and positive relationships with her students. Before school starts, she interviews two experienced teachers to see what experience has taught them. Mac, a long-time second grade teacher, tells her to earn children's respect by having fair, clear, and consistent classroom rules. Mattie, who has taught kindergarten for three years tells Shawndra that being well prepared but flexible are the keys to good relationships with students.

These conversations prompt Shawndra to reflect on her own life as a student and look at her former teachers and how they created a respectful and supportive classroom atmosphere. One teacher stands out in her mind, her preschool teacher when Shawndra was 5-years-old. Mrs. Olivera's classroom was fun and fascinating (Ah, Mattie's point about preparation and flexibility!) and classroom rules were at a minimum (Mac is right: consistency is important). Most of all, Shawndra felt involved in the life of the classroom.

During the first week of school, Shawndra and her students had several brainstorming sessions about classroom behaviors and what kind of a climate they would like to create. By the end of the second week, the students unanimously agreed to a short list of rules they felt were important. What Shawndra succeeded in doing, by asking the class for their opinions and taking ownership of the rules, was to let students know she respected them and believed in their innate abilities to work together and got them involved.

Think About This
1. Do you think Shawndra's solution worked? Why? Why not?
2. What do you think were the most important suggestions that formed Shawndra's decision?
3. How can Shawndra's experience help you plan for creating successful relationships with children in your class?

---

at home, whereas some attend school part of the time (National Center for Educational Statistics, 2011).

Three reasons why parents select homeschooling are for the school environment, to provide religious instruction, and dissatisfaction with the academic instruction available elsewhere. From 2003 to 2007, the percentage of students whose parents reported that religious instruction was the most important factor increased from 73 to 83 percent (National Center for Education Statistics, 2011).

The educational philosophies and methods used in homeschooling are widely diverse and range from prepackaged curriculum that parents buy to "relaxed homeschooling" and "unschooling" (Cloud & Morse, 2001). The "relaxed" or "natural" homeschooling method involves real-life projects as teaching opportunities, such as taking care of the farm animals or building a table. "Unschooling" uses no curriculum plans, and children pursue their own interests. If some of this seems familiar, you might want to look back at Chapter 1 and review the various educational philosophies on which early childhood programs are based.

Some concerns expressed by educators regarding homeschool educational programs include: 1) lack of quality control due to varying regulations; 2) lack of socialization opportunities for students; 3) lack of sports opportunities; 4) the extreme time commitment demanded of parents; 5) lack of accountability, regulations, and policies surrounding homeschooling; and 6) the loss of revenue for public education.

Assessing Program Quality

Each week, more than 12 million children younger than the age of 5 are in some type of child care arrangement (U.S. Census Bureau, 2010) and each of these early childhood settings differs in the level of quality they provide. What does it mean to have a "high quality" program that benefits children and their families?

Indicators of Quality

Early childhood programs vary greatly in their educational goals and practices, their methods of instruction, and even in the kind of social "mood" or atmosphere they create.

Yet the quality of these programs is based on three essential factors:

1. The teacher–child ratio; that is, the number of children cared for by each staff member
2. The total size of the group or class
3. The education, experience, and training of the staff

The importance of these three factors cannot be underestimated, and they underscore each of the criteria in the DAP box "High-Quality Programs = DAP." The following 10 criteria are found in every chapter throughout this text.

DAP High-Quality Programs = DAP

The National Association for the Education of Young Children (NAEYC) has established a list of criteria for high-quality early childhood programs. These criteria are used for accreditation of programs by NAEYC and are based on a consensus of thousands of early childhood professionals (NAEYC, 2005).

1. *Relationships*. Positive relationships help children develop personal responsibility, self-regulation, constructive interactions, and academic mastery. Warm sensitive relationships help children feel secure and develop a positive sense of self, respect for others, and the ability to cooperate.
2. *Curriculum*. The curriculum draws on research for concepts, skills, and methodology that fosters children's learning and maximizes learning through time and materials as well as provides learning opportunities for children individually and in groups.
3. *Teaching*. Developmentally, linguistically, and culturally appropriate teaching practices enhance children's learning, as does multiple instructional methods, including teacher-directed, child-directed, and structured and unstructured learning opportunities. Teachers reflect the children's backgrounds, needs, interests, and capabilities in their instructional approaches. When more than one teacher is in the classroom, a team teaching approach is used.
4. *Assessment of Child Progress*. Appropriate and systematic assessment measures, which are culturally sensitive, inform needs. Assessments aid in identifying children who need additional instruction and/or intervention and further assessment.
5. *Health and Safety*. A healthy state of well-being enhances a child's ability to learn. Adults help protect children from illness and injury and help them make healthy choices for themselves.
6. *Teachers*. The teaching staff is educationally qualified, knowledgeable, and professionally committed to supporting children's learning and development, as well as families' diverse needs and interests. The teachers who have specific preparation in child development and early childhood education are more likely to have warm, positive interactions with children, promote richer language experiences, and create a higher quality

learning environment. Ongoing professional development ensures that teachers reflect current research and best practices.

7. *Families*. Good family relationships are collaborations between home and school and reflect family composition, language, and culture. They are based on mutual trust and respect in recognition of the primacy of the family in the life of the child.
8. *Community Relationships*. The program establishes relationships with and uses the resources of the community to realize program goals. By helping to connect families with a variety of resources, the children's health and development is enhanced.
9. *Physical Environment*. A safe, healthy, and accessible environment and well-maintained indoor and outdoor areas foster learning, health, and safety for young children. The design of the facilities and the activities support a high-quality program.
10. *Leadership and Management*. The program effectively administers policies, procedures, and systems that support a stable staff and strong personnel, fiscal, and program management. Effective governance and structure, program accountability, positive community relations, and a supportive workplace create a high-quality environment for all.

Visit an NAEYC accredited early childhood site and a nonaccredited program. Use these 10 criteria to assess the overall quality of the program. How do these programs compare? What issues seem to be the most challenging in meeting the standards for high-quality in both settings? Do you think accreditation based on these criteria is useful in creating high-quality? In promoting DAP? Why? Why not?

Quality early care and education contribute to the healthy cognitive, social, and emotional development of all children but particularly those from low-income families. The cost of child care is disproportionately high for poor families, so those who might benefit the most have the most difficult time affording quality care. Good, affordable, accessible child care that meets the increasing needs of American families is one of today's most crucial issues. Observation tools that measure quality in early childhood programs is discussed later in the chapter under "How to Evaluate a Program."

Research Studies on Quality

Every day, scores of parents search for affordable programs and reliable providers. A study by the National Association of Child Care Resource and Referral Agencies (NACCRRA, 2008) polled more than 1,000 parents nationwide to find out what parents want in child care. Quality was mentioned more than any other issue.

Issues That Affect Quality

The focus of the child care issues centers on a few core problems that threaten the *quality* of child care throughout the country:

● The annual turnover rate for child care staff is more than 30 percent (Whitebook & Sakai, 2004). Minimal benefits, lack of health care, and low wages account for this high rate of turnover.

Twenty percent of child care center teachers have a high school diploma or less and 43 percent of assistant teachers have a high school diploma or less. Forty-four percent of family child care providers have only a high school diploma (NCCRRA, 2010).
Average earnings of child care workers are $9.70 per hour or $20,350 annually. Preschool teachers earn $12.80 per hour or $26,610 per year (NCCRRA, 2010).

The triple threats to child care—quality, cost, and compensation—are discussed further in Chapter 15.

Highlights from three long-range research projects support the premise that high-quality child care programs have lasting impact on children's lives:

1. The Abecedarian Project, conducted by the Frank Porter Graham Child Development Center at the University of North Carolina, is the first study to track participants from infancy to age 21. The children were considered at risk for potential school failure.

   Important factors in determining quality were in place to ensure success: staff experience and education, little or no staff turnover, small teacher–student ratios, group size, and parent participation. Significant benefits for the children enrolled in the program for five years included the likelihood of attending a four-year college and delaying parenthood until after high school. Moreover, by age 15, twice as many of the children who did not receive intervention services had been placed in special education programs than those who had been in child care. By age 21, most subjects were either gainfully employed or in college. Only 30 percent of the child care children had to repeat a grade in school compared with 56 percent of the others.

2. The Children of the Cost, Quality, and Outcomes Study Go to School (Whitebook, Sakai, Gerber & Howes, 2001), tracked children from child care years through second grade. The findings noted that:
   - Children who receive good, quality child care had better social and cognitive skills in kindergarten and beyond.
   - Children who were at risk gained the most from positive child care experiences and sustained these gains through second grade.
   - Children who had closer relationships with their child care teachers had better behavior and social skills through second grade.

3. A 25-year federally funded study at the Child-Parent Centers in Chicago is the longest follow-up ever of an established large-scale early childhood program. According to Reynolds, Temple, Ou, Arteaga, and White (2011), the participants showed

higher levels of education, socioeconomic status, and better jobs, as well as lower rates of substance abuse, grade retention, drop-out rates, arrest, and incarceration than those who did not attend an early childhood program that offered comprehensive services to children and families.

All three of these studies show positive economic benefits of quality early childhood education.

The Process of Assessing Programs

As educators, we are constantly evaluating, judging, and rating areas such as:

- *Curriculum.* Will this language game help develop the listening skills of 3-year-olds?
- *Materials and equipment.* If we order the terrarium, will there be enough money for the math lab?
- *The environment.* Should the children begin school with free play or a group time? Where can we store the nap cots? Do the cubbies create a hazard out in the hallway?
- *Children's behavior.* Evan and Francie interrupt each other too much. Should they be placed in separate work groups?
- *Teacher effectiveness.* Yolanda still finds it difficult to lead a group time. How can she be supportively challenged?

As a process, an assessment involves making decisions, choices, and selections. In its simplest form, it is a process of appraisal. A good assessment encourages positive change. It is easy to continue the same program, the same teaching techniques, year after year when a school is operating smoothly. Sometimes it is not clear what—or how—improvements could be made. A regular assessment process keeps a system alive and growing and helps to give meaning and perspective to children, teachers, and programs. An assessment that helps clarify issues and ideas brings renewed dedication and inspiration.

Why Program Assessment is Important

There are four major reasons for making an annual assessment of a program for young children.

To Gain an Overview Evaluating a program gives an overview of how all the various components function together. The fundamental questions are: Is this a good place for children? Would you want your child to be here? What is a high-quality program for young children? Looking at children, teachers, and the total environment, a program evaluation reveals the environment as an integrated whole. These assessments add an awareness of how one area is

Evaluations are part of everyday life in an early childhood setting. Observations highlight ways to improve the program.

related to another and how the parts mesh in a particular setting. Such evaluations, then, are the standards of quality and include:

- Children's progress
- Teacher performance
- Curriculum development
- The financial structure
- Family involvement
- The community at large
- The governing organization of the school

In program evaluations, each of these is assessed for how it functions alone and how each works in concert with the others.

To Establish Accountability A program evaluation establishes accountability. This refers to a program's ability to answer to a controlling group or agency, for instance, the school board or the government office or the parents and the community in which the program operates. These groups want to know how their funds are being spent and how their philosophy is being expressed through the overall program.

To Make Improvements Program evaluations are an opportunity to take an objective look at how the goals of the school are being met. A good evaluation supports the strengths of the existing program and suggests areas in which changes might improve overall effectiveness. An in-depth assessment increases the likelihood that program goals and visions are realized. The evaluation helps determine the direction the program may take in the future.

To Acquire Accreditation Evaluations are a necessary step for some schools that wish to be approved for certification or accreditation by various organizations or government agencies. Such groups require that a school meet certain evaluation standards before the necessary permits are issued or membership is granted. Agencies, such as a state department of social services or department of education, often license family child care homes, whereas private schools may need to follow certain criteria to be affiliated with a larger organization (such as the American Montessori Society).

The National Academy of Early Childhood Programs, a division of NAEYC, has established an accreditation system for improving the quality of life for young children and their families. The accreditation system articulates standards for physical, social, emotional, and cognitive development of children in group care. The academy established goals for accreditation on the basis of 10 criteria, which are outlined on page 57.

Essential Steps Before You Begin

To ensure the most productive assessment, take the following steps:

1. *Set goals.* Without evaluation, goals are meaningless. Evaluation helps shape a goal into a meaningful plan of action. To be useful, an evaluation must include suggestions for improving the performance or behavior. The assessment tool that only describes a situation is an unfinished evaluation; goals for improvement must be established.

2. *Define expectations.* In every early childhood setting, more than one set of expectations is at work. The director has job expectations of all the teachers. Teachers have standards of performance for themselves, the children, and parents. Parents have some expectations about what their children will do in school and about the role of the teachers. Children develop expectations regarding themselves, their parents, teachers, and the school. A good evaluation tool outlines clearly and specifically how expectations have been met in a system of mutual accountability. Evaluations provide information by which to rate performance, define areas of difficulty, look for possible solutions, and plan for the future.

3. *Be inclusive.* A good evaluation instrument should be culturally appropriate and recognize the many ways that a program can be multicultural and anti-biased in its operations. In Chapter 9, you will learn about anti-bias and inclusive environments. (See Figure 9-4 for a checklist for creating an inclusive setting.)

4. *Define the objectives.* A program evaluation begins with a definition of the program's objectives. Knowing why a program is to be evaluated indicates how to tailor the procedure to the needs and characteristics

Checklist for Program Evaluation

The Physical Environment

_____ Are the facilities clean, comfortable, safe?

_____ Are room arrangements orderly and attractive?

_____ Are materials and equipment in good repair and maintained?

_____ Is there a variety of materials, appropriate to age levels?

_____ Are activity areas well-defined?

_____ Are cleanup and room restoration a part of the daily schedule?

_____ Are samples of children's work on display?

_____ Is play space adequate, both inside and out?

_____ Is personal space (e.g., cubby) provided for each child?

The Staff

_____ Are there enough teachers for the number of children?

_____ How is this determined?

_____ Are the teachers qualified? What criteria are used?

_____ Is the staff evaluated periodically? By whom and how?

_____ Does the school provide/encourage in-service training and continuing education?

_____ Do the teachers encourage the children to be independent and self-sufficient?

_____ Are the teachers genuinely interested in children?

_____ Are teachers aware of children's individual abilities and limitations?

_____ What guidance and disciplinary techniques are used?

_____ Do teachers observe, record, and write reports on children's progress?

_____ Are teachers skilled in working with individual children, small groups, and large groups?

_____ Does the teaching staff give the children a feeling of stability and belonging?

_____ Do teachers provide curriculum that is age-appropriate and challenging?

_____ How would you describe the teachers' relationships with other adults in the setting? Who does this include, and how?

_____ Can the teaching staff articulate good early education principles and relate them to their teaching?

Parent Relationships

_____ How does the classroom include parents?

_____ Are parents welcome to observe, discuss policies, make suggestions, help in the class?

_____ Are different needs of parents taken into account?

_____ Where and how do parents have a voice in the school?

_____ Are parent-teacher conferences scheduled?

_____ Does the school attempt to use community resources and social service agencies in meeting parents' needs?

The Organization and Administration

_____ Does the school maintain and keep records?

_____ Are scholarships or subsidies available?

_____ What socioeconomic, cultural, and religious groups does the school serve?

_____ What is the funding agency, and what role does it play?

_____ Is there a school board, and how is it chosen?

_____ Does the school serve children with special needs or handicaps?

_____ Is the classroom group homo- or heterogeneous?

_____ What hours is the school open?

_____ What age range is served?

_____ Are there both full- and part-day options?

_____ Is after-school care available?

_____ Does the school conduct research or train teachers?

_____ What is the teacher-child ratio?

The Overall Program

_____ Does the school have a written, stated educational philosophy?

_____ Are there developmental goals for the children's physical, social, intellectual, and emotional growth?

_____ Are the children evaluated periodically?

_____ Is the program capable of being individualized to fit the needs of all the children?

_____ Does the program include time for a variety of free, spontaneous activities?

_____ Is the curriculum varied to include music, art, science, nature, math, language, social studies, motor skills, etc.?

_____ Are there ample opportunities to learn through a variety of media and types of equipment and materials?

_____ Is there ample outdoor activity?

_____ Is there a daily provision for routines: eating, sleeping, toileting, play?

_____ Is the major emphasis in activities on concrete experiences?

_____ Are the materials and equipment capable of stimulating and sustaining interest?

_____ Are field trips offered?

_____ Do children have a chance to be alone? In small groups? In large groups?

Cultural Responsiveness

_____ Are multicultural perspectives already incorporated throughout the school, classroom curriculum, and classroom environment?

_____ Do my attitudes (and those of all staff) indicate a willingness to accept and respect cultural diversity? How is this demonstrated?

_____ Do classroom materials recognize the value of cultural diversity, gender, and social class equity?

_____ Do curricular activities and methods provide children opportunities to work and play together cooperatively? In mixed groups of their choice or at teacher direction?

_____ Do schoolwide activities reflect cultural diversity? How is this noticed?

_____ Does the program planning reflect the reality (views and opinions) of families and the community?

_____ Does the curriculum include planning for language diversity? For full inclusion? (Adapted from Baruth and Manning, 1992, and de Melendez and Ostertag, 1997.)

FIGURE 3-7 Checklist for areas of program evaluation.

Ⓢ This checklist can be downloaded from the Education CourseMate website.

of an individual school. With the objectives defined, the choice of evaluation instrument becomes clear. If, for example, a program objective is to provide a healthy environment for children, the evaluation tool used must address the issues of health, safety, and nutrition.

5. *Choose an evaluation instrument.* Evaluation instruments vary with the purpose of the program evaluation. NAEYC's accreditation guidelines are effective (described as 10 essentials for high quality programs on pages 57), as are four rating scales developed by the Frank Porter Graham Child Development Institute at the University of North Carolina at Chapel Hill. Each focuses on a specific early childhood setting:

   - Infant/Toddler Environment Rating Scale (ITERS-R), which is designed to assess programs for children from birth to 21 years of age
   - Early Childhood Environment Rating Scale (ECERS-R) for preschool through kindergarten programs serving children from 5 to 21 years of age
   - Family Child Care Environment Rating Scale (FCCERS-R) for use in homes that serve infants through school-age
   - School-Age Care Environment Rating Scale (SACERS) assesses group care programs for children from 5 to 12 years of age

See Chapter 9 for details of how these elements are used in planning environments. Figure 3-6 is a checklist that includes the program areas to include in an evaluation.

Implement the Findings

The evaluation process is complete when the results are tabulated and goals are set to meet the recommendations of the evaluation. Program administrators meet with the teaching staff to discuss the challenges highlighted by the evaluation. A process is put into place for addressing the issues, a calendar is established to create a timeline for improvement, the appropriate staff members are assigned the responsibility for making the changes, and the process begins anew. Evaluations are only as useful as the implementation plan. They can help identify specific concerns, determine the areas of growth and potential development, and be a blueprint for the future.

Summary

LO 1 High-quality early childhood programs reflect the core elements of developmentally appropriate practices (DAP) by basing the program on what is known about child development and learning, what is known about each individual child, and what is known about the child's social and cultural context. By following DAP guidelines, early childhood programs maximize the benefits children gain from attending an early education program. Following the guidelines for developmentally and culturally appropriate practice (DCAP) ensures equal and fair teaching and learning experiences for all students.

LO 2 The traditional nursery school and its sister programs of child care centers and family child care form the core of early childhood programs. Each has unique characteristics, scheduling, hours of operation, licensing requirements, and a combination of child care and education. The teacher's role in each setting differs according to the length of day that children attend, the number of caregivers, and the needs of parents and families.

LO 3 Early childhood programs reach a broad population and parents have a range of delivery systems from which to choose. An array of programs in parent cooperatives, laboratory schools, faith-based settings, and before/after school are available and serve children from infancy through elementary school. These programs are under the sponsorship of public and private schools; community organizations; churches; synagogues; local, state, or federal governments; corporations; and colleges and universities.

LO 4 A good assessment process evaluates quality according to established professional criteria that serves as a reference for making changes that improve the teaching and learning in that setting. The assessment includes a clear purpose, knowing who and what will be evaluated, and what use will be made of the results. Teachers, children, and the program must be assessed individually and then evaluated as a whole. Each supports and depends upon the other. An evaluation is a way to look at how these relationships are working. The result is a better prepared staff and a program of greater quality.

Key Terms

developmentally appropriate practice (DAP)
mixed-age grouping
looping
traditional nursery school
child care center

licensing
family child care
comprehensive
educaring
attachment
kindergarteners

school readiness
alignment
self-care
assessment
accountability

Review Questions

1. What are the three core considerations of developmentally appropriate practices? How do they contribute to children's learning?
2. What are the core programs of early childhood education? How are they similar? How are they different?

3. What are the variations of the core programs and who do they serve?
4. What are three factors that affect the quality of early childhood programs? How do they influence program assessment?

Observe and Apply

1. Choose one program and describe why you would like to teach in it. What are the most attractive elements of the program? What are some of the challenges you would have working in such a program?
2. Visit a family child care home. Look at the home as if you were a prospective parent. What did you like most? Least? Is the home licensed? If so, for how many children? After talking with the family child care provider, what do you think are the challenges of this type of program? What do you think are possible solutions to these problems?
3. Visit a Head Start program and a local kindergarten. Compare their programs in terms of appropriate or

inappropriate curriculum. What are the major concerns of the teaching staff in each type of setting? What are the controversies about each of these programs in your community?

4. As you reflect on the various options for teaching in an early childhood program, what are the most important factors a program must have for you to teach in that setting?
5. What aspect of an assessment process gives you the greatest concern? How do you think you will handle criticism?

Helpful Websites

Bureau of Labor Statistics, **www.stats.bls.gov**

U.S. Department of Education, **www.ed.gov**

Families and Work Institute,
  www.familiesandwork.org

National Institute on Out-of-School Time,
  www.niost.org

National Network for Child Care, **www.nncc.org**

National Association for Family Child Care,
  www.nafcc.org

Child Care Information Exchange, **www.ccie.com**

National Center for Education Statistics,
  www.nces.ed.gov

Culturally and Linguistically Appropriate Services,
  www.clas.uiuc.edu

Center for Child Care Workforce, **www.ccw.org**

International Nanny's Association, **www.nanny.org**

Head Start/Early Head Start,
  www.acf.hhs.gov/programs/ohs

ChildStats, **www.childstats.gov**

U.S. Census Bureau, **www.census.gov**

Children's Defense Fund, **www.childrensdefense.org**

About Homeschooling, **www.homeschooling.about.com**

National Association for the Education of Young Children, **www.naeyc.org**

⊙ The Education CourseMate website for this text offers many helpful resources and interactive study tools. Go to CengageBrain.com to access the TeachSource Videos, flashcards, tutorial quizzes, direct links to all of the websites mentioned in the chapter, downloadable forms, and more.

References

Afterschool Alliance. (2010). *America After 3 PM: Key findings*. (2010). http://www.afterschoolalliance.org. Retrieved August 5, 2011.

Baker, K. R. (1950). *The nursery school: A human relationships laboratory*. Philadelphia, PA: Saunders.

Bureau of Labor Statistics. Frequently asked questions, 2010. http://www.bls.gov. Retrieved August 2011.

(The) Carolina Abecedarian Project. (1999). The Frank Porter Graham Child Development Institute. The University of North Carolina at Chapel Hill: Author.

Cloud, J., & Morse, J. (August 27, 2001). Home sweet school. *Time*, pp. 47–54.

Copple, C., & Bredekamp, S. (2009). *Developmentally appropriate practice in early childhood programs serving children from birth through age 8*. Washington, D.C.: National Association for the Education of Young Children.

Cost, Quality, and Child Outcomes Study Team. (1995). *Cost, quality and child outcomes in child care centers*. Denver, CO: Department of Economics, University of Colorado at Denver.

Gerber, M. (1979). Respecting infants: The Loczy model of infant care. In E. Jones (Ed.), *Supporting the growth of infants, toddlers, and parents*. Pasadena, CA: Pacific Oaks.

Harms, T., Clifford, R. M., & Cryer, D. (1998). *Early Childhood Environmental Rating Scale* (Rev. Ed.). New York: Teachers College Press.

Hatch, J. A. (2005). *Teaching in the new kindergarten*. Clifton Park, NY: Thomson Delmar Learning.

Head Start. (2010). *2010 Head Start fact sheet*. Washington, D.C.: Head Start Bureau, Department of Health and Human Services.

Hyun, E. (2007). Cultural complexity in early childhood: Images of contemporary young children from a critical perspective. *Childhood Education*, 85(5), pp. 261–266.

Hyun, E. (1998). *Making sense of developmentally and culturally appropriate practice (DCAP) in early childhood education*. New York: Peter Lang.

Kagan. S. L., & Kauerz, K. (2006). Making the most of kindergarten: Trends and policy issues. In D. F. Gullo (Ed.) *Teaching and learning in the kindergarten year*. Washington, D.C.: National Association for the Education of Young Children.

McCartney, K., Dearing, E., Taylor, B., & Bub, K. (2007). Quality childcare supports the achievement of low-income children: Direct and indirect pathways through caregiving and the home environment. *Journal of Applied Developmental Psychology*, 28, pp. 411–426.

National Association of Child Care Resources and Referral Agencies (NACCRRA). (2010). Leaving children to chance: 2010 update. Retrieved July 2011. www.naccrra.org.

National Association for Family Child Care. (2011). *NAFCC accreditation and information*. Salt Lake City, UT: Author.

National Association for the Education of Young Children Position Statement. (2009). Developmentally appropriate practice in early childhood programs serving children from birth through age 8. In Copple, C. & Bredekamp, S. (Eds.), *Developmentally appropriate practice in early childhood programs*. Washington, D.C.: Author.

National Association for the Education of Young Children. (2005). *NAEYC early childhood program standards & accreditation criteria*. Washington, D.C.: National Association for the Education of Young Children.

National Association of Early Childhood Specialists in State Departments of Education and the National Association of Education for Young Children. (2001, September). Still unacceptable trends in kindergarten entry and placement. *Young Children*, pp. 59–62.

National Center for Education Statistics. (2011). *Fast facts: homeschooling*. Washington, D.C.: Author. Retrieved July 9, 2011. www.nec=es.ed/gov/fastfacts.

National Coalition for the Homeless. (2007). *How many people experience homelessness?* NCH Fact Sheet #2. National Coalition for the Homeless, June, 2008.

Neugebauer, R., Wilson, M., & Ballas, T. (2007, September/October) School-age child care trend, part II. *Child Care Information Exchange*, pp. 28–39.

Program for Infant/Toddler Care (PITC). (2011). http://www.pitc.org. Retrieved August 5, 2011.

Reynolds, A. J., Temple, J. A., Ou, S. R., Arteaga, I. A., and White, R. A. B. (June 9, 2011). School-based early childhood education and age-28 well-being:

Effects by timing, dosage, and subgroups. *Science*. http://www.sciencedaily.com. Retrieved August 5, 2011.

Rhode Island KIDS COUNT. (2005). Getting ready: Findings from the National School Readiness Indicators Initiative: A 17 State Partnership. http://www.gettingready.org. Retrieved August 5, 2011.

U.S. Bureau of Labor Statistics. (2011). *Labor force statistics from the Current Population Survey: Women in the Labor Force: a Databook (2009 Edition)*. Washington, D.C.: U.S. Bureau of Labor: Author. Retrieved August 7, 2011.

United States Census Bureau. (2007). *Who's minding the kids? Child care arrangements: Spring, 2005*. Survey of Income and Program Participation (SIPP). Internet release date February 2008. Washington, D.C.: Author.

Schweinhart, L. J. (n.d.). *The High/Scope Perry Preschool Study Through Age 40*. Ypsilanti, MI: High/Scope Educational Research Foundation.

Whitebook, M., Sakai, L., Gerber, E., & Howes, C. (2001). *Then and now: Changes in child care staffing, 1994–2000*. Washington, D.C.: Center for the Child Care Workforce.

History of Early Childhood Education

Learning Objectives

LO1 List the major historical contributions from outside the United States that influence modern early childhood education.

LO2 Describe the primary influences within the United States on early childhood education.

LO3 Identify the three professions that closely connect to the field and their major contributions to early childhood education.

LO4 Define the four major themes that shape practices and policies of early childhood education.

naeyc Standards For Professional Development

The following NAEYC Standards for early childhood professional development are addressed in this chapter:

Standard 1 Promoting Child Development and Learning
Standard 2 Building Family and Community Relationships
Standard 5 Using Content Knowledge to Build Meaningful Curriculum
Standard 6 Becoming a Professional

naeyc Code of Ethical Conduct

These are the sections of the NAEYC Code of Ethical Conduct that apply to the topics of this chapter:

Core Values: We have committed ourselves to appreciating childhood as a unique and valuable stage of the human life cycle.
Section I. Childhood is a unique and valuable stage of the human life cycle.
Section I I-1.3. To recognize and respect the uniqueness and the potential of each child.
Section III I-3B.2. To do nothing that diminishes the reputation of the program in which we work unless it is violating laws and regulations designed to protect children of the provisions of this Code.

Please refer to Figure 4-2, *An Abbreviated Timeline for Early Childhood Education,* and online at the Education 🔅 CourseMate for an expanded timeline as you read this chapter.

Introduction

Early childhood education has a rich and exciting history. The stories of our field chronicle courageous people who took steps toward improving children's lives. Critical events have had a hand in shaping the history of early childhood education. As the conditions of childhood and early education have changed through the centuries, its educators have also adapted to those challenges.

While reading this chapter, imagine yourself as a time traveler. As you go back in time, you span the centuries and meet the people whose vision helped to shape our profession. You learn how Froebel's own unhappy childhood inspired a new way of teaching called the kindergarten. You see the passion and struggle of Montessori as she convinces the world that "slum children" can learn and succeed. In the 1960s, you witness the dedication of America to create a program for preschoolers known as "Head Start." You see early childhood teaching become a profession that includes infants and toddlers, as well as kindergarten and early primary grades.

There is more than one right way to educate young children. Every culture has the task of socializing and educating their young. The historical record may document several educational philosophies, but there is no single monopoly on ideas about children. People inside the United States and across the world have influenced our ideas about children and their education. Other disciplines (medicine, education, and psychology) inform early childhood teaching. Current issues always influence what is happening for young children and their teachers. What emerge are some consistent themes over time.

All professions have a canon of beliefs and practices. As you acquire this knowledge, you begin to develop your own *philosophy of teaching* (based, in part, on information gathered in this chapter). As you do, be sure to constantly rethink your practices. See "Teaching With Intention" to delve into why knowing the history of early childhood education is important.

All professionals should re-examine themselves on a regular basis because although understanding historical records makes sense for professional development, recognizing that they are a reflection of certain cultural norms is also crucial. For example, mainstream educational philosophy claims the following areas are "universal," but cross-cultural research has shown them not to be:

- Early attainment of individuality and independence.
- The necessity of early and free exploration.
- The critical importance of the early stimulation of intellect and language.

The first reflects a priority of many Western European cultures, but it is not a common practice in societies that promote group harmony and interdependence. Second, many indigenous groups hold their very young children close, carrying them along while they work; there is no data that indicate these children develop poorly. Third, although American educational systems of the early 21st century are building on increasing academic and intellectual standards, there is no universal mandate for an exclusive focus on this developmental domain in the early years. Figure 4-1 offers other traditional educational practices, their historical context, and alternatives to consider as you create your own educational philosophy. Perhaps some of the mistakes of the past can be avoided if history is remembered.

Defining the Terms

The term early childhood education refers to group settings deliberately intended to affect developmental changes in children from birth to 8 years of age. In school terms, it includes group settings for infants through the primary years of elementary school, kindergarten through 3rd grade in the United States. In programmatic terms, the education of young children includes formal and informal group settings regardless of their initial purpose. For instance, after-school programs for elementary ages are included, as are their formal academic sessions.

Early childhood educators thus build bridges between a child's two worlds: school (or group experience) and home. It is during these years that the foundation for future learning is set; these are the building block years, during which a child learns to walk, talk, establish an identity, print, and count. In later years, that same child builds on these skills to be able to climb mountains, speak a second language, learn to express and negotiate, write in cursive, and understand multiplication.

Influences from Abroad

When did early childhood education first begin? Refer to Figure 4-2, *An Abbreviated Timeline for Early Childhood Education,* and to the expanded timeline on the

Why Does History Help?

Most early childhood education students and many educators know little about the origins of their chosen profession. To better build your philosophy of teaching, note the links between the past to *your* present:

Support: Learning the works of others gives us validation of our ideas. The philosophies of Froebel, Montessori, and Dewey are part of the foundation of our educational practices. Traditional early childhood practices reflect European values and beliefs, and looking beyond the dominant culture to writings of Africa, Asia, and South America broadens your viewpoint.

Inspiration: Knowing our deep roots helps develop professional expression. Ideas of past educators offer you more methods of teaching. An historical overview clarifies how children and learning are viewed based on the religious, political, and economic pressures.

Identity and Commitment: Accepting the mission of our field commits you to enhancing the education, development, and well-being of young children. Such identity brings with it an awareness of the diversity in cultural norms. Be cautious of theories or opinions claiming to be "universal." For instance, history notes that schools of the past were overwhelmingly created for boys; this gender bias of past practices adds to the underdevelopment of girls and prevails today in parts of the world.

Add your voice to those crusaders for education as you create your personal philosophy of education. Include an element of reform in making the work of teaching into a legitimate profession. Listen to their voices, so you can develop your own.

Think About This

1. If you didn't know anything about the history of the field, what mistakes would you likely make in your first year of teaching?
2. Which historical figures interest you in developing a personal philosophy of teaching?
3. What are the strongest ideas that draw you into this work? Why would finding historical roots for your professional identity help you in your career?

---

accompanying Education CourseMate as you read this chapter. Getting a visual sense of when and where things happened can help you make sense of the various threads in our tapestry of early childhood educational history.

Looking at the timeline lets you see how impressive the accomplishments really are. For instance, there are many anniversaries to celebrate at this time (Fanjul, 2011):

- Forty-five years ago: Congress passed bills that authorized both Head Start and Elementary and Secondary Education Act/Title 1.
- Twenty-five years ago: NAEYC's accreditation for programs serving young children was launched.
- Twenty years ago: The Child Care and Development Block Grant was created to help working families afford child care.

In addition, the timeline helps us see that it is impossible to pinpoint the origins of humankind. There are few records from millions of years ago. Some preparation for adult life was done informally, mostly through imitation. As language developed, communication occurred. Children learned dances, rituals, and ceremonies, and both boys and girls were taught skills for their respective roles in the tribe. Ancient historical documents seem to indicate that child-rearing practices were somewhat crude;

DeMause (1974) even suggests that the further one goes back in history, the more likely the case of abandonment and brutality.

European Roots

The definition of childhood has varied greatly throughout history. For example, in ancient times children were considered adults by age 7. A society's definition of childhood influences how it educates its children.

In Ancient Times

Many of our own practices are founded on those developed in Greece and Rome. Greek education—and virtually all classical European schooling—was provided for the boys of wealthy families, while girls and working-class children received training for domestic work or a trade.

Education began by age 6 or 7, although Plato and Aristotle both spoke of the need to educate the younger child. Some ancient Romans felt that education should begin at home as soon as a child began to talk, and they highlighted the use of rewards and the ineffectiveness of corporal punishment (Hewes, 1993).

Probably the first education in schools outside the home or homelike apprenticeship was in ancient Greek

Reflecting on Practices: Building Your Philosophy of Teaching

Educational Practice	Historical Context and ECE Trend/Practice	Think Again . . .
Same-age grouping	K–12 schools in the United States since 1850s target curriculum goals.	▪ Learning takes place with "guided collaboration," which often occurs with an older "expert." ▪ Children learn when challenged to accommodate to higher level thinking, likely to occur with a mixed-age range. ▪ Developing values of caring and responsibility happen best when children practice helping and protecting younger children. ▪ Reduced family size indicates that multi-age experiences should happen in schooling. ▪ Diversity (gender, culture, exceptionality, etc.) makes strict target goals unrealistic.
Daily schedules	Routines are the framework for programs, offering security and predictability.	▪ Children's sense of time is unlike that of adults, so rigid schedules do not correspond to their development. ▪ Brain research indicates a need for stimulation, change, and challenge rather than the same structure constantly.
Curriculum is at the center of good programs.	A plan for learning should be driven by specific outcomes in order to be assured that children are learning.	▪ Not following an adult-planned and driven curriculum worked well for geniuses such as Einstein, Erikson, and Bill Gates. ▪ Educators as diverse as Dewey and Steiner promoted curricula based on children's interests or innate spirit. ▪ Children appear to learn well through a curriculum that emerges, following their interests and timetable.

FIGURE 4-1 As you develop a philosophy of teaching, be sure to examine common beliefs and practices of the profession.

© Cengage Learning 2011

and Roman times. Plato (427 BC), Aristotle (384–323 BC), Cicero (143–106 BC), and Polybius (222–204 BC) founded schools, with the model of small-group tutoring, teaching wealthy boys thinking skills, governing, military strategy, and managing commerce. Our word *educate* comes from a Latin verb *educare*, through a French verb *educere*, to draw forth or to lead.

As the Roman Empire deteriorated and society fell apart (400–1200 AD), childhood lasted barely beyond infancy. Although education was the responsibility of

parents, most were busy fighting for survival. Childhood was not seen as a separate time of life, and children were used in the labor force. People left villages and towns for the safety of a local baron or king, and schools ceased to exist. Few members of the ruling class could read or write their names, and the monastery schools were for priests and religious instruction only.

The education of children was fairly simple before the 15th century; there was no educational system, and the way of life was uncomplicated as well. The

An Abbreviated Timeline for Early Childhood Education

Authors' Note: A debt of gratitude is owed to D. Keith Osborn for his outstanding historical research and to James L. Hymes, Jr., for his generous time and perspective.

5th–3rd centuries BC to AD 1400s Few records exist concerning child-rearing practices; the development of cities gives rise to schooling on a larger scale.

1423 & 1439 The invention of printing and movable type allows knowledge to spread rapidly; ideas and techniques become available to large numbers of people; printing is credited with bringing about the end of the Middle Ages and the beginning of the Renaissance.

1657 *Orbis Pictus,* by Comenius, is the first children's book with pictures.

1690 John Locke published his essay, which postulated that children are born with a tabula rasa, or clean slate, on which all experiences are written.

1740–1860s Sabbath Schools and Clandestine Schools are established as facilities to educate African Americans in the United States.

1762 *Emile,* by Rousseau, proclaims the child's natural goodness.

1801 *How Gertrude Teaches Her Children,* by Pestalozzi, emphasizes home education.

1826 *Education of Man,* by Froebel, describes the first system of kindergarten education as a "child's garden," with activities known as "gifts from God."

1837 Froebel opens the first kindergarten in Blankenburgh, Germany.

1860 Elizabeth Peabody opens the first English-speaking kindergarten in Boston.

1861 Robert Owen sets up infant school in New Lanark, England, as an instrument of social reform for children of parent workers in his mills.

1871 The first public kindergarten in North America opens in Ontario, Canada. (First public American kindergarten: 1873).

1873 The Butler School at Hampton Institute is opened as a free school for black children, including kindergarten curriculum for five-year-olds.

1880 First teacher-training program for kindergartners, Oshkosh Normal School, Pennsylvania.

1892 International Kindergarten Union founded; becomes the Association for Childhood Education in 1930, increasing its scope to include elementary education.

1896 John Dewey establishes a laboratory school at the University of Chicago and develops a pragmatic approach to education, becoming the father of the Progressive Movement in American education.

1897 *My Pedagogic Creed* is published, detailing the opposition to rote learning and the philosophy of educating "the whole child."

1903 The Committee of Nineteen, a splinter group of the International Kindergarten Union, forms to report various philosophical concepts. Members include Patty Smith Hill, Lucy Wheelock, and Susan Blow.

1907 Casa di Bambini (Children's House) is opened by Maria Montessori in a slum district in Rome, Italy. She later develops an educational philosophy and program to guide children's growth through the senses and practical life experiences.

1909 First White House Conference on Children is held by Theodore Roosevelt, leading to the establishment of the Children's Bureau in 1912.

1911 Deptford School, an open-air school in the slums of London, is opened by Margaret McMillan. The school emphasizes health and play, thus coining the phrase "nursery school."

1915 First U.S. Montessori school opens in New York City.

1916 The Bureau of Educational Experiments, which becomes Bank Street College of Education (and laboratory school) in 1922, is founded by L. S. Mitchell, who is a leading proponent of progressive education at the early childhood level.

FIGURE 4-2 An abbreviated timeline for early childhood education (see the Education CourseMate for an expanded version).

1916 First Cooperative Nursery School opens at the University of Chicago.

1918 First public nursery schools are opened in England.

1921 A. S. Neill founds Summerhill school in England, which becomes a model for the "free school" movement (the book entitled *Summerhill* is published in 1960).

1922 Abigail Eliot opens Ruggles Street Nursery School and Training Center.

1925–1926 The National Committee on Nursery Schools is founded by Patty Smith Hill; it becomes NANE and eventually NAEYC.

1926 Gesell establishes the Clinic of Child Development at Yale University and studies norms of child growth and behavior.

1926–1927 Research facilities are founded at several American universities and colleges (e.g., Smith College, Vassar College, Yale University, and Mills College).

1927 Dorothy Howard establishes the first Black Nursery School in Washington, DC, and operates it for over 50 years.

1929 Lois Meeks Stolz names the first President of the National Association for Nursery Education (later to become National Association for the Education of Young Children), and joins the Teachers College (Columbia University) faculty to start the laboratory school and Child Development Institute. Stolz later becomes the Director of the Kaiser Child Service Centers during World War II.

1929 Susan Isaacs publishes *The Nursery Years*, which contradicts the more scientific psychological view of behavior shaping and emphasizes the child's viewpoint and the value of play.

1929–1931 Hampton Institute, Spellman College, and Bennett College open Black laboratory nursery schools, emphasizing child development principles as in other lab schools and serving as training centers.

1933 WPA (Works Projects Association) opens emergency nurseries for Depression relief of unemployed teachers.

1935 First toy lending library, Toy Loan, begins in Los Angeles.

1936 The first commercial telecast is shown in New York City, starring Felix the Cat.

1943–1945 Kaiser Shipyard Child Care Center, run by Lois Meeks Stolz, James Hymes, and Edith Dowley, operates 24-hour care in Portland, Oregon.

1944 *Young Children* is first published by NAEYC.

1946 Dr. Spock's *Baby and Child Care* is published. It advocates a more permissive attitude toward children's behavior and encourages exploratory behavior.

1946 Loris Malguzzi starts school of Reggio Emilia, Italy, emphasizing the child's individual creative expression.

1948 USNC OMEP, the United States National Committee of the World Organization for Early Childhood Education, is founded to promote the education of children internationally and begins to consult with UNICEF and UNESCO in the United Nations. It starts publishing a journal, *The International Journal of Early Childhood*, in 1969.

1954 U.S. Supreme Court ruled in *Brown v Board of Education* that in public education the doctrine of "separate but equal" has no place.

1956 La Leche League is established to provide mothers with information on breast-feeding, childbirth, infants, and child care.

1960 Katherine Whiteside Taylor founds the American Council of Parent Cooperatives, which later becomes the Parent Cooperative Pre-schools International.

1960 Nancy McCormick Rambusch founds the American Montessori movement.

1962 Perry Preschool Project, directed by David Weikart, opens in Ypsilanti, Michigan, and conducts longitudinal study to measure the effects of preschool education on later school and life.

1964–1965 The Economic Opportunity Act of 1964 passes, becoming the foundation of Head Start Programs in the United States, as part of a federal "War on Poverty."

1966 The Bureau of Education for the Handicapped is established.

1966 NANE becomes National Association for the Education of Young Children (NAEYC).

1969 Pediatrician T. Berry Brazelton publishes *Infants and Mothers*, along with several other books and numerous articles advocating a sensible and intimate relationship between parents and children. ·

(continues)

1969   The Ford Foundation, Carnegie Corporation, and the Department of Health, Education, and Welfare subsidize the Children's Television Workshop, which develops *Sesame Street*.

1971   Stride-Rite Corporation of Boston opens a children's program on site, becoming a vanguard for employer-supported child care.

1972   The Child Development Associate Consortium is started by Edward Ziegler to develop a professional teacher training program (now known as CDA).

1975   PL 94-142, the Education for All Handicapped Children bill, passes, mandating appropriate education for special needs children in the "least restrictive environment" possible, thus defining the concepts of "mainstreaming" and "full inclusion."

1979   The United Nations declares an International Year of the Child.

1982   Marion Wright Edelman establishes the Children's Defense Fund, a Washington-based lobby on behalf of children, and particularly children of poverty and color.

1983   *A Nation at Risk* is published, which concluded "If an unfriendly foreign power had attempted to impose on America the mediocre educational performance that exists today, we might well have viewed it as an act of war."

1984   NAEYC publishes a report entitled "Develomentally Appropriate Practices," which outlines what is meant by "quality" work with young children from infancy through age 8.

1985   NAEYC establishes a National Academy and a voluntary Accreditation system for centers, in an effort to improve the quality of children's lives, and confers its first accreditation the next year.

1986   U.S. Department of Education declares the Year of the Elementary School. PL. 99-457, amending 94-142, establishes a national policy on early intervention for children as young as infants.

1990   The Child Care Development Block Grant is established to improve the quality, availability, and affordability of child care programs.

1990   U.N. Children's World Summit includes the following goals to be reached by the year 2000: (1) to reduce child mortality below age 5 by one third; (2) to provide universal access to basic education; and (3) to protect children in dangerous situations.

1990   The Americans with Disabilities Act (ADA) is passed, requiring programs of all sizes to care for and accommodate the needs of children with disabilities whenever they are reasonably able to do so.

1991   "Ready to Learn/America 2000," part of the U.S. government's educational strategy for reforming American public schools, is published.

1991   The first Worthy Wage Day, organized by the Child Care Employee Project, is held on April 9, drawing attention to the inadequate compensation of early childhood workers and how this affects the retention of a skilled and stable work force.

1993   The Family and Medical Leave Act (FMLA) passes, providing new parents with 12 weeks of unpaid, job-protected leave.

1996   The first "Stand for Children" demonstration is held in Washington, DC, drawing 200,000 participants.
Rethinking the Brain, published by the Family and Work Institute, summarizes the new research on children's brain development.

1997   The Child Development Permit Matrix is adopted by the California Commission on Teacher Credentialing, introducing the career ladder concept into early childhood public education.

1998   The 100,000th CDA Credential is awarded by Carol Brunson Phillips, Executive Director of the Council for Early Childhood Professionals.

2002   In the U.S., the "Leave No Child Behind" legislation is passed.

2003   Universal preschool is considered as a next step in providing equal access to quality early educational experiences for all children under 5 years of age.

2007   State-funded preschools rose in per-child funding, expanded access, and moved toward higher quality standards.

2008   12 states in the US still provide no state preschool for their children.

2010   Common core state standards for grades K-12 in English language arts and mathematics is published.

FIGURE 4-2 *(continued)*

church control of school in the medieval period meant that education projected a view of children as basically evil in their natural state. The value of education was in preparation for an afterlife. Children learned mostly through their parents or by apprenticeship outside the family. The child was expected and encouraged to move into adulthood as fast as possible. Survival was the primary goal in life. Because the common religious belief was that people were naturally evil, children had to be directed, punished, and corrected constantly.

What little we know of systematic learning developed during the Dark Ages through the policies of Charlemagne—who proclaimed that the nobility should know their letters—and from monastery schools that maintained libraries. A new social class in the form of craft guilds began to grow as apprenticeships expanded. Although education was sparse, the seeds of learning were planted, including the introduction of the concepts of equality and brotherhood, a continuing concern of educators today.

In the Renaissance and Reformation

The European Renaissance and Reformation (1400–1600) brought more ease and freedom for the common person. Children were seen as pure and good. The printing press, invented by Johannes Gutenberg in 1439, made books more available to the common person rather than exclusively to the domain of monks and church-sponsored schools. Martin Luther (1482–1546) urged parents to educate their children by teaching them morals and catechism.

The first humanist educators began to advocate a basic education for all children, including girls and the poor. The call for a *universal education* and *literacy* are two fundamental effects of this period on education as we know it today. Concern for the common man was on the rise, as skilled craftsmen formed a kind of middle class. By the 1500s, schools that taught subjects such as reading, writing, arithmetic, and bookkeeping were fairly common throughout Europe.

The German school system was established at this time and would influence education in all parts of Europe. People changed the way they looked at children and their education. Towns grew and expanded, and there was an opportunity to move to new lands. Living conditions improved and infant mortality waned. Children were living longer. The acquisition of knowledge and skills at an earlier age became important. If educated, children could be expected to help their family improve its situation. Parents found they needed help in teaching their children.

Cornix cornicatur,	à à	A a
The *Crow* crieth.		
Agnus balat,	b è è è	B b
The *Lamb* blaiteth.		
Cicàda stridet,	cì cì	C c
The *Grasshopper* chirpeth.		
Upupa dicit,	du du	D d
The *Whooppoo* saith.		
Infans ejulat,	è è è	E e
The *Infant* crieth.		
Ventus flat,	fi fi	F f
The *Wind* bloweth.		
Anser gingrit,	ga ga	G g
The *Goose* gagleth.		
Os halat,	hà'h hà'h	H h
The *Mouth* breatheth out.		
Mus mintrit,	ì ì ì	I i
The *Mouse* chirpeth.		
Anas tetrinnit,	kha, kha	K k
The *Duck* quaketh.		
Lupus ululat,	lu ulu	L
The *Wolf* howleth.	[mum	
Ursus murmurat,	mum-	M m
The *Bear* grumbleth.		

Orbis Pictus, by Johann Comenius, is considered the first picture book written for children.

Into Modern Times

Johann Amos Comenius Comenius (1592–1670), a Czech educator, wrote the first picture book for children. Called *Orbis Pictus* (*The World of Pictures*, 1658), it was a guide for teachers that included training of the senses and the study of nature. Comenius fostered the belief that education should follow the natural order of things. His ideas included the "school of the mother's lap," in which children's development follows a timetable of its own and their education should reflect that fact. Comenius advocated approaching learning based on the principles of nature. He believed that "in all the operations of nature, development is from within," so children should be allowed to learn at their own pace. He also proposed that teachers should work with children's own inclinations, for "what is natural takes place without compulsion" (Gianoutsos, 2011). Teachers must observe and work with this natural order—the timetable—to ensure successful learning. This idea was later reflected in Montessori's sensitive periods and Piaget's stages of development. Today it is recognized as the issue of school readiness.

Comenius also stressed a basic concept that is now taken for granted: learning by doing. He encouraged parents to let their children play with other children of the same age. Rather than pushing a standard curriculum, Comenius said that "the desire to know and to learn should be excited ... in every possible manner" (Keatinge, 1896). He also reflected the growing social reform that would educate the poor, as well as the rich.

In summary, probably the three most significant contributions of Comenius are *books with illustrations,* an emphasis on *education with the senses,* and the *social reform* potential of education.

John Locke An English philosopher of the 1600s, Locke (1632–1714) is considered to be the founder of modern educational philosophy. He based his theory of education on the scientific method and the study of the mind and learning. Locke theorized the concept of tabula rasa, the belief that the child is born neutral, rather than evil, and is a "clean slate" on which the experiences of parents, society, education, and the world are written. He based his theory on the scientific method and approached a child as a doctor would examine a patient. He was one of the first European educators to discuss the idea of individual differences gleaned from observing one child rather than simply teaching a group. Education needed to take the individual learner into account.

The purpose of education, he claimed, is to make man a reasoning creature. A working knowledge of the Bible and a counting ability sufficient to conduct business was the fundamental education required of adults, so children were taught those basics. Locke suggested that such instruction should be pleasant, with playful activities, as well as drills. Locke's influence on education was not felt strongly at the time. Later, however, his best ideas, such as the notion that the teacher must work through the senses to help children reach understanding, were popularized by Rousseau. Today, teachers still emphasize a sensory approach to learning.

In summary, Locke's contribution is felt most in our acceptance of *individual differences,* in *giving children reasons* as the basis for helping children to learn, and in his *theory of a "clean slate"* that points to the effect of the environment on learning.

Jean-Jacques Rousseau After Comenius, new thoughts were everywhere in Europe. Locke offered some educational

Rousseau advocated that children were naturally good and should have a flexible and less restrained school atmosphere.

challenges, and Darwin brought a change to science. The time was ripe for new ideas about childhood. Rousseau (1712–1778), a writer and philosopher, proposed that children were not inherently evil, but naturally good. He is best known for his book *Emile* (1761) in which he raised a hypothetical child to adulthood. He reasoned that education should reflect this goodness and allow spontaneous interests and activities of the children. "Let us lay it down as an incontrovertible rule that the first impulses of nature are always right; there is no original sin in the human heart ... the only natural passion is self-love or selfishness taken in a wider sense."

Rousseau's ideas on education in and of themselves were nothing short of revolutionary for the times. Making what might be considered the first comprehensive attempt to describe a system of education according to nature, his concern for the learner led him to the idea that children learn from firsthand information and their views are different from those of adults. Moreover, a child's mind develops in distinct phases and teachers should adjust their instruction accordingly.

Although he was not an educator, Rousseau suggested that school atmosphere should be less restrained and more flexible to meet the needs of the children. He insisted on using concrete teaching materials, leaving the abstract and symbolism for later years. His call to *naturalism* transformed education in such a way that led educators to eventually focus more on the early years. For instance, he encouraged others to "sacrifice a little time in early childhood, and it will be repaid to you with usury when your scholar is older" (*Emile*, 1761). Pestalozzi, Froebel, and Montessori were greatly influenced by him. The theories of developmental stages, such as of Jean Piaget and Arnold Gesell (see Chapter 4), support Rousseau's idea of natural development. In Europe, his ideas had a ripple effect that sent waves across the Atlantic Ocean.

Rousseau's ideas are still followed today in early childhood classes. *Free play* is based on Rousseau's belief in *children's inherent goodness* and ability to choose what they need to learn. Environments that stress autonomy and self-regulation have their roots in Rousseau's philosophy. Using *concrete rather than abstract materials* for young children is still one of the cornerstones of developmentally appropriate curriculum in the early years.

Johann Heinrich Pestalozzi   Pestalozzi (1746–1827) was a Swiss educator whose theories on education and caring have formed the basis of many common teaching practices of early childhood education. Like Rousseau, he used nature study as part of the curriculum and believed that good education meant the development of the senses. Rather than simply glorify nature, however, Pestalozzi became more pragmatic, including principles on how to teach basic skills and the idea of "caring" as well as "educating" the child. Pestalozzi stressed the idea of the integrated curriculum that would develop the whole child. He wanted education to be of the hand, the head, and the heart of the child. Teachers were to guide self-activity through intuition, exercise, and the senses. Along with intellectual content, he proposed that practical skills be taught in the schools. He differed from Rousseau in that he proposed teaching children in groups rather than using a tutor with an individual child. Pestalozzi's works, *How Gertrude Teaches Her Children* and *Book for Mothers*, detail some procedures for mothers to use at home with their children. Probably his greatest contribution is the blending of Rousseau's strong romantic ideals with his own egalitarian attitude: "I wish to wrest education from the outworn order of doddering old teaching hacks as well as from the new-fangled order of cheap, artificial teaching tricks, and entrust it to the eternal powers of nature herself" (in Silber, 1965).

In summary, Pestalozzi's contributions are strongest around the *integration of the curriculum* and *group*

teaching. He initiated *sensory education* and blended both *freedom* and *limits* into working with children.

Friedrich Wilhelm Froebel   Froebel (1782–1852) is one of the major contributors to early childhood education, particularly in his organization of educational thought and ideas about learning, curriculum, and teacher training. He is known to us as the "Father of the Kindergarten," not only for giving it a name, but for devoting his life to the development of a system of education for young children. The German word kindergarten means "children's garden," and that is what Froebel felt best expressed what he wanted for children less than 6 years of age. Because his own childhood had been unhappy, he resolved that early education should be pleasant. He attended a training institute run by Pestalozzi and left to promote children's right to play, to have toys, and to be with trained teachers by founding a Play and Activity Institute. Early childhood historian Dorothy Hewes (1993) notes:

> Froebel started his kindergarten in 1836, for children aged about two to six, after he had studied with Pestalozzi in Switzerland and had read the philosophy promoted by Comenius two hundred years earlier. His system was centered around self-activity and the development of children's self-esteem and self-confidence. In his *Education of Man,* he wrote that "Play is the highest phase of child development—the representation of the inner necessity and impulse." He had the radical idea that both men and women should teach young children and that they should be friendly facilitators rather than stern disciplinarians.

More than 100 years ago, Froebel's kindergartens included blocks, pets, and finger plays. Froebel observed children and came to understand how they learned and what they liked to do. He developed the first educational

A Froebelian kindergarten at the end of the nineteenth century.

toys, which he termed "gifts" (*gaben* in German), as seen in Figure 4-3.

Angeline Brooks (1886), a teacher in an American Froebelian kindergarten in the late 1800s, described the gifts this way:

> Froebel regarded the whole of life as a school, and the whole world as a school-room for the education of the [human] race. The external things of nature he regarded as a means to making the race acquainted with the invisible things of the minds, as God's *gifts* for use in accomplishing the purpose of this temporal life. Regarding the child as the race in miniature, he selected a few objects which should epitomize the world of matter in its most salient attributes and arranged them in an order which should assist the child's development at successive stages of growth."Froebel wanted teachers to see how children developed as they manipulated specific objects (gifts and occupations he designed for their education), such as blocks for design construction, parquetry shapes for picture creation, and drawing forms" (Reifel, 2011).

Some of his theories about children and their education later influenced Montessori and were reflected in the educational materials she developed, as well as modern kindergarten (Brosterman, 1997).

Every day, teachers in centers and homes across the country practice the Froebelian belief that one's first educational experiences should be a *child's garden*: full of pleasant discoveries and delightful adventure, where the adults' role is to plant ideas and materials for children to use as they grow at their own pace.

Maria Montessori designed materials, classrooms, and learning methods for young children.

Maria Montessori At the turn of the century, Montessori (1870–1952) became the first female physician in Italy. She worked in the slums of Rome with poor children and with mentally retarded children. Sensing that what they lacked was proper motivation and environment, she opened a preschool, *Casa di Bambini*, in 1907. Her first class was 50 children from 2 to 5 years of age. The children were at the center all day while their parents worked. They were fed two meals a day, given a bath, and provided with medical attention. Montessori designed materials, classrooms, and a teaching procedure that proved her point to the astonishment of people all over Europe and America.

Before her, no one with medical or psychiatric training had articulated so clearly the needs of the growing child. Her medical background added credibility to her findings and helped her ideas gain recognition in this country. The Montessori concept is both a philosophy of child development and a plan for guiding growth, believing that education begins at birth and the early years are of the utmost importance. During this time, children pass through "sensitive periods," in which their curiosity makes them ready for acquiring certain skills and knowledge.

Froebelian Gifts

When the children are just making friends with the teacher and with each other, it is very interesting and profitable for them to formulate their mite of knowledge into a sentence, each one holding his ball high in the air with the right hand and saying:

My ball is red like a cherry.
My ball is yellow like a lemon.
My ball is blue like the sky.
My ball is orange like a marigold.
My ball is green like the grass.
My ball is violet like a plum.

FIGURE 4-3 When introducing the gifts, the teacher in Froebelian settings would teach children rhymes and finger plays.

Montessori was an especially observant person and used her observations to develop her program and philosophy. For instance, the manipulative materials she used were expensive, so they were always kept in a locked cabinet. One day the cabinet was left unlocked, and the children took out the materials themselves and worked with them quietly and carefully. Afterward, Montessori removed the cabinet and replaced it with low open shelves. She noticed that children liked to sit on the floor so she bought little rugs to define the work areas. In analyzing how children learn, she concluded that they build themselves from what they find in their environment, so she designed the school around the size of the children. Because of her enlightenment, a carefully prepared environment with child-sized furniture and materials are common features of early educational classrooms.

By focusing on the *sequential steps of learning*, Montessori developed a set of learning materials still used widely today. One of her most valuable contributions was a theory of how children learn: children teach themselves if only we will dedicate ourselves to the self-creating process of the child. She believed that any task could be reduced to a series of small steps. By using this process, children could learn to sweep a floor, dress themselves, or multiply numbers.

After Montessori was introduced in the United States in 1909, her methods received poor reception and were often misunderstood. Chattin-McNichols (1993) notes that "adaptation of her methods in a variety of ways, a focus on academics by demanding middle-class parents, and a flood of 'trainers' and authors eager to capitalize on Montessori contributed to a rapid downfall of Montessori schools in the United States by 1925 or so." A second American Montessori movement began in the late 1950s and early 1960s. Differences between European and American society and education generated the American Montessori Society, founded by Dr. Nancy McCormick Rambusch. According to Chattin-McNichols (1993):

> Today with a much wider range of children than ever before, the majority of Montessori schools are private preschools and child care centers, serving 3- to 6-year-old children. But there are many which also serve elementary students and a small (but growing) number of programs for infants, toddlers, and middle-school students. . . . The word *Montessori*, however, remains in the public domain, so that Montessori in the name of a school or teacher education program does not guarantee any adherence to Montessori's original ideas.

To summarize, Montessori's contributions were substantial to all we do in early childhood programs today. *A prepared environment, self-correcting and sequential materials,* teaching based on *observation,* and a trust in *children's innate drive to learn* all stem from her work. (Montessori education as a curriculum model is discussed in Chapter 10.)

Rudolf Steiner Steiner (1861–1925) was an Austrian philosopher, scientist, and artist whose lectures for the German factories of Waldorf-Astoria led to the establishment of schools now known as Waldorf Schools. This system has influenced mainstream education in Europe, and its international reputation is felt in North America today. A growing independent school movement, Waldorf schools number more than 1,000 worldwide (www.waldorfanswers.org, 2004).

Steiner theorized that childhood is a phase of life important in its own right, and the environment must be carefully planned to protect and nurture the child (see Figure 4-4). His philosophy, known as *anthroposophical spiritual science,* emphasized the children's spiritual development, imagination, and creative gifts. As did Froebel and Montessori, Steiner emphasized the whole child and

Steiner's Ages of Childhood

Age	Span	Child Learns by...	Emphasis
The Will	0-7	Imitation	Role models and beautiful environment
The Heart	7-14	Authority	Consistency with enthusiasm and feeling
The Head	14+	Challenge	Intellectual study for real mastery

© Cengage Learning 2011

FIGURE 4-4 Rudolf Steiner created a system of education in the early 1900s that was based on educational goals for the whole child and the transformation of the spirit/soul.

believed that different areas of development and learning were connected into a kind of unity. The role of the teacher is that of a mother figure, and her goal is to allow the child's innate self-motivation to predominate. The teacher is to understand the temperament of each child, and to go with it; thus, play has a large place in Waldorf classrooms.

Self-discipline emerges from the child's natural willingness to learn and initiate, and the classroom needs to support this self-regulation process. Yet, although the child's inner life is deeply valued by Steiner, experiences in early childhood must be carefully selected. For instance, fairy stories help children acquire time-honored wisdom; modern Waldorf followers insist that television be eliminated.

In summary, for Steiner, the people with whom the child interacts are of central importance. (Waldorf schools are addressed with curriculum models in Chapter 10.)

Nontraditional Perspectives

You can likely notice how traditional early childhood educational practices reinforce European-American values and beliefs. Education is often built from the knowledge base of its teachers; curriculum usually draws from the system—cultural, economic, or political—that is most familiar. If teachers are trained on European writings and the ideas of university-educated Americans, then their own teachings would likely reflect those philosophies.

But there have always been other influences on our child-rearing and educational practices, especially those of our upbringing or of the communities whose children and families we teach. We know that there is more than one "right way" to care for and educate children.

What nontraditional perspectives influenced early childhood education? As mentioned before, information about non-Western early childhood history is not easily accessible (see "Additional Resources" for a reading list). Gonzalez-Mena (2001) summarizes some of these perspectives in this way:

Historically, attitudes toward childhood in China and Japan were influenced by Confucius' writings (551–479 B.C.), which stressed harmony. Children were seen as good and worthy of respect, a view not held in Europe until more recently.

Native-American writings show close ties and interconnectedness, not only among families and within tribes but also between people and nature. Teaching children about relationships and interconnectedness are historical themes of early education among many indigenous peoples. Strong kinship networks are themes among both Africans and African Americans; people bond together and pool resources for the common good. Whether these contemporary tendencies come from ancient roots, historic, and modern oppression, or all three, remains unclear.

Latin American and Hispanic cultures value children highly and emphasize the importance of cooperation and sensitivity to authority figures. Families from the Pacific Islands stress the connection to family, as well as the importance of respecting one's elders.

Early education practices have been influenced by many of these perspectives. For instance, understanding and accepting each child's family and cultural perspectives includes a working knowledge of the variations in attitudes and child-rearing practices. Learning about nontraditional cultures and behaviors has become critical for professional teachers to honor diversity both in the classroom and in the larger societal context (see Chapters 3 and 9–15).

Whether or not an activity or program is developmentally suited to a particular age or individual was put into more modern context in the mid-1980s when specific descriptions were required to support NAEYC's efforts to accredit early education programs. Defining what is appropriate now includes as much about the family and culture of a child as the age and even the individual characteristics. Developmentally appropriate practices (DAP) are defined and expanded in the next chapter. The dynamic nature of "DAP" allows for both basic principles and variation. This means that it can reflect the best, most current thinking of the field, and it requires periodic evaluation and revision. Personal application of nontraditional perspectives is part of your professional identity (see the Diversity, "Finding Your Place at the Table").

American Influences

Significant moments in American history have served as turning points in education in general, as well as for early childhood education in particular. As you will read, the American educational system has been dynamic, from its onset in Colonial America to developmentally appropriate practices and common core standards of today.

Colonial Days

When thinking of Colonial America, people often envision the one-room schoolhouse. Indeed, this was the mainstay of education in the New England colonies. Although home-teaching of the Bible was common, children of elementary

DIVERSITY

Finding Your Place at the Table

"The field of Early Child Education eagerly awaits, with hopeful expectation, your special contribution. 'What could I possibly have to offer?' you ask. Your history, or life story, is your greatest asset. Tucked away in your early years are special experiences that can shape the lives of small children" (Williams, 2011).

The challenges from your childhood can enhance your work with children as you add your own sensitivity and perspective. In that way, you make your place at the table of early childhood education, in whatever workplace it may be, both your own and an opening for children. Drawing on the stories and memories may require you to check with your family and others who knew you then. Again, Williams prompts you to consider:

1. What expectations does your culture have for young children? (Consider what messages society sends to families about the activities in which these children should participate.)

2. In which activities did you participate as a child younger than 8 years old? (Remember the toys with which you played or activities your family said you liked.)

3. Did you participate in preschool? If so, what was the setting? Was it in your home, the home of others, a neighborhood childcare facility, or a larger group center? (You might consider how it was physically organized and the people involved.)

4. Were your contacts with others ethnically diverse or localized to one cultural group? (Cultural identity can be defined in many ways such as geographical, religious, racial, and so forth. Many of our identities include many cultures; that is, they are multicultural.)

5. What did you gain from those early years that will help you as an early childhood educator? (Look for a way this can be passed to others.)

6. Describe one way you would like to improve the early childhood education you received. (By rethinking what you did not receive, you can change this in the lives of those you are involved with.)

Finding your own personal diversity helps you find uniqueness within the diverse experiences of your life, which brings richness to your work and treasures to share with the children, families, and professionals that you serve.

---

age were sent to school primarily for religious reasons. Everyone needed to be able to read the Bible, the Puritan fathers reasoned. All children were sent to study, though historically boys were educated before girls. Not only was the Bible used in school, however; new materials like the *New England Primer* and the *Horn Book* were also used.

Early life in the New England colonies was difficult, and estimates run as high as 60 percent to 70 percent of children younger than age 4 dying in colonial towns during the "starving season." Discipline was harsh, and children were expected to obey immediately and without question. Parents may have loved their children, but Puritan families showed little overt affection. Children were important as economic tools, and they worked the land and were apprenticed into trades early.

In the South, it was a different story. Plantation owners imported tutors from England or opened small private schools to teach just their sons to read and write. Although the reasons were different from those in New England, the results were similar: a very high percentage of adult readers. From these came the leaders of the American Revolution and the new nation. History can provide us with reminders of the strides that have been made in American history and

The *Horn Book* was a common reading primer in colonial American schools.

that the challenge of overcoming bias and unequal access continues.

The Revolutionary War brought the establishment of both the Union and religious freedom. By affirming fundamental principles of democratic liberty, the Founding Fathers paved the way for a system of free, common, public school systems, the first the world had seen (Cubberly, 1920). However, after the Revolutionary War, there were no significant advances in education until the late 1800s. Leaders such as Thomas Jefferson felt that knowledge ought to be available to all, but that opinion was not widely shared. Most of the post-Revolutionary period focused on growing crops and pioneering the frontier, not teaching and educating children. Even by the 1820s, education for the common man was not readily available. Industrialization in both the North and South did little to encourage reading and writing skills. Manual labor and machine-operating skills were more important. Although public schools were accepted in principle, in reality, no tax basis was established to support them.

Children in Enslavement

The first African Americans were not slaves but indentured servants, whose debts repaid by their labor would buy them their freedom. However, by 1620, Africans were brought to the New World as slaves. In many states, children of slaves were not valued as human beings but rather as property of the owner. During the Revolutionary War, many Americans turned against slavery because of the principles of the natural rights of the individual, as embodied in the Declaration of Independence and, later, in the United States Constitution. By the early 1800s, most northern owners had freed their slaves, although living conditions for them were generally poor.

Because of the high economic value of children as future laborers, there was a certain level of care given to pregnant women and babies. Osborn (1991) tells of a nursery on a South Carolina plantation around 1850 in which

> . . . infants and small children were left in a small cabin while the mothers worked in the fields nearby. An older woman was left in charge and assisted by several girls 8–10 years of age. The infants, for the most part, lay on the cabin floor or the porch—and once or twice daily, the mother would come in from the field to nurse the baby. Children of toddler age played on the porch or in the yard and, at times, the older girls might lead the group in singing and dancing.

Before the Civil War, education was severely limited for African Americans. Many southern states prohibited literacy instruction for enslaved Africans, so female African American teachers helped establish Clandestine Schools, also known as midnight schools, because plantation owners banned teaching (Jones-Wilson, 1996). After the Civil War, most education came through the establishment of Sabbath schools because literacy training was considered part of religious instruction. Because of its necessary secretive existence, few records are available, although it is reasonable to conclude that the curriculum was similar in both types of schools.

After the Civil War, private and public schools were opened for African Americans. Major colleges and universities were founded by the end of the 1800s. Booker T. Washington, born into slavery, founded the Tuskegee Normal & Industrial Institute in Alabama in 1881 and emphasized practical education and intercultural understanding between the two races as a path to liberation. Many former slaves and graduates established schools for younger children. Of integrated schools, Osborn (1991) reports:

> Generally, however, if the schools accepted Blacks at all, it was on a strictly quota basis. . . . Blacks were often excluded from kindergartens. Thus as the early childhood education movement began to grow and expand in the years following the Civil War, it grew along separate color lines.

Hampton Institute of Virginia established a laboratory kindergarten for African Americans in 1873, and by 1893 the Institute offered a kindergarten training school and courses in child care. The graduates of Hampton Institute became the teachers at the laboratory school because, in the words of its principal, "[the] students know the children and the influences surrounding them. . . . Their people are proud to see them teaching. They furnish what has always been a missing link between me and the parents" (Pleasant, 1992). It would be worth investigating whether all laboratory schools for African Americans copied European models, as did those of most American universities, or if they reflected some African influences.

A Progressive Era

By the end of the 1800s, however, a nationwide reform movement had begun. The Progressive Movement of the late 1800s and first half of the 20th century changed the course of education in both elementary and nursery schools in America. Coinciding with the political progressivism in this country, this philosophy emphasized a child-centered approach that gained

Music time at Hampton Institute kindergarten.

advocates from both the scientific viewpoint (Dewey, Hall) and those of a psychoanalytic bent (Hill, Isaacs). Some of the major features of the educational progressive philosophy were:

1. We must recognize individual needs and individual differences in children.
2. Teachers [must be] more attentive to the needs of children.
3. Children learn best when they are highly motivated and have a genuine interest in the material.
4. Learning via rote memory is useless to children.
5. The teacher should be aware of the child's total development—social, physical, intellectual, and emotional.
6. Children learn best when they have direct contact with the material (Osborn, 1991).

These beliefs were instrumental in changing the old traditional schools from a strict and subject-based curriculum to one that centered on children's interests as the foundation for curriculum development. Progressives wanted educators to work on "how a school could become a cooperative community while developing in individuals their own capacities and satisfying their own needs" (Dewey, 1916). Although Dewey (1858–1952) and others did not reject the teaching of basic skills, the shift was away from such subject matter education.

John Dewey

Dewey was the first real American influence on American education. Raised in Vermont, he became a professor of philosophy at both the University of Chicago and Columbia University. In the years that followed, Dewey was responsible for one of the greatest impacts on American education of all time.

Dewey believed that children were valuable and that childhood was an important part of their lives. Like Froebel, he felt that education should be integrated with life and should provide a training ground for cooperative living. As did Pestalozzi and Rousseau, Dewey felt that schools should focus on the nature of the child. Until this time, children were considered of little consequence. Childhood was rushed. Children as young as 7 were a regular part of the work force—on the farms, in the mines, and in the factories. Dewey's beliefs about children and learning are summarized in Figure 4-5.

Dewey's ideas of schooling emerged from his own childhood and his family life as a parent. Jane Dewey, his sixth child, offered that "his own schooling had bored John; he'd disliked the rigid, passive way of learning forced on children by the pervasive lecture-recitation method of that time" (Walker, 1997). Furthermore, the Dewey's parenting style caused a stir among friends and neighbors; the children were allowed to play actively in

My Pedagogic Creed—John Dewey	What It Means Today
1. "...I believe that only true education comes through the stimulation of the child's powers by the demands of the social situations in which he finds himself."	This tells us that children learn to manage themselves in groups, to make and share friendship, to solve problems, and to cooperate.
2. "...The child's own instinct and powers furnish the material and give the starting point for all education."	We need to create a place that is child-centered, a place that values the skills and interests of each child and each group.
3. "...I believe that education, therefore, is a process of living and not a preparation for future living."	Prepare children for what is to come by enriching and interpreting the present to them. Find educational implications in everyday experiences.
4. "...I believe that ... the school life should grow gradually out of the home life ... it is the business of the school to deepen and extend ... the child's sense of the values bound up in his home life."	This sets the rationale for a relationship between teachers and parents. Values established and created in the home should be enhanced by teaching in the schools.
5. "...I believe, finally, that the teacher is engaged, not simply in the training of individuals, but in the formation of a proper social life. I believe that every teacher should realize the dignity of his calling."	This says that the work teachers do is important and valuable. They teach more than academic content; they teach how to live.

FIGURE 4-5 John Dewey expressed his ideas about education in an important document entitled "My Pedagogic Creed." (Washington, D.C.: The Progressive Education Association, 1897.)

the same room as adult guests, to ignore wearing shoes and stockings, and even to "stand by during the birth [of brother Morris] while Mrs. Dewey explained the process" (Walker, 1997). His passionate belief in the innate goodness of children, in the principle of mind-body unity, and in the encouragement of experimentation shaped John Dewey's ideals.

A new kind of school emerged from these ideals. Even the buildings began to take on a different look. Movable furniture replaced rows of benches. Children's projects, some still under construction, were found everywhere. The curriculum of the school began to focus on all of the basics, not just on a few of the academics. If a group of 6-year-olds decided to make a woodworking table, they would first have to learn to read to understand the directions. After calculating the cost, they would purchase the materials. In building the table, geometry, physics, and math were learned along the way. This was a group effort that encouraged children to work together in teams, so school became a society in miniature. Children's social skills were developed along with reading, science, and math. The teacher's role in the process was one of ongoing support, involvement, and encouragement.

The contribution of John Dewey to American education cannot be underestimated. Dewey's ideas are part of today's classrooms in several ways. His child-oriented schools are a model of child care centers and family child care homes, as learning and living are inseparable. The teacher's role served as a model for current *intentional teaching* methods (see Teaching With Intention feature in every chapter). As the following sections on kindergarten and nursery schools illustrate, John Dewey had a vision that is still alive today.

The Field Expands: Kindergarten

The word **kindergarten**—German for "children's garden"—is a delightful term. It brings to mind the image of young seedlings on the verge of blossoming. The similarity between caring for young plants and young children is not accidental. Froebel, the man who coined the word *kindergarten,* meant for that association to be made. As a flower opens from a bud, so too does a child go through a natural unfolding process. This idea—and ideal—are part of the kindergarten story.

The first kindergarten was a German school started by Froebel in 1837. Nearly 20 years later, in 1856, Margaretha Schurz, a student of Froebel, opened the first kindergarten in the United States. It was for German-speaking children and held in her home in Wisconsin.

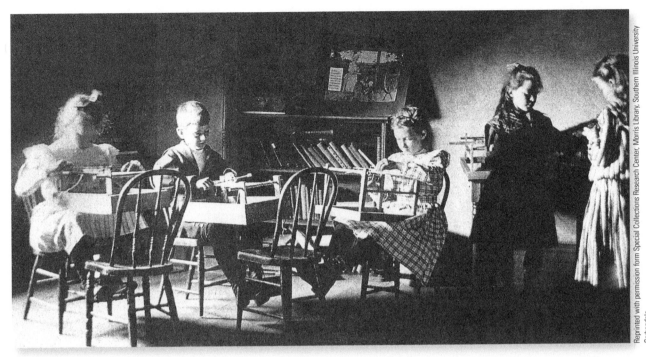

John Dewey's lab school involved children in activities of a practical, real-life nature, such as weaving small rugs to use in the classroom.

Schurz inspired Elizabeth Peabody (1804–1894) of Boston, who opened the first English-speaking kindergarten there in 1860. Peabody, in turn, after studying kindergartens in Germany, influenced William Harris, superintendent of schools in St. Louis, Missouri. In 1873, Harris allowed Susan Blow (1843–1916) to open the first kindergarten in the United States that was associated with the public schools. By the 1880s, kindergarten teachers such as Eudora Hailmann were hard at work inventing wooden beads, paper weaving mats, and songbooks to use with active 5-year-old children.

Look at kindergarten in a historical perspective to trace the various purposes of this specialized educational experience. At first, Froebel's philosophy (see section on Froebel earlier in this chapter) was the mainstay of kindergarten education. At the same time, kindergartens began to become an instrument of social reform. Many of the kindergartens started in the late 1800s were established by churches and other agencies that worked with the poor and were called charity kindergartens. For instance, "in the early kindergartens, teachers conducted a morning class for about 15 children and made social calls on families during the afternoon. The children were taught to address the teachers as 'Auntie' to emphasize her sisterly relationship with their mothers" (Hewes, 1993).

Moreover, by early 1900, traditional kindergarten ideas had come under the scrutiny of G. Stanley Hall and others who were interested in a scientific approach to education. Dewey advocated a community-like (rather than garden-style) classroom. A classic clash of ideals developed between followers of Froebel (conservatives) and those of Dewey's new educational viewpoint (progressives). For those who saw kindergartens as a social service in an era of rising social conscience, the reasons for helping the less fortunate were similar to the rationale that led to the creation of Head Start 60 years later.

The emphasis in a Froebelian kindergarten was on teacher-directed learning. Dewey's followers preferred a more child-centered approach, with teachers serving as facilitators of children's learning. This is the same tension that exists today between the "back to basics" movement and the supporters of child-centered education. The progressives found fault with the "gifts" of Froebel's curriculum. Those who followed Dewey believed that "real objects and real situations within the child's own social setting" should be used (Read & Patterson, 1980). Froebel was viewed as too structured and too symbolic; Dewey was perceived as child-oriented and child-involved. Even the processes they used were different. Froebel believed in allowing the unfolding of the child's mind and learning, whereas Dewey stressed adult intervention in social interaction.

The reform of kindergarten education led to the creation of the modern American kindergarten. By the 1970s, the trend was to focus on the intellectual development of the child; thus there was an emphasis on academic goals for 5-year-olds. By the late 1990s, the concept of developmentally appropriate practices advocated a shift toward more holistic, broad planning for kindergarten. (Today's kindergarten programs are discussed in Chapter 2.)

Patty Smith Hill

Hill (1868–1946) of Teacher's College, Columbia University, was an outstanding innovator of the time and one of the Progressive Movement's most able leaders. It was she who wrote the song "Happy Birthday," created sets of large blocks (known as "Patty Hill blocks," now known as hollow and unit blocks) and founded the National Association for Nursery Education (NANE). The largest association of early childhood educators, it is known today as the National Association for the Education of Young Children (NAEYC). Trained originally in the Froebelian tradition, she worked closely with G. Stanley Hall and later with John Dewey. Thus her philosophy of classroom teaching was a blended one. She believed strongly in basing curricula and programs on the nature and needs of the children, and she was one of the major education experimenters of her day. She was:

> . . . guided by principles of democracy and respect for individuals. She argued for freedom and initiative for children, as well as a curriculum relevant to children's lives. It was she who originated large-muscle equipment and materials suitable for climbing and construction, a departure from the prescribed small-muscle activities of the Froebelians. Patty Hill also urged unification of kindergarten and first-grade work, but her objective was not to start 5-year-olds on first grade work, as we today might readily assume. Rather, emphasis was on giving six-year-olds the opportunity for independent, creative activities before embarking on the three R's. (Cohen & Randolph, 1977)

These ideas became the backbone of kindergarten practice. Moreover, Hill did not work for kindergarten alone. In fact, during the 1920s, Hill rekindled Froebel's early ideas to promote nursery schools for children too young to attend kindergarten. Regardless of controversy within, kindergartens were still on the fringes of the educational establishments as a whole. In fact, Hill (1941) herself commented that "adjustment to public-school conditions came slowly . . . [and] until this happy adjustment took place, the promotion of the self-active kindergarten children into the grades has made it possible for the poorest and most formal first-grade teacher to criticize and condemn the work of the best kindergarten teacher as well as the kindergarten cause, because of the wide gap that existed between kindergarten and primary ideals at that time."

As Hill and others prevailed and made continual improvements in teaching methods, materials, guidance, and curriculum, the interests of kindergarten and primary education could be seen as more unified.

Nursery Schools

The very phrase "nursery school" conjures up images of a child's nursery, of a carefully tended garden, and of a gentle place of play and growing. In fact, the name was coined to describe a place where children were nurtured (see the section later in this chapter on the McMillan sisters). Nursery schools have always been a place of care, for the physical needs, the intellectual stimulation, and the socio-emotional aspects of young children's lives.

Establishment in America

Early childhood educators took Dewey's philosophy to heart. Their schools reflected the principles of a child-centered approach, active learning, and social cooperation. By the 1920s and 1930s, early childhood education had reached a professional status in the United States. Nursery schools and day nurseries went beyond custodial health care. They fostered the child's total development. The children were enrolled from middle- and upper-class homes, as well as from working families. However, until the 1960s, nursery schools served few poor families.

Parent education was acknowledged as a vital function of the school and led to the establishment of parent cooperative schools. Brook Farm, a utopian cooperative community in the 1840s, had "the equivalent of an on-site child care center 'for the use of parents doing industrial work' or for mothers to use 'as a kindly relief to themselves when fatigued by the care of children'" (Hewes, 1993). The first of these parent participation schools was developed in 1915 at the University of Chicago, where a group of faculty wives started the Chicago Cooperative Nursery

Traditional nursery and kindergarten included circle time.

Golden Gate Kindergarten Association

School. Research centers and child development laboratories were started in many colleges and universities from about 1915 to 1930. These laboratory schools were active in expanding knowledge of the importance of a child's early years. As Stolz (1978) describes it, "the [preschool] movement from the beginning was integrated with the movement for child development research. The purpose . . . was to improve nursery schools, and, therefore, we brought in the people who were studying children, who were learning more about them, so we could do a better job." It is noteworthy that professionals such as Hill, Stolz, Dowley, and others encouraged researchers to share their findings with classroom teachers to integrate these discoveries into the daily programs of children.

These schools followed one of two basic models. One model, patterned after the first psychological laboratory in Leipzig, Germany, in 1879, was formed to train psychologists in the systematic training of child study. This model adopted a scientific approach to the study of human beings, as the field of psychology itself attempted to become more like the biologic sciences. The second approach, like the Butler School of Hampton Institute and later Spelman College, was established primarily for training teachers. The latter model took its influence almost exclusively from educational leaders. The nursery school laboratory schools attempted a multidisciplinary approach, blending the voices from psychology and education with those of home economics, nursing, social work, and medicine. By 1950, when Katherine Read Baker first published *The Nursery School: A Human Relationships Laboratory* (now in seven languages), the emphasis of the nursery school was on understanding human behavior and then building programs, guidance techniques, and relationships accordingly. In her estimate,

> . . . the nursery school is a place where young children learn as they play and as they share experiences with other children. . . . It is also a place where adults learn about child development and human relationships as they observe and participate in the program of the school. . . . Anyone working in an educational program for children, even the most experienced person, needs to be learning as well as teaching. The two processes, learning and teaching, are inseparable.

Lucy Sprague Mitchell

Early childhood education in the United States grew out of John Dewey's progressive movement largely because of Lucy Sprague Mitchell (1878–1967) and her contemporaries. Raised in an environment of educational and social reform, Mitchell developed the idea of

schools as community centers, as well as places for children to learn to think. As Greenberg (1987) explained, Mitchell gathered together, in a democratic, cooperative venture, many talented people to brainstorm, mastermind, and sponsor:

- A remarkable Bureau of Educational Experiments
- A school to implement and experiment with these principles
- A laboratory to record and analyze how and why they function as she knew they did (and as we know they do!)
- A teachers' college to promote them
- A workshop for writers of children's literature (a new genre—a number of currently famous authors of juvenile books attended)
- A bulletin to disseminate it all, as well as to disseminate what a plethora of progressive educators were up to elsewhere, *beginning* in 1916!

Strongly influenced by John Dewey, she became a major contributor to the idea of "educational experiments," that is, trying to plan with teachers the curriculum experiences that would then be observed and analyzed "for children's reactions to the various learning situations [and] the new teaching techniques" (Mitchell, 1951). For instance, Mitchell suggested that teachers expand on what they knew of children's "here-and-now" thinking by making

> . . . trips with kindergarteners to see how work was done—work that was closely tied up with their personal lives . . . the growth in thinking and attitudes of the teachers had moved far . . . toward the conception of their role as a guide as differentiated from a dispenser of information.

By establishing Bank Street College of Education (and its laboratory school), Lucy Sprague Mitchell emphasized the link between theory and practice—namely, that the education of young children and the study of how children learn are intrinsically tied together.

Abigail Eliot

The nursery school movement was pioneered by Eliot (1892–1992). A graduate of Radcliffe College and Harvard University, Eliot had worked with the McMillan sisters (see section in this chapter) in the slums of London. A social worker by training, she became interested in children and their relationships with their parents. Eliot had a lively and clear view of what good schools for children could be. She is generally credited with bringing the nursery school movement to the United States. She founded the Ruggles Street Nursery

School in the Roxbury section of Boston, teaching children and providing teacher training, and served as its director from 1922 to 1952, when it was incorporated into Tufts University. Today, it is known as the Eliot-Pearson Department of Child Study.

Eliot became the first woman to receive a doctoral degree from Harvard University's Graduate School of Education and, after retiring from Tufts, moved to California where she helped establish Pacific Oaks College. In all her work, she integrated Froebel's gifts, Montessori's equipment, and the McMillans' fresh air, as well as her own ideas. As she put it (Hymes, 1978):

> . . . the new idea—was program. I had visited many day nurseries in Boston as a social worker. I can remember them even now: dull green walls, no light colors, nothing pretty—spotlessly clean places, with rows of white-faced listless little children sitting, doing nothing. In the new nursery school, the children were active, alive, choosing.

Mid-century Developments

Even as the economic crisis of the Depression and the political turmoil of World War II diverted attention from children's needs, both gave focus to adult needs for work. Out of this necessity came the Works Progress Administration (WPA) nurseries of the 1930s and the Lanham Act nurseries of the 1940s. The most renowned

Celebrating a birthday in a WPA (Works Progress Administration) nursery program, provided by the Lanham Act for women in the workforce during World War II.

Courtesy of WPA (Works Progress Administration)

program of the mid-century was the Kaiser Child Care Centers.

Kaiser Child Care Centers

During World War II, funds were provided to deal with the common situation of mothers working in war-related industries. Further support came from industry during World War II. An excellent model for child care operated from 1943 to 1945 in Portland, Oregon. It was the Kaiser Child Care Centers. Kaiser became the world's largest such center and functioned "'round the clock" all year long. A number of services were made available on-site. An infirmary was located nearby for both mothers and children. Hot meals were made available for mothers to take home when they picked up their children. Lois Meek Stolz was the director of the centers, and James L. Hymes, Jr. was the manager. He describes the centers this way:

> . . . The centers were to have three distinctive qualities. One, they were to be located not out in the community but right at the entrance to the two shipyards, convenient to mothers on their way to and from work. They were to be industry-based, not neighborhood-centered. Two, the centers were to be operated by the shipyards, not by the public schools and not by community agencies. They were to be industrial child care centers, with the cost borne by the Kaiser Company and by parents using the service. Three, they were to be large centers, big enough to meet the need. In the original plan, each center was to serve a thousand preschool children on three shifts. (Hymes, 1978)

These centers served 3,811 children. As Hymes points out, they provided 249,268 child care days and freed 1,931,827 woman work-hours.

Once the war had ended, though, the workers left. Child care was no longer needed, and the centers closed. The Kaiser experience has never been equaled, either in the universal quality of care or in the variety of services. However, it left us a legacy, which Hymes has stressed ever since (in Dickerson, 1992): "It is no great trick to have an excellent child care program. It only requires a lot of money with most of it spent on *trained* staff."

The model Kaiser Child Care Centers provided for child care remains exemplary.

Civil Rights

As early as the beginning of the 20th century, the United States Supreme Court upheld laws concerning "the core of the Jim Crow system, the public schools in which white and black children first experienced the reality of

Genevieve Naylor/CORBIS

Kaiser Shipyard operated a model child care center during World War II.

segregation . . . Jim Crow schools—which taught their students only those skills needed for agricultural work and domestic service—fit the needs of the whole economy and society" (Irons, 2004). The term itself comes from a character in a late 1880s minstrel show and refers to the complete system of segregation.

World War I played an important role in moving large numbers of blacks from the rural South to the cities of the North and West, beginning what has been called the Great Migration. By 1930, the reported literacy rate for blacks had doubled from 1900 to just more than 80 percent, but "the educational status of blacks in the Jim Crow states remained abysmally low in 1950" (Irons, 2004). The Depression was a particularly difficult time for African Americans, as the living standards for those Americans in poverty plummeted. President Franklin Roosevelt's administration and the emerging industrial union movement gave impetus to blacks looking for both employment and political change. World War II continued the process of transformation for many adults, but for children, the situation was still bleak.

The stage for another legal challenge to segregation was set. As Weinberg (1977) states, "Midcentury marked a turning point in the history of black America. The movement for equality came under black leadership, embraced unprecedented numbers of Negroes, and became national in scope. A persistent black initiative forced a reformulation of public policies in education." Children were starting to be considered citizens with rights.

The attack against the segregation system had begun. As seen in the historic cases of *McLaurin v Oklahoma* (1950) and *Brown v Board of Education of Topeka* (1954) the concept of "separate but equal" was overturned. Furthermore, the Civil Rights Act of 1964 continued to address the struggle for equality of opportunity and education, one that persists today in our schools and society (see "Ethic of Social Reform" later in this Chapter).

The Free School

A. S. Neill (1883–1973) was the most famous proponent of the "free/natural school" movement of the mid-century. His book *Summerhill* describes 40 years of that educational program, of which he was headmaster. Neill claimed that most education was defective because it arose from the model of original sin. Assuming children were inherently evil caused educators to force children into doing what was contrary to their nature. Neill shared Rousseau's belief in noninterference, as he states, "I believe that a child is innately wise and realistic. If left to himself without adult suggestion of any kind, he will develop as far as he is capable of developing" (1960).

Neill's belief in freedom was practiced in his school, where children governed themselves and worked toward equal rights with adults. The benefits from such liberties were touted as highly therapeutic and natural, an escape from repression and guilt. Several influences are clear in these educational programs: Rousseau's belief in the *child's innate goodness*, Freud's idea of the *dangerous effects of guilt*, and some of the *social idealism* of Dewey and the Progressives.

Sputnik and the War on Poverty: Head Start

After World War II, few innovations took place until a small piece of metal made its worldwide debut. Sputnik, the Soviet satellite, was successfully launched in 1957 and caused an upheaval in educational circles. Two questions were uppermost in the minds of most Americans: Why were we not first in space? What is wrong with our schools? The emphasis in education quickly settled on engineering, science, and math in the hope of catching up with Soviet technology.

The Civil Rights struggle in the early 1960s soon followed. In pointing out the plight of the poor, education was highlighted as a major stumbling block toward equality of all people. It was time to act, to declare a "war on poverty" that robbed America of its pre-eminent position in the world.

Project Head Start was conceived as education's place to fight the "war on poverty." The same goals of Froebel and Montessori formed the basis of Head Start: helping disadvantaged preschool children. This was a revolution in American education, not seen since the short-lived child care programs during World War II. This project was the first large-scale effort by the government to focus on children of poverty.

Head Start began in 1965 as a demonstration program aimed at providing educational, social, medical, dental, nutritional, and mental health services to preschool children from a diverse population of low-income families. In 1972, it was transformed into a predominantly part-day, full-year program. Key features included offering health services, small groups, parent-teacher collaboration, and the thrill of communities getting involved with children in new ways. Osborn (1965) tells us:

> I wish I knew how to tell this part of the story . . . the bus driver in West Virginia who took time off from his regular job and went to the Center to have juice and crackers with "his" children because they asked him to. . . . The farmer who lived near an Indian Reservation and who each morning saddled his horse, forded a river and picked up an Indian child—who would not have attended a Center otherwise . . . they represent the true flavor of Head Start.

Over the years, Head Start has provided comprehensive developmental services to more than 10 million children and their families.

This was an exciting time, a national recognition of the needs of young children and a hope for a better quality of life. Head Start was an attempt to make amends, to compensate poor children by preparing them for school and educational experiences. Parents, who were required to participate at all levels, were educated along with their children. The purpose of the community-based governing boards was to allow the program to reflect local values and concerns. Concurrently, underprivileged, poor people were being encouraged to take part in solving some of their own problems.

The spirit of Head Start was infectious. As a result of community interest in Head Start, there was a burst of enthusiasm for many programs for the young child. Thanks to Head Start, there is national attention to the need for providing good care and educational experiences for young children. The Head Start program is recognized as an effective means of providing comprehensive services to children and families, serving as a model for the development of the ABC Child Care Act. (The program is discussed in Chapter 2.)

Infant-Toddler Care

Some people say we are in the midst of a second child care revolution for young children, as two parents, single parents, and step-parents all leave the home to work in greater numbers than ever before. Parents must rely on educators to teach their children from a very young age, including infants. While many European industrialized nations have addressed these issues, the United States has not completely faced this reality or risen to the challenge.

The roots of infant-toddler care stem from the women's movement of the 1920s, which brought attention to deeply held beliefs about child-rearing and early education practices. When America was mobilized around World War II, children's care was addressed so as to enable mothers to work while fathers were in the armed forces. With the advent of 1960s, women once again soared into the workplace, and both parents once again focused on work outside the home. Care for children by extended family, family child care homes, and centers is on the rise.

The American public is unclear about what is the best way to raise our very young children, especially those younger than age 2. Women, by and large, are working outside of the home and are not available around the clock to care for infants and toddlers; men are not, by and large, electing to stay home or raise their children full time. There are not nearly enough properly funded centers or family child care homes for very small children, and the patchwork system of parents, extended family, and neighborhood adults fragments the care. As we learn more about the critical time period of 0–2 years of age for brain development, we need to look carefully at quality child care for infants and toddlers.

More Recent Developments

In the late 20th and into this century, three practices are serving as turning points for contemporary early education.

● **DAP.** Developmentally Appropriate Practices (DAP, 1997, 2003, 2007) articulated early education's

National Archives

Head Start is the largest publicly funded education program for young children in the United States.

principles of standard teaching practices that enhanced the growth of the whole child and included age, family, and individual elements. Look for the DAP box in each chapter.

- **NCLB.** The No Child Left Behind Act (NCLB, 2001) reauthorized the Elementary and Secondary Education Act, calling for extensive implementation of state educational standards. Chapter 15 discusses educational reform.
- **Common Core Standards.** Common Core State Standards (CCS, 2010) call for new standards in English language arts and mathematics for grades K-12. These may be as significant as *Brown v Board of Education* in changing the direction of education for years to come (Weber, 2011). Learn more about these standards in the curriculum in Chapter 10 and 15.

Interdisciplinary Influences

Several professions enrich the heritage of early childhood. This diversity was apparent from the beginning as the first nursery schools drew from six different professions: social work, home economics, nursing, psychology, education, and medicine. Three of the most consistent and influential of those disciplines were medicine, education, and child psychology.

Medicine

The medical field has contributed to the study of child growth through the work of several physicians. These doctors became interested in child development and extended their knowledge to the areas of child rearing and education.

Maria Montessori

Maria Montessori (1870–1952) was the first woman in Italy ever granted a medical degree. She began studying children's diseases and, through her work with mentally defective children, found education more appealing. Her philosophy is discussed earlier in this chapter and is part of the Chapter 10 curriculum models.

Sigmund Freud

Sigmund Freud (1856–1939) made important contributions to all modern thinking. The father of personality theory, he drastically changed how we look at childhood. Freud reinforced two specific ideas: 1) a person is influenced by his early life in fundamental and dramatic ways, and 2) early experiences shape the way people live and behave as adults. Thus psychoanalytic theory is mostly about personality development and emotional problems. Freud's work set into motion one of the three major strands of psychological theory that influence the developmental and learning theories of early childhood today. Though he was not involved directly in education, Freud and psychoanalytic theory influenced education greatly. Chapter 4 expands on the theory and its application in early childhood education.

Arnold Gesell

Arnold Gesell (1880–1961) was a physician who was concerned with growth from a medical point of view. Gesell began studying child development when he was a student of G. Stanley Hall, an early advocate of child study. He later established the Clinic of Child Development at Yale University, where the data he collected with his colleagues became the basis of the recognized norms of how children grow and develop. He was also instrumental in encouraging Abigail Eliot to study with the McMillan sisters in England.

Gesell's greatest contribution was in the area of child growth. He saw maturation as an innate and powerful force in development. "The total plan of growth," he said, "is beyond your control. It is too complex and mysterious to be altogether entrusted to human hands. So nature takes over most of the task, and simply invites your assistance" (Gesell, Ames, & Ilg, 1977).

Through the Gesell Institute, guides were published using this theory. With such experts as Dr. Frances Ilg and Dr. Louise Bates Ames, Gesell wrote articles that realistically portrayed the child's growth from birth to adolescence. These guides have sharp critics regarding their overuse and inappropriate application to children of cultures other than those studied. Moreover, their approach can be limiting, particularly as we think of developmentally appropriate practices and the importance of both individual variation and family and cultural diversity (Copple & Bredekamp, 2010). Chapter 3 uses Gesell's "ages and stages" material to develop the word pictures used widely as a yardstick of normal development, and Gesell's maturation theory is discussed in Chapter 4.

Benjamin Spock

Benjamin Spock's book *Baby and Child Care* was a mainstay for parents in the 1940s and 1950s. In a detailed "how-to" format, Dr. Spock (1903–1998) preached a common-sense approach that helped shape the childhood of many of today's adults. By his death in 1998, the book had sold almost 50 million copies around the world and had been translated into 42 languages.

Medical doctors such as Benjamin Spock have contributed to early care and education in significant ways.

Spock saw himself as giving practical application to the theories of John Dewey (see this chapter) and Sigmund Freud (see this chapter and chapter 4), particularly in the ideas that children can learn to direct themselves, rather than needing to be constantly disciplined.

Spock suggested that mothers use the playpen less and allow children freedom to explore the world first-hand. To that end, he asked parents to "child proof" their homes—a radical thought at the time. The word *permissiveness*, as it relates to child-rearing, became associated with Dr. Spock's methods, although Spock himself described his advice as relaxed and sensible, while still advocating for firm parental leadership.

Dr. Spock became an outspoken advocate for causes that extended his ideas. He was an active critic of those forces—economic, social, or political—that destroy healthy development. Dr. Spock noted:

> Child care and home care, if well done, can be more creative, make a greater contribution to the world, [and] bring more pleasure to family members, than 9 out of 10 outside jobs. It is only our mixed-up, materialistic values that make so many of us think the other way around (1976).

T. Berry Brazelton

Dr. T. Berry Brazelton (1918–) is a well-known pediatrician who supports and understands the development of infants and toddlers. He developed an evaluation tool called the Neonatal Behavioral Assessment Scale (the NBAS is also known as "the Brazelton") to assess newborns. Co-founder of the Children's Hospital Unit in Boston, professor emeritus of pediatrics at Harvard Medical School, and a former president of the Society for

Research in Child Development, he is also a well-known author. His pediatric guides for parents deal with both physical and emotional growth. His writings speak to the parents' role in child-raising, such as setting limits, listening to what children say, and observing what they do, as in the following discussion:

> I think many working parents have a very tough time thinking about limits. They find it difficult to say no, to set behavior standards. . . . Parents tell me, "I can't stand to be away all day and then come home and be the disciplinarian." We have to realize how hard it is for parents to discipline these days. They need a lot of reinforcement to understand how important reasonable discipline is to the child. Teachers can be very important here, helping parents see the need to expect more adequate behavior (2001).

Brazelton advocates a national parental leave standard and is involved in a federal lobbying group known as "Parent Action." He hosted the nationally syndicated show *What Every Baby Knows*; is co-founder of *Touchpoints*, an educational training center focusing on teacher/parent communication about early development; and writes about key areas of need for children to develop well (Brazelton & Greenspan, 2001).

Education

Early childhood is one part of the larger professional field known as education. This includes elementary, secondary, and college or postsecondary schools. Along with Rudolf Steiner, John Dewey, and Abigail Eliot, several other influences from this field bear attention.

The McMillan Sisters

In the first three decades of this century, these two sisters pioneered in early education. Nursery schools in Britain and America probably were developed because of the drive and dedication of the McMillan sisters.

Both women had broad international backgrounds. They grew up in North America and Scotland. Margaret studied music and language in Europe. She was well read in philosophy, politics, and medicine. Rachel studied to become a health inspector in England.

Health studies of 1908 to 1910 showed that 80 percent of children were born in good health, but by the time they entered school, only 20 percent could be classified that way. Noticing the deplorable conditions for children younger than age 5, the McMillan sisters began a crusade for the slum children in England.

Queen Mary (left) with some of the children from the nursery school attached to the Rachel McMillan Training College in Deptford (1930).

Their concern extended beyond education to medical and dental care for young children. In 1910, they set up a clinic in Deptford, a London slum area, which became an open-air nursery a year later. The McMillans called it a "nurture school." Later, a training college nearby was named for Rachel. With no private financial resources, these two women faced tremendous hardships in keeping their school open. It is to their credit that Deptford still exists today.

The McMillans' theory of fresh air, sleep, and bathing proved successful. "When over seven hundred children between one and five died of measles, there was not one fatal case at Deptford School" (Deasey, 1978). From the school's inception, a primary function was to research the effects of poverty on children.

Of the two sisters, Margaret had the greatest influence at the school at Deptford. After Rachel died in 1917, Margaret continued to champion early education issues beyond Deptford. "Her clinics, night camps, camp school, baby camp, open-air nursery school, and training college all reflected her conviction that health was the handmaiden of education" (Bradburn, 2000). Abigail Eliot writes of her:

> Miss McMillan invented the name [nursery school]. She paid great attention to health: a daily inspection, the outdoor program, play, good food—what she called "nurture." But she saw that an educational problem was also involved and she set to work to establish her own method of education for young children. This was why she called it a "school" (Hymes, 1978).

Susan Isaacs

Susan Isaacs (1885–1948) was an educator of the early 20th century whose influence on nursery and progressive schools of the day was substantial. In 1929, she published *The Nursery Years*, which emphasized a different point of view than that of the behaviorist psychologists of the times. She interpreted Freudian theory for teachers and provided guidance for how schools could apply this new knowledge of the unconscious to the education of children. She proposed:

> . . . the opportunity for free unhindered imaginative play not only as a means to discover the world but also as a way to reach the psychic equilibrium, in working through wishes, fears, and fantasies so as to integrate them into a living personality (Biber, 1984).

The teacher's role was different from that of a therapist, she asserted, in that teachers were to encourage play as a bridge in a child's emotional and intellectual development.

Isaacs's influence is felt today in schools whose philosophy emphasizes the child's point of view and the notion of play as the child's work.

The Child Study Movement

A survey of education influences is incomplete without mentioning the Child Study Movement in the United States beginning in the 1920s. It was through this movement that education and psychology began to have a common focus on children. Besides the Gesell Institute, many research centers and child development laboratories were established at colleges and universities around the country. The Merrill-Palmer Institute, for example, began in 1920 as a school to serve Detroit, Michigan's, urban children and later served as a model for the Head Start Program; in addition, it sponsored research and training about children and families. Schools of psychology looked for children to observe and study; schools of education wanted demonstration schools for their teachers-in-training and for student-teacher placement. Schools of home economics wanted their students to have firsthand experiences with children. Schools of education hoped to develop leadership from among its teaching and research staff. These on-campus schools provided a place to gather information about child development, psychology, and educational innovation (Harms & Tracy, 2006).

This period of educational experiments and child study led to an impressive collection of normative data by which we still measure ranges of ordinary development. The Child Study Movement was the impetus that began the search for the most appropriate means of educating young children. Laboratory schools reflect the interest of several disciplines in the growth of the young child.

On campus schools have a legacy from the Child Study Movement of early- to mid-20th century where students can learn in a laboratory setting.

The British Infant Schools

Developed by Robert Owen in the early 19th century, the British infant schools had a strong commitment to social reform. Owen was a self-made businessman whose philosophy extended to the creation of an ideal community. Like Rousseau, he believed that people were naturally good but were corrupted by harsh environment and poor treatment. He took his ideas to the British House of Commons, speaking against the common practice of child labor. He then was invited to take over the building of a school in New Lanark, a 2,000-person community near several textile mills. Once there, he stopped employment of children younger than 10 years, sent younger children to nursery and infant schools he built, and required the mills to allow secondary-age children to reduce their labor time to go to school. His son and a daughter immigrated to the United States and founded the community of New Harmony. Both utopian communities were built on Owen's ideas of a new social order built on experimentation and reform.

In England, the term *infant school* refers to the kindergarten and primary grades. In 1967, the Plowden Report proposed a series of reforms for the schools. These changes paralleled those of Owen and mainstream American early education. Three aspects of this open school style that received the most attention were:

1. *Vertical (or mixed age) groupings.* Children from 5 to 8 years of age are placed in the same classroom. Several teachers may combine their classes and work together in teaching teams. Children may be taught by the same teachers for two or three years.

2. *Integrated day.* The classroom is organized into various centers for math, science, and the arts. The teacher moves from one child or center to another as needed. Play is often the central activity, with an emphasis on follow-through with children's ideas and interests as they arise.

3. *Thinking over facts.* There is an underlying concept that the process of thinking takes precedence over the accumulation of facts. Learning how to think rather than stockpiling data is encouraged. How to identify and solve problems is valued more than having a finished product. Teachers focus on the child's current learning rather than on the future.

The Infant School model of mixed age range is used widely in early learning centers and school-age programs in the United States, while elementary schools still hold primarily to the one-year/one-grade model.

Reggio Emilia

In the last part of the 20th century into the present time, another educator and educational system have influenced early childhood thinking. Loris Malaguzzi (1920–1994) developed his theory of early childhood education from his work with infants, toddlers, and preschoolers while working as the founder and Director of Early Education in the town of Reggio Emilia, Italy. His philosophy includes creating "an amiable school" (Malaguzzi, 1993) that welcomes families and the community and invites relationships among teachers, children, and parents to intensify and deepen to strengthen a child's sense of identity. Malaguzzi continually asked teachers to question their own practices and listen to the children, as we can hear in his letter (Gandini, 1994) excerpted below:

> My thesis is that if we do not learn to listen to children, it will be difficult to learn the art of staying and conversing with them. . . . It will also be difficult, perhaps impossible, to understand how and why children think and speak; to understand what they do, ask, plan, theorize or desire. . . . Furthermore, what are the consequences of not listening? . . . We adults lose the capacity to marvel, to be surprised, to reflect, to be merry, and to take pleasure in children's words and actions.

Reggio Emilia has attracted the attention and interest of American educators because of its respect for children's work and creativity, its project approach, and its total community support. Its focus on child self-expression and the emergent curriculum model are discussed in Chapter 10.

Psychology

The roots of early childhood education are wonderfully diverse, but one taproot is especially deep: the connection with the field of psychology. In this century particularly, the study of people and their behavior is linked with the study of children and their growth.

Initially, child development was mostly confined to the study of trends and descriptions of changes. Then, the scope and definition of child development began to change. Psychodynamic theories of Freud and Erikson were contrasted by behaviorist theories of Watson and Skinner and by the cognitive theories of Piaget and Vygotsky. Bowlby and Ainsworth studied attachment, Kohlberg and Eisenberg moral development, and Maccoby and Gilligan gender differences.

Developmental psychologists now study the processes associated with those changes. Specifically, child development focuses on language acquisition, the effect of early experiences on intellectual development, and the process of attachment to others, and how neuroscience discoveries reveal developmental processes. Such is the world of early childhood—it is no wonder that we are so closely tied to the world of psychology, as discussed in depth in Chapter 4.

Themes in Early Childhood Education

When we review the colorful and rich history of early childhood education, four major themes emerge. Each is reflected in the many influences on early childhood education.

Ethic of Social Reform

The first theme, the ethic of social reform, expects that schooling for young children leads to social change and improvement. Maria Montessori, Robert Owen, the McMillans, Patty Smith Hill, Abigail Eliot, and the Head Start program all tried to improve children's health and physical well-being by attending first to the physical and social welfare aspects of children's lives. Other more recent examples, including Marian Wright Edelman, Louise Derman Sparks, Robert Coles, and Jonathan Kozol, illustrate how important this theme is to our work.

Marian Wright Edelman is an outstanding children's advocate. A graduate of Spelman College and Yale Law School, Edelman began her career as a civil rights lawyer. (She was the first black woman to be admitted to the Mississippi state bar.) By the 1960s she had dedicated herself to the battle against poverty, moving to Washington, D.C., and founding a public interest law firm that eventually became the Children's Defense Fund (CDF). CDF has become the United States' strongest voice for children and families (see Figure 4-6).

The author of several books, including *Families in Peril*, *The Measure of Our Success*, and *The Sea Is So Wide and My Boat Is So Small*, Edelman advocates for equity in social reform:

> [We] seek to ensure that no child is left behind and that every child has a Healthy Start, a Head Start, a Fair Start, a Safe Start, and a Moral Start in life with the support of caring families and communities (Edelman, 2006).

CDF: Child Advocacy as Social Reform

1975	Assisted in passing the Education for All Handicapped Children Act
1979	Blocked attempts to eliminate $200 million for Social Services
1980	Supported Adoption Assistance & Child Welfare Act
1982	Helped forward the Children's Mental Health Program
1990	Supported Act for Better Child Care (Child Care & Development Block Grant)
1994	Reauthorized Head Start with Quality Improvements
1997	Promoted Children's Health Insurance Program (CHIP)
2001	Expanded Child Care Tax Credit
2002	Food Stamp provisions preserved
2003	Preserved CHIP funding to all states
2007	Evaluation of the CDF freedom schools, summer enrichment programs, find that children score higher on standardized reading achievement tests.
2008	Published its annual State of America's Children, reporting that it lags behind nearly all industrialized nations in key child indicators.
2010	Established its online research library, using data from a wide range of sources, primarily federal data systems such as the Bureaus of the Census and of Labor Statistics, and from nonprofit and educational entities such as the Kaiser Family Foundations and National Association of Child Care Resource and Referral Agencies.

© Cengage Learning 2014

FIGURE 4-6 Children's Defense Fund, led by Marian Wright Edelman, has successfully advocated for children with research and persistence for more than three decades.

What Is Neuroscience and Why Should We Care?

When the field of psychology began to develop in the 1800s, new questions began to surface about the brain and the mind. Freud's ideas about the subconscious mind, Piaget's concepts of the thinking mind, and behaviorists' work on changing thoughts and attitudes via shaping behavior all led to the emergence of cognitive science in the late 1980s. A landmark report by the National Academy of Sciences entitled *From Neurons to Neighborhoods: The Science of Early Childhood Development* (Shonkoff & Phillips, 2000) joined early childhood education with neuroscience. Since then, the development and availability of brain-imaging techniques provide glimpses of brain activity as an individual thinks and feels.

We are now in what might be called the "century of the brain." If the human brain is like the hardware of a computer, the mind may be seen as the software. Further, this software changes as it is used; people assign different meaning to the inputs and outputs of things. Brain structures can now be mapped on a matrix. The work of cognitive neuropsychologists allows us to link specific regions of the brain with specific cognitive processes such as verbal and memory skills, attention, emotional responding, and motor coordination. Experimental techniques used on animals (that could not be ethically used with humans) have revealed the brain regions that connect with psychological processes. Combining computed tomography (CT) and magnetic resonance imaging (MRI) developed during the late 20th century with the more recent functional magnetic resonance imaging (fMRI) and positron emission topography (PET) allows us to determine the location of tumors or lesions as well as study the genetic basis of differences (Byrnes, 2001).

The new frontier of neuroscience is showing us the remarkable plasticity of the brain, as well as the critical nature of the early years. "Early experiences determine whether a child's developing brain architecture provides a strong or weak foundation for all future learning, behavior and health" (CDC/Harvard, 2007). Neuroscience, hand-in-hand with child development research, can address questions about why you—and society—must invest in young children.

Questions
1. If this is the "century of the brain," what do you think will change in educational practices?
2. What do you think parents should know about brain development in the first five years of a child's life?
3. What would "investing in young children" look like in your community? In your state?

This reform work is being carried on by her son, Jonah, who now organizes the annual Washington, D.C., rally "Stand for Children."

Louise, in collaboration with Betty Jones and the Anti-Bias Task Force of Pacific Oaks and Julia Olsen Edwards of Cabrillo College, has published several books and countless articles about anti-bias education. These works outline several areas in which children's behavior is influenced by biases in our society and suggests a host of ways that teachers (and parents) can begin addressing these issues. These professionals have added an important dimension to the notion of social reform, for they focus attention on ourselves, the school environment, children's interactions, and the community of parents and colleagues in educational settings.

Finally, social reform in contemporary times has been championed by educators and citizens beyond early childhood education. Robert Coles, a psychiatrist and educator, has written and lectured extensively about his observations and work with children of poverty and is best known for *Children of Crisis: A Study of Courage and Fear* (1971). Jonathan Kozol has spoken extensively about segregation in the schools, most notably in his books *Letters to a Young Teacher* (2007) and *Savage Inequalities: Children in America's Schools* (1991), in which he writes:

> Surely there is enough for everyone in this country. It is a tragedy that these good things are not more widely shared. All our children ought to be allowed a stake in the enormous richness of America. Whether they were born to poor white Appalachians or to wealthy Texans, to poor black people in the Bronx or to rich people in Manhasset or Winnetka, they are all quite wonderful and innocent when they are small. We soil them needlessly.

A challenge of our profession is to create funding mechanisms to provide early educational experience for *all* children regardless of family income. Founded in 1948, the Annie E. Casey Foundation, one of the largest private foundations in the United States, is based on helping vulnerable kids and families succeed. Educators today still assert that tired, undernourished children are not ready to learn or to be educated. Social reform can go further as described in Chapter 15.

Importance of Childhood

The second theme is the importance and uniqueness of childhood. In fact, the entire concept of the child as a special part of human existence and, therefore, a valuable part of the life cycle rests on this theme.

The saying "As the twig is bent, so grows the tree" could apply to all children and their early childhood learning experiences, as well as to an individual child. When people accepted the importance of childhood, they began to take responsibility for a quality life for children. From Comenius, Rousseau, and Froebel of earlier centuries to Neill, Russell, and the Child Study Movement of the 1900s, society began to provide for the health and physical welfare of children and come to understand the necessity to care for their minds. Reflecting on public thinking about childhood over the past four centuries reveals these patterns (Mintz, 2004):

- Premodern childhood (through 17th century)—children as adults in training
- Modern childhood (18th–20th centuries)—children as innocent and fragile creatures

Childhood is a special time of life.

© Cengage Learning

- Postmodern childhood (late 20th to 21st centuries)—children as participants/consumers of culture and the common life

We believe the early years form the foundation for later development, physically, intellectually, socially, and emotionally. This viewpoint takes a holistic approach; that is, all developmental areas of a child matter and blend together to form a complete child. Even as we teachers outline the separate developmental domains, we must take into account the whole child, for each part influences the whole. Current trends that support this theme are developmentally appropriate practices (DAP) and the contexts of culture and family that we are becoming familiar with in our global community (see Diversity feature in every chapter). Children come to us with a genetic history and from families that identify with a range of racial, ethnic, cultural, language, and socioeconomic groups.

Moreover, early childhood educators believe that play is essential to children's development. Of increasing concern to childhood advocates is the pushing of children toward adulthood too fast and away from childhood too quickly. Spurred by the advent of technology and social media and the rush to academic content, young children are pushed unnecessarily out of a relaxed childhood by a fast-paced society whose pressure to succeed puts children of all ages at risk. The classic comments of Dr. David Elkind (1982) ring true today:

> We should appreciate the value of childhood with its special joys, sorrows, worries, and concerns. Valuing childhood does not mean seeing it as a happy, innocent period but rather as an important period of life to which children are entitled. They have a right to be children, to enjoy the pleasures and to suffer the trials of childhood that are infringed upon by hurrying. Childhood is the most basic human right of children.

Children need special attention during these years. Childhood is fundamentally different from adulthood; it needs to be understood and respected as such. Children's styles of learning, of letting the child "learn by doing" and "learn by discovery," are part of the essential respect for children and childhood. Public recognition of that need has created a wealth of programs for the young not dreamed of at any other time in history.

Transmitting Values

The third recurrent theme in our educational heritage is that of transmitting values. What children should ultimately *do* and *be* is at the core of all child-rearing practices, whether in the home or the school. Values—whether social, cultural, moral, or religious—have been the essence of education for centuries.

- Puritan fathers valued biblical theology, so schools of their time taught children to read the Bible.
- Rousseau and Froebel valued childhood, so they created special places for children to express their innate goodness and uniqueness.
- The works of Montessori, Dewey, and Steiner reflected a belief in the worth and dignity of childhood.
- Ed Ziegler of Head Start and Derman-Sparks of the Anti-Bias Curriculum realized that the child's self-worth would be enhanced by valuing one's culture or origin.

These educators all transmitted their values into the educational practices we have inherited.

Many issues clamor for our attention. Information overload threatens to drive us to distraction and inertia. "People are so overwhelmed," wrote Brazelton and Greenspan (2001). "While they're whirling around, they don't have time to stop and think, 'What are my values? Do my children really come first? Am I making time for them in my life?'" Many young families today are aware of this situation and are looking for spiritual and moral direction for themselves and their children.

Children learn what they live. Valuing and connecting home cultural knowledge with an early childhood program is challenging. Successful teaching practices must reflect teaching practices at home in substantial ways; blending basic life skills, ethics, culture, and traditions builds substance in our children and in our society. This teamwork is possible if (and this is a big *if*) adults can find a way to honor diversity and still form a cohesive culture. "An ability to reach unity in diversity will be the beauty and test of our civilization," said Mahatma Gandhi. It is our ethical responsibility to articulate our values as educators and to include those of the families we teach.

Teaching children to live in a democratic society has always been valued in the United States. In the curriculum from early education through college, this belief is reflected as we educate our children for citizenship. Being an early childhood educator provides you with the opportunity to be an agent for social change—to actually translate the values of democracy into practice. Successful teaching practices include the process of defining our values and working on how we teach them; both are the critical issues in education.

Professionalism

The fourth recurrent theme is professionalism. "If you are thinking about working with young children as a career, perhaps you are wondering how early childhood education compares in prestige and importance with elementary or secondary education," wrote Stanford's Edith Dowley (1985). As one of the original Head Teachers of the Kaiser Child Care Centers, Dowley had seen many changes in her nearly half-century in the field: "Is it truly a profession for growth and change? Can a student preparing to work with young children today look forward to a challenging, intellectually stimulating, and rewarding future in an early childhood profession?"

If you have read this chapter, then you already know the answer. The early years are a special time of life, and those who work with young children can openly declare their calling. There are four aspects of this sense of professionalism:

- *Sense of identity.* Early childhood professionals see themselves as caregivers who strive to educate the

Early educational experiences transmit society's values to children.

TeachSource Video

Watch the TeachSource Video entitled "Teaching as a Profession: An Early Childhood Teacher's Responsibilities and Development." After you study the video clip, view the artifacts, and read the teacher interviews and text, reflect on the following questions:

1. How does preschool teacher Samantha Brade show her sense of the importance of early childhood education, and what values is she trying to transmit?

2. How does Samantha demonstrate professionalism, and why should this inform one's teaching?

whole child, taking into consideration the body, the mind, and the heart and soul (see Chapter 3).

- *Purpose to engage in developmentally appropriate practices* (DAP). What constitutes quality care and education calls for blending three knowledge bases:

  1. Child development and learning.
  2. The strengths, interests, and needs of each child.
  3. The social and cultural contexts in which children live.

  (See the DAP Box in each chapter.)

- *Commitment to ethical teaching and to child advocacy.* Being a professional means behaving with a child's best interests in mind, keeping confidentiality when discussing issues in the classroom and about families, upholding a code of ethics, and taking one's self and work seriously. (See Chapter 5 and connections to the Code of Ethical Conduct in all chapters.)

- *Participation in the work as a legitimate livelihood.* Early childhood education is more than glorified babysitting; the people who provide care and education to young children deserve wages and working conditions that are worthy of their efforts. The

Center for the Study of Child Care Employment, led by Marcy Whitebook and others, is attempting to both define and highlight the issues of labor and employment of early childhood workers as a profession (see Chapter 15).

"In the last decade and a half, the boundaries of the profession have changed rather dramatically for teachers. As we have become a more complex and diverse society, the roles traditionally ascribed to teachers have taken new meaning and significance. In the case of teachers of young children, their role has expanded to encompass many, heretofore, duties and responsibilities that were often considered to be part of the home" (Cruz, 2008). The challenges we face in meeting our professional obligations are considerable. Cruz continues:

Aside from the traditional roles that teachers have assumed, they are now expected to serve as curriculum specialists, diagnosticians, health care providers, family counselors, adult educators, program managers, child development experts, child advocates, mental health specialists, nutrition specialists, and many others too numerous to list. At the same

---

DAP · Making Good Teaching a Professional Enterprise

As you look to making teaching your profession, you need to be familiar with developmentally appropriate practice (DAP). The foundation of good teaching for young children is based in engaging in practices, regardless of the setting, that are appropriate to the children in front of you. A blend of the familiar and the novel, with the challenges of meaningful and relevant experiences that are full of play and focus, helps all children grow and learn.

At the same time, making this a profession includes articulating what DAP is and ensuring that the public understands and endorses these priorities. The *Save Our Schools March* on Washington, D.C., on July 30, 2011, was an event that did just that. Luminaries such as Jonathan Kozol, Diane Ravitch, and Matt Damon spoke out on behalf of teachers. "Teachers are my heroes," stated Kozol. "I always feel safe in a group of teachers." Ravitch added, "We join together—parents, students, school leaders, teachers—to insist that the public schools are the public trust. . . . [E]ducation is a right, not a race. . . . Our goal is to prepare all children to be winners in their own lives."

To inspire is part of a teacher's commitment to DAP, as Damon's comments point out (www.washingtonpost.com [2011]):

I was raised by a teacher. My mother is a professor of early childhood education. And from the time I went to kindergarten through my senior year in high school, I went to public schools. I wouldn't trade that education and experience for anything.

I had incredible teachers. As I look at my life today, the things I value most about myself—my imagination, my love of acting, my passion for writing, my love of learning, my curiosity—all come from how I was parented and taught. . . .

But it's more than that. My teachers were EMPOWERED to teach me. Their time wasn't taken up with a bunch of test prep—this silly drill and kill nonsense that any serious person knows doesn't promote real learning. No, my teachers were free to approach me and every other kid in that classroom like an individual puzzle. They took so much care in figuring out who we were and how to best make the lessons resonate with each of us. They were empowered to unlock our potential. They were allowed to be teachers.

Making good teaching a professional enterprise asks you to speak out about what YOU know is good for children.

time, the teaching profession is confronting new notions of pedagogy and more intense scrutiny by professional groups. With the focus on standards, readiness initiatives, assessment, and other forms of accountability, the field of early education is truly being reinvented.

So where do we go from here? We have professional organizations to guide us (see Figure 4-7). These organizations have made improvements in the status of children, and they have begun to outline standards and practices for the people who call themselves "early childhood professionals."

The four themes—an ethic of social reform, the importance of childhood, the transmission of values, and professionalism of the field—have been at the center of early education for centuries. Occasionally one theme dominates, as it did in the 1960s when the desire for social reform led to the creation of Head Start. At other times, they seem indistinguishable from one another. Together, they have shaped the direction of early childhood education as we know it today. As we learn more about children, society, and ourselves, the 21st century will be a time to reconsider and redefine our aims and directions. It is a formidable challenge—and one for us to meet in flexible, innovative ways.

Guides to the Early Childhood Profession

Document	Goal	Source/Access
Code of Ethical Conduct	Provide a moral compass for early childhood educators	Feeney & Freeman (1999), Feeney (2011), Gordon & Browne, Appendix A
Developmentally Appropriate Practices	Provide guidance about current understandings, values, and goals for working with children in group settings	Copple & Bredekamp (2010), Gordon & Browne, Chapters 2 and 9
Program Accreditation Criteria & Procedures	Establish recommended standards for practice, serving as benchmarks	NAEYC Academy (2006) Gordon & Browne, Chapters 2 and 15
Early Childhood Professional Preparation	Guidelines for teacher education	NAEYC Standards for Professional Preparation Programs (2009), CA ECE Competencies (2011), Gordon & Browne, Chapters 5-8

© Cengage Learning 2014

FIGURE 4-7 Documents that promote professionalism in early childhood education.

SUMMARY

LO 1 Major contributions to the field of early childhood education have come from Europe. Since the mid-1700s, philosophers such as Comenius, Locke, Rousseau, and Pestalozzi wrote about children and their education. From the 1800s, educators such as Froebel, Montessori, and Steiner opened schools based on their interpretations and innovations. Other perspectives from China, Japan, Native Americans,

and Africa have added to the educational thinking of our time.

LO 2 American influences began in the days of colonialism and slavery. The Progressive era of the late 1800s and early 1900s expanded the field with the work of Dewey, Hill, Mitchell, and Eliot. Parent cooperatives and the Child Study Movement expanded the types of schooling for young children, as did child care centers at the Kaiser Shipyards and Head Start for low-income families. Recent developments in the United States include developmentally appropriate practices, No Child Left Behind, and common core standards.

LO 3 The disciplines of medicine, education, and psychology have made profound influences on the field. Theories of doctors like Montessori, Freud, and Gesell established a base on which Spock and Brazelton built. The MacMillan sisters and Isaacs helped spur the inclusion of health and play into early childhood settings, and the multi-age range of the British Infant Schools and creativity of Reggio Emilia today adds important

educational components. Psychology has a rich history (elaborated in Chapter 4), which today includes work with neuroscience.

LO 4 Four themes emerge in early childhood education throughout history. They are the ethic of social reform, the importance of childhood, the transmission of values, and professionalism. These themes make good teaching a professional enterprise that is worthy of advocacy and dedication. The contributions of many pioneers leave us dreams for the young children of our society. This can give meaning to our lives as teachers as we continue to create a climate for the child who will make history tomorrow.

Key Terms

professional
early childhood education
building block years
readiness
tabula rasa
concrete
integrated curriculum

kindergarten/children's garden
self-correcting
child-centered approach
kindergarten
custodial
parent cooperative schools
open school

vertical groupings (mixed age)
integrated day
ethic of social reform
importance and uniqueness of childhood
transmitting values
professionalism

Review Questions

1. Match the name with the appropriate phrase. Put them in the order that best matches your own theory of early childhood education. State your reasons.

   Rousseau   "prepared environment"
   Montessori   "nurture" school
   Froebel   children are naturally good
   Malaguzzi   father of kindergarten
   Dewey   common-sense approach
   Spock   first picture book for children
   McMillan sisters   Progressive Movement
   Comenius   Reggio Emilia

2. Read the following list of some nontraditional and mainstream perspectives as described in the chapter. After each, trace its original root and put at least one example of how this perspective could be practiced in an early childhood classroom today.

Perspective	Roots in Early Childhood Practice
Harmony	
Kinship networks	
Close ties to nature	
Respect for elders	
Cooperative work	
Expressiveness	

3. Maria Montessori made several contributions to education. What are some of her theories, and how did she adapt them for classroom use? How are Montessori materials or teaching methods used in your classroom?

4. Name the four themes that have guided early childhood education throughout its history. Include a person and a concept for each theme and explain why they match the theme.

Observe and Apply

1. Choose a school or center near you, and interview the director or lead teacher. What philosophies are important? What were some of the social, economic, and political issues of the times when it was founded? Ask to look at any old photos, handbooks, or newspaper clippings. Why would documenting the history of a program be useful?

2. Identify and describe five key people who influenced the field of early childhood education. With whom would you like to have studied or worked? Why? Ask your professor, a teacher, and a principal/director and compare your findings with your own.

3. Write your own pedagogic creed. List what you consider to be the most important beliefs you hold about educating young children. How do you see those beliefs expressed in school today?

4. Make a list of the values you think are important to teach children. In an adjoining column, add the ways in which you would help children learn those values. In other words, list the materials and curriculum you would use.

Helpful Websites

American Federation of Teachers Educational Foundation **www.aft.org**

Annie E. Casey Foundation **www.aecf.org**

Association for Childhood Education International **www.acei.org**

British Infant School **www.sparatcus.schoolnet.co.uk**

Center for the Study of the Child Care Workforce **www.irle.berkeley.edu/cscce**

The Children's Defense Fund **www.childrensdefense.org**

National Association for the Education of Young Children **www.naeyc.org**

National Center for Children and Poverty **www.nccp.org**

National Institute for Early Education Research **www.nieer.org**

North American Reggio Emilia Alliance **www.reggioalliance.org**

Society for Research in Child Development **www.srcd.org**

Waldorf Schools **www.waldorfanswers.org**

The Education CourseMate website for this text offers many helpful resources and interactive study tools. Go to CengageBrain.com to access the TeachSource Videos, flashcards, tutorial quizzes, direct links to all of the websites mentioned in the chapter, downloadable forms, and more.

References

Aries, P. (1962). *Centuries of childhood.* New York: Knopf.

Baker, K. R. (1950). *The nursery school: A human relationships laboratory.* New York: Saunders.

Biber, B. (1984). *Early education and psychological development.* New Haven, CT: Yale University Press.

Bradburn, E. (2000). Margaret MacMillan: 1860-1933. In A. Gordon & K. W Browne (Eds.), *Beginnings and beyond* (5th Ed.). Clifton Park, NY: Thomson Delmar Learning.

Brazelton, T. B., & Greenspan, S. (2001). *The irreducible needs of young children: what every child must have to grow, learn and flourish.* Cambridge, MA: DaCapo Press.

Brooks, A. (1886). *Four active workers.* Springfield, MA: Milton Bradley.

Brosterman, N. (1997). *Inventing Kindergarten.* New York: Harry N. Abrams.

Byrnes, J. P. (2001). *Minds, brains, and learning.* New York: Guilford Press.

Center on the Developing Child at Harvard University. (2007). *A science-based framework for early childhood policy: Using evidence to improve outcomes in learning, behavior and health for vulnerable children.* http://www.developingchild.harvard.edu.

Chattin-McNichols, J. (1993). In A. Gordon & K. W Browne (Eds.), *Beginnings and beyond* (3rd Ed.). Clifton Park, NY: Thomson Delmar Learning.

Cohen, D. H., & Randolph, M. (1977). *Kindergarten and early schooling.* Englewood Cliffs, NJ: Prentice-Hall.

Coles, R. (1971). *Children of crisis: A study of courage and fear.* New York, NY: Houghton Mifflin.

Comenius. (1658). *Orbis Pictus* (The World of Pictures). Pressburg, Bratislava.

Copple, C. C., and Bredekamp, S. (Eds.). (2010). *Developmentally appropriate practice in early childhood programs serving children birth through age eight.* (3rd Ed.). Washington, D.C.: NAEYC.

Cottrol, R.J., Diamond, R. T., & Ware, L. B. (2004, Summer). The Decline of the Idea of Caste: Setting the Stage for *Brown v. Board of Education. American Educator,* AFT.

Cubberly, E. P. (1920). *A brief history of education.* Boston: Houghton Mifflin.

Damon, M., Kozol, J., and Ravitch, D. (July 30, 2011). "Save Our Schools: March & Rally on Washington, D.C.-*Washington Post.* http://www.washingtonpost.com.

Deasey, D. (1978). *Education under six.* New York: St. Martin's Press.

DeMause, L. (1974). *The history of childhood.* New York: Psychohistory Press.

Derman-Sparks, L. (1988). *The anti-bias curriculum: Tools for empowering young children.* Washington, D.C.: NAEYC.

Derman-Sparks, L. & Olsen Edwards, J. (2010) *Anti-bias education for young children and ourselves.* Washington, D.C.: NAEYC.

Dewey, J. (1897, 1916). *My pedagogic creed.* Washington, D.C.: The Progressive Education Association and Democracy and Education.

Dickerson, M. (1992, Spring). James L. Hymes, Jr.: Advocate for young children. *Childhood Education.*

Dowley, E. (1985). Early childhood education in the shipyards. In A. Gordon & K. W Browne, *Beginnings and beyond* (1st Ed.). Clifton Park, NY: Thomson Delmar Learning.

DuBois, W E. B. (1995). The talented tenth. Published in The Negro Problem (1903), excerpted in F. Schultz (Ed.), *Sources: Notable selection in education.* Guilford, CT: Dushkin.

Edelman, M. W (2006). *The state of America's children.* Washington, D.C.: Children's Defense Fund.

Elkind, D. (1982). *The hurried child.* Reading, MA: Addison-Wesley.

Fanjul, S. (2011, January). Many anniversaries. *Young Children,* 66(1).

Feeney, S. (2011). *Professionals in early childhood education: Doing our best for young children.* Upper Saddle River, NJ: Pearson.

Feeney, S., & Freeman, N. K. (1999). *Ethics and the early childhood educator: Using the NAEYC Code.* Washington, D.C.: NAEYC.

Froebel, F. (1887). *The education of man* (M. W. Hailman, Trans.). New York: D. Appleton.

Gandini, L. (1994, July). Tribute to Loris Malaguzzi. *Young Children,* 49(5).

Gesell, A. L., Ames, L. A., & Ilg, F L. (1977). *The child from five to ten.* New York: Harper & Row.

Gianoutsos, J. (2011). Locke and Rousseau: Early Childhood Education. *The Pulse,* 4(1). http//:www.baylor.edu./pulse.

Gonzalez-Mena, J. (2001). *Foundations: Early childhood education in a diverse society.* Mountain View, CA: Mayfield.

Greenberg, P. (1987, July). Lucy Sprague Mitchell: A major missing link between early childhood education in the 1980s and progressive education in the 1890s-1930s. *Young Children,* 42(5).

Harms, T. & Tracy, R. (2006, July). University laboratory schools in early childhood education. *Young Children,* 61(4).

Hewes, D. (1993). On doing history. In A. Gordon & K. W Browne (Eds.), *Beginnings and beyond* (3rd Ed.). Clifton Park, NY: Thomson Delmar Learning.

Hill, P. S. (1996). Kindergarten. From the American Educator Encyclopedia (1941). In Paciorek & Munro. *Sources: Notable selections in early childhood education.* Guildford, CT: Dushkin.

Hilliard, A. G., III. (1997, September). Teacher education from an African American perspective. In

J. Irvine (Ed.), *Critical knowledge for diverse teachers and learners*. Washington, D.C.: AACTE.

Hymes, J. L., Jr. (1978-79). *Living history interviews (Books 1-3)*. Carmel, CA: Hacienda Press.

Hyson, M. (Ed.) (2003). *Preparing early childhood professionals: NAEYC's standards for programs*. Washington, D.C.: NAEYC.

Irons, P. (2004, Summer). Jim Crow's Schools. *American Educator*, AFT.

Jones-Wilson, F. C. (1996). Westport, CT: Greenwood Press. *Encyclopedia of African-American Education*.

Keatinge, M. W. (1896). *The great didactic of John Amos Comenius* (Trans. and with introductions). London: Adams and Charles Black.

Kozol, J. (1991). *Savage inequalities: Children in America's schools*. New York: Crown Publishers.

Malaguzzi, L. (1993, November). For an education based on relationships. *Young Children*.

McMillan, M. (1919). *The nursery school*. London and Toronto: J. M. Dent & Sons; New York: E. P. Dutton.

Mintz, S. (2004). *Huck's raft: A history of American childhood*. Cambridge, MA: Belknap Press of Harvard University.

Mitchell, L. S. (1951). *Our children and our schools*. New York: Simon & Schuster.

Montessori, M. (1967). *The Montessori method* (Trans. A. E. George). Cambridge, MA.

National Academy. (2006). *Accreditation criteria & procedures (Revised)*. Washington, D.C.: NAEYC.

Neill, A. S. (1960). *Summerhill: A radical approach to child rearing*. New York: Hart.

Osborn, D. K. (1991). *Early childhood education in historical perspective* (3rd Ed.). Athens, GA: Education Associates.

Pleasant, M. B. B. (1992). *Hampton University: Our home by the sea*. Virginia Beach, VA: Donning.

Read, K., & Patterson, J. (1980). *The nursery school & kindergarten: Relationships and learning* (7th Ed.). New York: Holt, Rinehart, & Winston.

Reifel, S. (2011, March). Our proud heritage: Observation and early childhood teaching—evolving fundamentals. *Young Children*, 6(1).

Rousseau, J. J. (1761). *Emile* (Trans. by B. Foxley). London and Toronto: J. M. Dent & Sons..

Shonkoff, J. P., and Phillips, D. A. (Eds.). (2000). *From neurons to neighborhoods: The science of early childhood development*. Washington, D.C.: National Academies Press.

Silber, K. (1965). *Pestalozzi: The man and his works*. (2nd Ed.). London: Routledge and Kegan Paul.

Spock, B. (1947). *The common sense book of baby and child care*. New York: Duell, Sloan & Pierce.

Spock, B. (1976, April). Taking care of a child and a home: An honorable profession for men and women. *Redbook Magazine*.

Steiner, R. (1926). *The essentials of education*. London: Anthroposophical Publishing.

Stolz, L. M. (1978). In J. Hymes. *Living history interviews*. Carmel, CA: Hacienda Press.

Walker, L. R. (1997, Fall). John Dewey at Michigan. *Michigan Today*.

Weber, S. (September 5, 2011). ASCD edge in brief: Turning points. http://edge.ascd.org/_Turning Points/blog/4976758/127586.html.

Weinberg, M. (1977). *A chance to learn: The history of race and education in the United States*. Cambridge, MA: Cambridge University Press.

Williams, S. M. (2011). Insights from the field: A delightful story. *Beginnings & beyond*. (8th Ed.). Belmont, CA: Wadsworth Cengage Learning.

© Cengage Learning

5

Defining the Young Child

Learning Objectives

LO1 Describe what is meant by the whole child and define the major domains of development.

LO2 Demonstrate an awareness of developmental ages and stages using Word Pictures to recognize the major developmental milestones.

LO3 Recognize the characteristics of typical and atypical development and describe adaptations needed to support children with diverse abilities.

The NAEYC Standards for Initial and Advanced Early Childhood Professional Preparation addressed in this chapter are:

Standard 1 Promoting Child Development and Learning

Standard 2 Building Family and Community Relationships

Standard 3 Observing, Documenting, and Assessing to Support Young Children and Families

Standard 4 Using Developmentally Effective Approaches to Connect with Children and Families

Standard 5 Using Content Knowledge to Build Meaningful Curriculum

Standard 6 Becoming a Professional

These are the sections from the NAEYC Code of Ethical Conduct that apply to the topics in this chapter:

Ideals:

I-1.1   To be familiar with the knowledge base of early childhood care and education and to stay informed through continuing education and training.

I-1.2   To base program practices upon current knowledge and research in the field of early childhood education, child development, and related disciplines, as well as on particular knowledge of each child.

I-1.3   To recognize and respect the unique qualities, abilities, and potential of each child.

I-1.8   To support the right of each child to play and learn in an inclusive environment that meets the needs of children with and without disabilities.

I-1.9   To advocate for and ensure that all children, including those with special needs, have access to the support services needed to be successful.

Principles:

P-1.3.   We shall not participate in practices that discriminate against children by denying benefits, giving special advantages, or excluding them from programs or activities on the basis of their race, national origin, immigration status, preferred home language, religious beliefs, medical condition, disability or the marital status/family structure, sexual orientation, or religious beliefs or other affiliations of their families.

The Whole Child

The concept of "the whole child" is based on the accepted principle that all areas of human growth and development are integrated. It is only for the purpose of studying one area or another in depth that categories are created. In reality, all areas of growth are knitted together in a mutually supportive network creating the uniqueness of each child.

Teachers quickly learn what makes each child special, what they look like when they move their bodies, change expressions, or assume a posture. We can tell when Sonja is hurt, happy, or harried by the way she moves and looks. Rodrigo's face mirrors his distress or his delight. The observant teacher reads children through the ways they express the "whole child."

Developmental Domains

We use six **developmental domains** to define the "whole child" and express how children grow and develop:

1. *Social-emotional development*: includes a child's relationship with herself and others, self-concept, self-esteem, and the ability to express feelings.
2. *Physical–motor development*: includes gross motor, fine motor, and perceptual motor activity.
3. *Cognitive development*: includes curiosity, the ability to perceive and think, memory, attention span, general knowledge, problem solving, analytical thinking, beginning reading, and computing skills.
4. *Language development*: includes children's utterances, pronunciation, vocabulary, sentence length, and the ability to express ideas, needs, and feelings. It includes receptive language (do they understand what they hear?) and verbal ability (what do they say?).

   The interaction among the developmental domains is a key element to understanding the "whole" child. Figure 5-1 shows the connection of each developmental domain in relation to the others.
5. *Cultural identity development*. This suggests the interconnections between developmental stages and a growing awareness of one's attitudes toward others. Various cultural milestones appear in each age group which, when appropriately fostered, can increase a child's sensitivity to differences. The Word Pictures on pages 71–78 indicate cultural identity growth in the early years and are highlighted by an asterisk.
6. *Creative development*. This includes the usual creative activities such as movement, dance, music, and painting, as well as originality, imagination, divergent thinking, and problem solving.

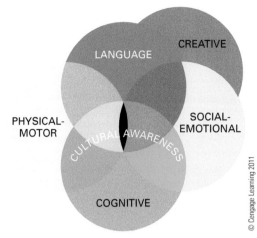

FIGURE 5-1 How areas of growth are interrelated: Each area of growth is affected by and influences every other area of development.

Children: alike, yet different.

Developmental Ages and Stages: Major Milestones

Descriptions of children's common characteristics date back to a classic collection of research by Gesell and Ilg. (See Chapters 1 and 4 for related discussions.) Age alone does not determine a child's capabilities, but it does provide a guideline for establishing appropriate expectations. Despite the wide range of individual differences at all ages, common behaviors lend a perspective to help teachers prescribe programs, plan activities, and create curricula.

DAP | Growth Is Interrelated

One area of development affects the other. Figure 5-1 helps us to visualize the interrelationship of the whole child. Think how each area might affect or interact with the others:

- Physical development affects how children feel about themselves. Children who appreciate their body and its power feel confident in what they can do (social-emotional).
- Intellectual skills interact with language development and creativity. When children have mastered their primary language, they can then clarify some of their thought processes.
- The kindergartner who masters using scissors (physical) is ready to try printing. The fine-motor skills enhance the cognitive task of learning the alphabet.
- A child with a hearing loss is likely to have language delay as well; thus the physical development affects the language part of growth.
- The child who has trouble making friends (social) is likely to exhibit his unhappiness (emotional) in the school yard (physical) and in the math period (intellectual).

Observe a classroom during free play or activity time. What interactions do you see between developmental domains? How does this affect the child's ability to learn? Describe yourself at this age, commenting on what developmental domains were your strengths.

The Value of Word Pictures

Each developmental phase has characteristics traits. These are described in the following pages as Word Pictures. Word Pictures are designed to help classroom teachers plan learning experiences for a group of children. Word Pictures are a valuable teaching tool because they help teachers know what to expect and when to expect it. The developmental and learning theories in Chapter 4 and their classroom applications help you understand the basis from which these Word Pictures are drawn. See "Teaching With Intention" box later on in this chapter for specific ways to use the Word Pictures. (Chapter 10 has more practical applications and examples for planning curriculum.)

In Behavior and Guidance

We use guidance and discipline strategies based on the expected behaviors common to a given age range. Many so-called problem behaviors are normal behaviors of the age at which they occur: 2-year-olds are easily frustrated as they grow increasingly independent. Four-year-olds test limits and are resistant to controls. The knowledgeable teacher accepts these characteristics and guides each child accordingly.

Word Pictures of a child, taken from age-level charts, help teachers know what to expect and when to expect it. By using the charts as a reference, teachers lessen the risk of expecting too much or too little of children at any given age. Age-level characteristics give a frame of reference for handling daily situations and a basis for planning appropriate guidance measures. When using Word Pictures, ask yourself which ones:

Are most common to the ages of the children in the class

Are appropriate for children in group settings

Suggest guidance and disciplinary measures

Have implications for planning a developmentally appropriate curriculum

Are culture milestones, *which are highlighted by an asterisk*, to suggest the interaction of children's development and their awareness of attitudes toward race and culture

In Curriculum

Word Pictures can be used to tailor curriculum planning to an individual child or a particular class or group on the basis of known developmental standards. A group cooking experience, for instance, allows children to choose their level of comfort and involvement. As an early reader at age 4, Darragh loves to read the recipe to others. Lourdes's favorite activity is to mix the ingredients together, refining her small motor skills. Von, who loves to play with mud and clay, spreads the cookie sheet with oil while Felicity helps the teacher adjust the oven temperature. Cooking is always a fun activity but serves a greater purpose when planned with individual children in mind. The skills and abilities of the specific age group helps to determine the

Adults see children through many filters. What is it like to look through children's eyes?

The Architecture of the Brain

Block play is one of the most popular activities in preschool programs. When young children first encounter blocks, they make piles, stack them, or lay them out in a row. As they have more experiences with blocks, more complex building emerges as children build walls and floors, bridges, and enclosures. At first, playing with blocks is an end in itself but with more experience, blocks are used in a larger architectural plan. "I need to put these blocks on top of each other to build a second story to my garage," says 5-year-old Gian-Francesco. It is almost as if the first year of block building was a practice period to lay the foundation for more complex work.

So it is with how the young child's brain develops. Foundational concepts of brain development (National Scientific Council on the Developing Child, 2010) help us understand three basic blocks on which brain development is based. (See the video series, "Three Core Concepts in Early Development," available at www.developingchild.harvard.edu/resources/multimedia/video/three_core_concepts/.)

Concept 1: Experiences build brain architecture. Through daily activities and experiences the brain cells (neurons) shape the neurological networks that create the foundation for emotions, logic, memory, motor skills, social-emotional behaviors, and vision. Each neuron creates an axon (which sends signals) and dendrites (which receive signals). Axons and dendrites join to form synapses. Simple circuits form the basis for more complex brain circuits. Electrical activity is triggered by sensory experiences and fine-tunes the brain's architecture. As you supervise block play, notice all the architecture there, and remember that the brain is being built as well.

Concept 2: "Serve and return" shapes the brain's architecture. If you have ever played tennis or ping-pong, you have participated in "serve and return." Your partner serves the ball to you and you hit it back, returning the serve. Now think of the image of new parents cooing, babbling, and smiling at their baby. That, too, is a "serve and return" activity and is key to forming strong brain architecture. The back and forth interactions between children and adults form the foundation of brain architecture on which all future development will be built. "Serve and return" interactions help create the neural connections between all the different areas of the brain, and they build the child's emotional and cognitive skills. The best advice for teachers and parents is to create "serve and return" interactions to enhance the child's growing brain.

Concept 3: Toxic **stress** hinders healthy brain development. Persistent adversity in young children, such as poverty, neglect, abuse, family violence, parental substance abuse, and severe maternal depression cause toxic stress. The body's stress management system is activated and sends the stress hormone cortisol into the body. The body's reaction to stress includes rapid increase of heart rate and a rise in blood pressure. These responses help the body deal with stress and then return to normal when the brain perceives that the stress is past. However, when stress is prolonged and the child is without supportive adult help, the stress level persists and affects the brain's architecture. The neural connections become reduced by stress overload at a time when they should be growing new ones. High levels of cortisol can disrupt the learning process by inhibiting reasoning abilities, which can lead to emotional and cognitive problems. These early experiences of deprivation and stress become hardwired into the brain.

Questions

1. Aside from block play, what other experiences in an early childhood program helps to build the brain's architecture? List those that are appropriate for infants and toddlers, for preschoolers, and for school-age children.

2. How would you "serve and return" with a 3-year-old? A school-age child?

3. What is our role as early childhood educators in reducing persistent stress in children's lives?

---

kind of activities at which children can succeed while still taking the next steps in their development. See the next section for guidelines on using the Word Pictures as tools for planning. Chapters 10 through 14 have more practical applications and examples for planning curricula.

In Cultural Awareness

Derman-Sparks and Edwards (2010) point out that children become aware of and form attitudes about racial and cultural differences at a very early age. Their experiences with their bodies, social environment, and cognitive development combine to help them form their own identity and attitudes. As they develop cognitively, children become aware of differences and similarities in people. These cultural milestones are included in the Word Pictures to indicate how, as children come to a sense of themselves as individuals, their attitudes and behaviors toward others can be influenced.

Using Word Pictures

Setting goals for individual children and for the group is an important part of a teacher's role. We intentionally observe all developmental domains—physical-motor, cognitive-language, social-emotional, creative—so that we have a picture of the whole child. To plan effectively, we reflect on what we know about each child, what we need to know, and what we know about the group. Assessing children's development and measuring their progress provides the information needed to create appropriate teaching strategies and curriculum. It tells us what children know and what they can do. Use the Word Pictures to find the baseline, the place where each child starts from, and that will be used at a later date to determine growth over time by measuring the child's progress against the original assessment. The following six guidelines will help you get started:

1. Balance your impression of the Word Pictures with your experiences of children. *Example: Toddlers are always on the move and prefer standing and squatting to sitting in a chair. Observe a toddler story time to see how many children are sitting on the floor, how many are standing, and how many are squatting on their haunches.*

2. Make a profile of the whole child to balance your impression of the whole child. *Example: At 3½-years-old, Chad's language skills were those of a 7-year-old. He tended to talk in long and convoluted sentences and other*

children had difficulty relating to him. After looking over Chad's profile, the teachers focused on his social development and worked with Chad's parents on finding him a friend. In class, the teachers modeled more appropriate ways to engage other children in conversation and play.

3. Get perspective on the range of developmental norms a child exhibits over time. *Example: Children have varying levels of development at any point in time. Look at the Word Pictures for the group just older and younger than the age level of the child you are observing. A typical child may have the physical development of a 3-year-old, the language skills of a 4-year-old, and the social coping skills of a 2-year-old. Children exhibit some of the behaviors appropriate in a two- to three-year range.*

4. Remember that these norms of development refer to average or typical behavior, and they should not be applied too literally. *Example: Use these examples with discretion. If Dixon and Emma are the only two children in the class reading at the next grade level, do not expect the rest of the class to achieve the same success. The Word Pictures are norms and will help you track Dixon and Emma's progress in developmental domains as well as cognitive-language. The Word Pictures are not intended for comparing children's abilities, but rather to provide a*

compilation of information on individual children.

5. Keep in mind that children go through most of the stages described and in the same sequence, but they do so at their own rates of growth. *Example: Individual differences occur as development follows its orderly and predictable path as children acquire the abilities and skills that are necessary to succeed in the next stages. Elaina may not yet have the writing skills of her peers, but with appropriate experiences and teaching strategies, we can help her progress over a period of time.*

6. Focus on what the children can do rather than on what they cannot do. Use the characteristics to compare the child's rate of growth. *Example: In observing Dwayne, it is important to assess where he is in relation to other 4-year-olds, but it is more important to know where he is six months from now, a year from now, and what he was like a year ago. From this, a clear picture of his rate of growth emerges.*

Think About This
1. How do Word Pictures help you understand the concept of the "whole child"?
2. How do Word Pictures help you work with parents and families?
3. What other use can you find for Word Pictures?

Applying Word Pictures to Teaching Strategies

The Word Pictures focus on the critical issues that teachers address when planning for a group of children. We have included six basic developmental areas to give a more complete picture of each age group. In Chapter 4, you will come to appreciate the importance of research and significant theories from which these Word Pictures are drawn.

Culture, Race, and Ethnic Considerations

The answer to "Who is the young child?" takes on new meaning as we look at the ethnic mix of American life. A multicultural explosion has swept across the nation, filling early childhood programs with children from many different cultural backgrounds. There are more students in the classroom who are culturally and linguistically different

(text continued on page 157)

Word Pictures

Infant

Social-Emotional

0–1 month: cries to express emotions; bonding begins

4–10 weeks: makes social smiles

2 months: begins social games

3 months: distinguishes familiar faces*; turns head toward human voice; smiles in response to a smile; kicks, smiles, waves in response; cries when left alone; recognizes parent

4 months: has a genuine laugh; smiles when spoken to; loves attention

5 months to 1 year: begins to exhibit stranger anxiety*

6 months: distinguishes between voices; smiles; babbles at strangers; develops attachment to parents, caregivers; begins to play imitation games; plays peek-a-boo; sensitive to parental moods

8 months: laughs out loud

9 months: screams to get own way

Play is activity only for present moment

Fears unfamiliar: people, places, things*

Beginning sense of separate self*

Language

0–1 month: turns head in response to voices; cries to express needs

6–8 weeks: coos; gestures to communicate: pushes objects away; squirms; reaches out to people*; pouts; smacks lips; shrieks; points

2 months: makes voluntary vocal sounds

3 months: babbles

6–12 months: plays imitation sound games; responds to variety of sounds*; makes vowel sounds; acquires receptive language*; cries to communicate

12 months: says first words

Physical-Motor

By 1 year: grows 10 to 12 inches; triples birth weight; lengthens by 40 percent; doubles brain size; grows full head of hair; bounces in crib; uses whole-body motions

4 months: sees, grasps objects

5 months: examines fingers; sits when propped

6 months: rolls over; discovers feet; teething begins

7 months: crawls

8 months: sits up unaided; pulls to standing position; pincer grasp established

9 months: creeps

10 months: feeds self with spoon

11 months: stands alone; cruises

12 months: takes first steps

Late infancy: can move hands in rotation to turn knobs

Newborn motor activity is mostly reflexes

Creative

Discovers and explores hands and feet

Expresses and discovers emotion

Talks by babbling, cooing, and gurgling

Plays peek-a-boo

Responds to facial expressions

Courtesy of the author

Cognitive

0–1 month: responds to mother's voice; aware of senses, especially pain, touch*

10 weeks: memory is evident*

4 months: makes smiles of recognition

7–10 months: solves simple problems (knocks over box to get toy)

8 months: begins to believe in permanence of objects; follows a simple instruction

8–12 months: becoming intentional in behavior

11 months: begins trial-error experimentation

12 months: plays drop/retrieve games, pat-a-cake

Explores with hands and fingers

Smiles, vocalizes at image in mirror*

*Key characteristics of cultural awareness or identity.

Social-Emotional

Almost totally egocentric

Likes to be noticed; loves an audience

Lacks inhibitions

Insists on own way, assertive

Likes doing things by self

Independent, has self-identity*

Adapts easily

Refers to self by name

Laughs loudly at peek-at-boo

Cries when left alone

Curious*

Relates to adults better than children

Active, eager

Talks mostly to self

Usually friendly

Strong sense of ownership

Mimics adult behavior*

Experiences and shows shame*

Language

Some two-word phrases

Enjoys vocalizing to self

Babbles in own jargon

Uses "eh-eh" or "uh-uh" with gestures

Names closest relatives*

Repeats adults' words*

Points to communicate needs, wants

Shakes head "no" to respond*

Responds to directions to fetch, point

Obeys verbal requests

Asks "What's that?" or "Whassat?"*

Understands simple phrases

Uses five to 50 words

Physical-Motor

Awkward coordination; chubby body

Tottering stance

Creeps when in a hurry

Walks with increasing confidence

Walks with feet wide apart, arms out,
head forward

Finds it difficult to turn corners

Goes up and down stairs holding on

Backs into chair to sit down

Can squat for long periods of time

In constant motion

Loves to pull/push objects

Runs with stiff, flat gait

Uses whole-arm movements

Carry and dump becomes a favorite
activity

Scribbles

Turns pages two or three at a time

Zips/unzips large zipper

Likes holding objects in both hands

Creative

Responds to mood of music

Freely examines every object

Sings phrases of nursery rhymes

Loves to finger-paint and explore texture

Stares; takes it all in

"The age of exploration"

Makes up nonsense syllables

Cognitive

Points to objects in a book

Matches similar objects

Fits round block in round hole

Loves opposites: up/down, yes/no*

Imitates simple tasks

Interest shifts quickly

Short attention span

Follows one direction

Gives up easily but easily engaged*

Conclusions are important: closes
doors, shuts books

Thinks with feet; action-oriented

Builds tower of three or four small blocks

*Key characteristics of cultural awareness or identity.

© Cengage Learning

Social-Emotional

Self-centered

Unable to share, possessive

Clings to familiar; resistant to change*

Ritualistic; insists on routines*

Dependent

Likes one adult at a time*

Quits readily; easily frustrated

Goes to extremes

Impulsive; shifts activities suddenly

Easily distracted

Pushes, shoves

Finicky, fussy eater; some food jags

Refers to self by given name*

Treats people as inanimate objects*

Dawdles; slow-geared

Plays parallel to other children

Watches others*

Likes people*

Excited about own capabilities

Language

Uses two- or three-word sentences

Telegraphic sentences: "Throw ball"

Has difficulty in pronunciation

"Me," "Mine" most prominent pronouns*

Spontaneous language; rhythmic, repetitive

Constant talking; interested in sound

Sings phrases of song, not on pitch

Cannot articulate feelings

Frustrated when not understood

May stutter

Asks "Whassat?" about pictures*

Can match words with objects

Repeats words and phrases

Uses 50 to 300 words

Physical-Motor

Uses whole-body action: pushes, pulls, pokes

Climbs into things

Leans forward while running

Climbs stairs one by one

Dependent on adults for dressing

Can help dress/undress

Has reached one-half potential height

Bladder/bowel control begins

Feeds self

Thumb-forefinger opposition complete

Grasps cup with two hands

Awkward with small objects

Lugs, tumbles, topples; unsteady

Alternates hands; hand preference is developing

Can rotate to fit objects

Expresses emotions bodily*

Sensory-oriented

Cuts last teeth

Has difficulty relaxing

Creative

Imitates other children

Combines parallel play and fantasy play

Plays with sounds; repeats syllables over and over

Enjoys simple finger plays

Can follow simple melodies

Learns to scribble

Uses art for sensory pleasure

Cognitive

Recognizes, explores physical characteristics of objects*

Investigates with touch and taste

Intrigued by water, washing

Likes to fill and empty things

Has limited attention span

Lives in present

Understands familiar concepts*

Can tell difference between black and white*

Needs own name used

Likes simple make-believe

Does one thing at a time

Remembers orders of routines

Recalls where toys are left

Classifies people by gender*

Names familiar objects in books

*Key characteristics of cultural awareness or identity.

Social-Emotional

Highly imitative of adults*

Wants to please adults; conforms*

Responds to verbal suggestions

Easily prompted, redirected

Can be bargained with, reasoned with

Begins to share, take turns, wait

Avid "me-too"-er*

Exuberant, talkative, humorous

Has an imaginary companion

Has nightmares, animal phobias

Plays consciously, cooperatively with others*

Plays spontaneously in groups

Demonstrates fears

Goes after desires; fights for them

Asserts independence often

Often stymied, frustrated, jealous

Sympathizes*

Strong sex-role stereotypes*

Language

Talkative with or without a listener

Can listen to learn*

Likes new words*

Increases use of pronouns, prepositions

Uses "s" to indicate plural nouns

Uses "ed" to indicate past tense

Uses sentences of three or more words

Says "Is that all right?" a lot

Talks about nonpresent situations

Puts words into action

Moves and talks at the same time

Substitutes letters in speech: "w" for "r"

Intrigued by whispering

Uses 300 to 1,000 words

© Cengage Learning

Physical-Motor

Has well-balanced body lines

Walks erect; nimble on feet

Gallops in wide, high steps

Alternates feet in stair climbing

Suddenly starts, stops

Turns corners rapidly

Swings arms when walking

Jumps up and down with ease

Uses toilet alone

Loses baby fat

Achieves bladder control

Rides a tricycle

Puts on, takes off wraps with help

Unbuttons buttons

Has some finger control with small objects

Grasps with thumb and index finger

Holds cup in one hand

Pours easily from small pitcher

Washes hands unassisted

Can carry liquids

Has activity with drive and purpose

Can balance on one foot

Creative

Dramatizes play

Enjoys slap-stick humor

Laughs at the ridiculous

Experiments with silly language

Imaginary companion may appear

Tricycle becomes many objects in dramatic play

Acts out own version of favorite story

Enjoys simple poems

Learns color concepts

Cognitive

Matches people according to physical characteristics*

Estimates "how many"

Enjoys making simple choices

Alert, excited, curious

Asks "why?" constantly*

Understands "It's time to . . ."

Understands "Let's pretend . . ."

Enjoys guessing games, riddles

Has lively imagination*

Often over generalizes*

Carries out two to four directions in sequence

Often colors pages one color

Can't combine two activities

Names and matches simple colors

Has number concept of one and two

Sees vague cause-and-effect relationships*

Can recognize simple melodies

Distinguishes between night and day

Understands size and shape comparisons

*Key characteristics of cultural awareness or identity.

Four-Year-Old

Social-Emotional

Mood changes rapidly

Tries out feelings of power

Dominates; can be bossy, boastful, belligerent

Assertive, argumentative

Shows off; is cocky, noisy

Can fight own battles

Hits, grabs, insists on desires

Explosive, destructive

Easily over stimulated; excitable

Impatient in large groups*

Cooperates in groups of two or three*

Develops "special" friends* but shifts loyalties often

May exclude others from play*

Resistant; tests limits

Exaggerates, tells tall tales

Alibis frequently

Teases, outwits; has terrific humor

May have scary dreams

Tattles frequently

Has food jags, food strikes

Language

Has more words than knowledge

A great talker, questioner

Likes words, plays with them

Has high interest in poetry

Able to talk to solve conflicts*

Responds to verbal directions

Enjoys taking turns to sing along

Interested in dramatizing songs, stories

Exaggerates, practices words

Uses voice control, pitch, rhythm

Asks "when?" "why?" "how?"*

Joins sentences together

Loves being read to

Physical-Motor

Longer, leaner body build

Vigorous, dynamic, acrobatic

Active until exhausted

"Works": builds, drives, pilots

Can jump own height and land upright

Hops, skips

Throws large ball, kicks accurately

Hops and stands on one foot

Jumps over objects

Walks in a straight line

Races up and down stairs

Turns somersaults

Walks backward toe-heel

Accurate, rash body movements

Copies shapes such as a cross, square

Can draw a stick figure

Holds paint brush in adult manner, pencil in fisted grasp

Can lace shoes

Dresses self except back buttons, ties

Has sureness and control in finger activities

Alternates feet going down stairs

Creative

Is adventurous

Shows vivid imagination

Displays great interest in violence in imaginary play

Loves anything new

Demonstrates more elaborate dramatic play

Makes up new words, sounds, and stories

Enjoys complexity in book illustrations

Exaggerates and goes to extreme

Likes funny poetry

Tells spontaneous story with artwork

© Cengage Learning

Can put on elaborate plays with puppets

Finds ways to solve problems

Combines words and ideas

Cognitive

Does some naming and representative art

Gives art products personal value

Can work for a goal*

Questions constantly*

Interested in how things work

Interested in life-death concepts

Has an extended attention span

Can do two things at once

Dramatic play is closer to reality*

Judges which of two objects is larger

Has concept of three; can name more

Has accurate sense of time

Full of ideas

Begins to generalize; often faulty*

Likes a variety of materials

Calls people names*

Has dynamic intellectual drive*

Has imaginary playmates

Recognizes several printed words

*Key characteristics of cultural awareness or identity.

© Cengage Learning

Spells out simple words
Takes turn in conversation
Has clear ideas and articulates them*
Insists "I already know that"
Asks questions to learn answers*
Makes up songs
Enjoys dictating stories
Uses 1,500 words
Tells a familiar story
Defines simple words
Answers telephone, takes a message
Thinks out loud*

Social-Emotional
Poised, self-confident, self-contained
Sensitive to ridicule*
Has to be right; persistent
Has sense of self-identity*
May get silly, high, wild
Enjoys pointless riddles, jokes
Enjoys group play, competitive games*
Aware of rules, defines them for others*
Chooses own friends; is sociable*
Gets involved with group decisions*
Insists on fair play*
Likes adult companionship*
Accepts, respects authority*
Asks permission
Remains calm in emergencies

Language
Uses big words and complete
    sentences
Can define some words

Physical-Motor
Completely coordinated
Has adult-like posture
Has tremendous physical drive
Likes to use fine-motor skills
Has accuracy, skill with simple tools
Draws a recognizable person*
Handedness is evident
Dresses self completely
Cuts on a line with scissors
Begins to color within the lines
Catches ball from three feet away
Skips using alternate feet
Enjoys jumping, running, doing stunts
Rides a two-wheeler
Balances on a balance beam
Jumps rope, skips
Runs lightly on toes
Likes to dance; is graceful, rhythmic
Sometimes roughhouses, fights

Creative
Explores variety of art processes
Becomes engrossed in details of paint-
    ing, blocks
Fantasy is more active, less verbal
Thinks out loud
Has ideas; loves to talk about them
Can learn simple dance routine
Enjoys making patterns, designs
Puts on simple plays
Has idea of what to draw—wants to
    make something recognizable

Cognitive
Curious about everything*
Wants to know "how?" and "why?"*
Likes to display new knowledge, skills
Somewhat conscious of own
    ignorance*
Knows tomorrow, yesterday
Can count 10 objects, rote counts to 20
Sorts objects by single characteristic*
Knows own name, address, town
Makes a plan, follows it, centers on task
Sorts objects by color, shape
Concepts of smallest, less than, one-half
May tell time accurately, on the hour
Knows what a calendar is used for
Seldom sees things from another's
    point of view

*Key characteristics of cultural awareness or identity.

Social-Emotional

Six-year-old

Likes to work, yet often does so in spurts

Does not show persistence

Tends to be a know-it-all

Free with opinions and advice

Brings home evidence of good school-work

Observes family rules*

Gender-role stereotypes are rigid*

Friends easily gained, easily lost*

Tests and measures self against peers*

Makes social connections through play*

Friends are of same sex*

Believes in rules except for self*

Active, outgoing

Charming

Proud of accomplishments

Shows aggression through insults, name-calling*

Seven-year-old

More serious

Sensitive to others' reactions*

Eager for home responsibilities

Complaining, pensive, impatient

Shame is common emotion*

Leaves rather than face criticism, ridicule, disapproval*

Complains of unfair treatment, not being liked*

Shows politeness and consideration for adults*

Enjoys solitary activities

First peer pressure: needs to be "in"*

Wants to be one of the gang*

Relates physical competence to self-concept*

Self-absorbed; self-conscious

Language

Six- and seven-year-olds

Enjoy putting language skill to paper

Talk with adults rather than to them*

Chatter incessantly

Dominate conversations

Speech irregularities still common

Learning to print/write

Acquisition of new words tapers off

Bilingual capacities nearly complete* if English is second language

Ability to learn new language still present*

Physical-Motor

Six- and seven-year-olds

Basic skills need refinement

Like to test limits of own body

Value physical competence*

Work at self-imposed tasks

Need daily legitimate channels for high energy

Learn to ride two-wheeler, skate, ski

Use motor skills as a tool for socializing

Boisterous, enjoy stunts and rough-housing

Susceptible to fatigue

Visual acuity reaches normal

Hungry at short intervals, like sweets

Chew pencils, fingernails, hair

Creative

Six-year-old

Tries out artistic exploration seriously for the first time

Industrious

Greater interest in process, not product

Eager, curious, enthusiastic

Loves jokes and guessing games

Loves to color, paint

Understands cause and effect

Likes cooperative projects, activities, tasks

Interested in skill and technique

© Cengage Learning

Seven-year-old

Likes to be alone listening to music

Wants work to look good

The age for starting music lessons

Driven by curiosity, desire to discover and invent

Intensely interested in how things work; takes apart, puts back together

Uses symbols in both writing and drawing

Interested in all sorts of codes

Likes to select and sort objects

Cognitive

Six- and seven-year-olds

Work in spurts, not persistent

Letter and word reversal common

Learn to read, beginning math skills

Can consider others' points of view*

Use logic, systematic thinking*

Can plan ahead

Enjoy collecting: sorting, classifying

Can sequence events and retell stories

Concepts of winning and losing are difficult*

Like games with simple rules*

May cheat or change rules*

Want "real" things: watches and cameras that work

Sift and sort information*

Can conceptualize situations*

Enjoy exploring culture of classmates*

*Key characteristics of cultural awareness or identity.

Social-Emotional

Outgoing, enthusiastic

Enormously curious about people and things*

Socially expansive*

Judgmental and critical of self and others*

Ambivalent about growing up

Often hostile but attracted to opposite sex

Growing self-confidence

Learns about self through others: peers, parents*

Is aware of and sensitive to differences from other children*

Begins to evaluate self and others through clothing, physical attraction, social status*

Likes to meet new people, go new places*

Has emerging sensitivity to personality traits of others*

Eager for peer approval and acceptance*

Growing sense of moral responsibility

Joins clubs

Chooses same-sex playmates

Struggles with feelings of inferiority

Likes to work cooperatively

Responds to studies of other cultures*

Has growing interest in fairness and justice issues*

Language

Talks with adults

Attentive and responsive to adult communication*

© Cengage Learning

Teases members of opposite sex

Talks about "self"*

Talkative, exaggerates

Likes to explain ideas

Imitates language of peers

Enjoys storytelling and writing short stories

Physical-Motor

Beginning to engage in team sports*

Often a growth-spurt year

Speedy, works fast

Restless, energetic, needs physical release

Plays hard, exhausts self

Eye-hand coordination matures; learning cursive handwriting

Enjoys competitive sports*

Hearty appetite, few food dislikes

Repeatedly practices new skills to perfect them

Creative

Has great imagination

Enjoys riddles, limericks, knock-knock jokes

Likes to explain ideas

Visual acuity and fine-motor skills come together

Is most productive in groups

Shows interest in process and product

Cognitive

Criticizes abilities in all academic areas

Seeks new experiences*

Likes to barter, bargain, trade

Enjoys creating collections of things

Interested in how children from other countries live*

Thinks beyond the here-and-now boundaries of time and space

Enjoys role-playing character parts*

Tests out parents to learn more about them

Needs direction, focus

Enjoys all types of humor

Full of ideas, plans

Gaining competence in basic skills

Industrious, but overestimates abilities

Interested in process as well as product of schoolwork

Growing interest in logic and the way things work

Takes responsibility seriously*

*Key characteristics of cultural awareness or identity.

from the teaching staff and from each other. Unless teachers are informed and educated about these differences, they may misinterpret a child's abilities, learning, and needs. Too often, language barriers between a teacher and a child lead to the conclusion that the child is a slow learner or has a disability.

Many families are unfamiliar with school culture in the United States and the expectations schools have about family involvement and participation. Some parents are illiterate in their own language. An informed and supportive teacher can help children succeed under these circumstances.

A lack of understanding about the culture, history, beliefs, and values of the children is harmful to a child's self-concept (see Derman-Sparks and Edwards, 2010, and other references in this book). When there are no assessment tools or instructional materials in the language of the children or that depict their native heritage, children are placed at a distinct disadvantage and often eliminated from programs and services that could help them succeed.

Children of Mixed Heritage

One group of children and families who have often been neglected in the discussion of race are those who are biracial or interracial. Biracial children have parents who are of different races, for instance, a child of a Native American and a white person. All combinations of races can produce a biracial child, such as a Korean/African American child, or a Chinese American/Japanese American child. Interracial children have parents who represent more than two racial or ethnic backgrounds. These terms also apply to children who are adopted by parents of a different race.

Kelly (2009), a black woman married to a white man, writes about her newborn son, reflecting some of the emotion tied to children of mixed heritage: "I was worried that our son would be so light-skinned as to appear Caucasian, and I wanted him to look Black. . . . I wanted to claim [him] for "my" side—in league with [me] against small minds, casual racism, and discrimination. . . . at seven months after his birth, [my son] is the exact shade you'd get if you mixed his father and me up in a paint can—a color I call golden."

The election of Barack Obama, who is biracial, as President of the United States has evoked needed conversations that bring to light many of the issues facing children and families who are interracial.

Culturally Sensitive Teaching

It is important to help interracial children gain a positive self-concept and identity at an early age. Classroom environments and curricula should intentionally reflect images of interracial children and families to help children recognize and connect with people who share their heritages so that they learn to see and understand themselves.

Educators need to encourage open discussions of racial identification and give children some positive experiences in talking about their heritage. Consult with families about how they handle their mixed heritage and how they identify themselves and their children. Focus on their needs as a family to help them nurture their child in an interracial context.

Cultural sensitivity means that each child's heritage is honored, that it is understood as unique from other cultures, and that it is respected. It means that teachers must become familiar with the cultural norms of the children in their classes and build bridges for children and their families into the more dominant culture.

The culturally sensitive teacher gets to know each of the families as a separate entity and becomes familiar with their individual expressions of culture and values. Today's teacher recognizes that one family does not represent the totality of the culture (which would be stereotyping) and is careful not to overgeneralize from one example. The effective teacher is called on to integrate these insights into curriculum planning, as well as in their relationships with the children's families, in order to serve the best interests of the young child.

Children with Diverse Abilities

Watching and working with children exposes a range of diversity among the group. Megan is challenged by eye-hand coordination, Ariel has difficulty attending to tasks, and Hans stutters when he is excited. What accounts for these developmental differences?

Factors That Influence Developmental Differences

There are several factors that influence the way children grow and develop.

Genetic Makeup

Each child has a unique combination of genes that determine eye and hair color, height, body shape, personality traits, and intelligence. Certain diseases, such as Tay-Sachs, cystic fibrosis, and sickle cell anemia, are linked through heredity (Berk, 2009).

Environment

From conception, the brain is affected by environmental conditions. An individual child's rate and sequence of development reflects the interactions among the brain, the body, and the environment. The attitudes with which children are raised, their culture, socioeconomic status, the kinds of caregiving they experience, and their community combine in countless ways to affect growth. Nutrition, safety, play space, adult relationships, neighborhood, and family stability affect individual development. Whether a child lives in relative poverty or riches, environmental factors interact with genes to create a single, individual person.

Gender and Race Differences

Girls and boys differ in both the rate and the pattern of growth, especially during adolescence. Ethnic variations in growth are common. African American and Asian American children seem to mature faster than do North American Caucasian children (Berk, 2009). Growth "norms" should be used with caution and with respect to ethnic differences.

Learning Styles

Children exhibit a number of different approaches to learning that must be accounted for when planning programs. Some are quiet; others move around and talk, while others seem never to listen. While on a field trip to the farm, these children demonstrate three common learning styles:

- Lorenzo watches, looks around, and visually absorbs the environment. He calls to others, "See the goat!" and "Look at that." Lorenzo is a **visual learner**.
- Olivia chatters away to her friends as they enter the barnyard. "Listen to all the noise the sheep are making." "Hear the horses?" While she enjoys listening to what others have to say, Olivia has difficulty waiting for her turn to talk. Olivia is an **auditory learner**.
- As she runs ahead of the other children, Anna calls out, "Get over here so we can touch them!" Looking up at the teacher, she begs, "Take me closer. I want to see what sheep feel like." Anna is a **tactile learner**.

Each of the children responds to the experience in a way that reflects an individual learning style. Lorenzo interprets the field trip in pictures, by drawing or painting what he saw. Olivia repeats stories from her experience over and over again as she integrates her experience at the farm. Anna plays out her farm experience by making clay animals or dancing an "animal dance." (In Chapters 4 and 10, learning styles are further discussed in terms of Gardner's Multiple Intelligences.)

In our diverse world, teachers should be sensitive to the influence of sex, race, and individual patterns of development.

The implication for teachers is that programs are planned to meet the needs and challenges of the whole group. Individual differences are incorporated into the planning. Activities are selected to allow for a variety of responses from children at different stages of development and learning styles.

Planning for Diverse Abilities

When teachers are aware of the range of developmental differences and learning styles of the children in the class, they incorporate those variations into the planning process. Figure 5-2 suggests some strategies for how to plan for these types of variations.

Collaborating with Families

Families are usually the first to notice that their child is not developing according to the norms. They may ask the child's teacher to watch for signs of hearing impairments, lack of necessary motor skills, or language imperfections. Because early diagnosis and intervention are important, teachers assess the child's overall skills. If both the family and the teachers feel there is a potential

Planning for Developmental Differences and Learning Styles

The learning environment can be arranged so that children of every skill level can work and play together when you:

- Make sure the materials and activities are in a variety of formats. Art can be expressed in paints, crayons, markers, clay, wood, and paper.
- Address the variations of development within a one-year span. A selection of books would include wordless books, easy-reader books, picture books, short story books, Braille books, and alphabet and number books.
- Plan around the known similarities within the group and allow for the needs and interests of all the children. There is great interest in the 3-year-old class for three new baby siblings. Add more dolls, carriages, beds, and doll clothes to the dramatic play area.
- Small groups may help some children with a new learning experience. In preparation for an upcoming field trip to the fire station, hold small group discussion so that each child is able to listen, ask questions, and participate in the planning. Rehearse rules for walking with a buddy, staying with the group, and expected behavior while at the fire station.
- Modify materials and activities to make them accessible to all children. Make sure that all surfaces, indoor and out, are wide enough, stable, and safe for wheelchairs. Have multiples of popular items (shovels, telephones, dolls). Use a small tray for puzzle pieces or Legos to contain the activity and define the work space.
- Every classroom can be adapted for children with special needs. Consult with each child's family to explore together ways to enhance learning.

FIGURE 5-2 An inclusive classroom provides a way for every child—regardless of ability—to experience growth and learning.

© Cengage Learning 2014

problem, further resources and services are explored through social service agencies and public health offices. The early childhood professional is not an expert in diagnosing learning exceptionalities but can be effective in helping family's secure proper referrals and treatment.

State and federal laws require that when a child from 3 to 21 years of age is identified with having a disability, an individualized education program (IEP) is developed by a team composed of the child's parents, a special education teacher, a regular classroom teacher, a representative of the local education agency, and other specialists. They base the IEP on the strengths of the child and present level of functioning as well the goals and concerns of the family. The team establishes long-term goals and short-term objectives to meet those goals. Special education and related services are determined as well as where and when the inclusive programs take place.

For infants and toddlers younger than 3 years of age who receive early intervention services, an individualized family service plan (IFSP) is put in place. A significant difference between this plan and the IEP is the focus is on the whole family, who determine the goals. Family-centered as well as child-centered services are made available to enhance family functioning.

The IEP and the IFSP are part of IDEA, the Individuals with Disabilities Education Improvement Act, which stems from the Education for All Handicapped Children Act of 1986. The Diversity Box, "The Right to Be Included," outlines the important legislation that led to the creation of these programs.

Children With Special Needs

The term special needs includes many conditions that may or may not be noticeable. To be designated as having special needs, a child's normal growth and development is: 1) delayed; 2) distorted, atypical, or abnormal; or 3) severely or negatively affected (Allen & Cowdery, 2012). This definition includes the physical, mental, emotional, and social areas of development. The terms "exceptionality" and "disability" are both used to define atypical development.

Two types of children come under the category of children with special needs: 1) children who have some sort of exceptionality and 2) children who are gifted. They extend the definition of "Who is the child?" and are discussed separately in this section.

There are children who have some obvious characteristics that qualify them for special-needs status:

- Five-year-old Pete, blind from birth, has been in nursery school for three years.
- Chrissy, a 4-year-old with multiple exceptionalities, has her daily program in a special school supplemented by attending the child care center three afternoons each week.
- Travis is a child with Down syndrome, and this is his first experience in a school not restricted to atypical children.

Other children with less apparent exceptionalities are defined as children with special needs.

In the course of normal development, any one area of a child's growth is affected by the development of the whole child, and this holds true for children who do not develop according to the norms. Any single exceptionality may lead to other multi-handicapping conditions:

- A child with a profound hearing loss is often delayed in speech production or language abilities and suffers social isolation due to the inability to hear and speak with peers.
- A child with a speech impairment or cleft palate may have the intellectual capacity to put simple puzzles together but may not yet have the language to engage verbally in songs and finger play.
- A child with Down syndrome may have congenital heart defects, intellectual impairments, eye abnormalities, or poor physical coordination.
- Children who have cerebral palsy, a central nervous system disorder, often have other exceptionalities, such as intellectual delays, epilepsy, and hearing, visual, and speech problems (Kiernan, et al., n.d.).

Figure 5-3 lists a number of exceptionalities, from mild to severe, that teachers of young children may encounter.

Learning Disabilities

Children with learning disabilities are found in almost every classroom; they have no discernable condition but, nevertheless, are having problems with one or more basic skills or learning disabilities that keep them from storing, processing, and producing information. These conditions may include:

- Poor memory skills; difficulty in following directions; eye–hand coordination problems; and trouble discriminating between letters, numbers, and sounds.
- Dyslexia, the most common specific learning disability, causes children to reverse letters (such as *d* and *b*) or words (such as *was* and *saw*), although many children do this who are not dyslexic.
- A strength in another area, such as math, and yet have a learning difficulty with language. Learning difficulties are usually not a singular dysfunction. Children who exhibit problems with reading and writing often have difficulties with spatial relationships and body coordination.

Observations of these behaviors can give teachers some of the first warning signs of learning disorders.

A learning disability does not mean that a child is intellectually impaired or delayed. A child with a learning disability usually has a normal or above normal IQ (Allen & Cowdery, 2012) and tends to develop normally, but the task of reading seems to highlight several areas of difficulty: problems of visual perception, inability to integrate visual and auditory information, impaired memory, problems with language, and difficulty distinguishing the separate sounds in words. This wide range of symptoms, the number of potential causes, and the varying degrees to which children exhibit the symptoms make learning exceptionalities difficult to diagnose.

Teachers of Young Children May Encounter a Variety of Disabilities

- *Speech and language:* hearing impairment, stuttering, articulation problems, cleft palate, chronic voice disorders, learning disabilities.
- *Physical-motor:* visual impairment, blindness, perceptual motor deficits, orthopedic disabilities such as cerebral palsy, spina bifida, loss of limbs, muscular dystrophy.
- *Intellectual:* cognitive delays, brain injury, brain dysfunction, dyslexia, and learning disabilities.
- *Social-emotional:* self-destructive behavior, severe withdrawal, dangerous aggression toward self and others, noncommunicativeness, moodiness, tantrums, attention-deficit/hyperactivity disorder, severe anxiety, depression, phobias, psychosis, autism.
- *Health impairments:* severe asthma, epilepsy, hemophilia, congenital heart defects, severe anemia, malnutrition, diabetes, tuberculosis, cystic fibrosis, Down's syndrome, sickle cell anemia, Tay-Sachs disease, AIDS.
- *Specific learning disabilities:* difficulties with language use and acquisition, spoken and written language affected, perceptual handicaps, brain injury, minimal brain dysfunction, dyslexia, developmental aphasia.

© Cengage Learning 2011

FIGURE 5-3 These disorders may range from mild to severe, and children exhibit a variety of abilities and needs even if they are diagnosed with the same condition. For further information concerning a specific condition, the student should consult a special education textbook.

Use caution against early diagnosis of a young child as "learning disabled" because young children differ in their individual rates of growth, and many differences and delays are within the range of normal development.

Attention-Deficit/Hyperactivity Disorder (ADHD)

Do you know a child who never sits still—one who is constantly on the move, talks excessively, and disrupts classroom activities? This behavior is typical of children with a condition known as attention-deficit/hyperactivity disorder (ADHD), which, according to Berk (2009), affects up to 3 to 5 percent of all school-age children, more often boys than girls. The median age at onset of ADHD is 7 years (National Institutes of Health, 2012).

The National Resource Center on ADHD (2011) notes three subtypes of ADHD that are common today:

1. ADHD predominately inattentive type (ADHD-1)
   - Makes careless mistakes
   - Does not pay close attention to details
   - Easily distracted; hard to maintain attention
   - Does not appear to listen; seems forgetful
   - Has trouble with follow-through
   - Loses things; has difficulty with organization
   - Might avoid tasks that take prolonged intellectual effort
2. ADHD predominately hyperactive-impulsive (ADHD-HI)
   - Fidgets, squirms
   - Has trouble staying seated, runs about

   - Talks excessively; difficulty with being quiet during activities
   - Blurts out answers; interrupts; intrudes on others
   - Has difficulty waiting to take turns
3. ADHD combined type (ADHD-C)
   - Child or adult meets criteria from both categories listed previously.

Children with ADHD can be difficult to manage both at home and in the classroom. Their constellation of behaviors may apply at some level to many children, but teachers must be cautious about labeling the normally active, somewhat disruptive child as having ADHD. The child with ADHD exhibits these behaviors in extreme, usually before age 7 (Berk, 2009).

Medication is a common treatment for children with ADHD, but because its effects are short term and its side effects can be serious, it is controversial. The most effective approach appears to be a combination of medication and individual behavior management strategies (Allen & Cowdery, 2009; Berk, 2009). There is no easy solution for dealing with children who have ADHD; further research into the cause of this disability and development of safe effective treatments are clearly needed. Figure 5-4 suggests guidance techniques that help children with ADHD.

Autism Spectrum Disorder

Autism spectrum disorder (ASD) is a neurological condition that includes autism, Asperger syndrome, and nonspecified pervasive developmental disorders (PDD). ASD is characterized by impaired language

---

Effective Guidance Strategies for Children with ADHD

Strategy	Example
Maintain regular and consistent routines and rules.	"Remember, Sitara, always wash your hands before eating lunch."
Have realistic expectations.	"I know it is hard for you to wait. Why don't you go over to the math lab and work until I am ready."
Make eye contact when giving directions, using clear and simple explanations.	"Look at me Toby, so I know that you are listening. Good. Now let's go over the assignment together."
Allow time for transitions by giving a plan for the next step.	"In three minutes it will be time to have small groups, so please finish your snacks."
Select jobs in which the child will be successful.	"Richy, please get enough rulers for everyone at this table."
Recognize accomplishments.	"Good job. You counted out enough for each of us."

© Cengage Learning 2014

FIGURE 5-4 These examples help children with ADHD modify their behavior.

and communication skills as well as repetitious behaviors. The symptoms are evident by age 3 and may appear as early as 18 months of age. ASD is more common in boys than girls and in siblings of a child with ASD (National Institutes of Health, 2012).

Children with ASD commonly have problems with 1) verbal and nonverbal communications, making eye contact, holding conversations, and smiling; 2) social skills, such as sharing emotion and grasping how others think and feel; and 3) repetitive routines and behaviors, repeating words and phrases over and over, and obsessively following schedules (National Institutes of Health, 2012).

Some ASD symptoms are severe and cause a child to appear very differently from other children; other children may exhibit only mild forms of ASD symptoms and not be noticeably different. Every child with ASD is different from every other child with ASD, depending on the severity of the symptoms.

There is no cure or single treatment for children with ASD. Some of the solutions that help to manage the symptoms so that children may learn are behavior management therapy (see Chapter 7), speech and language therapy, and physical and occupational therapy. There are no medications to treat ASD, but some medications can treat some of the symptoms. As noted in the Diversity Box on page 86 the law requires free public education from age 3 to 21 for children with special needs, such as ASD. A team composed of parents, teachers, caregivers, school psychologists, and other child development specialists collaborate to create an IEP best suited to each child (National Institutes of Health, 2012).

As of this writing, the American Psychiatric Association is redefining ASD. The new guidelines may eliminate some of those who are currently getting special education services. Check the National Institutes of Health at www.nichd.nih.gov/health/topics/asd.cfm for updates.

Many children with ASD attend schools with normally developing children. The following strategies are useful in guiding children with ASD:

- Use simple, direct, and short statements.
- Demonstrate actions: show the child the puzzle and where it goes in the shelf.
- Encourage social interactions with other children.
- Foster interactions with adults by encouraging the child to use simple words when he or she wants something.
- Maintain an environment with a predictable schedule and minimal distractions.
- Establish frequent communication with the family.

TeachSource Video

Watch the TeachSource Video entitled, "Programs for Children with Autism." After you study the video clip, reflect on the following questions:

1. Why do you think there is such a low child/adult ratio? In what ways was it successful? Unsuccessful?

2. Would you like to teach children with ASD? Why or why not? What would be the most challenging aspect of teaching young children with ASD?

Children Who Are Gifted and Talented

The U.S. Department of Education's time-tested definition of gifted and talented children is: "children and youth with outstanding talent who perform or show the potential for performing at remarkably high levels of accomplishment when compared with others of their age, experience, or environment. Outstanding talents are present in all cultural groups . . . and across all economic strata" (USDE, 1993). The National Association for Gifted Children (2011) identifies six areas of giftedness. A child may be gifted in more than one but not in all six areas:

Creative thinking: Independent and original thinker in speech and writing, creates and invents, improvises, challenged by problem solving and creative tasks, has sense of humor, and does not mind being different from the crowd.

General intellectual ability: Observant and inquisitive, hypothesizes, formulates abstractions and processes information in complex ways, excited about new ideas, learns rapidly, uses a large vocabulary, and is a self-starter.

Specific academic ability: High ability in memorization and comprehension, acquires basic skill knowledge quickly, widely read and high academic success in special interest area, pursues special interest with enthusiasm and vigor.

Leadership: Fluent and concise in self-expression, self-confident, well-liked by peers and has high expectations for self and others, assumes responsibility and is well organized, has good judgment and foresees consequences and implications of decisions.

Psychomotor: Enjoys participation in various athletic opportunities, well coordinated, good manipulative and motor skills, high energy level, exhibits precision in movement, and challenged by difficult athletic activities.

Visual/Performing Arts: Unusual ability to express self, feelings, and mood through dance, drama, and music; outstanding sense of spatial relationships; a high level of creative expression; observant; and likes to produce rather than copy.

Ford et al. (2002) have long promoted the view that the percentage of blacks and Hispanics are underrepresented in identification as gifted and that this oversight is linked to standardized tests that are often culturally and linguistically inappropriate for many students. They further note that the inclusion of the word "potential" in the definition of gifted is a critical factor that will enhance the inclusion of children who are ethnically and culturally in the minority, children with special needs, and children of poverty. It serves as a reminder that giftedness is a trait that cuts across all socioeconomic and cultural groups.

Early childhood teachers should be aware of some traits children who are gifted display so that they can recognize potentially gifted children in their care. Further, because the majority of children in the early years are too young for IQ or standardized tests, teachers are likely to have unidentified gifted children in their programs.

The Teacher's Role

The teacher's role with children who are gifted is that of providing challenge and stimulation. Children who are gifted may need scaffolding strategies to support their learning. In early elementary grades, children who are gifted may be advanced to an older group, or spend part of the day in special classes where they can interact with like-minded peers. A more common approach in early childhood has been in the area of curriculum enrichment. In this way, the child remains with age-level peers to develop social skills. Children who are gifted often feel isolated from their nongifted peers and may have social and emotional difficulties. These factors must also be considered in planning programs.

Curriculum areas are developed in more complex ways. The child who is gifted needs a learning environment that supports intellectual risk-taking, the use of logic and abstract concepts, and curiosity and enhances their specific talents. All the children in the classroom benefit from this enrichment; each responds according to his or her abilities and a rich curriculum benefits the whole class.

Families of children who are gifted need support and encouragement as well as guidance in dealing with their child's exceptionality. Together, teachers and parents can explore what best suits each individual child so that this giftedness may be nurtured and challenged at home and at school.

The Inclusive Classroom

In the past, children with special needs were integrated into classrooms only after they had met certain standards and expectations. Often they were assigned to separate special education classes. When ready, they were mainstreamed into classrooms with typically developing children. Inclusion means that a child with special needs is a full-time member of a regular classroom, a more natural environment, with children who do, as well as those who do not, have special needs.

More than a word definition is at stake, however. Inclusion is the right to belong, to have worth, and be accepted as a valuable part of society. Teachers are a key factor in the successful integration of children with exceptionalities. Their attitude is critical; they must be committed to teaching all children with equal caring and concern, regardless of their intelligence or skill levels. Some strategies to enhance inclusion in the classroom are:

- Support social encounters between children who have special needs and those who do not by encouraging them to get involved in a wide variety of activities together. Some children with special needs require assistance and modeling for successful social play and interactions.
- Build a play-based curriculum on the strengths of each child—those who have disabilities and those who do not—that include materials and activities that challenge their capabilities. Work with individual families to integrate each child's IEP into the overall plan.
- Teachers who work with children who have special needs should have specific training and guidance to ensure that each child is challenged developmentally.

Inclusion is a critical concept for all children. For typically developing children, it is an opportunity to learn to

All children, regardless of abilities, learn and grow through play.

DIVERSITY

The Right to Be Included

During the past 50 years there has been significant public recognition of and funding for education programs for persons with special needs. Previously, pubic and private attitudes were ones of shame and segregation. Past generations hid adults and children with special needs in their homes or secluded them in institutions. Keeping special populations out of sight gave way to providing separate opportunities for them. Public consciousness is now sufficient to understand that not all people with special needs are necessarily mentally impaired. The current practice of integrating children with varying exceptionalities into ongoing programs in schools—and into the mainstream of American life—is a more humane practice. Significant legislation and practices that fostered the practice of inclusion are:

1972: Head Start required that a minimum of 10 percent of its enrollment be reserved for children with disabilities and led the way toward large-scale inclusion.

1975: Public Law 94-142, the Education for All Handicapped Children Act—the so-called Bill of Rights for the Handicapped was passed and guarantees free public education to disabled persons from three to 21 years of age "in the least restrictive" environment. Parents of children with special needs are an integral part of the development of their child's individualized education plan (IEP) in which the strengths and needs of the family are taken into consideration.

1986: Public Law 99-457, the Education of the Handicapped Amendments provides funding for children who were not included in the previous law: infants, toddlers, and 3- to 5-year-olds. This law also allows for the inclusion of "developmentally delayed" youngsters and leaves local agencies the opportunity to include the "at-risk" child in that definition.

1990: Congress reauthorized Public Law 94-142 and renamed it the Individuals with Disabilities Education Act (IDEA) (Public Law 101-576). The law covered two new categories: autism and traumatic brain injury.

1990: Public Law 101-336, the Americans with Disabilities Act (ADA), makes it unlawful to discriminate against people with disabilities and requires that they have equal access to public and private services, as well as reasonable accommodations.

Each step taken during the past 50 years has given thousands of children the right to be included and promotes the dignity and worth of all individuals.

accept differences in people. For the child with special needs, typically developing children serve as age-appropriate behavior models. Some children with special needs may not have an opportunity to hear the language of their normal peer group. They may not know how to play with another child or how to communicate in socially acceptable ways. In the inclusive classroom, with sensitive and knowledgeable teachers, children with exceptionalities are helped to realize their potential as growing and learning children.

Dealing with Bias and Stereotypes

One of the most important issues for a child with special needs is to be accepted. Young children are known for their forthrightness in commenting on and asking questions about what confuses or frightens them. Children without special needs may be anxious about what another child's exceptionality may mean to them. Although this is a common reaction and age appropriate, we cannot allow an individual to be rejected on the basis of his or her abilities. Derman-Sparks and Edwards (2010) suggests the following strategies:

- The rejection must be handled immediately with support and assurance given to the child who was rejected that this type of behavior is not permitted.

  Example: "No, Rachel. You cannot tell Gina that she can't play because she is in a wheelchair. Let's look at ways you can include her in your play."
- It is important to help children recognize how they are different and how they are alike.

  Example: "Gina is very good at writing stories, just like you, Rachel. Perhaps you could write a story together."

Educators must help all children develop a pride in their cultural heritage.

Mitch Kezar/Stone/Getty Images

- Children need to have their fears about other children's abilities and exceptionalities taken seriously and to have adults understand their concerns.

  Example: "I'm glad you told me that Emma frightened you because she is blind. You don't have to be afraid that you, too, will be blind. Emily was born without sight and when you were born, you were able to see. You could use your eyes to help Emily walk to the playground."

- Questions must be answered promptly, truthfully, and simply. Use the children's own curiosity, and let the child with special needs answer questions, whenever possible.

Example: "Yes, Emily, Janice has some questions about being blind. Would you like to tell her how you are able to read with Braille?"

All children benefit when adults are willing to confront bias and deal with children's prejudice and misconceptions. When we provide opportunities for children to interact with people who look and act differently than they do, we actively foster acceptance and respect for the individual. (More gender diversity issues are found in Chapter 15.)

Summary

LO 1 The concept of the whole child means that you include all developmental dimensions: the physical, cognitive, social, emotional, and linguistic areas of growth. Although they may be discussed separately, each area of growth is affected by and affects every other development area.

LO 2 Word Pictures describe the common behaviors and characteristics typical to an age group that helps teachers look at specific areas of a child's development to plan appropriate experiences for the group as well as the individual child. Changing demographics bring more culturally and linguistically diverse children into early childhood classrooms who call for culturally sensitive teaching and efforts to work with parents from a multicultural perspective.

LO 3 Children may share many typical characteristics while displaying wide individual differences. Atypical development includes a variety of exceptionalities, such as learning disabilities, dyslexia, Attention deficit/hyperactivity disorder (ADHD), autism spectrum disorder (ASD), and children who are gifted and talented. In an inclusive classroom, the environment and the curriculum are adapted to fit the needs of each student who has an exceptionality. All children require a learning environment that supports their unique needs. Federally mandated programs for children from birth through age 21 offer early intervention services for children diagnosed with a disability.

Key Terms

Word Pictures
developmental domains
age-level characteristics
stress
biracial
interracial
genes
visual learner
auditory learner

tactile learner
disability
exceptionalities
Down syndrome
attention-deficit/hyperactivity
    disorder (ADHD)
gifted and talented children
Public Law 94-142
Public Law 99-457

individualized education program
    (IEP)
individualized family service plan (IFSP)
special needs
inclusion
mainstreaming
prejudice

Review Questions

1. What are some of the reasons for using the concept of the whole child in early education? How is each child unique?
2. How can Word Pictures be a valuable tool for planning programs for young children? What role does cultural considerations play when discussing developmental stages?
3. Who are the children with special needs? Why is it important for teachers to know about the variety of special needs? What are some of the difficulties that must be overcome for successful inclusion of children with special needs?
4. What do educators need to consider when teaching children who are gifted and/or talented?

Observe and Apply

1. Select two children who are approximately the same age. Using the Word Pictures, compare their physical, cognitive, language, creative, and social development. How are they alike? How are they different? What conclusions do you draw about their developmental level?
2. Observe a class of children with special needs in an inclusive classroom. What would you do to foster interactions between the children who have exceptionalities and the children who do not? What verbalizations are used about a child's exceptional condition, and do other children seem to understand how their friends are similar to them as well as different?
3. Survey a classroom for its cultural, racial, and ethnic mix. How do the classroom and the curriculum reflect the various heritages of each child? What suggestions would you make to enhance cultural sensitivity in this class? How do you think this information affects your teaching?
4. Have you ever experienced feeling "different"? In what context? How does this inform your work with children? With families?
5. What would do you if a child made racial slurs against another child in the class? How did it make you feel? What can you do to affirm the feelings of the child who was called names?

Helpful Websites

National Resource Center on AD/HD
www.help4adhd.org

National Society for the Gifted and Talented
www.nsgt.org

National Institute of Neurological Disorders and Strokes   **www.ninds.nih.gov**

Individuals with Disabilities Education Act
www.idea.ed.gov

The Division of Early Childhood for Exceptional Children   **www.dec-sped.org**

The ARC (formerly National Association of Retarded Citizens)   **www.thearc.org**

The Center for the Study of Biracial Children
csbchome.org

🔊 The Education Course Mate website for this text offers many helpful resources and interactive study tools. Go to CengageBrain.com to access the TeachSource Videos, flashcards, tutorial quizzes, direct links to all of the websites mentioned in the chapter, downloadable forms, and more.

References

Allen, K. E., & Cowdery, G. (2012). *The exceptional child: Inclusion in early childhood education.* Belmont, CA: Wadsworth Cengage Learning.

Berk, L. E. (2009). *Child development.* Boston: Allyn & Bacon.

Derman-Sparks, L., & Olsen Edwards, J. (2010). *Anti-bias education for young children and ourselves.* Washington, D.C.: NAEYC.

Ford, D.Y., Harris III, J. J., Tyson, C.A., & Frazier Trotman, M. (2002, revised). *Theory into practice: Providing access for culturally diverse gifted students: from deficit to dynamic thinking.* Columbus: The Ohio State University, on behalf of its College of Education (2003).

Hirsch, E. (Ed.) (1974). *The block book.* Washington, D.C.: National Association for the Education of the Young Child.

Kelly, R. Beyond just black and white. (February 2, 2009). *Newsweek,* Volume CLIII, 41.

Kiernan, S., et al. (not dated). *Mainstreaming preschoolers: Children with orthopedic handicaps.* Washington, D.C.: U.S. Department of Health, Education, and Welfare.

National Association for Gifted and Talented. (2011). Giftedness defined: What is gifted and talented? http://www.nsgt.org. Retrieved August 11, 2011.

National Institutes of Health. Autism spectrum disorders (ASDs). http://www.nichd.nih.gov/health. Retrieved January 23, 2012.

National Resource Center on ADHD. (2011). About ADHD: Statistical prevalence. http://www.help4adhd.org. Retrieved August 13, 2011.

National Scientific Council on the Developing Child (2). Video Series. *Three core concepts in early development.* http:developingchild.harvard.edu/activitiescouncil/

United States Department of Education website. The Jacob K. Javits Gifted and Talented Student Education Act of 2001, Section 5464. Retrieved July 31, 2011. www.2.ed.gov/javits/index.html

6

Creating Environments

© Cengage Learning

naeyc Standards For Professional Development

The following NAEYC Standards for early childhood professional development are addressed in this chapter:

Standard 1 Promoting Child Development and Learning

Standard 4 Using Developmentally Effective Approaches to Connect with Children and Families

Standard 5 Using Content Knowledge to Build Meaningful Curriculum

naeyc Code of Ethical Conduct

These are the sections of the NAEYC Code of Ethical Conduct that apply to the topics in this chapter:

Section I:

P-1.2. We shall care for and educate children in positive emotional and social environments that are cognitively stimulating and that support each child's culture, language, ethnicity, and family structure.

Section II:

I-2.5 To respect the dignity and preferences of each family and to make an effort to learn about its structure, culture, language, customs, and beliefs to ensure a culturally consistent environment for all children and families.

Section III:

Based upon our core values, our primary responsibility to colleagues is to establish and maintain settings and relationships that support productive work and meet professional needs.

Learning Objectives

LO1 Outline the major criteria that are used in creating a developmentally appropriate learning environment.

LO2 Examine the central elements of children's health, safety, and well-being when planning environments.

LO3 Analyze basic arrangements and materials for the physical, temporal, and interpersonal aspects of the environment.

Criteria for Creating Environments

What does it mean to create an environment appropriate for young children? The environment is the stage on which children play out the themes of childhood: their interests, triumphs, problems, and concerns. An environment for children includes all of the conditions that affect their surroundings and the people in it.

Each environment is unique. Rather than a single model, there are many good settings for all children. Each program has goals that reflect the values and priorities of its teachers, families, and communities. When growth goals and the setting mesh, the atmosphere encourages enthusiasm and engagement.

Definition and Characteristics

The environment speaks volumes to children, and their development is strongly influenced by settings and materials. Our ideas about the environment have been influenced by educators such as Montessori, Vygotsky, and Malaguzzi (see Chapters 1 and 4). As Wurm (2009) notes:

> Each of these educators has left their own influence: from child-sized furnishings, to the creation of social spaces for language development, and the importance of a stage for storytelling. These details, when woven together, have shown us both in theory and practice that schools for young children are spaces that attend to social interaction, problem solving, dramatic play, storytelling, fantasy, conflict and its resolution, and communication as a few of the vehicles for children to build their repertoire and further their understanding of the world.

Definition

The **environment** is the sum total of the physical and human qualities that combine to create a space in which children and adults work and play together. Environment is the content teachers arrange; it is an atmosphere they create; it is a feeling they communicate. Environment is the total picture—from the traffic flow to the daily schedule, from the numbers of chairs at a table to the placement of the guinea pig cage. It is a means to an end. The choices teachers make concerning the **physical** environment (the equipment and materials, the room arrangement, the playground and the facilities available), the **temporal** environment (timing for transitions, routines, activities), and the **interpersonal** environment (number and nature of teachers, ages and numbers of

The environment includes not only physical space and materials but also aspects of time and interpersonal relationships such as who plays together and how much time they need to engage deeply in the play.

children, types and style of interactions among them) combine to support the program goals.

Teachers arrange the environment to promote what they feel is best in children. Whether the environment is an adapted church basement, an elementary school classroom, or a space made especially for young children, it is a powerful force in their lives. After the family and teacher, it is the child's third teacher. It is the canvas on which children create their work.

Characteristics

All settings for the care and education of young children have similar basic environmental components and goals—meeting the needs of children—despite the fact that programs vary widely in the size of the group, age of children, length of day, program focus, and number of staff. Although physical environments vary on the surface, all high quality, **prepared environments**:

- Convey a welcoming feeling
- Give clear cues about what can be done in each area
- Provide varied spaces that let children concentrate, as well as letting them experience lively group interactions and vigorous physical activity (Hyson, 2008)

Such variation on this common educational theme is one of the reasons why our field is so diverse and interesting. Caution must be exercised, however, to ensure a quality experience for all children. For instance, *size does matter*. Research conducted more than 40 years ago (Prescott, Jones, & Kritschevsky, 1972) found that when a center gets too large, rules and routine guidance are emphasized, outdoor areas often have little variety, and children are often less enthusiastically involved and more often wandering. *Group size* is now recognized as one of the most important indicators of quality child care (Howes, Phillips, & Whitebook, 1992; Copple & Bredekamp, 2009). Too many of us know the problems associated with crowding and cramped conditions, little rooms that become institutions that dehumanize.

The National Association for the Education of Young Children (NAEYC) continues its work with program accreditation of programs and developmentally appropriate practices (DAP). In addition, standards have been set both for group size and for optimal adult–child ratios (see Figure 6-1).

Physical Plant

Before creating an environment for children, the early childhood teacher must analyze the physical plant. The building that is inviting and beautiful beckons children to enter; a space with color and light encourages children to play with both. The size and shape of the designated space determine how to plan for safe and appropriate use.

To rescale the space, teachers shift from an adult perspective to a child's scale. Getting on one's knees provides a glimpse of the environment from the child's point

Teacher[a]–Child Ratios within Group Size

Age Group	Group Size									
	6	8	10	12	14	16	18	20	22	24
Infants										
Birth to 15 months[b]	1:3	1:4								
Toddlers/Twos (12–36 months)[b]										
12 to 28 months	1:3	1:4	1:4[c]	1:4						
21 to 36 months		1:4	1:5	1:6						
Preschool[b]										
2.5–3s (30–48 months)				1:6	1:7	1:8	1:9			
4-year-olds						1:8	1:9	1:10		
5-year-olds						1:8	1:9	1:10		
Kindergarten								1:10	1:11	1:12

NOTE: In a mixed–age preschool class of 2.5-year-olds to 5-year-olds, no more than two children between the ages of 30 months and 36 months may be enrolled. The ratios within group size for the predominant age group apply. If infants and toddlers are in a mixed–age group, the ratio for the youngest child applies.

Ratios are to be lowered when one or more children in the group need additional adult assistance to fully participate in the program (a) because of ability, language fluency, developmental age or stage, or other factors or (b) to meet other requirements of NAEYC Accreditation.

A group or classroom refers to the number of children who are assigned for most of the day to a teacher or a team of teaching staff and who occupy an individual classroom or well-defined space that prevents intermingling of children from different groups within a larger room or area.

Group sizes as stated are ceilings, regardless of the number of staff.

Ratios and group sizes are always assessed during on–site visits for NAEYC Accreditation. They are not a required criterion. However, experience suggests that programs that exceed the recommended number of children for each teaching staff member and total group sizes will find it much more difficult to meet each standard and achieve NAEYC Accreditation. The more these numbers are exceeded, the more difficult it will be to meet each standard.

[a]Includes teachers, assistant teachers, and teacher aides

[b]These age ranges purposely overlap. Programs may identify the age group being used for on–site assessment purposes for groups of children whose ages are included in multiple age groups.

[c]Group sizes for this age group would require an additional adult.

FIGURE 6-1 Group size and staff–child ratio are two aspects of the environment that affect the quality of children's experience. (*NAEYC Early Childhood Program Standards and Accreditation Criteria: The Mark of Quality in Early Childhood Education*, Table 2, p. 83. Reprinted with permission from the National Association for the Education of Young Children.)

of view; child space is measured from the floor and playground up. A child's stature determines what is available to and noticed by that child. For crawling infants, space consists primarily of the floor, whereas school-aged children can use and learn from the space up to about five feet, roughly their own height. It is this perspective that teachers must remember as they plan the physical space for children.

Resources

In planning the environment, the teacher must know what kinds of resources are available. Rarely do teachers have unlimited dollars: "This year we can only afford . . ." determines many of the decisions made about the environment. Priority must be given to teachers' salaries and benefits, equipment and materials for the school, and other related services (maintenance, office help, bus service). Despite budget constraints, teachers must beware of operating on too low of a materials budget. Lack of necessary materials can create increasingly passive, angry, and unhappy children out of sheer boredom. Only by knowing the extent of the fiscal boundaries and budget limits can a teacher plan a complete environment.

There are ways to stretch the budget. Good environmental principles do not depend on numerous or expensive equipment, materials, or buildings. A creative child-centered environment can happen in any setting, regardless of financial resources.

- Some equipment can be made, borrowed, or purchased secondhand. In church-based schools, annual rummage sales at the church provide a wealth of dress-up clothes, books, toys, and some appliances.
- Resource books are filled with ideas for recycling materials into usable equipment for young children.
- Parents can provide computer paper, wood scraps, photo paper.
- Community sources, such as the public library storyteller or a senior citizens group, may be available for extended experiences for the children.
- Effective fund raising provides an added source of revenue in many schools and centers.

The human resources must also be identified. Adults do their best with children when their abilities, experience, and availability are matched with what is expected of them. Volunteers, for instance, feel satisfied if their time is organized and spent in ways meaningful to them. A first-year teacher's resources are best expended in the classroom rather than on administrative projects. A master teacher is ready for the challenges of orienting parents or evaluating curriculum materials. When the entire community values its children, as in the case of Reggio Emilia, the school is a showcase, sending a strong message of how important children are in the life of its citizens. Just as we try to match children's developing skills to the tasks at hand, so, too, should we consider individual people as part of an environment's resources.

Program Goals

The goals and objectives of the program are expressed directly in the arrangement of the environment. Three general goals in designing environments are:

1. To have responsive settings that avoid behavior problems;
2. To establish predictable environments that encourage independence;
3. To create stimulating spaces for active learning.

The physical space and materials should tell the children exactly what is going to happen and how they are to go about their work. In every program, consideration of what children are to accomplish puts goals and environments together. For example, if cognitive and fine motor skill development are the program goals, a space with games using pre-reading and writing materials should be prominent. Puzzles and table toys should have a central place in the classroom. Enough time should be dedicated to these activities every day, and teachers should be available to reinforce and encourage children as they play.

The goals of an early childhood program vary widely. Some programs are housed in large centers, others in homes; children may attend all day or part of it; the purpose may be educational, recreational, or even custodial. In every case, good environments for children must reflect clear and reasonable program goals. Once we know what we wish to do and why we want to do it, we can create space, timing, and an atmosphere in which to meet those goals.

Goals into Action

Creative teachers plan a program directed toward goals for each dimension (physical, temporal, and interpersonal) of the environment (see later in this chapter).

1. The room and yard are arranged to give maximum exposure to the materials and equipment they want children to use.
2. They take care to arrange the daily schedule in ways that provide the time blocks needed to teach content when and how they want to teach it.
3. They see that a warm relationship exists among the teachers and in their interactions with children.

When children walk into a center, the environment should communicate how they are to live and work in that setting. Children should receive clear messages about what they can and cannot do there as well as cues that tell them:

- Where they are free to move to and where they cannot go.
- How they will be treated.
- Who will be there with them.
- What materials and equipment they can use.

- How long they have to play.
- That they are safe there.
- What is expected of them.

The teacher is the key element in creating the environment. It is not the facility alone that counts, as much as it is the teacher's understanding of all the environmental factors and how they are related to one another (see Figure 6-2). A room is just a room and a yard is just a yard until a teacher makes them environments for learning. The teachers are the most responsive part of the

Messages from the Environment

Children Need to...	So the Environment Should...
Be treated as individuals, with unique strengths and developmental goals.	Have low teacher–child ratio for one-to-one interactions. Provide private as well as public spaces for group and solitary play. Place teachers and materials for ready access. Be staffed by teachers who set goals for each child based on observation and assessment. Have materials that match the developmental level of the group. Provide a balance of quiet and active times.
See themselves and their family culture represented positively and be exposed to cultural diversity in meaningful ways.	Include pictures, books, dolls, dramatic play materials, activities, and people that reflect many cultures and life experiences. Have teachers who understand and value home cultures and diverse family practices. Provide opportunities for various cultural habits, activities, and celebrations to occur.
Make choices and independent learning.	Be arranged with clearly marked available choices. Offer a variety of activity centers for exploration. Allow large blocks of time for child-initiated choices. Provide an adequate number of trained teachers to support self-discovery.
Learn to be part of a group.	Be set up for group play—several chairs around tables, easels next to each other, more than one telephone and wagon. Regularly schedule small and large group times and encourage participation. Include trained staff who can create engaging group activities. Allow children to use each other as resources. Provide activities that emphasize cooperation and social interaction.
Become responsible for the setting.	Schedule cleanup times as part of the daily routine. Include teachers and children working together to restore order. Allow time for children to be instructed in the proper use of materials and care.
Be aware of the behavioral limits.	Ensure that teachers and the daily schedule reflect important rules of behavior. Have teachers who deal with behavior problems in a fair and consistent way. Allow plenty of time during transitions that reduces stress during changes. Be arranged to avoid runways and dead ends.
Be with adults who will supervise and facilitate play and encourage learning throughout the day.	Be set up before children arrive so teachers are free to greet them. Encourage teacher–child interactions through the use of small groups. Create a daily schedule that allows time for in-depth interactions.

FIGURE 6-2 The goals of the program are mirrored in the environment.

environment; they converse, hug, appreciate, give information, and see the individuality of each child. They are the ones who create the space, time, and atmosphere that engages children's curiosity and involvement. Indicators of program quality, such as group size, adult–child ratio, the stability, education, and experience of the caregiver all contribute to an environment that meets its goals for children (see Chapters 2 and 5).

Developmentally Appropriate Learning Environments

Because children live in the world of the senses, actions, and feelings, they are greatly influenced by their immediate surroundings. Therefore, we must pay attention to what is in their environment and what happens during their stay there. The following are 15 elements of developmentally appropriate learning environments:

1. *Create brain-compatible environments.* Positive neurological changes occur when a child is engaged in a learning experience. "By immersing a child in a highly motivating and challenging room, we may be able to engage the brain, especially the pre-frontal cortex [where] higher-order thinking skills take place such as comparing and contrasting or making connections between size and shape" (Rushton et al., 2010). A child at the sand table adds water to build a castle [stimulating the motor cortex], sizes it up [occipital lobe], then gauges how high to build it before it collapses [prefrontal lobe]. Children with language or learning disabilities are often over stimulated by excessive noise or harsh lighting. Acoustics, light, colors, and other stimuli may affect the brain.

2. *Build culturally responsive environments.* The environment reflects the cultures of the children in the program and introduces them to those outside of their experience. A self-help focus reinforces a Euro-American cultural value of independence; an anti-bias goal brings in values of group harmony and interdependence. Even if the teachers do not look like the children, or the space does not look like home, it is critical that the environment complement children's home culture. (See Figure 6-3 and the next sections of this chapter.)

3. *Consider children's developmental levels.* Recognize that there are many things young children are not able to do on their own, but allow them the chance to do all they can. Be developmentally aware—know what children in the class are capable of, at what point they are now in their development, and what

the next step should be. Three-year-old Sophie can only zip her jacket now, so having dressing frames helps her put the zipper in the housing. Kindergartener Andrew needs time for both independent work and cooperative peer play

4. *Give families ways to identify their children's space.* Label cubbies, storage bins, or baskets with names, a photo, or a familiar picture so that children can see where to put jackets, artwork, and other personal belongings.

5. *Provide access to enough toys and materials.* Make sure that supplies are stored in such a way that adults do not have to hand them to children each time they are used. "A developmentally appropriate learning environment is designed for individual children to be messy, noisy and quiet, alone and social, and active and still," says Greenman (2000). "It is designed to accommodate much *stuff*—loose parts—the raw materials of discovery for active hands and minds." Equipment placed at a child's height on open, low shelving permits children to proceed at their own pace and to select materials without depending on adults to serve them.

6. *Give opportunities for making choices.* Both indoors and out, children should be given an abundance of materials and a range of activities from which to choose so that they may decide how to spend their time. Choosing to feed the hamster instead of painting at the easel helps 2- to 7-year-olds practice self-regulation. Choosing who to play with and which teacher to join gives children experience in establishing close relationships.

7. *See that children are responsible for caring for the environment.* Have a clean up time in the daily schedule and allow children time to help restore the room and yard. Label shelves and cupboards with pictures or symbols of what is stored there so that children can readily find and return things. Outline the specific shapes of the blocks that are stored on each shelf and make a "parking lot" for wheel toys. An accessible drying rack with large clothespins tells children that they are expected to care for their own artwork.

8. *Involve children in planning and setting up the environment.* Let the children help decide what they want to learn. When Sarita's cat had kittens, the center encouraged a visit to school, then sent a newsletter asking for other pets, arranged a field trip to a pet store, and organized a pet hospital for dramatic play.

9. *Provide children with enough time.* One of the ways children learn is to repeat an activity over and over

Culturally Responsive Environment Checklist

Overall Environment

1. In general, is the classroom hospitable?

2. What is on the walls?
   *If there is work done by children, does it all look alike? For example, are there teacher-made shapes that the children colored, or is the art *genuinely* done by the children?
   *Are all of the pictures for children and the art hung *at children's eye level*?
   *Are the pictures of people hanging on walls or bulletin boards representative of a multicultural community?
   *Even if pictures *do* represent a diverse population, are they stereotypic in any way? For example, is there an alphabet chart that uses "Indian" to symbolize the letter "I"?

3. Is there evidence of families in the environment?

Social Studies

1. Does the curriculum as a whole help the children increase their understanding and acceptance of attitudes, values, and lifestyles that are unfamiliar to them?

2. Are materials and games racially or sex-role stereotypic—for example, black people shooting dice or boys playing war games? Are women depicted only as caregivers while men do lots of exciting jobs?

Music and Games

1. Do the music experiences in the curriculum reinforce the children's affirmation of cultural diversity?

2. Are fingerplays, games, and songs from various cultural groups used in the classroom?

3. Are there many varieties of musical instruments, including ones made by children?

Dramatic Play

1. Is there a wide variety of clothes, including garments from various cultural groups?

2. Are the pictures and the props representative of a diversity of cultures?

3. Are the dolls representative of a broad variety of racial groups?
   *Are they just white dolls with changed skin color?

Blocks

1. Are the accessories representative of various cultural groups and family configurations?

2. Are the people block accessories stereotypic in terms of sex roles?

Language Arts

1. Does the classroom have a wide variety of age-appropriate and culturally diverse books and language-arts materials?

2. Are there stories about a variety of people from each of the following groups in the book corner?
   _____ Native-American cultures
   _____ Asian-American cultures
   _____ Black cultures
   _____ White ethnic cultures
   _____ Spanish-speaking cultures
   _____ Biracial or multiracial people
   _____ Family configurations, including biracial and multiracial families and gay and lesbian families

3. Are there any books that speak of people of diverse cultures in stereotypical or derogatory terms (e.g., describing Latinos as "lazy" or Japanese as always taking photographs)?

Cooking

1. Do the cooking experiences in the classroom encourage the children to experiment with foods other than those with which they are familiar?

2. Are the cooking experiences designed to give young children a general notion of the connections between cultural heritage and the process of preparing, cooking, and eating food?

FIGURE 6-3 An environment checklist provides questions for teachers to evaluate and monitor progress toward an anti-bias environment for children. (Adapted from Frances E. Kendall, *Diversity in the Classroom: New Approaches to the Education of Young Children.* New York: Teachers College Press. Copyright © 1995 by Teachers College Press, Columbia University. Reprinted with permission.)

🔘 You can download a copy of this checklist from this text's Education CourseMate website.

again. They explore, manipulate, experiment, and come to master a puzzle, to shape a lump of clay, or how to brush their teeth. Large blocks of time in the daily schedule—especially for routines—let children learn at an unhurried pace (see Temporal Environment section).

10. *Make expectations clear and consistent.* Use both the environment and your words to let children know what you want them to do. Putting on a clean up song that lasts several minutes communicates both verbally and nonverbally, without pressure. Give clues that indicate how to proceed. For example, Isaac usually has someone dress him at home, yet when he comes to the toddler class, he sees the poster of a child dressing himself, then plays a dressing game in circle time. So when the teacher prompts him, "If you pull up your underpants first, it will be easier to get your pants up," and then gives feedback on what is working, "Good. You've got the back up. Now reach around the front," he hears the teacher's confidence in his ability to finish the task.

    Be sure staff expectations are consistent. The teaching team should set common goals for each child and reinforce them consistently. Children become confused if one teacher expects children to get their cots ready for nap, then another does it for them.

11. *Let children teach one another.* Encourage children to share the skills they have mastered with their peers. Actively seek out each child's way of doing things; support a diversity of approaches. Those who can tie shoes enjoy helping their friends with stubborn laces or slippery knots. Whether reading or telling stories to one another, or showing a friend a fast way to put on a jacket, children benefit from helping each other.

12. *Allow children to solve their own problems whenever possible.* Piaget reminds us that we rob a child of the joy of self-discovery when we do things for them. See how far a child can go in discovering how to manipulate a pin so that it closes, or to work out with another child who uses the red paint first. A good teacher tries not to intervene too early and can let a child struggle sufficiently with a problem before stepping in to help.

13. *Accept children's efforts.* To support children in their quest for independence, the adult must be satisfied with children's efforts. Be ready to accept that Shelley put her boots on the wrong feet, if they are right to her.

14. *Make it safe to make a mistake.* Children learn from their own actions and their own experiences. Let them know it is perfectly acceptable, indeed inevitable, that they at times make mistakes. Help them deal with the consequences of their mistakes. When Chelo spills her juice, she is encouraged to find a sponge and clean up the table, then reinforced by commending her for scrubbing ability and swift action.

15. *Give credit where it is due.* Provide feedback so that children know when they have been successful. Compliment Chaz on how carefully he sorted through the nails to find the one he wanted. Let children take pride in their own accomplishments.

A final note: *Include beauty in your planning.* The environment in which children grow and learn should also be visually appealing and relaxing. There are so many assaults on our visual senses in schools: concrete, barred windows, heavy doors, clutter, to name a few. People become numbed to balance, shape, form, line, and color. While resources are limited, beauty does not need to be ignored. The environment is one of the few things that teachers can control and use to everyone's advantage.

Three Core Aspects of DAP Environments

When creating engaging, appropriate environments for young children, teachers keep in mind the concepts of anti-bias, self-help, and inclusion.

The Anti-Bias Environment

One of our ethical responsibilities is to create and maintain settings for children that respect their dignity and their contributions. Children learn to value one another's uniqueness, the differences as well as the similarities when culturally relevant experiences are embedded in the environment and curriculum.

The anti-bias curriculum, developed at Pacific Oaks College, encourages children and adults to:

- Explore the differences and similarities that make up our individual and group identities.
- Develop skills for identifying and countering the hurtful impact of bias on themselves and their peers. (Derman-Sparks & Edwards, 2010)

The physical and interpersonal environment can be used to help children see that culture consists of the various ways people do similar activities. This approach is different from the "tourist curriculum," which provides only superficial information that is often detached from the child's own life. It is also different from an approach that is based only on the interests of the class and gender, racial, and cultural groups represented therein. The anti-bias environment incorporates the positive aspects of a multicultural curriculum and uses some of the activities that highlight other cultures, but it provides a more inclusive, ongoing approach. This approach avoids patronizing or emphasizing trivial, isolated, exotic differences. There is an inherent feeling of fairness to self and others in the anti-bias approach, as children explore the many ways people do the basic human tasks of everyday life. Think of the diverse cultures expressed in how babies and things are carried from place to place in different parts of the world. How many ways do people eat? Cook? Shop for food?

The anti-bias approach to creating environment has its roots in the theories of Maslow, Piaget, and Erikson (see Chapter 4). Research data reveal that children begin to notice and construct classifications and evaluative categories very early; indeed, 2-year-olds begin to notice gender and racial differences and may even notice physical disabilities (Froschl, Rubin, & Sprung, 1984). Early childhood programs must develop a child's basic sense of trust and mastery so that children can learn to understand themselves and become tolerant and compassionate toward others (see Figure 6-3).

With the prevalence of stereotyping in society, and the impact of bias on children's development, early childhood educators have a responsibility to find ways to prevent, even counter, the damage done by such stereotyping. Teachers do this by arranging an anti-bias physical environment, as well as creating an atmosphere of problem solving and learning in the day-to-day conflicts and interactions that arise naturally. Think about how teachers provide the materials and encourage an atmosphere of trust and time for conflict resolution in these examples:

- A kindergarten teacher shows the children a magazine picture entitled "Brides of America." All of the women pictured are Caucasian. She asks, "What do you think of this picture?" Sophia responds, "That's a silly picture. My mom was a bride, and she's Mexican" (Derman-Sparks & Edwards, 2010).
- A toddler teacher sets up the water play table for washing babies. Choosing dolls that represent several racial and ethnic groups, she invites the children to soap and rinse them. One 2-year-old begins to wash the teacher's arm, then scrubs it hard. "Do you wonder if my color will wash off?" the teacher asks. The child nods, and several others look up. "Does it? Go ahead and try . . . See, a person's color is her own and stays with her. Try yours, too. That's one way people look different: we all have skin, and yet we

each have our own color" (Gutierrez, personal communication, 1987).

The anti-bias approach takes a broad view of a classroom, as a kind of "mini-society" in which children and adults work together. Injustices from the outside world are sometimes addressed. For instance a teacher helps children ticket parents' cars who improperly park in the class-made handicapped parking space (Derman-Sparks, 1989). An anti-bias classroom fosters:

- *Positive self-concept.* Curiosity and creativity stem from being able to affect the environment and what is in it. When Jamal says his baby's hair is fuzzy like his, his smile tells how good he feels about the similarity.
- *Awareness.* All people have interests and feelings, both about themselves and about others. Yoko notices that her classmate Julie runs and throws her arms around her dad, but she prefers a less demonstrative greeting.
- *Respect for diversity.* This stems from the ability to classify similarities and differences and then to appreciate both. For example, when the children create self-portraits for their class books, some choose different colors of paper for drawing faces, but all of them use the same markers to draw in their features.
- *Skills in communication and problem solving.* Learning how to express thoughts and feelings includes being able to hear others and finding peaceful ways to resolve conflicts. Jim and LaNell are quick to tell Eben he cannot play, but they find out that telling him he is "too little" does not work. He does not accept that simply being 3 years old is enough reason to leave him out, so they must either try to include him or make a claim for privacy.

Self-Help Environment

A **self-help** environment has as one of its fundamental goals the development of children's own skills—fostering their mastery of basic abilities that allow them to become responsible for their personal care, learning, emotional controls, problem solving, and choices and decisions. A self-help environment gives children the feeling that they are capable, competent, and successful. It allows children to do for themselves, to meet the challenge of growing up. A self-help environment reflects the belief that autonomy and independence are the birthright of every child.

I Can Do It Myself "I can do it myself" is heard frequently in preschoolers. Nothing renders people more helpless than not being able to maintain their own needs or to take care of themselves in basic ways. Children are

© Cengage Learning

The anti-bias environment encourages girls and boys to play together, respecting differences and including others in new ways.

still in the process of learning about what they can and cannot do. They need many different kinds of experiences to help them learn the extent of their capabilities. Most of all, they need adults who understand their tremendous drive to become self-reliant, adults who not only encourage their abilities and provide the time for them to practice skills, but adults who understand that it is the nature of the child to develop this way.

Self-concept is based on what we know about ourselves, which includes the ability to take care of our own needs. To care for oneself, to feel capable of learning, to solve problems, are all related to feelings of self-esteem. Self-esteem is the value we place on ourselves; how much we like or dislike who we are. Helping children achieve a positive self-concept and self-esteem is the most important part of teaching. The development of a strong sense of self-esteem is a lifelong process; its origins are in the early years.

A program designed to promote self-help skills uses every aspect of the environment, from the room arrangement to the attitudes of the teachers. Each activity is designed to foster self-reliance, thereby building self-esteem. A supermarket is a real-world example of an environment created for maximum self-reliance. Shelves are accessible and the products are clearly marked and attractively displayed.

That kind of thoughtful preparation can create spaces that say to children, "Try me. Master me. You are capable." Teachers want to communicate to children that they value self-help skills as much as they appreciate an art project or science experiment. If Claudia feels that

learning to tie her shoes is worth doing just because of the pleasure it gives her to manipulate the strings, weave them through the holes, and bring them together in a knot, then that becomes her reward. She becomes capable of reinforcing herself.

The Inclusive Environment

In 1975, the Education for All Handicapped Children Act (Public Law 94-142) called for an end to segregation for disabled students from kindergarten through high school. This policy filtered down to preschools and child care centers with an amendment (Public Law 99-457, 1986) that mandated all preschoolers with special needs be placed in the least restrictive environment (LRE). The practice of placing children with disabilities in the same classroom as children without disabilities is called mainstreaming. A more comprehensive method is known as full inclusion, in which both typically developing children and children with diverse abilities are taught together by a teaching staff with expertise in both normal child development and special education (see Chapter 3). The "Americans with Disabilities Act" (1990) prohibits child care centers from denying admission to a child simply because the child has a disability. Together, these federal laws form part of the rationale for early childhood centers to become more inclusive environments.

Children with diverse abilities need the same things in their environment as their more typically developing peers. They need an environment that is safe, secure, and predictable and one that provides a balance of the familiar and novel so that there are materials and activities that

DIVERSITY

A Place at the Table

The pluralistic view assumes that 1) people are different from each other and 2) differences are valuable; they add to the richness of everyone's experiences. The anti-bias aspect of the environment is the message that all children are included. The environment and the activities are derived from three sources: the children and their activities, the teachers' awareness of the developmental needs and learning styles of the group, and societal events.

All of the children are asked to bring something that shows their culture, so we have foods, clothing items, and toys throughout the environment on a daily basis. We ask about regular routines and special days in their cultures, such as Kwanzaa, Ramadan, and Hanukkah. Children share to educate us on why these days are special and what they do to celebrate them. We try to be sensitive; for example, during Ramadan you are not allowed to eat while the sun is up. If a family wants their children to participate in a cultural ritual, you have to make accommodations. And you watch the other children's reactions; if they seem to view it as "not normal," you take this opportunity to teach everyone so that it becomes familiar.

The various cultural learning moments include families.

- One of our African American families came in to educate us on black history month;
- Two Hispanic families explained Dia de los Muertos, and we all made a place in our environment for photos and items of special family members;
- Our new family from Shanghai helped us learn to make *zongzhi* and celebrate the Dragon Boat Festival by making boats to race.

Teachers make general selections of what children are to learn and arrange the environment for learning to begin. If unity is the completed puzzle, then diversity are the many pieces—with a place at the table for everyone. (Special thanks to Professor Elizabeth Jones and Student Leah Navarre Johnson.)

---

provide for their development. At the same time, a child with disabilities may be at a different level or need special help, so accommodations must be made. These may require either adding something to the environment that is not already there or using something in the environment in a different way. As noted at the chapter opening, we make adaptations in teaching strategies, learning environment, and curriculum so that each child can play and learn in an inclusive environment that meets the needs of children with and without disabilities.

Environmental adaptations are changes that make the environment fit the child better, so they vary with the children. Children with motor disabilities need different adaptations than those with hearing or language disabilities or with visual impairments. Physical changes may be necessary, modifications in the schedule may be recommended, or individualizing activities may be best. Parents are the best source of information about the child; other readings or specialists can be further guides (see Figure 6-4).

Three key concepts are helpful to remember—access, usability, and maximizing learning:

1. Can the child get where s/he needs to be in the classroom to learn something?
2. Once the child is in that location, can s/he use the materials and equipment and participate in the activity as independently as possible to learn something?

3. Are the learning activities arranged and scheduled to meet the individual learning needs of the children, including the child with disabilities?

Come Together for a Child "Come together for a child" is an adage for including children with special needs. Consider Andrew, who at 5 years of age had a motor/muscle disability with some speech difficulties. His cognitive skills were very strong and his social skills very weak. Andrew's mother talked to everyone during "Kinder Circle" about Andrew's needs and fears. If he fell down, he had a hard time righting himself. He needed help sitting and standing. He was afraid of getting bumped because he could not catch himself before falling very hard and then could not get up. The children all agreed to be careful about roughhousing around him. *The setting for success was being created.*

Because Andrew did not have much control of his fine motor skills, the teachers provided him with painting and play dough. They set up a crafts table; soon he was gluing pictures on paper, with or without order, and was very proud of his accomplishments. He even started using scissors on simple patterns. *The physical environment was responding to his needs.*

He was a wonderful puzzle builder, and the other children asked for his help often when they were stuck. It was wonderful to watch how they included him in

Checklist for an Inclusive Environment

Physical Environment:

Visual Environment

Questions to think about:
- How can we enhance or adapt the physical environment for children who have difficulty moving (or who move too much)
- How do different children use their bodies or the space around them for learning?
- How can we capitalize on the physical environment for children who learn by moving?

Accessing the environment safely:
_____ Doorway widths in compliance with local building codes
_____ Ramps in addition to or instead of stairs
_____ Low, wide stairs where possible (including playground equipment)
_____ Hand rails on both sides of stairs
_____ Easy handles on doors, drawers, etc.
_____ Kids' chairs with armrests, "cubes" or footrest and/or seat strap
- When adapting seating, mobility, and/or motor activities for a specific child with physical disabilities, consult a physical therapist.

Learning through the environment:
_____ Toys and equipment physically accessible
_____ Magnets glued to backs of puzzle pieces and attribute blocks and use on a steel cookie tray
_____ Large knobs or levers attached to toys with lids, movable parts
_____ Tabs attached to book pages for easier turning
_____ Tray for boundaries for art activities

- An occupational therapist can provide specific suggestions for adapting materials and activities.

Questions to think about:
- How do different children use their vision for learning?
- How can we enhance the visual environment for a child with low or no vision?
- How can we capitalize on the visual environment for children who learn by seeing?

Accessing the environment safely:
_____ Contrasting colors are used on edges and when surfaces change (e.g., tile to carpet, beginning of stairs, etc.)
_____ Windows shaded to avoid high glare
_____ Darker nonglossy floors and tabletops.
_____ Visual clutter is avoided on walls, shelves, etc.
_____ "Spot lighting" (e.g., swing arm lamp) available on some table tasks
- Orientation and mobility specialists help children with visual impairments learn to navigate the environment.

Learning through the environment:
_____ Large-print materials, textured materials, and auditory materials available (e.g., big books, sandpaper letters, books on tape)
_____ Daily schedule represented in words and pictures (e.g., a Velcro schedule with photos/pictures for children to post the schedule, then remove items as activities are completed)
_____ Children with low vision are seated close to the center of activity and away from high glare

FIGURE 6-4 When designing an inclusive environment, providing environmental support means altering the physical, temporal, and interpersonal environment to promote participation and learning. (Based on Brault et al., 2009, and Haugen, 1997.)
🔁 You can download a copy of this checklist from this text's Education CourseMate website.

Auditory Environment

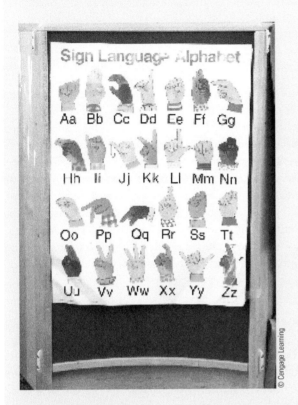

© Cengage Learning

Questions to think about:
- How do different children use their hearing for learning?
- How can we enhance the auditory environment for a child who is deaf, hearing impaired, or has poor auditory discrimination skills?
- How can we capitalize on the auditory environment for auditory learners?

Accessing the environment safely:
- _____ Eliminate or dampen background noise (using carpeting, closing windows and doors, etc.)
- _____ "Auditory competition" is avoided (e.g., instead of raising one's voice to get attention, use a "silent signal," such as holding up a peace sign and encouraging children who notice to do the same until the room is focused)
- _____ Nonauditory signals, such as turning lights on and off, are used to alert children

Learning through the environment:
- _____ Auditory messages are paired with visual ones (e.g., simple sign language, flannel boards, picture schedules)
- _____ Children with hearing impairments are seated so they can see others' faces and actions

Social Environment

© Cengage Learning

Questions to think about:
- How do different children use social cues for learning?
- How can we adapt the social environment for children with impulsive behavior, attention deficits, or other behavior problems?
- How can we capitalize on the social environment for children who learn by relating to others?

Accessing the environment safely:
- _____ Predictable schedule with children informed of changes
- _____ Schedule provide a range of activity levels (e.g., adequate opportunities for physical activity, activities simplified into small steps)

Learning through the environment:
- _____ Environment has a positive impact on self-esteem (capitalizing on child's interests and favorites, inviting adaptive equipment, invites peer support)
- _____ Learning materials and toys include representations of all kinds of people, including children and adults with disabilities
- _____ Schedule includes opportunities for a variety of groupings (pairs, small groups, whole class) as well as quiet time or time alone
- _____ Schedule provides both structured and open activity times
- School psychologists and behavior specialists can help analyze misbehavior and modify the environment or schedule.

FIGURE 6-4

many things. They accepted his differences right from the beginning and treated him just like all the rest—except they were careful when running and playing around him. His fear was apparent, and they respected it. *Thus, the interpersonal environment was emerging.*

There was a regular physical education time each day in the big room where the group jumped rope, played "Simon Says," played "Red Light, Green Light," and ran obstacle courses. At first, Andrew sat on the sidelines and watched. He cheered and looked interested, so one teacher started asking him if he'd be her partner because she was a little afraid. At first he refused and told her to use someone else. The teacher kept asking but would drop it as soon as he gave his answer; then one day he said, "OK." The two of them ran and jumped over the snake (rope), and all the kids laughed. They hugged and that was the beginning. *When given the time that is needed (the temporal environment), the child triumphs.* (Special thanks to Cindy Rogers)

Central Elements In Environment Planning

Planning environments is a complex task for early childhood teachers. There are many people who use the environment, and the children's health, safety, and well-being are the primary focus.

Who Is in the Environment?

Many people live and work in the early childhood environment. Cooks, bus drivers, office personnel, and yard and building maintenance people are but a few. Each person has special demands on the environment to do the job they are hired to do. Three key groups of people are the children, their teachers, and the families.

Children

Children's needs are met through the environment. The physical, social, emotional, and intellectual requirements of children suggest the type of building, the size of the furniture, the choice of equipment, the size and age range of the group, the number of teachers who lead and supervise, and the budget allocations. Guided by child development principles, teachers match the setting to the children who learn and play there. The individuality of a particular group of children, of a school, and of its philosophy is expressed by the arrangement of the environmental factors. Who are the children who use this space? What are their needs? How can those needs be met in this particular setting?

Teachers

The working environment is a predictor of the quality of care children receive. What has been done to meet the needs of the teachers? Do they have an office? A teachers' room? A place to hold conferences? Where do they keep their personal belongings or the materials they bring to use at school? Do they have a place to park? All teachers need room to create curriculum materials, to evaluate their programs, to review other educational materials, and to meet with their peers. The general context of the setting, opportunities for professional development, status, and wages are factors of how well teachers are provided for in an educational setting.

Families

The needs of children's parents and other adults vary, depending on whom the program serves. Adults who bring their children to child care or school need adequate and safe parking facilities. In settings in which adults are free to stay, a reading room, resource library, or a comfortable place to talk with others is desirable. Those who participate in the class are welcomed by a teacher, shown a place to put their belongings, and given a name tag and appropriate directions.

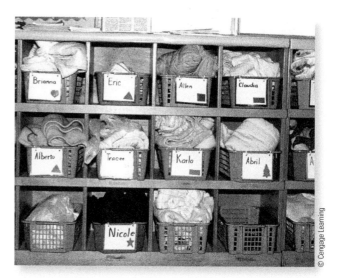

Children develop a sense of self when they have their own space, labeled with a photo or other visual clue so that they can easily identify it as their own.

There are many reasons families may need to contact the school or center. Are there ways to reach teachers and children in emergencies? How welcoming is the environment as they enter the building? The office? The classroom? What does the environment say about family involvement and interest?

The environment can be accessible and welcoming in several ways.

- Post contact information for school authorities and teachers where they can be reached after hours or in an emergency.
- Have a bulletin board for community notices, pertinent announcements, and for family use, along with mail pockets.
- Provide a place for families to talk with each other or wait outside the classroom.

The center that offers parents both an authoritative teacher and other useful resources helps them feel that their children are important. (See Chapter 8 for more suggestions.)

Regardless of how many children are in the setting and for how long, the first priority is to provide for their health and safety. Health, safety, and nutrition are closely related because the quality of one affects the quality of the others (Marotz, 2009). Programs for children must establish policies that provide for the protection, service, and education of child health and safety at all times. Government regulations and professional recommendations vary, but all establish some kind of standards to ensure good health and safety practices.

TeachSource Video

Watch the TeachSource Video Case entitled "Creating a Safe Physical Environment for Toddlers." After you study the video clip, view the artifacts, and read the teacher interviews and text, reflect on the following questions:

1. List five safety practices you noticed in the video. What potential problems might arise in implementing these practices into a program?

2. Choking hazards are a particular risk when working with children younger than 3 years of age. Identify three circumstances when there might be choking hazards and how to address them.

3. Director Doreen Dubique talks about being "a second set of eyes" in an environment. Create a 10-point safety checklist and observe a center or home.

Keeping Children Healthy
Sanitation

When groups of people live in close quarters, proper sanitary conditions are imperative to prevent the spread of disease. For an early childhood center, the physical plant must have adequate washing and toileting facilities for both children and adults. The number and size of toilets and wash basins are usually prescribed by local health or other regulatory agencies. Children do not realize their role in spreading germs, especially as their moist and warm hands touch and handle everything. Set regular times, use gentle reminders, and role model hand washing to help children learn the habit of washing their hands at important times.

Sanitation depends on frequent, systematic cleaning. The classrooms require daily cleaning, and equipment

that is used regularly should be sanitized on a periodic basis. Nontoxic paint must be used in all circumstances, including on outdoor equipment, cribs, and for art activities with children. Classroom dress-up clothing, pillows, nap blankets, and cuddle toys all need regular laundering, either at school or at home.

The nature of preventive health care in educational settings has expanded in the last decade. Knowledge of how disease is spread and concern over communicable diseases (see following discussion) have increased awareness of the kinds of practices teachers must en-

Spaces should be arranged according to the needs—and dimensions—of the children, so they can see and relate to things of interest at *their* level.

gage in on a daily basis. These include hand washing (the number-one way to prevent unnecessary spread of germs) and an approach known as universal infection control precautions. All teachers should receive training in using universal health precautions with all children.

Because we cannot be guaranteed of the infectious state of an individual, it is very important to always follow universal safety procedures with all children. The steps that keep a barrier between persons and blood can apply to more than blood-borne infections. All programs should be equipped with sets of latex gloves and plastic bags to properly handle and dispose of anything with blood or fecal material. Because intact skin is a natural barrier against disease, it may not always be necessary or possible to use gloves, but it is essential that hands be washed immediately after any toileting activity. All areas for eating, diapering, and toileting must be cleaned and sanitized, using a water-diluted bleach solution after cleaning away visible soiling.

Temperature, Ventilation, and Lighting

Heating and ventilation should be comfortable for the activity level of the children and should change when weather conditions do. Adequate, nonglare lighting is a necessity. Uniform, fluorescent lighting may not be the best environment for children; therefore, a mixture of lighting, such as is in homes, is preferable. Rooms should have some means of controlling light (e.g., shades, blinds). Cross-ventilation is necessary in all rooms where children eat, sleep, or play. Proper heating and insulation are important.

Communicable Disease

This is an important issue when dealing with young children in group care. Some people question the advisability of early group care on the grounds that it exposes children to too much illness. Others claim that such exposure at an early age helps children build up resistance and that they are actually stronger and healthier by the time they enter primary grades. In the largest U.S. study to date on children's health, the Environmental Protection Agency and Centers for Disease Control and Prevention concluded that, although infants and toddlers face a higher risk of colds and viruses, day care was not seen as increasing children's illnesses at older ages and not a risk overall (CDC, 2010).

Families should be notified when normal childhood diseases (such as chicken pox) or common problems (such as head lice) occur in the classroom. Infections of special concern to adults include chicken pox, hepatitis, cytomegalovirus (CMV), and human immunodeficiency virus (HIV). Regular education about disease is helpful; a handout on a specific infection that describes symptoms, dates of exposure, and incubation informs families who can then help prevent the spread of infectious disease.

In group care, children can contract a fair number of colds and viruses, especially when they are eating and sleeping close to each other (see Figure 6-5). The school and its staff have responsibility to ensure that good health standards are instituted and maintained to keep illness to a minimum.

Health Assessment and School Policies

Every early childhood center should establish clear health policies and make them known to families. A daily inspection of each child helps adults spot nasal discharge, inflamed eyes, and throat and skin conditions of a questionable nature. This daily check screens out more serious cases of children too ill to remain at school and may be done by a teacher, nurse, or administrator. Educating families about the warning signs of illness encourages sick children to be cared for at home.

It is very important for the school to inform families about what happens when children are refused admittance or become ill during the school day. Every school should provide a place for sick children where they can be isolated from others, kept under supervision, and be made comfortable until they are picked up. For their part, parents must arrange to have sick children cared for elsewhere if they are unable to take them home. School policies on these issues must be explicit and upheld consistently and compassionately for the sake of all the children.

Teachers must be sensitive to families' feelings and situations when sending a sick child home. This situation often produces guilt feelings in parents and work-related stress. Working families may need school assistance in locating alternatives for care of a sick child.

Most schools require, under state or local laws, a doctor's examination and permission to participate in an early childhood education program before a child can enter the program. This includes a record of immunizations and the child's general health. Parents, too, should submit a history of the child, highlighting eating, sleeping, and elimination habits. It is critical to note any dietary restrictions or allergies and then post them in the classrooms for a reminder.

Tips for Common Children's Health Problems

Condition	Tips
1. Allergies and asthma	Post a list of all children with chronic conditions; check ingredient lists on foods; watch what triggers reactions.
2. Scrapes and cuts	Reassure and sympathize with child; supervise child's washing with soaped pad and caring comments; use packs of ice or frozen peas in towel for swelling.
3. Bumps on the head	Notify parents of any loss of conciousness and watch for signs for two to three days.
4. Sand in eyes	Remind child "Do not rub!," have child wash hands and cover eyes with tissue; normal eye tearing will bring sand to inside corner of eye; remove with clean tissue.
5. Splinters	Clean area with alcohol and remove with tweezers or cover with adhesive strip and let parent remove.
6. Conjunctivitis	"Pinkeye" is highly contagious; watch for excess eye rubbing and red eyes; have child wash hands; isolate with washable toys until parent takes child home and gets treatment.
7. Head lice	Distressing but not dangerous; wash shared clothing, stuffed animals, bedding; vacuum rugs and furniture; remove hats, combs, and brushes from dramatic-play area; send notices home and inspect children's hair for two to three weeks.
8. Chicken pox	Isolate child until parents pick up; alert all parents about contagious period; watch for signs on all children for three weeks after exposure.
9. Strep throat	Send home notices; wash all equipment that might carry germs.
10. Lingering coughs	At onset, send child home until evaluated; frequent drinks will soothe; coughs may last up to two weeks; if longer, may suggest infection or allergy.

FIGURE 6-5 Common health problems require effective solutions. (Adapted from Needlman, R., & Needlman, G. [1995].)

Nutrition

What children eat is also important for proper health. Places where food is prepared and stored must be kept especially clean. The child who has regular, nutritious meals and snacks is likely healthier and less susceptible to disease. Many children do not have the benefits of healthy meals and snacks. Some do not receive adequate food at home; others are used to sugar-laden treats and fast foods. Education about child nutrition is needed for families and teachers in all programs, regardless of social or economic status. Some centers establish food regulations in an attempt to ensure that nutritionally sound meals are served to children. Most schools attempt to provide a relaxed atmosphere at meal and snack time. Children are asked to sit and eat, sharing conversation as well as food. Because lifelong eating patterns are established early in life, teachers of young children have a responsibility to understand the critical role nutrition plays in the child's total development.

Clothing

The health and safety of children are affected by the clothing they wear. A simple way to be sure children stay healthy is to encourage them to dress properly for play and for varying weather conditions. Children need clothing in which they can be active—clothing that is not binding and is easy to remove and easy to clean. To promote a self-help environment, parents and teachers should provide clothes the children can manage themselves (elastic waistbands, Velcro™ ties, large zippers). Pants are a good choice for both boys and girls; long dresses can become a hazard when climbing, running, or going up and down stairs. The safest shoes for active play should have composition or rubber soles. Whenever possible, it helps to keep extra clothes at school.

© Cengage Learning

Children need clothing in which they can be active, playful, and messy!

Health of the Staff

A responsible early childhood center is one that supports and maintains a healthy staff. Teachers should be in good physical and mental health to be at their best with children. It is wise to check the health regulations and benefits of the individual center when employed there. Many states require annual chest X-rays and tuberculosis clearance as a condition of employment. Sick leave policies should be clearly stated in print. Early childhood education is an intense job involving close interpersonal contact. Most teachers work long hours, often with low wages and few health benefits, and with clients in various stages of health. Such working conditions produce fatigue and stress, which can lead to illness or other stress-related problems.

Guarding Children's Safety

Beyond the continual supervision of indoor and outdoor space, everything is planned with the children's safety in mind. Creating a hazard-free environment that still allows for risk and challenge for children takes careful observation and attention to detail. A quick walk around the room and yard reveals potential problems. Sharp corners, loose rug edges, and gated stairwells are sample indoor items; fences and broken equipment in the playground, use of scissors/hammers, and appliances everywhere are just some of the examples (see Figure 6-6).

Most importantly, there must be safety rules that are explained to children and upheld by adults. Outdoors is especially important because children are physically active. Approximately 200,000 children are sent to an emergency room every year as a result of a playground accident (Consumer Product Safety Commission, 2009). With an estimated 27 to 30 million children between 5 and 14 years of age participating in organized sports each year, safety issues are paramount for school-aged children. The adults serve as the link between children and sports and are the chief means of prevention of injuries and accidents (see Chapter 11).

Field trips are an extension of the program, and "safety first" is the motto. Preparing children for the trip includes rehearsal of safety procedures.

First Aid

Every school should establish procedures for dealing with children who are injured on the property. First aid and CPR training should be required of all teachers and made available as part of their in-service training. Teachers should know how to handle a child who is not breathing as well as treat bumps and bruises, minor cuts and abrasions, bleeding, splinters, bites and stings, seizures, sprains, broken bones, and minor burns. Each classroom should be equipped with two first aid kits. One is for use in the classroom and yard; the other should be suitable for taking on field trips. Each kit should be readily available to adults but out of children's reach, and supplies should be replenished regularly.

Emergency numbers to be posted near the telephone in each room include those of the ambulance squad, fire department, police, health department, nearest hospital, and a consulting physician (if any). All families enrolled at the school should be aware of center policy regarding injuries at school and should provide emergency information for each child: the name of their physician, how to locate the family, and who else might be responsible for the injured child if the parents cannot be reached. The program, in turn, must make sure they notify families of any injuries the child has incurred during the school day.

Natural Disaster

Most adults are familiar with the most common disaster preparation: the fire drill. Most local fire regulations require that fire extinguishers are in working order and placed in all classrooms and the kitchen area. Exits, alarms, and escapes should be well-marked and functioning properly. Children and teachers should participate in emergency drills regularly. Other natural disasters vary by geographical location; helping children prepare for earthquakes, tornadoes, hurricanes, floods, and snowstorms includes participating in drills for those disasters. Proper preparedness includes eliminating potential hazards (e.g., bolting down bookcases); establishing a coordinated response plan (a "Code Blue!" emergency plan should involve children, parents, all staff, and local emergency agencies); and, in some areas of the country, conducting

Safety List for Indoor Environments

_____ Person monitoring children (at entrances, indoors, outdoors)

_____ First aid and emergency

    _____ Materials readily available to adults, out of children's reach, and regularly stocked and updated

    _____ Adults trained in first aid and CPR regularly and familiar with emergency routines

_____ Safety plugs on all outlets

_____ Cords

    _____ Electrical cords out of children's reach; avoid using extension cords

    _____ Curtain and window cords, window pulls and poles out of children's reach

_____ Floormat and carpet tacked down to avoid slippage

_____ Doors

    _____ Made to open and close slowly

    _____ All clear access, marked exits, and not blocked

_____ Cubbies and storage cabinets

    _____ Bolted to walls (or back-to-back together)

    _____ Any dangerous materials in locked area

_____ Toys

    _____ In good repair; no splinters or sharp, broken edges

    _____ Check for size with younger children (purchase safety-sizing gadget or estimate to keep at the size of a child's fist)

    _____ Check for peeling paint

_____ Plants and animals

    _____ Nonpoisonous plants *only*

    _____ Check animal cages regularly

    _____ Supervise animal handling carefully

    _____ Store animal food away from children's reach

_____ Adult materials

    _____ Keep adult purses, bags, and so on, away from children

    _____ Avoid having hot beverages around children

    _____ No smoking in children's areas

_____ Kitchen and storage

    _____ Children allowed in *only* with adult supervision

    _____ Poisonous or hazardous materials stored in a locked area

© Cengage Learning 2011

FIGURE 6-6 Children's safety is of primary importance to teachers and caregivers. Careful evaluation and regular safety checks eliminate dangerous materials and conditions in children's spaces.

You can download a copy of this checklist from this text's Education CourseMate website.

regular earthquake and tornado drills. These experiences can reinforce in parents the need for establishing similar procedures at home.

Automobile Safety

Automobile safety is a related concern when considering potential hazards for preschool children. The use of approved car seats and restraints for children riding in automobiles has received national attention in recent years. Some states have passed legislation requiring the use of specific devices to ensure safer travel for young children. Whether or not they walk to school, children should also be aware of basic rules for crossing streets. The street and parking lot can be a source of danger unless the program articulates policies to parents regarding the safety needs of children. There are potential risks when cars and children occupy the same space. Children should not be left unattended in parking lots.

Maintaining Children's Well-Being

The overall environment for children takes into consideration many factors. To provide for children's health and safety, teachers look at the physical environment carefully, then review the schedule, and finally assess the overall atmosphere of well-being. Young children are growing up in a world threatened by violence abroad and at home, drug abuse, unresolved conflicts among adults, and constant bombardment of television and other media.

Because young children do not easily separate the home and school parts of their lives, early childhood educators learn about children's lives and family details readily. They are often at a loss as to what to do, either with information that a child shares or with the child's behavior in the program. Yet, a situation does not need to be a crisis to affect a child's well-being. As a rule of thumb, when you feel the child's physical or emotional development is in jeopardy, you have a responsibility to take further action.

Difficulties in the Program

Children's well-being can be threatened by a difficult situation at school, such as being bitten, left out, or ridiculed. Although the situation may be remedied quickly and seem resolved, it may linger in a child's mind and get triggered later or when looking ahead to another day in the program.

Problems at Home

Children are at risk for myriad crises from home—problems with family members, separation or divorce, violence, or substance abuse. Community problems, such as closure of a local grocery store or a neighborhood crime incident, can affect children. Bronfenbrenner's ecological theory (see Chapter 4) is applicable to conditions of well-being. Although much of our response is with adults—families, community resources, professional supports—we are also responsible for trying to provide a psychologically safe and positive environment. By design (physical and temporal) and by responsiveness (interpersonal), teachers provide an environment that soothes and cares for young children.

Basic Arrangements and Materials for Creating the Environment

The environment is more than just the space provided or even the things put into it. When planning a place for children's growth and development, teachers consider three aspects of the environment: the physical elements, the temporal (time) dimensions, and the interpersonal atmosphere.

The Physical Environment

Every educational setting is organized fundamentally around physical space. The building itself may be new and designed specifically for young children. In Reggio Emilia, for example, it is the environment that creates an atmosphere of discovery. As founder Louis Malaguzzi explains (Edwards et al., 1993):

> There is an entrance hall, which informs and documents, and which anticipates the form and organization of the school. This leads into the dining hall, with the kitchen well in view. The entrance hall leads into the central space, or piazza, the place of encounters, friendships, games, and other activities

that complete those of the classrooms. The classrooms and utility rooms are placed at a distance from but connected with the center area. Each classroom is divided into two contiguous rooms . . . to allow children either to be with teachers or stay alone. . . . In addition to the classrooms, we have established the atelier, the school studio and laboratory, as a place for manipulating or experimenting.

More than likely, however, the space is a converted house or store, a parish hall, or an elementary classroom. Sometimes a program shares space with another group so that furniture has to be moved. Family child care programs are housed in a private home, so adaptations are made in the space both for the children and for the family that lives there. There may be a large yard or none at all. Some playgrounds are on the roof of the building, or a park across the street may serve as the only available playground (see Chapter 11).

Constraints also come in the form of weather conditions. Outside play—and therefore large-muscle equipment—may be unavailable during the winter, so room for active, vigorous play is needed inside during that time. Hot summer months can make some types of play difficult if there is little or no shade outdoors. Weather conditions must be considered when planning programs for children.

Early childhood programs have specific needs that must be met by the buildings they occupy. Although the choice of building is generally determined by what is available, at a minimum the setting should provide facilities for:

playing/working	food preparation
eating	washing/toileting
sleeping/resting	clothing and wraps
storage	office/work space

Ideally, the setting should have enough space to house these various activities separately. In practice, however, rooms are multipurpose, and more than one event takes place in the same space. A playroom doubles as an eating area because both require the use of tables and chairs. When a room serves many functions (playing, eating, sleeping), convenient and adequate storage space is a necessity.

General Requirements

Ground floor classrooms are preferable for young children to ensure that they can enter and leave with relative ease and safety. For noise reduction, the walls and ceilings should be soundproofed. Carpeting, draperies, and other fireproof fabrics in the room help absorb sound. Floors must be durable, sanitary, and easily cleaned. They should be free from drafts. Rugs should be vacuumed each day. Room size should be sufficient to allow for freedom of movement and the opportunity to play without interference.

Many local and state agencies have regulations regarding the use of space for children in group care settings. Licensing agencies often recommend or mandate minimum room and yard size standards. The fire marshal, health department, and similar agencies must be consulted and their regulations observed.

The National Academy of Early Childhood Programs (NAEYC, 2005) has developed guidelines for indoor and outdoor facilities that promote optimal growth. Besides floor and play space (minimum 35 [and recommended 50] square feet indoors and 75 square feet outdoors), the guidelines suggest how to arrange activity areas to accommodate children and what kinds of activities and materials are safe, clean, and attractive. This document, along with *Inspiring Spaces for Young Children* (Deviney et al., 2010), *The Creative Curriculum* (Heroman et al., 2010), and the *Environmental Rating Scales* (Harms et al., 2005-2009) are used extensively to develop this material. There are several key dimensions to any environment that are helpful to consider. If we are to offer children both balance and variety, these criteria need to be included in developing space both indoors and out (see Figure 6-7).

Indoors

Interest Areas/Learning Centers Interest areas or learning centers are activity centers, with a classic definition that holds today.

Key Environmental Dimensions

1. **Softness/Hardness**

   Soft: rugs, pillows, play-dough, finger paints, grass, sand, swings

   Hard: tile floor, wooden furniture, asphalt, cement

2. **Open/Closed**

   Open (no one right way to use it): sand and water, dress-up, collage materials, painting

   Closed (manipulated only one way to come out right): puzzles, many board games, most Montessori equipment

   In between: many manipulatives such as Legos®, Tinkertoys®, blocks, balls

3. **Simple/Complex**

   "Play equipment can differ in its holding power; i.e., the capacity to sustain attention . . . A simple unit has one manipulable aspect; a complex unit has two different kinds of materials combined; and a super unit has three different kinds of materials that go together."

   Simple: swings, climbers, sand pile with no toys

   Complex: dramatic play with only a kitchen

   Super: climbers with slides and ropes, playhouse with kitchen, dress-up clothes, dolls, and/or play-dough; sand area with equipment and/or water

   As you add more features to a unit, you increase its complexity and the children's interest in it. To simple play-dough, add cookie cutters; then add toothpicks or a garlic press and it becomes a super unit.

4. **Intrusion/Seclusion**

   Intrusion: places where children can enter or go through easily; blocks, housekeeping, even the entire environment are often highly intrusive areas

   Seclusion: places where children can be alone or with only one child or adult; cubbies, a fort, or under a table become secret places

5. **High Mobility/Low Mobility**

   High: whole-body places and activities, outdoors, climbers, trike lanes, gym mats

   Low: sitting-still places and activities; puzzles and games, story and group times, nap time

   In-between: dramatic play, block corner, woodworking

FIGURE 6-7 Key dimensions when considering an early childhood environment. (Adapted from *Exchange Magazine*, E. Prescott, 1994.)

"An activity area has five defining attributes. Physical *location*, with visible *boundaries* indicating where it begins and ends, within which are placed *work and sitting surfaces*, and the *storage and display of materials* used to execute the activities for which the area is intended. An area, like a room, has a *mood* or personality distinguishing it from contiguous spaces" (Olds, 1989).

Deciding what interest centers you want, reflective of program philosophy and children's interests, and what kind of space you need is good preparation to making a basic floor plan and sketching in the interest centers.

Start with an assessment of the way space is set up now. "First draw a simple floor plan of the room you are currently working in, one you are familiar with, or one you imagine using in a new job. As you sketch out the arrangements of the room, do not include a lot of detail. . . . Put yourself in the shoes of the children who spend their days in your space" (Carter & Curtis, 2003).

You consider their ages and needs of the group, and make a list of "I can" and "I like to" statements as if *you*

are those children. Now check your floor plan; if you had trouble finding any of the components in your room, make some changes.

Most programs include basic areas for play and engagement in a variety of dimensions. Learning centers are areas of the environment focused on different activities for different developmental experiences. For infants and toddlers, areas for movement and for sensory experiences dominate; preschoolers want more creative and manipulative choices; school-age children might include areas for academic stimulation or practice.

Teachers must create learning centers that are interesting; accurately reflect the goals for children; and take into consideration space, traffic flow, the number of people, and availability of equipment and materials. Teachers use environmental cues to communicate to children what may happen there, and make good use of the learning centers as places for observation and assessment (see Figure 6-8). Creating learning centers is a standard early childhood practice that has tremendous potential in school-age and primary settings.

Environmental Components that Frame the ECE Curriculum

Infants, Toddlers & Twos

Routines

Hello/goodbye, diapering/toileting, eating

Sleeping/napping, getting dressed

Experiences

Playing with toys, imitating/pretending

Enjoying stories, connecting with music

Creating with art, tasting food, exploring

Sand and water, going outdoors

Partnering with Families

Plenty of display space

Preschoolers

Physical learning environment

Time for play, routines, transitions, groups of several sizes

Interpersonal considerations with peers and teachers

School-Agers

Being with Friends

Quiet area for just talking, tables for being in groups, large area for whole group

Completing Homework

Place with lighting, computer access, teacher availability, away from noise

Special places for either older [10+] or younger [K only]

Preschoolers

Interest and Activity Centers
Art
Blocks
Cooking/sensory
Discovery/science
Dramatic play
Library/literacy
Media/computers
Music and movement
Outdoors/garden and pets
Toys and games/math

Infants, Toddlers & Twos | School-Agers

Research & Theory

FIGURE 6-8 Environmental features in the environment are set in a framework that helps build appropriate experiences for children in the early years.

Bathrooms Bathrooms should be adjacent to the play and sleeping areas and easily reached from outdoors. Child-sized toilets and wash basins are preferable, but if unavailable, a step or platform may be built. In most settings for children younger than age 5, the bathrooms are without doors, for ease of supervision. Toileting facilities for children should be light, airy, attractive, and large enough to serve several children at a time. An exhaust fan is desirable. Paper towel holders should be at child height and wastebaskets placed nearby.

If diapering is part of the program, areas for this purpose should be clearly defined and close to hand washing facilities. Hand washing regulations for the staff should be posted, and an area should be provided for recording children's toileting and elimination patterns. Closed cans and germicidal spray must be used, and diapering materials should be plentiful and handy.

Room to Rest Room to rest means providing nap and sleeping facilities with adequate storage space for cots and bedding. Movable screens, low enough for teacher supervision, allow for privacy and help reduce the noise level. Cots or cribs should be labeled with children's names and washed regularly. They should be placed consistently and in such a way that children feel familiar, cozy, and private—not in the center of the room or in rows. Teachers can develop a "nap map" that places children so that they can get the rest or sleep they need while still feeling part of the group.

Food Service This aspect includes routines and choices around food. "Good nutrition affects the health and well-being of individuals of all ages," states Marotz (2009). "Small children need nutrients for growth and energy . . . regardless of the guideline selected, the common factor necessary for good nutrition is the inclusion of a wide variety of foods." As early childhood classrooms have become more diverse and multicultural, educators must take into consideration families' cultural practices and preferences.

Feeding young children and teaching toddlers and older children about good food choices can be a challenge throughout the early childhood span. In an infant

Early childhood programs provide for children to play and work alone and together, with friends and teachers, indoors and out.

program, storing formula and milk is a necessity. As toddlers assert their independence, they begin to make their preferences known. Care must be taken to offer a variety of foods at regular times, but avoid a battle of wills over what the child eats. Preschoolers are influenced by a teacher who sets a good example of eating with balance and variety. School-aged children can understand nutritional concepts better but are more influenced by what their peers are eating.

Whether involved in a light snack or full meal program, the center must adhere to the most rigid standards of health protection and safety provisions. Every precaution must be taken to ensure maximum hygienic food service. Daily cleaning of equipment, counters, floors, and appliances is a necessity. Proper disinfecting of high chairs and tables requires an appropriate bleach-to-water ratio, and bottles of this solution should be stored away from children's reach yet handy for teachers. Consult NAEYC or local referral agencies for guidelines on serving nutritional foods and incentives or subsidies.

Each age has its unique food-service needs. Infants need to be held or seated near an adult with enough high chairs or low tables to prevent an unreasonable wait for eating. Toddlers should not be fed popcorn, nuts, or raw carrots because of the hazard of choking. All children must be served food on disposable dishes or on dishes cleaned in a dishwasher with a sanitation cycle. Lunches brought from home by school-age and full-day children must be checked for spoilage. Information about eating patterns, proportions, and nutritional needs should be regularly shared with families.

Adult Space Adult space is rare in early childhood centers. "Oh, for a real 'teacher's desk,'" the early childhood caregiver moans. "I'm lucky if I can find a place to stash my bag in the morning!" A common issue for early childhood education programs is to donate nearly all the available space to child use and materials storage. Yet, the personal and professional needs of adults deserve environmental support. Early education programs sometimes have an adult space in the director's area. An adult bathroom is also common. Elementary classrooms include a desk and a bookshelf for the teachers and a workroom or lounge for staff in the school office. However, in programs for children younger than age 5, even a desk can seem a hazard, taking up precious space for children.

Still, early childhood professionals deserve environmental support for their work. A safe place for their belongings, space for first aid/emergency materials and information for families, and an area for a special adult project goes a long way in respecting the teachers' lives in the classroom. We show our priorities by the space and time we give them.

Outside

Some of our deepest childhood joys—those of running in the grass, wading in a stream, exploring vacant lots, of privacy and secrecy—can only be experienced outside, and nowhere else. Free and fresh air and open space to move about at will are often children's favorite spots in a program. Indeed, many a preschooler has been able to say good-bye easier when the great outdoors beckons.

Traditional playgrounds—typically on a flat, barren area with steel structures such as swings, climbers, a slide, perhaps a merry-go-round or seesaws, fixed in concrete and arranged—are poor places for children's play from both safety and developmental perspectives. Children as young as toddlers and through the primary years much prefer the adventure of a creative playground, spaces that have a variety of fixed and movable equipment. Raw materials, such as sand, water, tires, spools, sawhorses, bowls, or pans, in combination with larger superstructures or open-air "houses" with some flexible parts, stimulate a wide variety of both social and cognitive play (including constructive, dramatic, and games play).

A wide porch or covered patio is ideal for rainy days or days when the sun is too severe. Many activities can be extended to the outside area with this type of protection. The physical plant should include adequate playground space adjacent to the building. A variety of playground surfaces makes for more interesting play and provides suitable covering for outdoor activities. Tanbark can be used in the swing area, cement for wheel toys, and grass for under climbers. Sand is used for play in a large area and also in a sensory table.

No matter what the surface, the yard should be constructed with a good drainage system. Trees, bushes, and other plantings allow for both sunshine and shade. Fences are *mandatory*. They must be durable, an appropriate height, with no opportunity for a child to gain a foothold. Because there are no mandatory standards for the manufacture of play equipment, adults who work with children must assume responsibility for playground design. Given the importance that young children attach to the outdoors, teachers are well advised to concentrate their efforts by visiting high quality playgrounds and consulting with child development specialists when selecting equipment (see Chapter 11).

Materials and Equipment

Selection of materials and equipment is based on a number of criteria. Program budgets are limited, so to make every dollar count, teachers select materials that:

- Are age and developmentally appropriate.
- Are related to program philosophy and curriculum.

- Reflect quality design and workmanship.
- Are durable.
- Offer flexibility and versatility in their uses.
- Have safety features (e.g., nontoxic paints, rounded corners).
- Are aesthetically attractive and appealing to children (and adults).
- Are easy to maintain and repair.
- Reflect the cultural makeup of the group and the diversity of the culture overall.
- Are nonsexist, nonstereotypical, and anti-bias.

Materials should be appropriate for a wide range of skills because children within the same age group develop at individual rates. Simplicity of detail and versatile in use are practical watchwords (Community Products, 2011). Selecting equipment and toys to support development is important because young children typically try to play with everything in their environment. Many of the materials can be open-ended; that is, they can be used in their most basic form or they can be developed in a variety of ways. Using the key dimension of simple/complex (see Figure 6-7) elements, unit blocks, clay, and Legos® are examples of materials that children can use in a simple fashion and, as skills develop, these materials can be manipulated in a more complex manner.

Toys and materials need to reflect the diversity of the class, the families, and the community:

- From a DAP perspective, materials need to appeal to individual interests and also respond to children's cultural and linguistic strengths. Homemade materials and a variety of cultural artifacts help the environment feel familiar.
- From a self-help viewpoint, dressing frames and plenty of workable doll clothes help children learn those self-care tasks.
- Children's books that demonstrate social values and attitudes that expand gender roles and family lifestyles show a value for an anti-bias environment.
- An inclusive viewpoint might include materials to highlight tactile, auditory, and olfactory experiences for children with visual impairments.
- Educational philosophy, including broad curriculum models of Montessori or High/Scope (see Chapter 10), might determine materials. Consider how the Waldorf philosophy contributes to the kindergarten environment (Waldorf, 1995):

The feeling of warmth and security is largely created by using only natural materials—woods, cotton, wool—in the construction of the decor and toys. The curtains transmit a warm glow in the room.

Ideally, the walls and floor of the room are of natural wood. In this warm environment are placed toys which the children can use to imitate and transform the activities that belong to everyday adult life. In one corner stands a wooden scale and baskets for children to pretend they are grocery shopping; a pile of timber stands ready to be constructed into a playhouse, a boat, or a train; a rocking horse invites a child to become a rider; homemade dolls lie in wooden cradles surrounded by wooden frames and cloths the children can use to create a pretend family and play house. Pinecones and flowers are artistically dispersed. Lovely watercolors adorn the walls. The effect of this beautiful arrangement of decorations and toys is the feeling of stepping out of the business and clutter of modern life into a sanctuary where one can breathe easily, relax, and play according to the impulses of one's heart.

Basic materials form a foundation from which individual and program interests blossom (see Figure 6-9).

Try to avoid toys that have limited play value. The organization "Teachers Resisting Unhealthy Children's Entertainment" (TRUCE, 2011) suggests that we steer away from toys that:

- Make electronic technology the focus of play.
- Lure girls into focusing on appearance.
- Model violent and sexualized language or behavior.
- Are linked to commercial products and advertisements.

Children are active learners, and their materials should provide them with ways to explore, manipulate, and become involved. Young children learn through all their senses, so the materials should be appealing to many of the senses. All children need opportunities for quiet, private time and space as well, with materials that parallel the balance of key environmental dimensions.

Organizing Space

There are many different ways to arrange and organize space in an early childhood setting; the final result expresses the diversity of the program. Most early childhood centers are arranged by interest areas (learning centers or activity areas). The amount of space devoted to any one activity says a great deal about its value to the staff. For example, teachers at a child care center noticed the high interest in sociodramatic play with several new babies in children's families. They built up the housekeeping area, making sure there were at least six baby dolls, four telephones, and three doll buggies and countless bottles, tippy cups, and pretend baby food. As interests

Basic Materials for ECE Environments

Basic Materials for Indoor Environments

Floors and Seating: Various surfaces (carpet, linoleum or tile, wood floor) kept clean and draft-free, comfortable seating (chairs at tables, rocking chair or sofa, carpet squares)

Areas: Art, blocks, dramatic play, toys and games, library, discovery/science, music and movement, cooking, media

Equipment:
Art: Easels, paints, watercolors; playdough, clay; pens, pencils, brushes; scissors, hole punch; glue, paste; collage materials; assorted paper

Blocks: Unit, hollow blocks; props (people & animal figures); accessories (signage, doll furniture)

Dramatic play: Mirrors; furniture; clothing; dolls, cooking utensils, pretend food items; purses and backpacks; expanded materials beyond house as needed

Toys and games: Puzzles, constructions toys, math toys, Montessori materials, cooperative games

Library/book nook: Picture books; flannel board and items; photos; writing center materials; listening post items

Discovery/science: Nature materials; pets; sensory materials; water/sand table; magnifying glasses and scales, etc.; textured materials or other 'theme/interest' related displays

Music and movement: CD/tape player and items; instruments, dancing scarves (may also be used in circletime)

Cooking: Food preparation materials (may also be used in discovery or art areas)

Media: Computers, tape/cd deck; TV

Infant-toddler: Limit materials and reduce number of interest areas; offer fewer choices in each area; substitute soft blocks and push/pull toys; have knobbed puzzles and stacking toys

School-age: Increase game area, vary units, add self-help in art and chapter books in library

Basic Materials for Outdoor Playgrounds/Yards

Grounds: Various surfaces (grass, asphalt, gravel/sand, tanbark), as much natural habitat as possible

Areas: Climbing place, sand/water space, wheel toy/riding place, games & dramatic play spot, building space, pet/garden area

Equipment: Climbing apparatus with ramps, slide, pole, ladder; swings (various types); house/quiet area; ramps and supports to build; tires, "loose parts"

- Sand and water toys
- Various wheel toys
- Large building blocks
- Dramatic-play props
- Balls and game materials
- Workbench and woodworking/clay materials

Infant-toddler: Have plenty of simple riding toys, eliminate woodworking, have apparatus correct size and simplicity and/or foam wedges

School-age: Increase game area, may eliminate number or kinds of wheel toys; substitute a stage, mural, boat, creek; increase "loose parts" for child-created forts

FIGURE 6-9 All programs should stock both indoor and outdoor environments with developmentally appropriate basic materials.

change, so do the room and yard—someone brings in a hamster and the discovery area blossoms or a family camping trip brings out the tents.

Room and Materials Arrangement Room arrangement and choice of materials play an important role in children's educational experience. A developmentally appropriate room invites children in and welcomes them at their level, as seen in these four examples:

1. *Toddler Class.* Simplicity is a watchword in a toddler room. Room arrangement changes with the age range.
   - A large-motor zone is essential for children aged 12 to 24 months.

   - The dramatic-play area for pretend play is advisable for children aged 24 to 30 months.
   - The messy zone for liquid materials is recommended for children aged 18-30 months.
   - Every toddler room needs a quiet zone, a haven to relax and step back.

2. *Family Child Care Home.* Having a program in a home presents special challenges, both in the space and the mixed age ranges of children. Beyond the general spaces for indoor and outside play, retreats (such as an empty cabinet without its door or behind the couch) allow moderate privacy while still ensuring supervision.

DAP · Inventing Toys for Tots

Toys can be used to support development in very young children, although their potential is often overlooked with a focus on safety or an inadequate understanding of infant and toddler development. "Teachers can build on children's play by providing engaging toys," advises Guyton, a special education teacher and infant/toddler specialist (2011). What needs to be kept in mind is the critical factor of engagement. "A little creativity combined with basic materials can stimulate play and facilitate a young child's development across all domains."

Using readily available materials of fabric, boxes, and safe kitchen items, teachers can create toys to stimulate DAP cognitive growth:

- *Use fabric scraps.* A scarf can be a toddler's costume in dramatic play or a cover for a surprise game with older infants.
- *Collect cardboard and paper.* Make boxes from shoeboxes or cereal boxes, even paper bags stuffed with newspaper, especially for toddlers younger than age 2.
- *Hunt for common household items.* Puzzles can be made combining a muffin tin with a variety of measuring cups, plastic jar tops, and clothespins that the 1- to 2-year-old fills and dumps out again.

"Developmentally appropriate" does not need to spell "expensive" or "impossible" when making cognitive connections with infants and toddlers.

3. *Preschool and Kindergarten.* Harms and others (2005) recommend these environmental areas for preschool and kindergarten:
   - Space and furnishings
   - Personal care routines
   - Language-reasoning
   - Activities (motor, cognitive, creative)
   - Interaction (social, emotional)
   - Program structure (schedules)
   - Parents and staff (personal and professional needs)
4. *School-Age Programs.* After-school programs for children from kindergarten through third and sometimes fifth or sixth grade have special requirements, as those environments have an extensive range of physical size, interests, and developmental needs. The National School-Age Core Competencies (NAA, 2011) recommends tables for projects and experiments, homework tables in a quiet corner, a place for snacks and club meetings, art, blocks, house corner, and large group activity area.

Placement of the interest centers is important. Balance the number of noisy and quiet activities, both indoors and out. Some activities are noisier than others, so place the noisier centers together and cluster the quieter ones together. Quieter activities, such as puzzles, language games, and storytelling, take place in areas away from blocks, water play, or dramatic play, because the last three tend to spark animated, active, and sometimes noisy behavior. Some programs create a kind of layered room—entry, quiet, messy, noisy.

Adult needs also should be met through proper organization. How can the teachers supervise all areas while ensuring cozy spots for children's privacy? Are the teachers deployed evenly throughout all the space? Is storage integrated so that equipment is located near the place where it is used? Is the space arranged for cooperation and communication among the adults as well as the children? In other words, is this a work and play place that is accepting, inviting, and challenging to all? (See Figures 6-10 through 6-12.)

Playground Designs Playgrounds must be arranged so that there are enough play spaces for the number of children in the group. Clearly defined boundaries and obvious pathways make it easy for children to live and work in the space. There should be enough space for larger groups to gather together as well as small groups (see Figure 6-13).

Calculating play prospects is part of analyzing the number of play opportunities in program settings. In their classic study, Prescott and others assigned areas and activities a value so that the overall richness of the environment can be calculated (Prescott, Jones, & Kritschevsky, 1972). A simple area (swings, climbers) counts as one play space, a complex area (housekeeping/dramatic play) counts as four play spaces, and a super area (sand and water play combined) counts as eight play spaces. The value assigned an area generally coincides with the number of children who might be accommodated in that space. When the total for the space is figured, it is matched against the actual number of children in the group to see if there is a place for everyone to play.

In summary, the physical environment should be organized around these criteria:

- *Availability.* Open, low shelving with visual cues for placement of toys and equipment aids in clean up and room set up.
- *Consistency in organization.* Neat, systematic, in logical order.
- *Compatibility.* Noisy activities are grouped away from quiet ones; art needs natural light when possible; water play near a bathroom or kitchen; messy projects done on washable floors.

Preschool Classroom

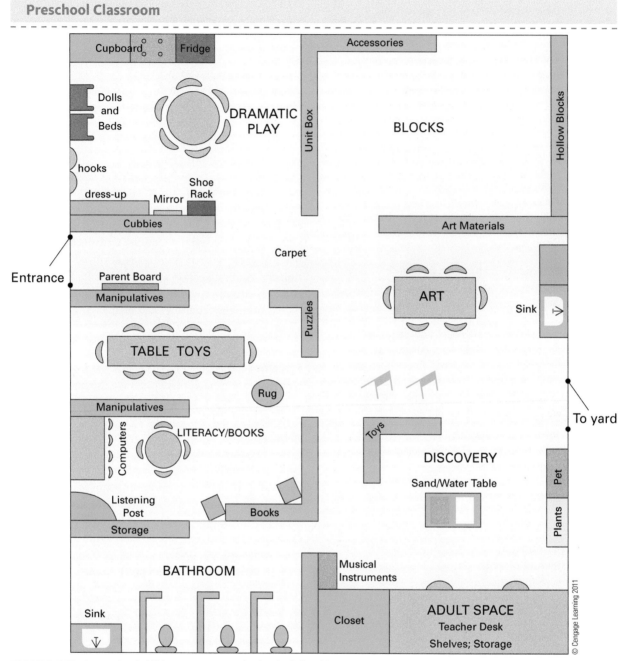

FIGURE 6-10 A preschool child care center needs clearly defined boundaries and obvious pathways so that children can use the space independently.

- *Definition.* Clearly defined boundaries indicating available space and what is to take place; obvious pathways outlined in class and yard; ways to get in and out of an area without disrupting activity in progress; no dead ends or runways.
- *Spacing.* Interest areas with enough space to hold the children who play there; one third to one half of the surface should remain uncovered; materials stored near space where they are used; storage and activity spaces have visual cues.

- *Communicability.* Tells children what to do instead of relying on adult to monitor activities; communicates to children what behavior is expected; arrangement suggests numbers of children, levels of activity.

The Temporal Environment

The second dimension of the environment to consider is the time and timing of a program. What happens, when

Toddler Room

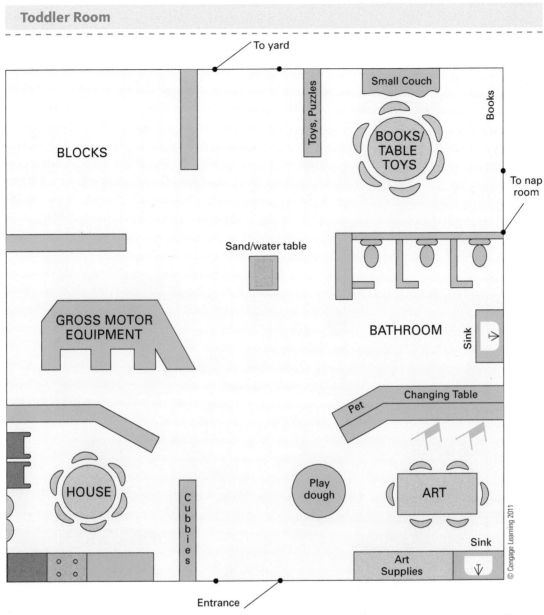

FIGURE 6-11 A toddler environment has safety and accessibility in mind so that children can be maximally involved with a minimum of distraction from others.

it occurs, and how long it takes all affect both individual children and group functioning.

Daily Schedule: Time to Learn

The **daily schedule** defines the structure of each program. It creates the format for how children experience the events of the day—in what order and for what length of time.

No two schedules are alike because each reflects the program it represents. The amount of time devoted to specific activities communicates clearly what value the school places on them. The amount of time given to certain aspects of the curriculum, the variety of events, and the level of flexibility tell children and adults what is important in this particular setting (see Figure 6-14).

Criteria for Scheduling Criteria is used to see how the schedule functions on a daily basis. Teachers first decide what is important for children to learn, how that learning should take place, and how much time to allow in the daily program. If small group work and individual attention are program goals, enough time is set aside to ensure their success. More time is needed to allow children several curriculum choices than if they had only one or

School-Age Center

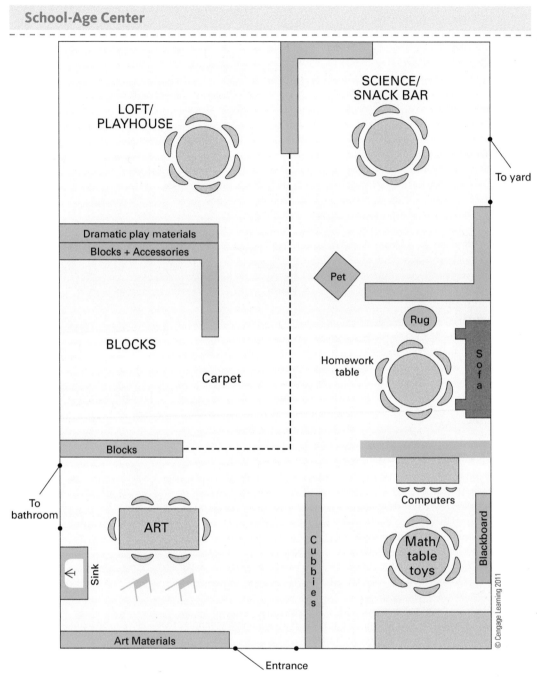

FIGURE 6-12 A school-age center has learning centers to allow children to engage in peer connections and homework constructively.

two activities from which to select. Three-year-olds need more time for toileting activities than do 5-year-olds, who are considerably more self-sufficient.

The physical plant itself may dictate a portion of the daily schedule. If toilet facilities are not located adjacent to the classroom, then more time must be scheduled to travel to and from the bathrooms. If the building or space is shared with other groups, some portion of the program may be modified. For example, a program housed in church buildings scheduled field trips during the annual church rummage sale to free up the space for the church's use.

Expectations and Flexibility Setting expectations and having flexibility are part of the golden rule for child care, which is to treat children as we want them to treat us. The children in child care today are the adults of tomorrow who will be taking care of us in our old age. Remembering that, it helps to think of how often

PreK-to-Grade 3 Yard

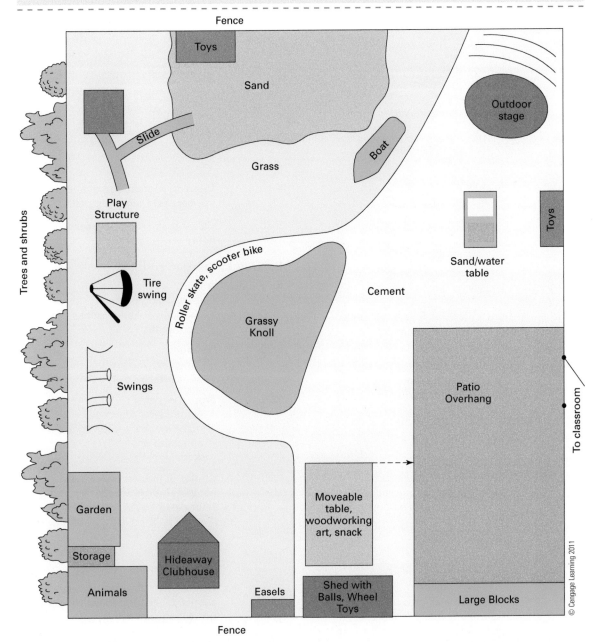

FIGURE 6-13 A playground/yard, suitable for ages 4 and older, gives children a sense of security and adventure, contact with nature, opportunities for social play, and freedom for active physical play. (Adapted from Themes, 1999.)

children are asked to do and finish their tasks on others' schedules, to ask permission to do what they wish, or to participate in activities of someone else's choice. A children's program must be *for* children, on their timetable as much as possible.

1. Suitable choices are built in as much of the time as possible, avoiding the expectation that everyone should do the same thing at the same time.

2. People need time to settle in, whether this is for a child to say good-bye in the morning or a group to get ready for lunch. Different people cope with change and new experiences in different ways.

3. Meaningless activities that simply keep children busy have no intrinsic value and should be avoided.

4. We need a healthy balance between an individual's need for autonomy, freedom, and independence on

Daily Schedules

Half-Day Toddler Program

9:00–9:30	Greet children Inside activities • playdough and art/easel • home living • blocks and manipulatives • books
9:30	Door to outdoors opens
9:45–10:20	Outdoor play • large motor • social play
10:20	Music/movement outdoors
10:30	Snack/"Here We Are Together" song • washing hands • eating/pouring/cleanup
10:45–11:45	Outside
11:15	"Time to Put Our Toys Away" song • all encouraged to participate in cleanup
11:20	Closure (indoors) • parent–child together • story or flannel board

Full-Day Program for Preschoolers

7:00	Arrival, breakfast
7:30	Inside free play • arts/easels • table toys/games/blocks • dramatic-play center; house, grocery store, etc.
9:00	Cleanup
9:15	Group time: songs/fingerplays and small group choices
9:30	Choice time/small groups • discovery/math lab/science activity • cooking for morning or afternoon snack • language art/prereading choice
10:00	Snack (at outside tables/cloths on warm days) or snack center during free play
10:15	Outside free play • climbing, swinging; sand and water, wheel toys, group games
12:00	Handwash and lunch

12:45	Get ready: toileting, handwashing, toothbrushing, prepare beds
1:15	Bedtime story
1:30	Rest time
2:30	Outdoors for those awake
3:30	Cleanup outdoors and singing time
4:00	Snacktime
4:15	Learning centers; some outdoor/indoor choices, field trips, story teller
5:30	Cleanup and read books until going home

Half-Day Kindergarten Plan

8:15–8:30	Arrival Getting ready to start • checking in library books, lunch money, etc.
8:30	Newstelling • "anything you want to tell for news" • newsletter written weekly
9:00	Work assignment • write a story about your news or • make a page in your book (topic assigned) or • work in math lab
9:30–10:15	Choice of indoors (paints, blocks, computer, table toys) or second-grade tutors read books to children • when finished, play in loft or read books until recess
10:15	Snack
10:30	Recess
10:45	Language: chapter in novel read or other language activity
11:15	Dance or game or visitor
11:45	Ending: getting ready to leave • check out library books • gather art and other projects
12:00–1:30	For part of group each day Lunch, then: • field trips • writing lesson • math or science lab

FIGURE 6-14 Daily schedules reflect the children's needs and ages; the time and timing of the day reflect the program's values and priorities.

the one hand, and the need for group connection and harmony with rules that help us get along together on the other.

5. Staff balances the need for a routine, for the comfort and reassurance of the familiar, with the need for variety and novelty for change. Flexibility makes for a more humane environment.

The daily schedule is important for everyone in the setting. Two important aspects of a schedule are routines and transitions.

Routines

The regular or habitual performance of an established procedure is a **routine**. Routines provide an important framework to a program. Each day, some events are repeated, providing continuity and a sense of order to the schedule. Routines are the pegs on which to hang the daily calendar. When should children eat? Sleep? Play? Be alone? Be together? These questions are answered by the placement of routines. The rest of the curriculum—art activities, field trips, woodworking—works around them.

Program Routines Program routines in an early childhood environment setting include:

- Self-care (eating, rest/sleeping, dressing, toileting)
- Transitions between activities
- Group times
- Beginning and ending the day or session
- Making choices
- Task completion
- Room clean up and yard restoration

Routines are an integral part of creating a good environment for children. All three environmental factors are influenced by routines:

1. *Physical.* Child-sized bathroom and eating facilities; storage of cots, blankets, and sleeping accessories; equipment for food storage and preparation.
2. *Temporal.* Amount of time in daily schedule for eating, resting, toileting, clean up.
3. *Interpersonal.* Attitudes toward body functions; willingness to plan for self-care tasks; interactions during activities and transitions; expectations of staff, parents, and children.

Most routines are very personal and individual rituals in children's daily lives. Children bring to school a history firmly established around routines, one that is deeply embedded in their family and culture. Routines are reassuring to children, and they take pride in mastering them; they are also a highly emotional issue for some.

Self-Care Tasks Self-care tasks include eating, sleeping, dressing, and toileting and can be difficult issues between adult and child, virtually from the moment of birth. Everyone can recall vivid memories associated with at least one routine. They seem to become battlegrounds on which children and adults often struggle. Many times this is where children choose to take their first stand on the road to independence.

The early childhood teacher must be able to deal with the issue of self-care routines in sensitive and understanding ways. Children adjust to routines when they are regularly scheduled in the daily program and when there are clear expectations.

Ordinary, everyday routines have learning potential because they teach the young child important skills and habits (see Figure 6-15). In the four curriculum chapters of this book (Chapters 11–14), there is specific planning for routines, transitions, and group times. It is these times that provide a sense of security for children. Beyond the planning for indoor and outdoor activities, careful teachers realize that helping children with the routines of daily living provides a solid underpinning so that other learning can take place.

Sequence with a "Loose Grip" Keeping a "loose grip" on sequencing is important because once the time sequence is clear to all, then everyone can go about the business of learning and teaching. Children are more secure in a place that has a consistent schedule; they can begin to anticipate the regularity of what comes next and count on it. In that way, they are then free to move, explore, and learn without hesitation. Children can freely involve themselves without fear of interruption. Adults, too, enjoy the predictability of a daily schedule. By knowing the sequence of events, they are then free to flex the timing when unforeseen circumstances arise.

It is the unforeseen that often does happen. Amidst the noise of children at work, the play is likely to be interrupted by a number of things that can affect the "best laid plans" of all teachers.

- Chad unexpectedly decides that he does not want Dad to go—just as the teacher was helping Shana onto the toilet for the first time.
- An argument breaks out in the block corner—at the moment a teacher was leaving with a group of children for the kitchen with several cookie sheets full of carefully constructed gingerbread people.
- A visitor comes in the door with a special group time activity—just as two children collide and bump heads.

Routines: Learning Opportunities in Self-Care

Eating Teaches:

Health: Introduction to new and different foods, good nutritional habits

Social Skills: How to manage in a group eating situation, how to focus on eating and conversing; what is acceptable mealtime behavior and manners

Fine-Motor Skills: Pouring; handling spoons, forks; serving self, drinking, eating without spilling

Independence Skills: Finding and setting one's place, serving self, making choices, cleaning up at snack and lunch

Respect for Individual Differences: Likes and dislikes; choices of food; pace of eating

Toothbrushing Teaches:

Health: How to keep teeth and tongue clean

Independence Skills: Self-awareness, perceptual-motor to use toothbrush in mouth.

Resting/Sleeping Teaches:

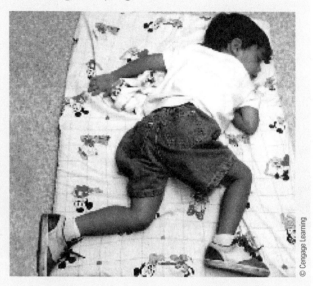

Health: Personal care skills; relaxation habits; internal balance; change of pace; alternating activity to allow body to rest

Dressing Teaches:

Independence Skills: Self-awareness, how to get one's own area ready—blanket, cuddly, book

Respect for Individual Differences: Comparisons between clothes for girls and boys, younger and older, larger and smaller children, and children in and out of diapers or training pants

Self-esteem: Caring for one's own body; choosing one's own clothes

FIGURE 6-15 Every routine can be used as a vehicle for learning within the environment.

Fine-Motor Skills: How to manage snaps, buttons, zippers; handling all garments; maneuvering in and out of a snowsuit or jacket; matching hands and feet with mittens and boots or shoes

Toileting/Handwashing Teaches:

Self-awareness: Body functions, learning the names and physical sensations that go with body functions

Self-identity: Comparisons between girls and boys (sit versus stand)

Self-esteem: Caring for one's own body without guilt, fear, shame

Human sexuality: In a natural setting, promotes healthy attitudes toward the body and its functions, and that adults can be accepting, open, and reassuring about the body and its care

FIGURE 6-15 *(continued)*

Teachers may then need to change the sequence to flex with the changing landscape. Further changes are at the heart of the next aspect of the temporal environment.

Transitions

Humans are known as a species for their adaptability. And yet we are resistant to change. For young children, too, change is difficult. Teachers and caregivers can make the necessary changes easier for children if they focus their attention on those times. Rather than trying to rush through quickly to get to the next event, provide enough transition time. Helping children anticipate, figure out, work through, and successfully manage the changes in their day guides them to maturity (see Figure 6-16).

Preparing children for upcoming transitions is useful, such as using a song or strumming of an instrument and the words, "Get ready to clean up soon." This helps children's perceptions of time, immediacy, and closure to collide with the schedule. Recall the unexpected chaos in the previous section on routines. If Chad does not want his Dad to go, perhaps getting Shana on the toilet has to wait; or Dad can read him another story until Shana's "All done now!" has taken place. The gingerbread sheets can be held up momentarily so that the quarrel can be resolved, or some of the "fighters" could be invited to be door-openers and help to march the group to the kitchen. Perhaps another teacher could help the visitor begin with the rest of the class on the rug while you get ice for the bumped heads.

These examples all illustrate the common clash of adult timetables and children's intentions. Programs need to be designed to allow for both consistency and **flexibility.** Consistency brings security and closure, allowing for teacher authority and expertise to assert themselves; flexibility invites sensitivity to individuals and respectful agreements to be reached. As teachers work with schedules, they continually balance the needs of individuals with those of the group.

Developmentally Appropriate Schedules

Just as the arrangement of space should reflect the group of children within, so does the daily schedule allow for appropriate growth at the developmental level of the group. There are common factors to consider for all children in the early years, as well as some developmental distinctions at the various ages.

There are common elements for all schedules:

- Include time for routines (to eat, rest, wash, toilet) as well as time for transitions (what happens when there is a change from one activity to another) and group times (circle time to begin the day, song time for announcements, or story time as closure).

Transition Times Made Easier

Questions for Planning

- Who is involved in the transition time (child, parents, teachers, other children, visitors, etc.)?
- What kind of activity has preceded the transition time and what will follow?
- What will the children be asked to do during transition?
- What will the teachers be doing during transition?
- How will the children be told or find out what to do *during* the transition?
- What do you know about child development and this particular child(ren) that can help with these questions?

Teaching Strategies

Arrival

- Greet each child with a smile, and welcome child and parent with what activities are available.
- Make name cards and/or an attendance sheet that child and parent can participate in as a starting point.
- Plan with parents, and alert the child, a simple and clear way for them to say goodbye and for the parents to leave (see Chapter 8 for details).

Cleanup Materials

- Give the children a five-minute "warning" to alert them to upcoming changes.
- Have a consistent and calm signal to start putting away toys.
- Use music as background and/or sing during cleanup.
- Consider having necklaces or cards of specific areas for children, or make teams.
- Construct the environment so that it is clear where things go and children can do the majority of it themselves.
- Occasionally thank the children publicly for cleaning up, noting individual efforts and specific chores done well.

Preparing Children to Attend

- Make a chart that shows the choices available.
- Sing a song or familiar fingerplay to get everyone's attention and participation.
- Ask the children to put on "elephant ears" (rabbit, etc.) or lock their lips and put the key in their pockets.

Ready to Rest/Nap Time

- Prepare the environment ahead of time to be restful—darkened room, soft blanket/cuddlies nearby, quiet music, teachers whispering and available to walk children to their places and stay with them.
- Read a story to the group in one place before they are to lie quietly, or split larger groups into small subgroups with a teacher reading to each.

Moving to Another Place/Building

- Gather the group and tell them exactly what will be happening.
- Ask for ideas of how to behave ("What will we need to remember? How can we stay safe and have fun together?") and reinforce with a few concrete rules.
- Have the children be a train, with adults as the engine and caboose, or a dragon with head and tail.
- Have the children choose a partner to stay with and hold hands.
- Ask preschoolers and early primary children to remember the "B" words ("beside or behind") in staying near adults.

Waiting for Others to Finish

- Prepare a part of the room for children to move to, such as a book corner or listening post, having an adult in that space with more than two children.
- Make an apron or hanging with several pockets filled with activity cards or small manipulatives for children to use alone.
- Plan a special table with folders or large envelopes with activities.
- Have a "waiting box" with special small items for these times only.

FIGURE 6-16 Transitions are a regular part of children's routines and should be learning times that are as well-planned as other parts of the day.

- Alternate quiet and active play and work to help children pace themselves.
- Provide opportunities for both inside and outside play.
- Allow children to participate in structured activities as well as those of their own choosing.
- Make it possible for children to work individually, in small groups, or in larger ones.
- Gear the time to the age and developmental levels of the group.
- Provide for flexibility so that children's interests can be maintained and emergencies met.
- Have a beginning and an end (meet and greet to start, close and review to finish, anticipate tomorrow).
- Involve the adults in planning and review (include a regular meeting time for more substantial discussion of children, long-range planning, and evaluation).
- Include time for clean up and room restoration.
- Incorporate the teachers' roles and assignments so that they know their area of responsibility.
- Be posted in an obvious place in the classroom for all to see.

Age-related differences should be taken into consideration as well. They call for schedules to reflect the development and needs of the group (see Figure 6-14). In general, these guidelines help to create a DAP schedule:

- *More choices* are available to children as they grow. *Example:* Two-year-olds could be over stimulated by the selection of materials that is appropriate for school-aged children.
- *Transitions* can be handled differently in the various age groups. *Example:* Older children can move through some transitions as a group, such as changing from one activity area to another or going out with a specialist in pairs or even in a single file. This is difficult for younger children, who would push or wander away. For them, the door to the yard opens quietly, allowing children to go out slowly. *Example:* A child care class of 3- and 4-year-olds is dismissed from song time to snack by the color of people's shirts or the first letter of their names, rather than as one whole group.
- *The structure* of the day changes with age. *Example:* The balance of free play and teacher-directed activities shifts from relatively few directed activities for younger children to more for preschool. A kindergarten schedule provides more structure both in individual work projects and teacher-focused time. A first grade schedule has more whole-group teacher instruction times.
- *The content of group activities* changes with age.

Example: A toddler circle time is simple, with a short finger play, flannel board or puppets story, and a good-bye song. Preschool group times include several songs, a dramatization of a favorite finger play, and a short story. By kindergarten, groups can last 15 to 20 minutes, with announcements and a weather board, children's "news telling," longer dramas, and even chapter stories.

The Interpersonal Environment

A child responds to everything in school: the color of the room, the way the furniture is arranged, how much time there is to play, and how people treat one another. To the child, everything is a stimulus. The feeling in a room is as real as the blocks or the books. Thus, the interpersonal or social aspects of an early childhood setting are powerful components of the environment.

Setting the Tone

Children are the most important people in the setting; they should feel safe and comfortable. A warm, interpersonal environment invites children to participate and to learn. When children feel secure with one another and with the setting, they are able to engage more fully in the total program.

Just how important is the interpersonal environment? Theories of Erikson, Bandura, and Vygotsky (see Chapter 4) emphasize the role of relationships in learning. Although most experts agree that the relationship between teacher and child is important, extensive research has only recently begun to document exactly how teacher–child interactions occur and how variations in such interactions might be related to behaviors or other outcomes in children. With a pattern of positive relationships between children's sensitive, involved interactions with teachers and other children, enhanced development is likely to be seen in cognitive, socio-emotional, and language domains. Brain research confirms that socialization plays a critical role in development. "The circuitry of the brain is developed through stimulations presented with adequate intensity, repetition, and duration to create and amplify the neural connection which are stored in short-term and, eventually, in long-term memory" (Marshall, 2011).

People are at the heart of early childhood education.

Defining Interpersonal Elements

The human component, the connections among the people in a center or home, makes all the difference to young children because they are the barometers of interpersonal tension or openness and freedom.

Noise and Busy-ness

Centers are very busy environments for children. So many things, so much learning, so much to do! Often the children's enthusiastic curiosity mixes with the teachers' focus on transmitting skills and information, creating an intensity that threatens to crush the spirit of play and compress the time.

- Reserve an area of your environment for those who want to sit quietly. This should include children and adults, both alone and with each other.
- Make meals a time for peace and quiet. This doesn't mean silence, but rather a rejuvenating break from the hustle of playtime.
- Wake up children from naps a little sooner than is needed. This gives them time to transition and allows wakeful children to learn to respect others' styles.
- Don't decorate every window with paintings. These are places to let in light and to contemplate the outdoors.
- Change room displays often. The room can get cluttered when projects are left up while more are added.

Avoid over-scheduling or making too many small time segments. Children may have short attention spans for adult-centered activities and "teacher talk." Yet they need and use longer periods of time to discover their interests and stay focused.

The intentional teacher shows respect for children when putting the temporal environment to work for them.

Think About This

1. Write a sample schedule for a preschool morning program. Mark the times for noise/busy-ness and those for quiet/respite. Count the minutes allotted for each. Is it balanced? Why or why not?
2. Many family child care homes have full-day schedules with children from newborns to 5-year-olds. How would you plan a day with eight children in this age range?
3. If you had an after-school program of 25 kindergarteners through third graders, what would be a balanced schedule for the afternoon? How many teachers would you need?

There are four elements of the interpersonal environment (Conventry, 2011):

Child–child relationship. Children learn from each other, observe and model other's behavior, and react to other children's expressions, especially emotional reactions.

Teacher–child relationship. Because it is understood that the single most important factor in determining the quality of a program is the teacher (see Chapter 5), it follows that teachers are the key ingredient in determining the interpersonal "flavor" of a class. The first component of the NAEYC's Academy criteria for high quality early childhood programs is the interactions among the staff and children (see Chapter 2).

Teacher–teacher relationship. The way staff feel about each other and how they express their feelings have an impact on children. How teachers solve conflicts with one another, how polite or kind they are, and how much positive communication flows makes a difference in the atmosphere.

Teacher–family relationship. Families matter in the life of a program, especially in the early years. Does the teacher know the family, share resources, and support their parenting?

Crafting the Teacher's Role

Young children develop best through close, affectionate relationships. Although this is true for all young children, it is particularly important for children younger than age 3 and those without facility in the dominant language spoken in the class. The interpersonal aspect of environment is the central element affecting the quality of toddler play. In addition, those who cannot talk about what is going on inside them show their feelings and conflicts through behavior. Teacher sensitivity and calm acceptance is critical. In this regard, every issue is a relationship issue.

The Reggio Emilia approach emphasizes relationships, as seen here (Caldwell, 2011):

I love Loris Malaguzzi's image of thinking with children as being a little like a game of tossing a ball back and forth. A child or a group of children have an idea or are drawn to something. If we are listening, we notice. Then perhaps we want to play a game, so we "toss" them a twist, a provocation, a wide-open question about their idea. They respond with something marvelous that we did not anticipate, and the game continues. We don't know where the next idea will come from, but the game is fun and challenging for both child and adult, and we get better at playing it in many situations and scenarios.

In a human and humane environment, people are respected, and the focus of the staff is on children's strengths and capabilities; limitations are seen as needs rather than liabilities. Children model their behavior on what they see others doing, so teachers engage children in interactions that include smiling, touching, listening, asking questions, and speaking on eye level. The language and tone of voice used are respectful and friendly, with children treated equitably across lines of culture, language, ability, and gender. Staff use positive guidance rather than punitive discipline techniques (see Chapter 7) and develop warm relationships with families (see Chapter 8).

Including Family Contributions

Teachers have to see children within the family context. To do so, they must establish stability and consistency through mutual learning, open dialogue, and exchange of information. Note the struggle, and ultimate shift, for these teachers:

- No matter how many times you tell Kai's grandfather that school starts at 9 AM, he continues to bring him between 9:30 and 10 . . . until you find out that in China, old people are often late and people respect their habits and sense of time. Now your realize you need to flex your schedule to allow for this late arrival and support this family custom.

- Elena's father speaks with such an accent you can hardly understand him. You would like to just avoid talking with him, but then you would connect only when there is a problem. You discover that, in his Central American culture, "good parents" are those that ask for teacher's opinions. You understand it is for you to overcome your discomfort and converse more, asking him respectfully to repeat what he is saying a bit more slowly so that you can understand.

- Every day Maryam brings her lunch, and it is so difficult to manage. These Iranian foods are not the same as the other children's, and the kindergartners tease each other about what they bring in their lunch boxes. You wonder if you should simply tell her auntie to send her with a sandwich. Only you realize that every child wants familiar foods, and letting Maryam eat what her parents send should be coupled with teaching tolerance to the other children. Now you move to use lunch as a time for everyone to get curious and interested in new foods.

The interpersonal connection between families and teachers cannot be overstated. Good relationships create a positive mood and can bolster what happens to the child within the classroom and can provide a smooth

The teacher's posture and facial expressions show respect for children and their learning pace and style.

© Cengage Learning

BRAIN
Research Says...

Space and Time for Brain Work

Advances in neuroscience have been touted in both the popular press and in educational conferences. Educators are urged to base their teaching practices on such research. But which research and what practices?

There are ways of improving learning based on brain research evidence. Good early childhood education has been implementing "teaching methods that respect the way the brain functions" (Jalongo, 2008):

- *An attentional mindset.* It is essential to pay attention. The more the mind wanders, the less it focuses on learning. Notes Jalongo (2008): "ECE has a long history of inventing materials to maximize the learner's attentional mind set. Whether it is unit blocks, outdoor play equipment, a dress up corner, toy animals or live classroom pets, early childhood is all about captivating children's attention and capitalizing on their curiosity."
- *Low to moderate stress.* Children need some choice over what they

engage with. DAP and early childhood traditions emphasize the whole child and do not focus on academic achievement only. "The physical learning environment is non-threatening, yet stimulating" (Rushton et al., 2009).
- *Engagement in coherent, meaningful tasks.* Hands-on, experiential learning gives children real toys and events to explore. Children are not bored, so they don't have to be convinced to engage in the tasks. Even the literature mirrors their lives.
- *Repetition for repeated practice.* Large blocks of time are made available to use materials over and over. Basic materials are available daily. "The brain will create new connections when there's new learning, but these connections must be reinforced and strengthened or they deteriorate" (Jensen, 2006).
- *Learner-controlled feedback.* Montessori materials are self-correcting, as is some of the best computer software, so that children can guide

both the pace and quantity of the "lessons" they are learning.

The study of the brain can now "assist educators in understanding how children learn best and what connects the learning environment with neurobiological changes in the child brain" (Rushton et al., 2009). We just need to give children the space and time so that they have a brain-friendly environment.

Questions

1. What parts of a physical environment might be considered "brain-friendly"? Why?
2. Which time blocks in a typical preschool program might be "brain-busters"? Why?
3. Look at the four components of the interpersonal environment, and list teacher behaviors that could be positive for brain compatibility and those that would be considered negative factors. Justify your list.

---

transition between school and home. Learning is enhanced when parents and teachers come to communicate in supportive, nonthreatening ways.

Noting Interpersonal Learning Moments

The attitudes and behaviors of teachers affect children's behaviors. Questions teachers can ask themselves as they evaluate the quality of the environment are:

- Is there a feeling of mutual respect between children and adults?
- Do teachers pick up on nonverbal and verbal expressions of both girls and boys? Of children with varying abilities? Of children of color?
- How do children treat one another?
- Do teachers model cooperative behavior with other adults and children? Do they show by example how to work through a disagreement or problem?
- Does the physical set up allow the teacher to focus on the children?
- Do housekeeping details keep teachers disconnected from children?

- Do teachers encourage children to use one another as resources?
- Do teachers take time to show children how to accomplish a task by themselves?
- Are girls complimented only on appearance and boys just for achievement? Are all children helped to appreciate similarities and differences?
- Do teachers use reasoning and follow-through?
- How and when do teachers interact with children?
- What are the teacher's posture and facial expression when involved in a problem situation?
- If I were a child, would I like to come here?

The answers to these questions provide a sense of the atmosphere of positive social interaction. The most important thing to remember is that the way people feel about each other and how they express their feelings have an impact on children. Teachers must focus as much attention on the interpersonal part of the environment as they do on buying equipment or arranging the room.

Summary

LO 1 The major characteristics of an environment are its physical plant, available resources, and program goals. Developmentally appropriate learning environments must adhere to several key principles that are expressed in the core aspects of anti-bias, self-help, and inclusion.

LO 2 The central elements in planning for the environment are children's health, safety, and well-being. Keeping children healthy has several components: Guarding children's safety involves first aid, natural disaster, and automobile safety and maintaining children's well-being means responding to both program and family challenges.

LO 3 Basic arrangements and materials for the environment revolve around three components. The physical environment addresses indoor and outdoor space, arrangement, and materials. The temporal environment refers to all aspects of time and schedule. The interpersonal aspects of the environment pinpoint the relationships and the tone created.

Key Terms

environment	self-concept	activity centers
physical environment	self-esteem	learning centers
temporal environment	least restrictive environment	open-ended
interpersonal environment	mainstreaming	interest areas
prepared environment	full inclusion	daily schedules
group size	environmental adaptation	routines
adult-child ratios	roughhousing	group times
anti-bias	universal infection control	transition
self-help	precautions	flexibility

Review Questions

1. What are the major principles in creating developmentally appropriate learning environments?
2. Who and what is involved in planning safe and healthy environments?
3. Write a definition of environment in early education including the three aspects to consider when planning programs for young children.

Observe and Apply

1. Hunch down on your knees and look at a classroom from the child's perspective. Describe what you see in terms of the principles of successful environments.
2. Discuss three school health and safety policies that help keep illness and injury to a minimum. Interview a director or head teacher about their policies, how they explain the guidelines to parents, and how they handle problems that have arisen.
3. Examine a daily schedule from an early childhood center. What do you think are the program goals of the school? How can you tell? Compare this with a daily schedule of a family day care home. How are they alike? How are they different?

Helpful Websites

American Alliance for Health, Physical Education, Recreation & Dance   **www.aahperd.org**

Canada Institute of Child Health   **www.cich.ca**

Centers for Disease Control and Prevention   **www.cdc.gov**

Children's Health   **www.kidshealth.org**

Consumer Product Safety Commission
www.cpsc.gov

National After School Association **www.naaweb.org**

National Association of Child Development
www.nacd.org

National Institute on Out-of-School Time
www.niost.org

National Program for Playground Safety
http://playgroundsafety.org

National Safety Council **www.nsc.org**

Teachers Resisting Unhealthy Children's Entertainment
www.truceteachers.org

Zero to Three **www.zerotothree.org**

The Education CourseMate website for this text offers many helpful resources and interactive study tools. Go to CengageBrain.com to access the TeachSource Videos, flashcards, tutorial quizzes, direct links to all of the websites mentioned in the chapter, downloadable forms, and more.

References

Brault, L. (2009). *Inclusion works! Creating child care programs that promote belonging for children with special needs.* Sacramento, CA: Child Development Division of California Department of Education.

Caldwell, L. (2011). Thinking about the environment: Inspirations from the Reggion approach. In A. Gordon & K. W. Browne, *Beginnings and beyond* (8th Ed). Clifton Park, NY: Thomson Delmar Learning.

Carter, M., & Curtis, D. (2003). *Designs for living and learning: Transforming early childhood environments.* St. Paul, MN: Redleaf Press.

Centers for Disease Control and Prevention. (2011). *The ABCs of raising safe and healthy kids.* Atlanta, GA: Author.

Community Products, LLC. (2008). *Children come first: Selecting equipment for early childhood education.* Rifton, NY.

Consumer Product Safety Commission. (2009). *Public playground safety checklist, CPSC Document #327.* Washington, D.C.: Author.

Conventry, A. (2011). Creating a calming environment in a preschool setting. http://www.brighthub.com/education/early-childhood/articles/65480.aspx. Accessed June 1, 2011.

Copple, C., & Bredekamp, S. (Eds.). (2009). *Developmentally appropriate practice in early childhood programs serving children from birth through age 8* (3rd Ed.). Washington, D.C.: National Association for the Education of Young Children.

de Melendez, R. W., & Ostertag, V. (2012). *Teaching young children in multicultural classrooms* (4th Ed.). Clifton Park, NY: Thomson Delmar Learning.

Derman-Sparks, L., and Olson Edwards, J. (2010). *Anti-bias education for young children and ourselves.* Washington, D.C.: NAEYC.

Deviney, J., Duncan, S., Harris, S., & Rody, M. A. (2010). *Inspiring spaces for young children.* Lewisville, NC: Gryphon House.

Froschl, M., Rubin, E., & Sprung, B. (1984). *Including all of us: An early childhood curriculum about disabilities.* New York: Educational Equity Concepts.

Greenman, J. (2000). What is the setting? Places for childhood. In A. Gordon & K. W. Browne, *Beginnings and beyond* (5th Ed). Clifton Park, NY: Thomson Delmar Learning.

Gutierrez, M. E. (1982). *Chicano parents' perceptions of their children's racial/cultural awareness.* Unpublished master's thesis, Pacific Oaks College, Pasadena, CA.

Guyton, G. (2011, September). Using toys to support infant-toddler learning and development. *Young Children, 66*(5), 50–56.

Harms, T., Clifford, R. M., & Cryer, D. (2005–2009). *The early childhood (revised), family day care, infant/toddler, and school age environmental rating scales.* New York: Teachers College Press.

Heroman, C., Dodge, D. T., Berke, K-L., & Bickart, T. (2010). *The Creative Curriculum® for preschool* (5th Ed). Washington, D.C.: Teaching Strategies.

Heroman, C., & Copple, C. (2006) Teaching in the kindergarten year. In D. F. Gullo (Ed.), *Teaching and learning in the kindergarten year.* Washington, D.C.: NAEYC, 59–72.

Howes, C., Phillips, D., & Whitebook, M. (1992). Thresholds of quality: Implications for the social development of children in center-based care. *Child Development*, 63(4), 449–460.

Hyson, M. (2008) *Enthusiastic and engaged learners: Approaches to learning in the early childhood classroom*. NY: Teachers College Press.

Jalongo, M. R. (2008). Editorial: Enriching the Brain—The link between contemporary neuroscience and early childhood traditions. *Early Childhood Education Journal*, 35, pp. 487–488.

Jones, E. (1984). *Personal notes about pluralistic and developmental viewpoints*. Unpublished.

Kendall, F. (1996). *Diversity in the classroom* (2nd Ed). New York: Teachers College Press.

Marotz, L. (2009). *Health, safety, and nutrition for the young child* (7th Ed). Clifton Park, NY: Thomson Delmar Learning.

Marshall, J. (2011, May). Infant neurosensory development: Considerations for Infant child care. *Early Childhood Education Journal*, 39, pp. 175–181.

National After-School Association (NAA). (2011). National School-Age Care Alliance Core Knowledge and Competencies for After-School and Youth Development Professionals. http://www.naaweb.org.

National Association for the Education of Young Children. (2005). *Position statement: Code of ethical conduct* (Appendix A is the entire text of the Code). Washington, D.C.: Author.

National Institute for Early Education Research. (December/January, 2006). Blueprint for new research: Classroom design and achievement. Volume 4, No. 1: 3.

Navarre Johnson, L. (2011). The interpersonal environment. Unpublished paper.

Needlman, R., & Needlman, G. (1995, November/December). Ten most common health problems in school. *Scholastic Early Childhood Today*.

Olds, A. (1989). Psychological and physiological harmony in the child care center design. *Children's Environments Quarterly*, (6)4, p. 13.

Prescott, E., Jones, E., & Kritschevsky, S. (1972). *Group care as a child-rearing environment*. Washington, D.C.: National Association for the Education of Young Children.

Ritchie, S., & Willer, B. (2008). *Accreditation performance criteria (revised)*. Washington, D.C.: National Association for the Education of Young Children.

Rogers, C. (1994, Spring). *Mainstreaming: Special needs—Special experiences*. Unpublished paper.

Rushton, S., Joula-Rushton, A., & Larkin, E. (2010). Neuroscience, play, and early childhood education: Connections, implications and assessment. *Early Childhood Education Journal*, 37, pp. 351–361.

Teachers Resisting Unhealthy Children's Entertainment (TRUCE). (2011-2012). *Toys and toy trends to avoid*. West Somerville, MA: Author.

Waldorf School (author unknown). (1995, January). *What is a Waldorf kindergarten?* Los Altos, CA: Author.

Wurm, J. (2009). *Working in the Reggio way*. Redmond, WA: Redleaf Press.

VPG/ Toddlers/Cengage Learning

7

Curriculum: Creating a Context for Learning and Play

Curriculum: The Framework for Teaching and Learning

Ira, a 2-year-old, is more interested in the process of pouring milk (especially what happens after the cup is filled) than in eating and conversing at snack time.

Kindergartners Bert and Leo become absorbed in watching a snail make its way across the sidewalk, ignoring for the moment the lesson on running relays. Each of these children are involved in the curriculum of an early childhood program.

What Is Curriculum?

In an early childhood setting, the curriculum consists of the art activity and language game; it is also the spontaneous investigation of pouring liquids at snack time, the song that accompanies digging in the sand, and the teacher's explanation of why the hamster died. Young children absorb everything going on about them. They do not discriminate between what is prepared and structured for them to learn and whatever else happens to them at school. It is *all* learning.

The curriculum is the framework around which planned and unplanned activities and lessons are created. The process of creating curriculum includes how, when, where, and why an activity or subject is being taught. Creating a good curriculum for young children is not simply a matter of writing lessons plans. It is understanding the process of how children interact with people and materials to learn. It is the sum of a teacher's knowledge about children's needs, materials, and equipment and what happens when they meet.

Curriculum must also be relevant to the child. Head Start classes on Native American reservations develop curricula that represent the history and traditions of the tribes the students represent. Relevant curriculum for a preschool in Seattle may include field trips to the Pike Street Market to see the recent salmon catch, whereas a transportation unit for inner city Boston children may include subway rides.

Developmentally Appropriate Curriculum

Appropriate early childhood curriculum is based on the theory, research, and experience of knowing how young children develop and learn. As noted in Chapter 2, developmentally appropriate programs, curricula, or practices

Children respond to curriculum materials that are inviting and accessible.

are defined by NAEYC (Copple & Bredekamp, 2009) as having the following core considerations:

- What is known about child development and learning of a particular age group so that the curriculum has appropriate experiences and learning activities to help children achieve and to challenge them.
- What is known about each individual child, the individual rate of growth, and the unique learning style so that the curriculum will reflect their needs, interests, and preferences.
- What is known about the social and cultural context of each child so that the curriculum provides meaningful and relevant learning experiences that are respectful of the backgrounds of the children and families in the group. The foundation for developmentally appropriate practices (DAP) and curriculum content is historically rooted in John Dewey's vision that schools prepare students to think and reason in order to participate in a democratic society (see Chapter 1). Figure 7-1 lists recommendations jointly endorsed by the National Association for the Education of Young Children and the National Association of Early Childhood Specialists in State Departments of Education to

---

Recommendations for Developmentally Appropriate Curriculum

NAEYC and the National Association of Early Childhood Specialists in State Departments of Education recommend implementing curriculum that is thoughtfully planned, challenging, engaging, developmentally appropriate, culturally and linguistically responsive, comprehensive, and likely to promote positive outcomes for all young children. The indicators of effectiveness for developing curriculum are:

- *Children are active and engaged.* Children of all ages and abilities can become interested and engaged, develop positive attitudes toward learning, and be supported in their feelings of security, emotional competence, and links to family and community.

- *Goals are clear and shared by all.* Curriculum goals are clearly defined, shared, and understood by program administrators, teachers, and families. The curriculum, activities, and teaching strategies are designed to help achieve the goals in a unified, coherent way.

- *Curriculum is evidence-based.* The curriculum is based on evidence that is developmentally, culturally, and linguistically relevant for each group of children and is organized around principles of child development and learning.

- *Valued content is learned through investigation, play, and focused, intentional teaching.* Children learn by exploring, thinking about, and inquiring about all sorts of things that are connected to later learning. Teaching strategies are tailored to children's ages, developmental capabilities, language and culture, and abilities or disabilities.

- *Curriculum builds on prior learning and experience.* The content and implementation builds on children's prior individual, age-related, and cultural learning, is inclusive of all children, and is supportive of the knowledge learned at home and in the community. The curriculum supports children whose home language is not English by building a base for later learning.

- *Curriculum is comprehensive.* All developmental domains are included in the curriculum, such as physical well-being and motor development, social and emotional development, language development, and cognition and general knowledge. Subject matter areas are included, such as science, mathematics, language, literacy, social studies, and the arts.

- *Professional standards validate the curriculum's subject-matter content.* Curriculum meets the standards of relevant professional organizations (for instance, The American Alliance for Health, Physical Education, Recreation and Dance, The National Council of Teachers of English, The National Science Teachers Association) and are reviewed so they fit together coherently.

- *Curriculum is likely to benefit children.* Research indicates that the curriculum, if implemented as intended, will likely have beneficial effects. These benefits include a wide range of outcomes.

FIGURE 7-1 NAEYC & NAECS/SDE (National Association of Early Childhood Specialists in State Departments of Education). 2003. *Early childhood curriculum, assessment, and program evaluation: Building an effective accountable system in programs for children birth through age 8*. Washington, D.C.: National Association for the Education of Young Children.

---

ensure developmentally appropriate curriculum. It can be used as a checklist as you move through the next three chapters, which focus on curriculum.

Culturally Appropriate Curriculum

If meaningful learning is derived from a social and cultural context (as Vygotsky asserts), then a multicultural atmosphere must be created in which awareness and concern for true diversity (including ethnicity, gender, and abilities) permeate the program. Multicultural education is about providing equal opportunities for all groups of students.

Culturally appropriate curriculum is also developmentally appropriate curriculum. The challenge is to develop a curriculum that reflects the plurality of contemporary American society in general and the individual classroom, in particular, and present it in sensitive, relevant ways.

Figure 7-2 highlights the differences between creating curriculum from a Eurocentric or dominant culture point of view and from a transformative curriculum approach.

Effective Curriculum: Five Basic Elements

Effective curriculum consists of any number of factors. Five important features of curriculum are that it is 1) inclusive, 2) integrated, 3) emergent, 4) based on multiple

 **DIVERSITY**

Transformative Curriculum

Creating a truly multicultural classroom calls into question the familiar ways of doing things and provides new insights and ways of thinking about culture. Banks (2006) describes this approach as transformative curriculum.

Transformative curriculum helps teachers develop critical thinking skills so that they question some of the opinions and images of people and cultures that are represented in the Eurocentric curriculum that dominates American schools. For instance, this approach encourages teachers to look at Christopher Columbus from the perspective of a Native American Indian before creating a curriculum about Thanksgiving, the pilgrim, or Native Americans. Transformation curriculum is a way to help develop more positive attitudes toward all racial, ethnic, and cultural groups.

The common practice in many early childhood programs of cooking ethnic foods or celebrating ethnic or cultural holidays as isolated experiences often trivializes or stereotypes groups of people. Folk tales, songs, food, and dress are symbols and expressions of a culture, not the culture itself. For children to gain any meaningful knowledge, the content must contribute to a fuller understanding of human diversity, not just a special occasion topic. Including diverse food, music, and clothing are important artifacts in the curriculum only when they expand a concept of diversity and serve as a link to discuss other aspects of a culture. Songs and dances of one culture could lead to a discussion of what games children play in different parts of the world.

Characteristics of a Multicultural Classroom

Common Practices of Dominant Culture	For a Multicultural Approach
Focuses on isolated aspects of the histories and cultures of ethnic groups	Describes the history and cultures of ethnic groups holistically
Trivializes the histories and cultures of ethnic groups	Describes the cultures of ethnic groups as dynamic wholes
Presents events, issues, and concepts primarily from Anglocentric and mainstream perspectives	Presents events, issues, concepts from the perspectives of diverse racial and ethnic groups
Is Eurocentric—shows the development of the United States primarily as an extension of Europe into the Americas	Is multidimensional and geocultural—shows how many peoples and cultures came to the United States from many parts of the world, including Asia and Africa, and the important roles they played in the development of U.S. society
Content about ethnic groups is an appendage to regular curriculum	Content about ethnic groups is an integral part of regular curriculum
Ethnic minority cultures are described as deprived or dysfunctional	Ethnic minority cultures are described as different from mainstream Anglo culture but as rich and functional
Focuses on ethnic heroes, holidays, and factual information	Focuses on concepts, generalizations, and theories
Emphasizes the mastery of knowledge and cognitive outcomes	Emphasizes knowledge formation and decision making
Encourages acceptance of existing ethnic, class, and racial stratification	Focuses on social criticism and social change

FIGURE 7-2 A comparison of two different approaches to multicultural curriculum, one from a Eurocentric point of view, the other from a culturally sensitive perspective. (Reprinted with permission of James A. Banks from James A. Banks, 2006, *Cultural diversity and education: foundations, curriculum, and teaching,* 5th Edition, Boston: Pearson Allyn and Bacon, page 238.)

intelligences, and 5) bears in mind differences in learning styles. With these in mind, the curriculum becomes more flexible and suited to all children in the class.

Inclusive Curriculum

Inclusive curriculum challenges teachers to provide opportunities for all children, regardless of gender, abilities, disabilities, language, culture, ethnicity, and religion. The activities and materials are chosen to enhance the potential of each child and are reflective of the diversity and abilities within the classroom. All activities are adjustable to a wide range of skills and abilities; are flexible enough to accommodate the needs of each child; and are ones in which children can participate at their developmental level, yet be challenged enough to help them learn. Chapters 3, 9, 10, and 11 have further information on inclusive classrooms.

Integrated Curriculum

The *whole child* approach that you learned about in Chapter 3 makes the point that interaction and relationship of the developmental domains are interconnected and work together to help children find meaning in and mastery of their world.

Developmentally appropriate materials fit the abilities of all children.

© Cengage Learning

Think of integrated curriculum in the same way because it weaves across many subject areas throughout the school day so that skills and concepts are developed in the context of other learning. Subjects such as math, science, reading, writing, and social studies are planned components of the daily curriculum and not taught as separate topics. An integrated curriculum makes it possible for teachers to include skill development activities in context, not in isolation. For instance, tracing square shapes in the Writing Center and cutting out squares with scissors can expand the concept of a square. A book about shapes shows squares in many configurations to make a picture; and in the Block Center, fences and building are constructed in square shapes. In this way, each activity center supports the concept of squares in different ways. The guidelines for developmentally appropriate curriculum found in Figure 7-1 contain many of the characteristics of an integrated curriculum.

It is easy to see how an integrated curriculum works. Experiencing a concept in a variety of contexts is a natural rather than a contrived way for children to learn. Unit blocks, a staple in most early childhood programs, are a good example of how much learning potential is available in one activity, as noted in the DAP Box.

An integrated curriculum supports developmentally appropriate learning by fostering children's wide range of abilities, skills, and knowledge and allowing them to proceed at their own level of development in meaningful activity.

Emergent Curriculum

Emergent curriculum is just what it says: curriculum that comes from or slowly evolves out of the child's experiences and interests. The emphasis is on children's interests, their involvement in their learning, and their ability to make constructive choices. Teachers set up materials and equipment in the room and the yard, sometimes planning a few activities each day that capture children's attention. For the most part, teachers then watch and evaluate what children do and support and extend what use children make of their experiences.

The curriculum begins with the children rather than with the teacher, who observes what children do, how they play, and what captures their interest and imagination. The point is to deepen and extend children's learning as they discover meaning and understanding in their play. The following example shows how emergent curriculum can be developed by following the children's lead.

Taking Cues from Children A lively group time discussion one day in the 4-year-old classes involved a new bridge that was being built near the school. The teachers had noticed

DAP | Integrated Learning Through Block Play

DAP includes engaging all of the developmental domains of the whole child. Social, emotional, cognitive, physical, language, and creative areas are drawn into action during block play. The significance of what children learn while building with blocks cannot be underestimated.

While playing with blocks, children learn about many concepts.

- *Science:* weight, gravity, balance, stability, height, inclines, ramps, interaction of forces
- *Mathematics:* classification, order, number, fractions, depth, width, height, length, fractions, size relationships, volume, area, measurement, shape, size, space, mapping
- *Social Studies:* symbolic representation, mapping, grids, patterns, people and their work
- *Art:* patterns, symmetry, balance, design, texture, creativity, drawing
- *Language:* making comparisons, recognition of shapes and sizes, labeling, giving directions, communicating ideas and needs, writing and drawing plans, using books as resources
- *Physical Development:* eye-hand coordination, clean up, hand manipulation, fine motor, visual perception
- *Social Development:* cooperation, sharing, clean up, conflict resolution, negotiation, respect for the work of others
- *Cognitive:* planning, naming, differentiation of sizes, shapes, inductive thinking, discovery

It is easy to see why one teacher has called block play "the perfect curriculum: It has everything children need to learn!"

Courtesy of the author

What math and science concepts did the 4-year-olds use while creating this block building?

that the block area had sat unused during the week, so they added books on bridges, paper, crayons, and scissors to the shelves near the blocks and put up pictures of different kinds of bridges. These additions drew children to the block area where they built bridges, made paper bridges, and counted the number of different kinds of bridges that were in the books nearby. Further conversations between the children and the teachers led to a woodworking project to create wooden bridges. Songs and poems about bridges became a routine part of circle time. Outdoors, the sand pit became a waterway with bridges and was soon followed by projects with boats and other water transportation. The curriculum content in this example is apparent, but an end product is not the focus. It is an example of integrated curriculum as well as emergent curriculum because the process children go through in creating knowledge through the

extension of bridge play fosters new insights and learning. The focus is on the child, not on the activity.

This practice of taking cues from children—noting what they play with, what they avoid, what they change—is one of the components of emergent curriculum and stems from the belief that in order to be a meaningful learning experience, the curriculum should come out of the daily life in the classroom. Based on the principles of Erikson, Piaget, and Vygotsky, emergent curriculum assumes that children are active, curious learners, capable of taking the initiative and constructing their knowledge through experience. Children are encouraged to use whatever style of learning is most natural to them, making use of the variety of materials in their own way. A materials-rich environment in which play is valued forms the foundation for the curriculum. For example,

- Anton, a first grader, noticed how dark the sky was as he and his classmates waited for the school bus to take him home. His teacher responded that the days were shorter in winter, so there was less daylight. The children began to ask questions about how this happened. The next morning many of the Activity Centers had materials for exploring light/dark;

charts for tracking the changes of light to dark; and a new outdoor thermometer. Over the next few months, children were immersed in the seasonal changes that occurred outside their windows.

- Four new babies were born to families with children in the 3-year-old class. The dramatic play area teemed with dolls, blankets, bottles, and baby beds. As the children talked about their new siblings, the teachers posed questions about the care and feeding of a newborn and how different it is from what the 3-year-olds ate. Children were asked to bring in pictures of themselves as babies and created a collage that was hung on the wall near the dramatic play area. During music, the children moved like babies and, outside, the wagons became baby carriages. As long as their interest held, the curriculum was deepened and extended.

In each instance, the curriculum followed the children's curiosity and became more complex in order to maintain their interests and learning potential. The teacher's role was to be a co-creator with the children to ensure that learning goals and objectives were met.

Planning emergent curriculum requires good observation and listening skills and the ability to interpret children's play. Webbing, which is discussed later in the chapter, is a good way to clarify with children what they know and what ideas they have for further exploration. Webbing also helps integrate the activity to include all learning domains.

Fostering Collaboration and Mutual Learning The emergent curriculum calls for collaboration on the part of the teachers with children and on the part of children with other children and with adults who offer suggestions and ideas. When children work collaboratively, they help each other succeed as well as to negotiate and solve problems together.

The accent is on mutual learning for both children and adults. For example, when the first grade class took a subway to the museum, this prompted a great many questions about subways and how they work. Because of the children's interest and the teacher's awareness of their developmental and educational needs, a project emerged and was developed over the next few weeks. Teachers learned more about what the students wanted to know about subways, so they could facilitate the children's learning and define the goals and objectives. The children helped plan the project. They asked questions; investigated; researched; explored; and, with the teacher's support and encouragement, formed small groups and completed assigned tasks. Books became an important

resource, as did people. The teacher, knowing what the children needed and were ready to learn, guided the discussion to ensure that educational goals would be met.

For emergent curriculum to be successful, teachers listen and observe carefully as children generate new ideas and then respond to what they hear and see that children have learned. Many observations methods were described in Chapter 6 and are appropriate ways to find ways and materials to advance and deepen what children learn. While emergent curriculum calls for collaboration and negotiation between children and teachers, it is the teacher who knows what is necessary for children's education and development and sets the goals for learning.

Finding Curriculum Ideas Children are only one of many sources of curriculum possibilities. A number of other sources feed into emergent curriculum, as noted by Jones (1994) in her classic work on emergent curriculum:

- Teachers' and parents' interests and skills
- Developmental tasks of the age group
- The physical and natural environment as well as people and things
- Curriculum resource books
- Family and cultural influences
- Serendipity or the unexpected
- Daily issues of living together, problem solving, conflict resolution, routines
- Values expressed by the school philosophy, the families, and the community

Emergent curriculum seems to capture the spontaneous nature of children's play and blend it with the necessary planning and organization. In the discussion of curricular models that follows in this chapter, you see that emergent curriculum has many applications.

TeachSource Video

Watch the TeachSource Video entitled "School Age: Emergent Curriculum." After you view the clip, reflect on the following questions:

1. What would you do to further the "cloud" discussion?

2. Describe the teachers' conversation regarding the weather. How would you have added to that conversation with regard to extending the children's interest?

3. How would you rate the teachers' planning process? Why?

Multiple Intelligences

In Chapter 4, you read about Gardner's theory of multiple intelligences (MI). According to this theory, children are capable of distinct categories of intelligence. That is, they have many different ways of knowing or of being "smart." Refresh your memory by reviewing Chapter 4. The potential for developing the various intelligences is based on the child's experience, culture, and motivation. The following is a summary of this theory (adapted from Armstrong, 2000 and The New City School, 1994). The MI categories with examples are:

1. *Linguistic Intelligence.* Sensitivity to the sounds, structure, meanings, and functions of words and language.

    Example: Children who enjoy word games, understand jokes, puns, and riddles, and enjoy the sounds and rhythms of language. They have a good vocabulary, spell easily, memorize readily, and are good storytellers.

    Examples: Adults such as Maya Angelou, Amy Tan, Martin Luther King, Jr.

2. **Logical-Mathematical.** Sensitivity to and capacity to discern logical or numerical patterns; ability to handle long chains of reasoning.

    Example: Children who notice and use numbers, patterns, and shapes and explore the relationships in them; they have a systematic approach to problem solving and organize their thoughts well. They think conceptually and are able to move easily from the concrete to the abstract. They like puzzles and computer games.

Logical-mathematical intelligence.

Examples: Adults such as Stephen Hawking, Madame Marie Curie, Bill Gates

3. **Spatial.** Capacity to perceive the visual-spatial world accurately and to perform transformations on one's initial perceptions.

    Example: Children who like to draw, build, design, and create things. They enjoy patterns and geometry in math as well as maps and charts. They think in three-dimensional terms and enjoy color as well as design. They love videos and photos.

Linguistic intelligence.

Spatial intelligence.

Examples: Adults such as I.M. Pei, Maria Martinez, Frank Lloyd Wright

4. **Bodily-Kinesthetic.** Ability to control one's body movements and to handle objects skillfully.

Example: Children who are agile, coordinated, have good body control and who take in information through bodily sensations. They are hands-on learners with good motor skills. They like to touch things, run, and use body language.

Examples: Adults such as Jackie Joyner-Kersee, Marcel Marceau, Kristi Yamaguchi

5. **Musical.** Ability to produce and appreciate rhythm, pitch, and timbre; appreciation of the forms of musical expressiveness.

Example: Children who like to sing, dance, hum, play instruments, and move their bodies when music is playing. They remember melodies, are able to keep and imitate a beat, make up their own songs, and notice background and environmental sounds. They enjoy listening and differentiating patterns in sounds and are sensitive to melody and tone.

Examples: Adults such as Stevie Wonder, Carrie Underwood, and Yo-Yo Ma

6. **Interpersonal.** Capacity to discern and respond to the moods, temperaments, motivations, and desires of other people.

Example: Children who have a lot of friends, who like to talk, who prefer group problem solving, and can mediate conflicts; who like to hear someone else's point of view; who volunteer to help when others need it.

Examples: Adults such as Marion Wright Edelman, Mother Teresa

Musical intelligence.

Bodily-kinesthetic intelligence.

Interpersonal intelligence.

7. **Intrapersonal**. Access to one's own feelings and the ability to discriminate among one's emotions; knowledge of one's own strengths and weaknesses.

Example: Children who pursue personal interests and set goals; who identify and label feelings; are insightful, sensitive, reflective, intuitive; who may daydream and are comfortable being alone. They know their own strengths and weaknesses.

Examples: Adults such as Sigmund Freud, the Buddha, Maria Montessori

8. **Naturalist**. Expertise in distinguishing among members of a species; recognizing the existence of other neighboring species; and charting out the relations, formally or informally, among several species.

Example: Children who enjoy all the features of the outdoor world. They recognize and classify plants, animals, rocks, clouds, and other natural formations; they garden and like to have animals at home and school to care for. They enjoy zoos, aquariums, and places where the natural world is on display and can be studied.

Examples: Adults such as John Muir, Jane Goodall, George Washington Carver

9. **Existential**. Individuals who think about the deeper aspects of life: questions such as the infinite or unexplained phenomenon and people who are drawn

Naturalist intelligence.

to issues of life and death, morality, and other matters of the spirit.

Examples: Children who ask questions about God, death, and war, and who raise questions about the ethics or "rightness" of a situation or discussion.

Examples: Adults such as Billy Graham, Bishop Desmond Tutu and other Nobel Peace Prize winners, Joan of Arc.

In a classroom it is easy to notice the different strengths children have in the MI categories. Some children excel at puzzles and manipulative games while others are busy dictating stories, building a boatyard with blocks, or holding the guinea pig. There are children who cannot be still for very long and need to be actively and physically involved in play and work for much of the day. We all have the capacities for the categories of MI, but we are not equally proficient in all of them.

Through a wide variety of meaningful learning experiences, children's strengths (and primary intelligences) can be assessed, and curriculum can be developed that fosters new knowledge and thinking. Jmel is strong in spatial intelligence, and that can serve as a context for other learning in different intelligence categories. Her intrapersonal and linguistic intelligences can be encouraged through activities that include her telling or writing stories about something she drew and what it means to her. Bodily-kinesthetic and music abilities can emerge through dancing and moving the body through space in different ways. This allows Jmel to experience and reinforce her own strengths and increase her strengths in other areas as well.

The relationship of curriculum based on MI to integrated curriculum is fairly clear from the example of Jmel and from Figure 7-4. If children have different ways of knowing, they should experience a concept, lesson, or subject matter in a variety of ways. As teachers

Intrapersonal intelligence.

Sounds of the City

Multiple Intelligences Context: Students from diverse communities need to develop an awareness and appreciation for the unique nature of the urban environment.

Learner Outcomes: Student will recognize the sounds of the city.

Procedure

1. Elicit from students the sounds that are unique to an urban area and list these sounds on chart paper. Show pictures of different urban settings to enhance the activity. Some sounds that might be included in this list are airplanes, traffic, emergency sirens, and street vendors.

2. Have students record city sounds on their empty playground if the school is located in an urban area. For homework, they could record city sounds from their neighborhoods or from the television.

3. Instruct the students to create a rhythm chant based on the sound word list created earlier, and use the taped examples to enhance the mood of the chants. Percussion instruments may be used to accompany portions of the chants. Students perform their musical numbers for the class.

Materials

Pictures of city scenes, tape recorders, cassette tapes, percussion instruments, chart paper, markers

Assessment/Reflection

Are the students able to identify urban sounds? How are the sounds the students collected from the various locations the same and different? What generalizations are the students able to make from this information?

Multiple Intelligences Extensions

Interpersonal: Help the students develop an awareness of how these city sounds affect their relationships with others.

Intrapersonal: How do city sounds affect moods?

Bodily-Kinesthetic: Use movement to complement the compositions.

Linguistic: Read *Apt. 3* by Ezra Jack Keats. List all the sounds that are heard within the story and who made those sounds. Use the sound hints to determine who lives on each floor.

Logical-Mathematical: Collect data on the number of times specific sounds can be heard within a community. Interview people and graph their reactions to these sounds. Propose a hypothesis as to how the frequency of sounds might affect the lives of the people they interviewed.

Spatial: Create cityscape murals that capture the city and its sounds.

A practical guide created by the faculty of The New City School © 1994

FIGURE 7-3 Planning curriculum around Multiple Intelligences. (From *Celebrating multiple intelligences: Teaching for success* [paper] by the faculty of the New City School. Copyright © 1994 New City School. Reprinted by permission.)

and caregivers expand their own thinking about children's abilities, they can vary what and how they teach and teach to many intelligences and developmental areas instead of just one. An integrated MI curriculum makes it possible to involve many intelligences in a wide range of activities and enable more children to succeed by drawing on their own capacities to learn. The lesson plan in Figure 7-3 is a good example of planning curriculum with an MI emphasis.

Gardner (Woolfolk, 2001) has written about the good uses of MI theory when it is applied to teaching. "Schools should cultivate those skills and capabilities that are valued in the community and the broader society," he says, and, "At the heart of the MI perspective—in theory and in practice—[is] taking human difference seriously." In both comments, Gardner affirms criteria for DAP.

Multiple Intelligences are also discussed in Chapter 4 and Chapter 12.

Learning Styles

Some people like going to lectures to learn about a new culture or country. Others prefer to watch a travelogue. Still others get the most out of traveling to that country and living among its people, eating the food, absorbing the atmosphere. Each of these is a legitimate method of learning and processing information, and each indicates the preferred style of that particular person. In Chapter 3, the discussion was about learning styles related to differences in children's behavior. In this chapter, we focus on how basic learning styles affect curriculum planning. These are the preferred mode of each child but not the only method by which the child can integrate knowledge.

Sensory Style

1. *The Visual Learner.* These are children who prefer pictures to words; photos, charts, and graphs provide the necessary clues; they like to represent their

learning by reading, writing, and drawing; the finished product is important.

2. *The Auditory Learner.* These are children who listen to others to learn and speak and discuss what they are learning. They are good at following directions in the appropriate sequence from one task to another.

3. *The Tactile-Kinesthetic Learner.* These children are active, full-body learners; they need hands-on activity and learn by doing, not listening or sitting still.

These modalities are the favored ways children learn through the use of their five senses. It seems clear that an integrated, emergent curriculum would be easily adaptable to all three learning modes. In fact, most early childhood experiences are heavily weighted toward the development of the five senses that provide many opportunities for children to learn through their preferred style.

Field Dependent/Independent Learning Style The two facets of this model, with examples (McNeely, 1997; Ramirez & Casteñada, 1974), are:

Field Dependent Learning Style (FD). These children are able to grasp broad distinctions among concepts, and they see relationships through a social context, working with others to achieve a common goal. They learn best through material that is related to their own experiences. FD learners are more person-oriented in their play and engage in social interactions sometimes for the sake of the interaction itself. They often use social conflict to make a social contact. They learn concepts through watching others, and their learning is reinforced by rewards such as verbal praise, helping the teacher, and showing the task to others. They depend on authority, seek guidance and demonstration from teachers, and need to have the performance objectives of the curriculum carefully explained.

Field Independent Learning Style (FI). These children look at things analytically, creating their own structure, and learn things for their own sake. They prefer self-defined goals and reinforcements and are motivated through competition and their own values and are more assertive than FD learners. FI learners prefer to work independently, and rarely seek physical contact with teachers; they are more idea-oriented than people-oriented. They like to try out new tasks without help. These children like the details of concepts because they find meaning in the various parts. They focus on the materials and their uses; social interactions are not as important to them.

A Teacher Provides Opportunities for:

Field Dependent Children to:	Field Independent Children to:
Engage in global thinking	Engage in analytical thinking
Follow a given structure	Generate own structure
Be externally directed	Be internally directed
Attend to social information	Be inattentive to social information
Resolve conflict	Think things through philosophically
Be social	Be distant in social relations
Work with others	Work alone
Have friends	Have acquaintances
Work with a provided hypothesis	Generate own hypothesis
Work with facts	Work with concepts
Use others' decisions	Use own decisions
Be sensitive to others	Be insensitive to others
Use stress for learning	Ignore external stress for learning

FIGURE 7-4 A teacher must make use of learning styles for field dependence/independence. (Adapted from McNeely, S.L. [1997], *Observing students and teachers through objective strategies.* Boston: Allyn & Bacon, Boston.)

Figure 7-4 suggests some curriculum approaches that work well for these two learning styles.

Play-Based Curriculum: Developing Skills, Knowledge, and Learning

In Chapter 4, you learned about the value and process of children's play. You may want to review that section to refresh your understanding of why play-based curriculum enhances children's potential for learning and is, in fact, the foundation for learning.

The vast knowledge of human development and behavior comes from researchers who spent countless hours observing and recording children playing. As noted by many, from Froebel to Vygotsky to Gardner, children need meaningful materials and activities in order to learn. They need to be physically as well as mentally and emotionally involved in what and how they learn, and they need to play. Through the use of activity centers, a variety of play opportunities that develop skills, knowledge, and learning are available throughout the school day (see Figure 7-5).

The Teacher's Role in Learning Through Play

Classroom teachers learn about children by listening to and observing spontaneous play activity and planning curriculum that encourages play. They discover each child's individual personality, learning style, and preferred mode of play.

Interest and Understanding

Genuine interest is one way teachers show their approval of the play process. Creating a safe environment in which children feel physically and emotionally secure is another. To establish play as an important part of the curriculum, teachers must:

Understand, appreciate, and value play experiences for young children;
Focus on the process of learning rather than on the process of teaching; and
Reflect on their observations in order to know what activities, concepts, or learning should be encouraged or extended.

Erikson (1972), one of the most notable contributors to the field of human development, advises that play has a very personal meaning for each individual. Perhaps the best thing that we as adults can do to discover this meaning is to go out and play; to reflect on our own childhood play; to once again look at play through the eyes of the child.

Involvement in Play

One of the most difficult tasks teachers face is knowing when to join children at play and when to remain outside the activity. They must ask themselves whether their presence supports what is happening or whether it inhibits the play. Sometimes teachers are tempted to correct children's misconceptions during play:

Abby and Salina, deeply involved in their grocery store drama, are making change incorrectly. A teacher must judge whether to explain the difference between nickels and quarters at that time or to create an opportunity at a later date. Teachers must be aware of what happens if they interrupt the flow of play and how they influence the direction it takes. If Abby and Salina begin to talk about their coins, showing an interest in learning how to compute their change, the teacher can move into the discussion without seeming to interfere.

Many adults enjoy playing with the children in their class; others feel more comfortable as active observers. But every teaching situation demands the teacher's involvement at some level. The hesitant child may need help entering a play situation; children may become too embroiled in an argument to settle it alone; play may become inappropriate, exploitative, or dominated by a particular child.

Vygotsky gives us other reasons to be involved with children as they play, particularly in relation to the interpersonal nature of teaching (see Chapter 4). The belief that learning is interpersonal and collaborative is exemplified by the teachers of Reggio Emilia (see Chapters 2 and 5), who guide and support children's learning by engaging in play and knowing what strategy best helps an individual child reach the next level of skill (zone of proximal development). The Reggio Emilia approach to curriculum (discussed at the end of this chapter under "Curriculum Models") finds an appropriate and appealing blend of Vygotsky's concern for individual exploration and assisted discovery.

The teacher's role in facilitating play is about balance: how to allow children the space and time to create their own play while still taking advantage of the teachable moments in which further learning is enhanced. Use the following guidelines to maintain a good balance:

- Guide the play, but do not direct or dominate the situation or overwhelm children by participation.
- Capitalize on the children's thoughts and ideas; do not enforce a point of view on them.
- Model play when necessary; show children how a specific character might act, how to ask for a turn, how to hold a hammer.

Play-Based Curriculum: Enhancing Children's Learning

Cognitive/Language

Distinguishes between reality and fantasy

Encourages creative thought and curiosity

Allows for problem solving

Encourages thinking, planning

Develops memory, perceptual skills, and concept formation

Learns to try on other roles

Acquires knowledge and integrates learning

Learns communication skills

Develops listening and oral language skills

Creative

Fosters use of imagination and make-believe

Encourages flexible thinking and problem solving

Provides opportunity to act upon original ideas

Supports taking risks

Learns to use senses to explore

Re-creates images in buildings and art media

Sharpens observational skills

Provides variety of experiences

Learns to express self in art, music, and dance

Develops abilities to create images and use symbols

Acquires other perspectives

Social

Tries on other personalities, roles

Learns cooperation and taking turns

Learns to lead, follow

Builds a repertoire of social language

Learns to verbalize needs

Reflects own culture, heritage, values

Learns society's rules and group responsibility

Shows respect for others' property, rights

Teaches an awareness of others

Learns how to join a group

Builds awareness of self as member of a group

Gives sense of identification

Promotes self-image, self-esteem

Experiences joy, fun

Physical

Releases energy

Builds fine- and gross-motor skills

Gains control over body

Provides challenges

Requires active use of body

Allows for repetition and practice

Refines eye–hand coordination

Develops self-awareness

Encourages health and fitness

© Cengage Learning

Emotional

Develops self-confidence and self-esteem

Learns to take a different viewpoint

Resolves inner fears, conflicts

Builds trust in self and others

Reveals child's personality

Encourages autonomy

Learns to take risks

Acts out anger, hostility, frustration, joy

Gains self-control

Becomes competent in several areas

Takes initiative

© Cengage Learning 2011

FIGURE 7-5 Play is the cornerstone of learning.

- Ask questions; clarify with the children what is happening.
- Help children start, end, and begin again.
- Give verbal cues to enable children to follow through on an idea.
- Focus children's attention on one another; encourage them to interact with each other.
- Interpret children's behavior aloud when necessary.
- Help children verbalize their feelings as they work through conflicts.
- Expand the play potential by making statements and asking questions that lead to discovery and exploration.

Setting the Stage for Play

Teachers set the stage for learning through play by developing curriculum that includes many forms of play, some of which is spontaneous, some of which is guided and/or directed by the teacher. The environment (physical, temporal, and interpersonal) is a key element in reinforcing a play-based curriculum.

Structuring the Environment

To structure the environment for play, teachers include uninterrupted time blocks in the daily schedule (at least 45 minutes to an hour) for free play time. This allows children to explore many avenues of the curriculum free from time constraints. It is frustrating to young children to have their play cut off just as they are getting deeply involved.

Established routines in the schedule add to the framework of a day planned for play. The raw materials of play—toys, games, and equipment—are changed periodically so that new ones may be introduced for further challenge:

- In choosing materials, teachers select dress-up clothes and accessories that appeal to all children's needs, interests, and emotions.

- Props are required for a variety of roles: men, women, babies, doctors, nurses, grocers, mail carriers, teachers, and firefighters.
- Hats for many occupations help a child establish the role of an airline pilot, tractor driver, construction worker, police officer, or baseball player.
- Large purses are used for carrying mail and babies' diapers; they also double as a briefcase or luggage.
- Simple jackets or capes transform a child for many roles.

Props that represent aspects of the child's daily life are important; children need many opportunities to act out their life stories.

For younger children, teachers make sure there are duplicates of popular materials. Group play is more likely to occur with three telephones, four carriages, eight hats, and five wagons. Social interaction is enhanced when three space shuttle drivers can be at the controls.

Materials that are open-ended further enlarge play. These are materials that expand the children's learning opportunities because they can be used in more than one way. Blocks, a staple of the early childhood curriculum, are a case in point. Children explore and manipulate blocks in many ways. The youngest children carry and stack blocks and also enjoy wheeling them around in wagons or trucks. They also enjoy the repetitious action of making small columns of blocks. Older preschoolers build multistoried structures as part of their **dramatic play**—offices, firehouses, and garages.

Classroom Activity Centers

The **activity centers** in most early childhood programs consist of:

Indoors	*Outdoors*
Creative arts	Climbing equipment
Blocks	Swings
Table toys	Sand/mud/water
Manipulatives	Wheel toys
Science/discovery	Woodworking
Dramatic play	Hollow blocks
Language arts/books	Music
Math	Nature/science
Music	Organized games

All of these centers offer activities and materials for children to choose from during free play time—the greatest portion of their school day. (See typical daily schedules in Chapter 2.) Paints are in the easel trays, puzzles on the tables, dress-up clothes and props in the housekeeping/dramatic play center, blocks and accessories in the block corner, and books and tapes in the language area. Teachers plan the resources and materials and place them so that children readily see the alternatives available to them. Some of these activities might be teacher-directed, such as cooking snacks in the housekeeping area. For the most part, however, these activities are self-initiating and child-directed. At all times, the emphasis is on providing a child-centered curriculum.

Whatever the activity center, it needs attention and planning. Wherever children are present, learning and playing are taking place. Because each play space makes a contribution to children's experiences, teachers should develop appropriate curriculum for that learning area.

Go back and review what Chapter 9 describes as the important principles in creating environments that reflect curriculum goals, and see Chapter 2 for daily schedules.

Just as focusing on the activity or learning centers can develop curriculum, so, too, can an early childhood program be planned around the skill levels of the children in the class. The next three chapters provide a more in-depth identification of the types of skills that children need to learn.

The first decision teachers must make concerns what particular skill they wish to help children develop. The skill can be in the area of physical, cognitive, language, creative, social, or emotional development.

The nature of the individual class and the program philosophy helps teachers establish priorities for these skills. Teachers then select the activities and materials that enhance the development of any one or more of those particular skills. Figure 7-6 shows how the cognitive skill of classification can be implemented in the classroom, making it the focus of the entire curriculum.

The next three chapters provide a more in-depth identification of the types of skills that children need to learn.

Planning Curriculum: Engaging Teaching and Learning

The aim of the curriculum is to help children acquire the skills and behaviors that promote their optimal growth physically, socially, emotionally, and intellectually. Teachers consider a number of factors in developing a curriculum to provide maximum learning opportunities. Among these are the *educational philosophy and goals* of the program. A family child care provider plans activities for a few children in an intimate setting while the kindergarten teacher arranges small working groups so that the large group does not seem overwhelming. The activities should support the goals of the program and result in the accomplishment of those goals.

Ways to Foster Skills, Knowledge, and Learning

1. The single most important determinant the teacher must consider is *the children themselves*. Their ages, developmental levels, individuality, and learning styles are barometers of what is a successful and stimulating curriculum.

2. The *number* of children in the class affects the teacher's planning as does the number of teachers, aides, and volunteers who help out in the classroom.

3. A prerequisite for planning is the *availability of people and material resources* and ways to use them. The strengths of the teaching staff, adequate supplies and equipment, and enough adults to supervise the activities are taken into consideration.

4. The *ethnic and cultural backgrounds* of the children must be taken into consideration. To be effective, curriculum experiences should draw on children's background and cultural experience.

5. Curriculum planning stems from *a knowledge of young children*. Teachers look at how, when, and what concepts children should learn and how they teach those concepts; what the child already knows, and how they can build on that. In many ways, teachers start at the end: They look at children's developmental levels as they focus on what they want the child to accomplish or to learn as a result of this experience and then plan the curriculum to lead toward those results.

6. Planning for a *broad range of developmental skills and interests* is important. Because the abilities of children even of the same age vary, activities must be open-ended and flexible enough to be used by a number of children with varieties of skills. Remember, too, that some children may not be interested in formal or organized art projects or science experiences. These children may learn more easily through self-selected play.

7. The developmental word pictures of children from birth through age 8 found in Chapter 3 can be useful in determining *what kinds of activities appeal* to young children. Activities should be conducted in a variety of modes so that all children can connect with what they need to learn.

8. The *amount of time* available in the daily schedule and *the amount of space* in the room or yard affect a teacher's planning. Finger painting requires time for children to get involved, proximity to water for clean up, and an area in which to store wet paintings.

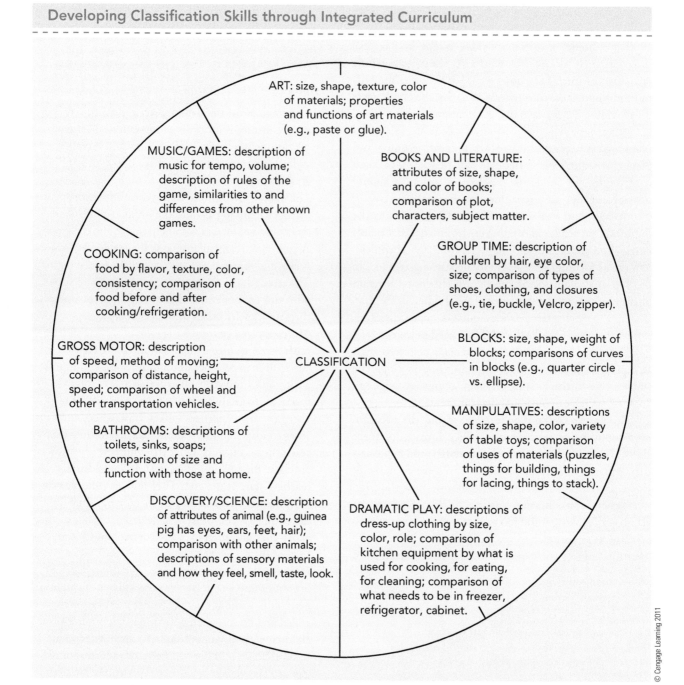

FIGURE 7-6 Curriculum can be developed with a focus on a particular skill. Classification skills can be enhanced throughout the curriculum and in activity centers. Note: This is a graphic way to demonstrate an integrated curriculum, not an example of how to write curriculum plans.

Culturally Responsive Teaching

Positive attitudes toward self and others emerge when children know they are valued for their individuality and appreciated as members of a family and a culture. The school environment can reflect this in a number of ways. Figure 7-7 lists ways in which an early childhood program can use culturally diverse materials on a daily basis to foster the relationship between home culture and school.

Banks (2006) identifies five important characteristics of the effective teacher in a multicultural society. They are teachers who:

1. Seek pedagogical knowledge of the characteristics of students from diverse ethnic, racial, cultural, and social class groups; of prejudice and prejudice reduction theory and research; and of teaching strategies and techniques.

Play Materials to Enhance Cultural Diversity and Inclusivity

Curriculum Area	Materials and Equipment
Music	Rainstick (Chile), marimba (Zulu), balaphon (West Africa), ankle bells (Native American), maracas (Latin America), Den-den (Japan), Shakeree (Nigeria), drums (many cultures), ocarina (Peru), songs of many cultures
Literature	Books on family life of many cultures, stories of children from far and near, legends and folktales from many countries, stories with common childhood themes from many lands, favorite books in several languages, wordless books, sign language, Braille books
Blocks and accessories	Variety of accessories depicting many ethnic people, aging people, community workers of both sexes in nonstereotyped roles and with various disabilities; Russian nesting dolls, Pueblo storytellers, animals from around the world
Art	Paints, crayons, markers, and construction paper in variety of skin-tone colors; child-size mirrors
Dramatic play	Anatomically correct dolls representing many ethnic groups; doll accessories, including glasses, wheelchairs, crutches, walkers, leg braces, and hearing aids; doll clothes, including cultural costumes and dress-up clothing from many cultures; cooking utensils, such as a wok, tortilla press, cutlery, chopsticks
Games	Language lotto, dreidel game, lotto of faces of people from around the world, black-history playing cards, world globe
Outdoors	Elevated sand and water tables and ramps for wheelchair access, lowered basketball hoops, sensory-rich materials
Classrooms	Carp banners (Japan), paper cuttings from Mexico and China, photographs and magazine pictures of daily life from many cultures, artwork by artists from a variety of ethnic backgrounds, pictures of children from many ethnic backgrounds and cultures

© Cengage Learning 2011

FIGURE 7-7 A child's family and culture can be brought into the classroom through a variety of curriculum materials; so, too, can children with disabilities be included.

2. Have reflected on and clarified an understanding of their own cultural heritage and experience and have knowledge of how it relates to and interacts with the experiences of other ethnic and cultural groups.
3. Have reflected on their own attitude toward different racial, ethnic, cultural, and social class groups.
4. Have the skills to make effective instructional decisions and reduce prejudice and intergroup conflict.
5. Devise a range of teaching strategies and activities that facilitate the achievement of students from diverse racial, ethnic, cultural, and social class groups.

Children with special needs also need their life mirrored in the school setting with dolls, books, and play accessories that signify acceptance and belonging.

Throughout this text, especially in Chapters 2, 5, and the upcoming chapters, cultural sensitivity on the part of teachers and curriculum goal is emphasized. Woolfolk (2001) suggests the following guidelines for culturally relevant teaching. They provide an accurate summary of many of the points found elsewhere in this book:

- Experiment with different group arrangements to encourage social harmony and cooperation.
- Provide a range of ways for children to learn material to accommodate a wide range of learning styles.
- Use direct teaching methods for important information that everyone should know, such as telling children how to take care of materials, acceptable ways to disagree, and how to get the teacher's attention.
- Learn the meaning of different behaviors of your students; find out how they feel when they are praised or corrected; talk with family members to discover the meaning of gestures, expressions, or other responses that are unfamiliar to you.
- Emphasize meaning in teaching; that is, make sure students understand the concept by using examples from everyday experiences.

● Get to know the customs, traditions, and values of your students; analyze different traditions for common themes; attend community fairs and festivals.

● Help students detect racist and sexist messages, analyze the curriculum for biases, and help children discuss ways that their communication with each other may be biased. Discuss expressions of prejudice.

A sound curriculum is the linchpin of a quality program for children. Curriculum planning and development is a creative act, one that is rewarding for teachers. Figure 7-8 highlights some of a teacher's thoughts in the planning process. In the next four chapters, curriculum implementations are explored from another perspective, that of the major areas of development in the child's growth. In Chapter 11, the focus is on how curriculum affects the growing body. Chapter 12 emphasizes the curricular role in developing the mind, and Chapters 13 and 14 explores the curricular issues surrounding social and emotional growth.

Integrating Learning Standards

Curriculum planning may be affected by a set of standards mandated by states. Most states have developed some sort of explicit learning expectations for children to meet at various age and grade levels, often termed "outcomes" or "desired results." At the federal level, there is the Head Start Child Outcomes Framework and the content standards that other national organizations have created for math, science, and literacy. Standards describe the kinds of learning that should take place and often, but not always, includes most areas of developmental domains.

There are several benefits of standardization (Gronlund, 2006). When linked to primary grade standards, early childhood standards may enhance school readiness. Standards help to define the foundational skills for learning and help teachers identify the next steps in their learning. To the public, they could reinforce the potential for learning in very young children and the importance of quality early childhood programs. Standards also provide a vehicle for demonstrating the breadth of learning that takes place in the early years and, if used with thought and planning, they can work hand in hand with developmentally appropriate practices.

Many early childhood professionals have concerns over the potential misuse of these standards. They may foster "teaching to the test" rather than a more developmental approach to teaching and cause pressure on the child through inappropriate expectations. They may promote testing and other assessment methods inappropriate for

How Teachers Plan Curriculum

Sets specific objectives

Integrates curriculum

Allows children meaningful choices

Uses environment as co-teacher

Knows what is worthwhile to teach

Uses people and materials as resources

Knows each child's capabilities

Expresses school philosophy and goals

Invites families and diverse cultures into curriculum

Balances child-initiated and teacher-directed learning

Plans activities

Uses play and active learning

Recognizes and accommodates individual differences

Uses knowledge about individual children's learning styles and intelligences

© Cengage Learning

FIGURE 7-8 The effective teacher's role in creating curriculum.

© Cengage Learning 2011

young children as noted earlier in Chapter 6. Too often, standards do not address all of the developmental domains but focus only on literacy and/or math and science. Children's sociocultural experiences are a significant part of their learning and standards need to recognize this when determining what children should know and be able to do (Bowman, 2006). We do not want to deprive children from recess and play because of the national emphasis on high stakes testing and the belief that play is less important than academics (Frost, Wortham, & Reifel, 2008).

A joint position paper by NAEYC and the National Association of Early Childhood Specialists in State Departments of Education (NAECS/SDE) (2002) cites four essential features that early learning standards should include: 1) significant, developmentally appropriate content and outcomes; 2) informed, inclusive processes to develop and review the standards; 3) implementation and assessment strategies that are ethical and appropriate for young children; and 4) strong support for early childhood programs, professionals, and families. By following these guidelines, standards could contribute to more positive outcomes for all children.

Today's teachers need to learn more about their own state's requirements and reflect with other early childhood professionals on the tension between meeting the standards and remaining true to developmentally appropriate practices. Figure 7-9 is an example of how a developmentally appropriate curriculum includes learning standards.

Setting Goals

The process of developing curriculum begins with setting goals and then choosing the most pressing ones for attention. The following five steps are guidelines to setting and achieving curriculum goals:

1. *Set goals.* Decide what it is you want children to learn. What do you want them to know about themselves? About others? About the world? State goals clearly, preferably in behavioral terms so that results can be measured.

2. *Establish priorities.* Make a list of three to five goals or objectives you consider most important. State the reasons for your choices; your own values and educational priorities will emerge more clearly.

3. *Know the resources.* A rich, successful, and creative curriculum relies on a vast number of resources. To create a health clinic in the dramatic play area, for instance, you might need the following resources:
   Materials. Props, such as stethoscopes, X-ray machines, tongue depressors, adhesive strips, medical gowns, and masks.
   People. Parents and/or community people in the health care professions to visit the class.
   Community. Field trips to a nearby clinic, hospital, dentist's office.

4. *Plan ahead.* Set aside a regular time to meet for curriculum planning. This may be on a weekly, monthly, or seasonal basis. Discuss the curriculum

Early Learning Standards

Standard	Activity	Demonstrates Mastery
Personal and social competence: Identifies self by categories of gender, age, or social group.	1. Graph children's ages. 2. Make an "All about Me" book. 3. Create self-portraits with dictation.	1. Says correct age and shows correct number of fingers. 2-3. Says, "I'm a girl," "I'm 4 years old," or "I'm Vietnamese."
Effective learner: Completes increasingly complex puzzles.	Play with knob-puzzles, puzzles with and without frames, and floor puzzles.	Uses puzzles with interlocking pieces without the help of frames.
Physical and motor competence: Manipulates two or more objects at the same time.	String beads; play with Legos or Duplos; practice buttoning, zipping, lacing cards, and cutting paper.	Two hands manipulate object at the same time to complete task successfully.

FIGURE 7-9 Early learning standards are beneficial when they can be linked to developmentally appropriate curriculum and have clear goals and outcomes. (Source: Adapted from Kim Yuen, San Mateo County Office of Education, San Mateo, CA. From Browne, K. W., & Gordon A. M., 2009. *To teach well: An early childhood practicum guide.* Upper Saddle River, NJ: Pearson Learning.)

activities as well as the daily routines in order to integrate the two.

5. *Evaluate*. Reflect on the outcome of your planning. Consider what worked and what did not, why it was successful or not. Look at the part of the experience that did not work as well as you would have liked. How can it be improved?

What can you change about it? An evaluation should be immediate, precise, and supportive. Teachers need feedback about their planning and implementing skills. The needs of children are best served when the curriculum is refined and improved. Figure 7-10 is a useful example of how to evaluate an activity.

Evaluating Classroom Activity

Activity _____

How many children participated?_____ Did any avoid the activity? _____

How involved did children become? Very _____ Briefly _____ Watched only _____

What were children's reactions? Describe what they said and did. _____
_____
_____
_____
_____

What did you do to attract children? To maintain their interest? _____
_____
_____
_____

How would you rate the success of this activity? Poor _____ Adequate _____ Good _____ Great _____
Why? _____

What skills/abilities were needed? Did the children exhibit the skills? _____
_____
_____

What parts of the activity were most successful? Why? _____
_____
_____

Describe any difficulty you encountered. Give reasons and tell how you would handle it if it happened again.
_____
_____
_____

If you did this activity again, what would you change? _____
_____

In light of your evaluation, what would you plan for a follow-up activity? _____
_____
_____

How did this activity compare with your goals and expectations? _____
_____
_____

FIGURE 7-10 Evaluating daily activities lets teachers use assessment as a curriculum planning tool. Although not every activity needs this scrutiny on a daily basis, careful planning and evaluation create effective classrooms. (Originally adapted from Vassar College Nursery school. From *Beginning Essentials in Early Childhood Education*. Figure 7-18, p. 393. Copyright © 2007 Wadsworth, a part of Cengage Learning, Inc. Reprinted by permission. www.cengage.com/permissions.)

⊡ You can download a copy of this form from this text's Education CourseMate website.

Teacher-Directed Learning

This text promotes teaching through active learning where children have a part in creating the curriculum. This does not exclude, however, the need for teacher-planned experiences in order to further the educational goals of the program. When materials and information are complex or the concept is unfamiliar to the children, teachers provide specific directions and knowledge to illustrate what they are teaching.

Teaching certain skills, such as cutting with scissors and writing lower and upper case letters, requires teacher guidance. The continuum that is shown in Figure 7-11 suggests a broad range of teaching behaviors, including teacher demonstration and directive teaching.

Different activities require different teaching strategies to meet the needs of all children. Helm and Katz (2001) observe that teachers using the project approach often use teacher-directed instruction for teaching certain skills and concepts while keeping a high degree of child choice and initiative in the project.

Group Times

There are certain times within the daily routine when teachers call children together. The size of the group is determined in part by how many teachers there are and how they want to present various learning experiences. The reverse is also true. Various types of learning experiences best lend themselves to small or large group discussions. In using the project approach, for instance, small group work seems to provide the best format for developing ideas and listening to one another's opinions. A presentation by a visiting parent or expert on the project theme would be more appropriate for the large group. Smaller groups could then form to discuss in greater detail the ideas presented.

Large group times are used for a variety of reasons. Teachers may use them as opportunities to bring the entire class together to:

- Provide transitions in the daily schedule.
- Bring in a special guest or presentation.
- Introduce new ideas and materials.
- Sing, dance, and do fingerplays.

A Continuum of Teacher Behavior

Nondirective			Mediating				Directive	
Acknowledge	Model	Facilitate	Support	Scaffold	Co-construct	Demonstrate	Direct

Give attention and positive encouragement to keep a child engaged in an activity

Display for children a skill or desirable way of behaving in the classroom, through actions only or with cues, prompts, or other forms of coaching

Offer short-term assistance to help a child achieve the next level of functioning (as an adult does in holding the back of a bicycle while a child pedals)

Provide a fixed form of assistance, such as a bicycle's training wheels, to help a child achieve the next level of functioning

Set up challenges or assist children to work "on the edge" of their current competence

Learn or work collaboratively with children on a problem or task, such as building a model or block structure

Actively display a behavior or engage in an activity while children observe the outcome

Provide specific directions for children's behavior within narrowly defined dimensions of error

FIGURE 7-11 There are many ways for teachers to respond to and support children's growth and learning. (From Bredekamp S. & Rosegrant, T., Eds. [1995]. *Reaching potentials: Appropriate curriculum and assessment for young children*, Vol. 2. Figure 2, p. 21. Reprinted with permission from the National Association for the Education of Young Children.)

Teaching With INTENTION

A Balancing Act: Child-Directed and Teacher-Directed Experiences

Intentional teaching involves deciding if a child-directed or adult-directed experience is best under particular circumstances. One researcher (Epstein, 2007) explored the similarities between both approaches to teaching and learning. It turns out that neither way is controlled exclusively by the teacher or by the child; both are actively involved in the activity and process. When the experience is teacher-directed, children are encouraged to make suggestions, ask questions, and otherwise actively participate. The teacher deliberately keeps the focus on the purpose of the lesson while responding to the children's involvement. For a child-directed experience, teachers are similarly intentional in their involvement. As children investigate and explore, the teacher is primed to observe and get involved when it seems appropriate. Neither teaching strategy is a passive approach, but in both, the teacher times suggestions and interactions with the children and the activity. The teacher's role is to help advance the experience and guide their learning to greater depths.

As we think about the learning experience, we ask ourselves:

Which method best suits the goals for learning?
Which method is best for this particular group?
Which method extends children's knowledge and deepens their understanding of this particular lesson or information?
Which method am I most comfortable with for this experience?

There is no right or wrong answer to these questions. Both methods are developmentally appropriate and children learn through both ways. Whether child- or adult-directed, teaching with intention fosters children's initiative and learning.

Think About This:

1. Describe a teaching situation where you would use teacher-directed methods. How would you get the class involved and keep interest high?
2. Describe a situation where you would interact with a child-directed activity. How would you establish your involvement and keep children focused without dominating the activity?

- Read stories.
- Plan activities with children.
- Review the day's events.
- Initiate group problem solving.

Small groups, on the other hand, are opportunities for teachers and children to have a closer and more personal experience. This setting provides the teachers with ample opportunities to:

- Help children practice a specific skill, such as cutting with scissors.
- Encourage children in their social interactions with one another.
- Enjoy conversations with children.
- Teach a new game to a few children at a time.
- Closely observe each child's growth and development.
- Hold discussions regarding their project work, and move the project along.
- Explore topics in depth.
- Eat a meal or have a snack with children and encourage the social process.
- Provide close supervision for some experiences, such as cooking.

What is common to all group times is the occasion for teachers to encourage listening and speaking skills; provide an arena in which children share thoughts and ideas with one another; and introduce any number of cognitive and social activities.

Written Curriculum Plans

A written plan is an organized agenda, an outline to follow, a framework for the curriculum. It may include a list of activities, goals for children's learning experiences, the

Group times are more meaningful when children's home language is used for story time. One teacher reads the book in English, the other reads it in Spanish.

process or method of instruction, the teacher's responsibilities, the time of day, and other special notations. A plan may be developed for a day, a week, a month, or a specific unit or theme. Figure 7-12 illustrates a weekly curriculum. The four chapters that follow also contain many examples of written plans.

Advantages of Written Plans

Setting lesson plans to paper helps teachers focus on the nature of the children they teach—their interests, their needs, their capabilities, and their potential. A written plan encourages thorough, in-depth planning of curriculum in a logical progression, provides a direction, and helps teachers clarify thoughts and articulate a rationale for what they do. Team teaching is more stimulating when teachers plan together, sharing their ideas and resources; everyone knows what is happening; in case of absences, a substitute teacher can carry out the plans. Changes can easily be made to allow for flexibility, adaptation, and on-the-spot decisions.

When plans are written down, it is easy to see what resources are needed and to have the time to prepare materials. Written plans serve as a communication tool for the teaching staff, for parents, and for the governing agency and provide a concrete format from which evaluation and assessment can be made.

A clearly written lesson plan serves as a curriculum map that guides the daily experiences and agendas. It should reflect the program's goals and priorities as well as the teachers' objectives for each student, such as what skills the activity fosters. The activities themselves should provide for first-hand learning experiences that promote discovery through active exploration of materials. A written lesson plan is a good way to demonstrate how well the curriculum is integrated, inclusive, and culturally sensitive.

The plan should present a balance to the day in which activity and play alternate with opportunities for quiet times, including the time spent outdoors. Large and small group times that are teacher-directed are included, as well as blocks of time in which children select their own activities. The plan should also note when and where teachers are able to work individually with children. Many written lesson plans also include any changes that need to be made to the environment or schedule.

Figure 7-12 demonstrates many of the key elements for a weekly lesson plans. Figure 7-13 shows a written plan for a curriculum that individualizes a child's specific needs and experiences, and Figure 7-14 is a lesson plan for an individual activity.

Planning by Objectives

One approach to curriculum development requires more formal, organized planning. Comprehensive lesson plans are developed, sometimes for the whole year, and usually include objectives, the stated concepts that children learn through this experience. These are commonly called behavioral objectives. The lesson plans include specific, stated, observable behaviors that children are able to demonstrate to show that the teaching objective has been met. In other words, a behavioral objective states clearly what children actually do (e.g., be able to hold scissors properly; grasp a pencil between thumb and first two fingers). If the behavioral objective is to improve fine motor skills, the lesson plan includes activities and events that foster children's use of their fine motor skills. Several objectives may apply to a given activity. It is then important to order the objectives so that the purposes of the lesson remain in focus. To plan successfully, the teacher needs to know developmental and behavioral theory (Chapter 4), to have good observational strategies (Chapter 6), and to possess tools to assess whether the objective has been accomplished (Chapter 6).

One example of using behavioral objectives is Figure 7-9, which shows the use of behavioral objectives when meeting learning standards. A more developed plan found in early childhood classrooms would include activities for the full range of curriculum areas, such as art, motor activities, and dramatic play, for each of the objectives. Important factors in developing curriculum objectives are how much knowledge and understanding children have, what children are interested in, and what standards are mandated by the individual state for the specific age group.

Webbing

Webbing is the process through which teachers develop a diagram based on a particular topic or theme, highlighting key ideas and concepts (Katz and Chard, 2000). Ideas generated from brainstorming sessions flesh out the topic with many subheadings and lists of curriculum possibilities. Webbing is a planning tool that provides depth to a topic and creates a map of possible activities and projects. A web may be organized around a theme (water), into curriculum areas (language arts, music), or around program goals (problem solving, cooperation). By their very nature, webs foster an integrated curriculum approach and help teachers extend children's learning and experiences.

Creating a web can be fun because it allows teachers to use their imaginations and calls into play their knowledge, resources, and experience. Katz and Chard (2000)

SAMPLE PRESCHOOL-KINDERGARTEN LESSON PLAN

TEACHER(S): _____ **DATES:** _____ **THEME:** Magnificent Me!

CONCEPTS: I am unique, special, and part of a family

SKILLS: Prewriting, writing, measuring, graphing, problem-solving, and-awareness of similarities/differences

CENTERS & ACTIVITIES	MONDAY	TUESDAY	WEDNESDAY	THURSDAY	FRIDAY
MORNING GROUP ACTIVITY	Sing "Good Morning." Introduce "My Body."	Take individual instant photos. Introduce "My ends."	Read **On the Day You Were Born.** Introduce "My Family."	Make breadsticks formed in initials. Introduce "My Home."	Healthy snack chart: finish & discuss.
AFTERNOON GROUP ACTIVITY	Identify body parts and what they do.	Animal friends: share stuffed animals and/or pets	Chart birthdays of the children and family members.	Read **How My Parents Learned to Eat.**	Bring and share something about yourself.
LANGUAGE & LITERACY	Begin "All About Me" books.	Write about photo and put into "Me" book with photo.	Add family photo to book. Write or draw about photo.	Write class story about field trip experience.	Finish "All About Me" books and share. Finish class story.
ART	Make life-sized self-portraits.	Make thumbprint and footprint pictures.	Make puppet papercup family pop-ups.	Make kitchen gadget puppets.	Mix playdough to match skin color.
MUSIC & MOVEMENT	"Name Song" Body parts move to music.	Sing "I'm A Special Person and So Are You" and "Friends Go Marching."	Beanbag toss and Kitchen marching band	Sing "So Many Ways to Say Good Morning" and dance.	Dance in hats with streamers to music.
DRAMATIC PLAY HOME LIVING	Home living center with a full mirror and baby pictures of children.	Add phones, paper, and pencils for message-taking.	Bathe baby dolls in warm sudsy water. Add stuffed animals to area.	Add a Wok and other cookware to center.	Add hats to dress-up clothes.
MATH MANIPULATIVE	Measure and record height of each child.	Graph the children's heights.	Use puzzles of family celebrations.	Gather items from home and play "What's missing?"	Estimate number of pennies in a jar, then count them.
SCIENCE & DISCOVERY	Listen to heart with stethoscope. Examine picture or model of skeleton.	Magnifying glasses to see thumbprints. Exploring shadows.	Food colors, eye droppers, and ice trays	Weigh on scales for "Me" book. "What's That Sound?"	Magnets and what sinks, what floats?

BLOCKS Add: people figures, animal figures, boxes, houses, cars

SENSORY CENTERS Water table with warm, soapy water Multicultural skin colored playdough. Healthy snacks "Tasting Tray"

OUTDOOR/LARGE MUSCLE Nature walk: obstacle course on playground Hop, run, skip, jump

SOCIAL STUDIES Invite family members to visit. Field Trip to grocery store. We are all alike. We are all different.

TRANSITIONS Puppet helper of the day Variations on "Name Song"

BOOKS OF THE WEEK My Five Senses, **Big Friend, Little Friend, Mommy's Office, William's Doll**

SPECIAL ACTIVITIES & NOTES Field trip to grocery store. Children decide which healthy snacks to buy. Explain decisions.

Week-long project: Make chart or diagram re: food groups. Prepare and eat snacks. Write class story.

FIGURE 7-12 Weekly lesson plan. (Source: Jackman, H.L., 2012. *Early education curriculum: A child's connection to the world*, 5th Ed. Belmont, CA: Wadsworth/Cengage Learning Inc., p. 66.)

Individualized Child Planning Form

Teacher: *Marlene* **Group:** *Fours*
Child's Name: *Rosie* **Date:** *Week of Jan. 7-11*

Developmental Information: *Rosie's physical/motor and cognitive skills seem to be age appropriate. Her language skills are well-developed with adults but Rosie does not speak to other children except in two or three-word sentences. Her social development seems limited with her peers but not her teachers.*

Current Observation: *Rosie prefers to play and work alone. She participates in groups but with limited response to her peers. She observes adults as they interact with other children and enjoys one-to-one conversations with teachers, telling them stories about her cat, Patches. Rosie was most animated last month during a project where she could work on her own along side others.*

Curriculum Plan:
- *Arrange a week-long small group experiences that include Rosie and 2 or 3 other children. Using animal photo cards, play a matching game to help Rosie begin to interact with others. Ask each child to talk about the animal on their card, making sure that Rosie gets one with a picture of a cat. Prompt her with questions and comments that help expand her discussion, especially about her own cat.*
- *Follow up with discussions about cat's names, their coloring, and their habits. As children become more involved in the topic, include larger members of the cat family. Make sure that Rosie has opportunities to contribute to the discussion.*
- *As Rosie becomes more comfortable with the group, ask her to work with Marley on an art project about wild cats. Support her interactions as she and Marley begin to work together.*
- *Teachers need to model for Rosie how to participate in an activity and to learn what to say and how to react to other children's suggestions.*
- *Suggest to Rosie's family that Marley be invited over to play. They are both quiet and enjoy less boisterous and crowded activities.*

© Cengage Learning 2014

FIGURE 7-13 The most effective curriculum grows out of the child's needs and experiences and the teacher's observations.

---

suggest the following process to develop a web about the fall season:

1. *Brainstorming.* Using small slips of paper, teachers write down theme or topic ideas that the children suggest—each idea on a separate piece of paper. For the topic "Things that happen in fall and winter," for instance, the slips would contain ideas such as "cut jack-o-lanterns" or "rake leaves."
2. *Grouping.* The slips of paper are organized into groups of similar ideas, and, on a colored piece of paper, a heading is given to each group. "Canning and preserving" and "seasonal recipes" fall under the heading of "Cooking." Subgroups can be created, if necessary.
3. *Sharing.* Teachers can share their ideas with one another, rearranging the headings and subheadings as they share skills, resources, and information with one another.
4. *Drawing.* The ideas can be transferred to a piece of paper, placing the topic or theme in the center and drawing lines radiating out to the headings (group time, manipulatives, dramatic play). *This creates a visual record* of the relationships between and among the ideas and becomes a flexible resource that changes and grows.

Jones and Nimmo (1994), in their early work with webbing, emphasize the organic nature of a web. First created as a response to children's ideas, it creates a picture in which ideas emerge and connect in any number of ways. It is, of course, a tentative plan, for what happens next depends on the children's responses. The web creates a flexible plan that can be altered and adapted as teachers observe children and evaluate their interests.

Figure 7-15 is an example of children and teachers working together on a curriculum web that grew out of the children's involvement with play animals. The project that evolved is featured in Figure 7-17 on page 326.

Themes

A traditional method of developing curriculum is to focus on a broad, general topic or theme, also known as a unit. Though used interchangeably, themes are generally a smaller part of a unit, allowing for a more specific focus. For example, a unit on the body may have "What I can do with my hands" as one theme. This mode of planning is used in many early childhood and elementary settings. Focusing on themes, however, can and

Lesson Plan for an Individual Activity

Teacher Name: _____
Date:_____

Name of Activity and Brief Description:_____
Classroom/Outdoor Location_____
Class or Group_____
Goal of Activity_____
Materials Needed_____
Changes Need in Environment_____
Teaching Methods and Process_____
Developmental Domains Included_____
Ways to Extend Learning_____

Evaluation:
Children's Involvement_____
Goals Realized_____
Problems that Emerged_____
Follow-up Suggestions_____
Clean Up_____

© Cengage Learning 2014

FIGURE 7-14 Good planning takes time and thought. A single activity can lead to other activities.

should be much more than an in-depth study of a topic and should be integrated into the whole curriculum.

A thematic approach can utilize many of the attributes of an integrated curriculum:

- Children can help choose and plan themes, thereby constructing their own learning.
- Activities can be chosen to reflect the curriculum goals.
- The emphasis is on active learning.
- The most appropriate themes are those that have a meaningful connection to children's lives.
- Many subject areas can be integrated in the different activities.
- The program lends itself to flexibility, teacher permitting.
- It provides for an in-depth study of a topic.
- It can support the use of multiple learning styles through different media.
- It adds coherence and depth to the curriculum.
- It has the potential for good multicultural curriculum emphasis.

Figure 7-16 is an example of a theme on the five senses for toddlers.

Gestwicki (2007) cites some disadvantages of using a traditional theme approach to curriculum. It can be restricted and narrow and too adult-directed, not allowing for children's curiosity and initiative. There is a danger of creating an artificial unit that has no relevancy to the children's experiences or interests. Teachers may find it hard to deviate from the curriculum plan and not be flexible enough to extend the topic further. When too rigidly applied, themes can isolate the experience into a particular subject or concept and miss the opportunities to broaden the learning potential. At its worst, a theme can be recycled every year without regard for the different group of children and their needs and interests.

Holiday Themes

An inappropriate use of themes is to limit them to specific times of the year, such as Thanksgiving or Valentine's Day, or to celebrate holidays. Themes are not just for special occasions because they tend to isolate and narrowly define the topic.

Some holiday themes may not be appropriate to every family represented by the group. One teacher decided that making Easter baskets on Good Friday (a religious day for many Christians) was offensive to those who practiced Christianity and was uncomfortable for the non-Christians in the class. The practice was dropped throughout the school in the name of cultural and religious sensitivity.

Some schools have adopted policies that do not permit celebrating holidays as part of the school curriculum. Holidays do provoke a particularly sensitive time for celebrating. There are many who believe that celebrating holidays from around the world brings a sense of multiculturalism to the curriculum. York (2003) suggests that when done with thought and care, holidays can be an important addition to the curriculum. To ensure the most positive outcomes, according to York, all holidays are celebrated with equal importance; only those that have importance to the children and families in the class are observed; parents are enlisted to help; the celebration takes place within the context of the daily life of people and families; and sensitivity to the children and families who do not celebrate a particular holiday is observed.

Others might say this is a tourist approach to cultural diversity or that it is a quick visit to another culture without follow-up and depth of exploration. Too often in early childhood programs, holiday curriculum units are the only expression of cultural diversity. According to Derman-Sparks & Edwards (2010), there are no meaningful developmental reasons for the strong emphasis on celebrating holidays in most early childhood programs today. She further argues that this overuse of holiday

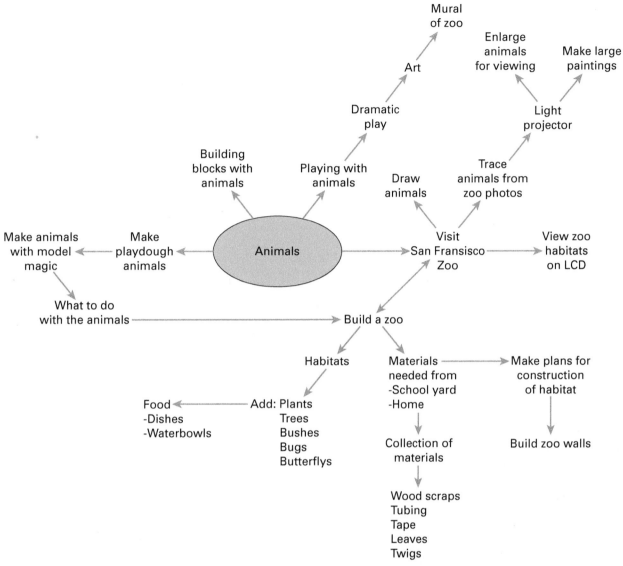

FIGURE 7-15 Web for elementary school children. (Tracy Pierce, Geo-Kids, Menlo Park, CA. Used by Permission.)

themes actually interferes with a developmentally appropriate curriculum because too many foods or songs are used, bypassing the opportunity for children to learn about common areas of life. It seems that holiday themes paint a flat picture of a cultural or religious event without taking into account how people in those cultures live, work, sleep, or play in ways that are familiar or similar to other cultures.

Life-Oriented Themes

Themes that are of great interest to young children are those that directly concern them. The body as a theme suggests many avenues for development: Body parts may be emphasized; exploration using the senses may be stressed; measuring and weighing children may be used to demonstrate growth of the body. Another subject to which children readily respond is that of home and family. Animals, especially pets, are appealing to young children and can lead into further curriculum areas of wild animals, prehistoric animals, and so on.

The more in touch with children the teachers are, the more their classroom themes should reflect the children's interests and abilities. Children who live in Silicon Valley in California, in Houston, Texas, or in Central Florida may have a local interest in computers and space shuttles. The urban child of New York, Detroit, or Washington, D.C., relates more readily to themes about subways, taxis, and tall buildings. Children's interests often focus on, but are not

Sensory Stimulation

Objective: To help toddlers begin to explore and understand the five senses.

	Activity	Small-Group Focus	Optional Activities
Monday	Soap painting	Guessing game: textures. Distinguish soft from hard using familiar objects.	Play hide-and-seek with two or three
Tuesday	Water table play	Guessing game: smells. Identify familiar scents in jars.	Blow bubbles.
Wednesday	Fingerpainting	Guessing game: weights. Distinguish heavy/not heavy using familiar objects such as book or doll.	Take walk to collect collage materials of different textures.
Thursday	Making collages of textures collected day before	Guessing game: shapes. Using puzzles of shapes and shape-sorting boxes.	Have a parade of sounds from many musical instruments.
Friday	Play dough	Food fest of finger foods: Try different textures, sizes, shapes, and flavors	Make foot or hand prints on large mural paper.

© Cengage Learning 2011

FIGURE 7-16 Example of teacher-directed activities to help toddlers explore their sensory skills.

necessarily limited to, what they have experienced. By choosing themes that coincide with children's daily lives, teachers promote connected and relevant learning. Take another look at Figures 7-4 and 7-8 from this perspective.

Some themes in an early childhood setting can address children's own issues. All young children share similar fears and curiosity about the world they do not know but imagine so vividly. The cues children give, particularly about their concerns, suggest to the observant teacher some important themes of childhood. During Halloween, for example, it can be helpful and reassuring to children if the theme of masks is developed. Select some masks that have a function, such as hospital masks, ski masks, safety glasses, sunglasses, snorkel masks, or wrestling and football helmets. Children can try them on and become comfortable with the way their appearance changes. They can laugh with friends as they look in the mirror to see how a mask changes the appearance but does not change the person.

Themes can be inclusive, integrated, and appropriate. It takes a teacher with a child-centered approach to respond to children's innate excitement and curiosity about learning.

The Project Approach

Much of what you have just learned about emergent and thematic curriculum as an integrated approach applies equally to projects. As you read ahead, keep in mind what you have learned about the advantages of an integrated curriculum (page 300), how to take cues from children as explained in the discussion on emergent curriculum (page 300), the concept of children and teachers collaborating (page 302), and the sources for curriculum ideas found on page 302. A project approach embodies these characteristics as well. On the continuum of teacher-directed versus child-directed learning, a project requires the greatest amount of child involvement.

Projects are the epitome of an integrated curriculum, embracing all of the key characteristics of integrated learning and allowing for the incorporation of a wide range of subject areas. In her now classic work, Katz (1994) defines the "project approach" as:

> . . . an in-depth investigation of a topic worth learning more about . . . usually undertaken by a small group of children within a class . . . the whole class . . . or even an individual child. The key feature . . . is

that it is a research effort deliberately focused on finding answers to questions about a topic posed either by the children . . . or the teacher.

A recent revival of this curriculum approach used in progressive schools (see Dewey, Chapter 1) is worth noting here. Based on the belief that "children's minds should be engaged in ways that deepen their understanding of their own experiences and environment" (Katz & Chard, 2000), the project approach consists of exploring a theme or topic (such as babies, dinosaurs, riding the school bus) over a period of days or weeks.

Preplanning by the children and teachers is the first step: They observe, question, estimate, experiment, and research items and events related to the topic. Together, they make dramatic play and display materials they need. Children work in small groups throughout the process and have the opportunity to make numerous choices about their level of participation. The teacher often records the activity on tapes and with photographs. Project work has different levels of complexity, so it meets the needs of children of different ages and abilities.

In the small town of Reggio Emilia in northern Italy, a similar approach to curriculum has received worldwide attention. The project approach is used in even greater depth as it permeates the entire curriculum and school environment. It will be discussed later in this chapter.

Projects emerge from children's own interests, teacher observations of children's needs and interests, and parents' suggestions. The topics reflect the local culture of the children. In fact, Chard (1998) suggests that because life experiences and interests of the teacher and of the children are so strongly reflected in the project itself, it is a singular occurrence relevant only to that group. Another group may adopt the same topic, but it is not a duplicate process due to the individual nature of the children and teacher planning the project.

This approach to teaching and learning easily lends itself to an inclusive classroom and curriculum, responding to diverse points of view as well as diverse cultures. Projects created by the children of Reggio Emilia, for instance, differ from those of American children due to many cultural influences—in particular, the children's ability to argue their point and defend their ideas to others as the project emerges. In the Italian culture, this is a natural part of discourse and is usual in the beginning of conversation between people; in American mainstream culture, it is usual when two people "agree to disagree" for the conversation to end.

The planning process is crucial to the success of the project approach as is the underlying philosophy that children can be co-constructors of their own education. This approach has much in common with the approaches of both Dewey and Neill's *Summerhill* (see Chapter 1). The teacher helps children explore what they already know about the topic, what they might need to know, and how they can represent that knowledge through various media, reinforcing Vygotsky's theory that interaction and direct teaching are important aspects of intellectual development. Teachers pose questions for children that lead them to suggest a hypothesis: What might happen if you do that? What do you think you could do to make that work? Children are encouraged to evaluate their own work and learn to defend and explain their creations to others. Figure 7-4 on field dependent/independent styles exemplifies this process.

The following is a summary of the process involved in a project approach as outlined by Chard (1998), Katz and Chard (2000), and Helm and Katz (2001). There are four phases to a project approach:

1. *Representation.* Children express and communicate their ideas. Through the use of drawing, writing, construction, dramatic play, maps, and diagrams, children share their experience and knowledge. Representation documents what children are learning.
2. *Fieldwork.* Investigations take place outside the classroom, through events, objects, places, and people so that children build on their own knowledge through direct experiences.
3. *Investigation.* Using a variety of resources, children explore and research the topic. This includes fieldwork as well as closely analyzing, sketching, and discussing what they find.
4. *Display.* Exhibits of children's work on the project serve as a source of information and provide an opportunity to share their work and ideas with others. As the project progresses, the children are kept up to date on their progress by displays of their work.

Using Technology in the Classroom

Many children come to early childhood settings having some knowledge and competency with today's technology tools. The digital age is part of their home setting as they see parents with cellphones, computers, cameras, DVD players, and a host of interactive tablets, games, and music devices. Many of these tools have found their way into the early childhood classrooms and challenge the early childhood professional to assess their usefulness and potential for learning. As with any other aspect of curriculum, teachers need to use their knowledge of child development principles and awareness of how children learn as guidelines for integrating technology and media into the curriculum. The National Association for the Education of Young Children and the Fred Rogers Center for Early Learning and Children's Media's

Playing with animals in classroom

Making animals from Model Magic

Making animals from Model Magic

Using their animals with blocks

Visiting the zoo

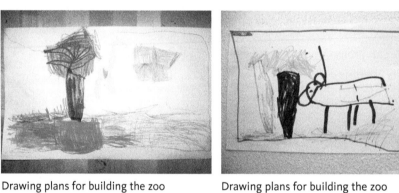
Drawing plans for building the zoo   Drawing plans for building the zoo

Building the zoo

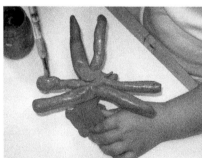
Making the zoo habitat

The zoo

FIGURE 7-17 This project evolved from the web shown in Figure 7-15 and took several months to accomplish. We thank the children at Geo-Kids in Menlo Park, CA, and photographers Tracy Pierce and Michele McMath.

position statement (2012), *Technology and Interactive Media as Tools in Early Childhood Programs Serving Children from Birth through Age 8*, sets out guidelines that help inform a teacher's decision of how and when to use technology and interactive media with children, noting that these activities should never replace "creative play, real-life exploration, physical activity, outdoor experiences, conversation, and social interactions."

1. Choose and evaluate interactive media tools intentionally, keeping in mind their developmental appropriateness and their potential for an interactive experience.
2. Use interactive media as a way to intentionally extend and support hands-on activities to enhance children's engagement with their real world and expand their ability to gain to new information.
3. Avoid the passive use of television, videos, DVD's and other non-interactive media in early childhood programs for children under age 2. Among two-to-five-year olds, discourage use of media in which children do not take an active part.
4. In programs for children under age 2, only use technology and interactive media that supports responsive and positive interactions between children and caregivers.
5. Follow screen time recommendations from public health organizations that limit how much time children should spend in front of media screens.
6. Help ensure equitable access to technology and interactive media for children and their families.

Chapter, 13, and 15 also include more in-depth discussions of this topic.

Play-Based Curriculum Models

Five distinct models demonstrate curriculum that embrace the five guidelines for developmentally appropriate practice: creating a caring community, teaching to enhance development and learning, planning curriculum to achieve important goals, assessing children's development and learning, and establishing reciprocal relationships with families. Each model is unique with its own strengths and characteristics, and each is play and development integrated.

High/Scope: Cognitively Oriented Model

The High/Scope curriculum stresses active learning through a variety of learning centers with plenty of materials and developmentally appropriate activities. The schedule includes extended periods of free play time and guidelines for teacher's intervention in play activities (Frost et al., 2008). Active problem solving is encouraged as children plan, with teacher's assistance, what they will do each day, carry out their plan, and review what they have done. Appropriately, this is known as the "plan-do-review" process. Teachers use small groups to encourage, question, support, and extend children's learning while emphasizing communication skills.

There is a balance between child-initiated experiences and teacher-planned instructional activities. Teachers use observational techniques to focus on children and to understand children's play. Teachers are responsible for planning curriculum organized around key experiences that reinforce and extend the learning activities the children select for themselves. These key experiences form the basis of the curriculum and include creative representation, language and literacy, initiative and social relations, movement, music, classification, seriation, number, space, and time (Hohmann & Weikart, 2002).

Children with special needs are integrated readily into High/Scope programs and with a curriculum developed especially for K–3 grades and early adolescents. High/Scope extends its active learning philosophy into further school years.

High/Scope's approach to children's learning is deeply rooted in Piagetian theory and supports Vygotsky's theory of social interaction and cognition: Children learn when interacting with the people and materials in their environment. The schools of Reggio Emilia share core elements of the High/Scope philosophy. Both philosophies stress the importance of children's constructing their knowledge from activities that interest them; team teaching is an important concept, to allow the children access to adult support; and the process of planning, acting, recording, and reassessing is one that both approaches use to foster critical thinking skills.

To document children's growth using a portfolio system (see Chapter 6), the High/Scope program uses the following categories (Schweinhart, 1993; Brewer, 1995):

- *Initiative:* Expressing choices, engaging in complex play.
- *Creative representation:* Making, building, pretending.
- *Social relations:* Relating to children and adults, making friends.
- *Music and movement:* Exhibiting body coordination, following a musical beat.
- *Language and literacy:* Showing interest in reading, beginning reading, beginning writing.
- *Logic and mathematics:* Sorting, counting objects, describing time sequences.

The Brainy Teacher

What does it mean to be a "brainy teacher"? How can we use current brain research to enhance children's learning and increase our own understanding of good teaching? One researcher (Jensen, 2005) developed a model that begins to answer some of these questions. The three-step model gives us an outline of what to do before, during, and after teaching that gives greater support to children's brain functions.

First Step: Preparation Before Class

The brain must be in the right "state" to activate the networks for learning. You learn more when you are in a clear and positive state of mind than when you are depressed or tired. To get yourself and children in the right "state" of mind, try the following:

Prepare yourself mentally, academically, and emotionally. Think about what students need and create a lesson plan that is appealing and involving.

Prepare the environment: Create a comfortable space, where children can move about, with bright lights and cool temperature.

Second Step: The Lesson

Teachers use a five-step approach to engage the brain to absorb knowledge. The steps and examples are outlined here:

Engage the whole child—mind and body. Get children ready for learning by capturing their attention and getting them excited about the lesson. This increases the heart rate and raises the dopamine and cortical levels of the brain and improves children's emotional state for learning. Engagement activates more of the pleasure structures in the brain than do tasks that require memorization (Poldrack et al., 2001).

Example: "Okay, everyone. Take a deep breath and hold it. Hold it. Hold it. Now let it out! Hold it again. Let it out! Hold it again."

"Good. Do it again, but think about this one thing when you begin to let your breath out: Alaska! Okay, breathe! Now look to your right and share with your friend what the word Alaska meant to you both. Good. Now stand up and show me with just your body what word you thought of. Aha, Carlos is walking like a big polar bear. Willy is walking like a penguin. Elsie is shoveling snow. Jacquie is fishing. Sit down now and let's make a list of all the words that come to mind about Alaska."

Frame the learning. Capitalize on children's curiosity and excitement:

Example: "Now that our list is made, we're going to focus on just one of these words today. Who has a guess?" "Those are all good guesses and Antony picked the right one, so he can come circle the word 'polar bear.' Do you remember the book about polar bears that Megan brought to school last week? You liked it so much I had to read it twice, so I thought we might learn more about polar bears today."

Knowledge acquisition. This is where the intentional teaching part of the lesson begins with teacher-directed learning. As children and teacher engage in dialogue, a more child-directed activity may emerge. Asking the brain to engage in nonstop attention hinders learning. For teacher-directed instructional learning of new content, Jensen (2005) suggests five to eight minutes for kindergarteners through second grade, and eight to twelve minutes for third through fifth grades.

Example: "You have a lot of questions about polar bears, so why don't we go on a bear hunt? Look around the classroom and find pictures and books, or draw something that bears like to eat or where they live. You have 10 minutes and then we'll talk some more about how polar bears hibernate."

Elaborate to extend the learning. Brain connections made at the synapse from the lesson solidify within the first hour of learning. Check to see if children have grasped the basic concepts and if they are correct in their understanding of the content. It is better to check for accuracy right away before the synapse sets with misinformation. The brain is also limited in how much a child can hold in short-term memory. Use quizzes, true/false statements, and other quick methods to ensure that the children have the correct information.

Strengthen the memory and correct the learning. The brain recalls more in the first hour after learning than in the next few days, so help the children recall the who/what/when/how of the lesson. An interactive method, such as acting out the story of the polar bear, helps the child retain the lesson.

Third Step: Settle and Review

The brain needs time for processing and rest after learning.

1. Plan the lesson just before snacks or lunchtime, recess, outdoor play, or nap time.
2. Give the children time to let the lesson settle.
3. The brain synapses have made connections, but you need to create time to review the lesson over the next few days in order to ensure that the synapses adapt to the new information the brain has received.

Questions

1. How does Jensen's model help teachers "teach with the brain in mind"? Why do you think the process works? Which stages is the most challenging for you?
2. How does Jensen's model relate to developmentally appropriate practices? Emergent curriculum? Integrated curriculum?

Teachers evaluate these abilities as they observe children's use of key experiences and plan the curriculum accordingly.

Bank Street: Developmental-Interaction Model

Bank Street was founded by Lucy Sprague Mitchell (see Chapter 1), and its roots reflect the thinking of Freud, Dewey, Erikson, Vygotsky, and Piaget, among others. It is a developmental approach as child development principles influence the curriculum planning, and it is an interactive model because of the connections made between children, adults, and the greater environment. The cognitive and social-emotional relationship stresses the link between education and psychology.

The Bank Street model originated the play-based approach used in many early childhood settings today through the use of interest centers, water and sand play, blocks, puzzles, painting, and small and large group play. Teachers use play to enhance children's cognitive and language skills through frequent conversations and interactions (Frost et al., 2008).

Children are seen as active learners who learn by interacting with and transforming the world about them. Play is the primary vehicle for encouraging involvement between and among children, adults, and materials. The teacher's primary role is to observe and respond to activities initiated by the children. Classrooms are organized into learning centers, in which children can work individually or in groups.

The Bank Street model exemplifies an integrated curriculum. Children learn about the world in which they live through concrete, first-hand experiences. Community and neighborhood connections are stressed. Units and themes are used to focus the curriculum, and children have access to materials and are free to choose where to play. A teacher's knowledge and understanding of child development principles is crucial to this approach. Educational goals are set in terms of developmental processes and include the development of competence, a sense of autonomy and individuality, social relatedness and connectedness, creativity, and an integration of different ways of experiencing the world.

The Schools of Reggio Emilia

Respect for children's investigative powers and for their ability to think, plan, criticize, collaborate, and learn from all they do is the hallmark of the Reggio Emilia approach and is an excellent example of an integrated and emerging

approach to learning. This collection of schools in Italy, with separate programs for infants to 3-year-olds and 3- to 6-year-olds, has commanded worldwide attention for its philosophy and practices. "Nowhere else in the world," states Gardner (in the classic work of Edwards, Gandini, & Forman, 1993), "is there such a seamless and symbiotic relationship between a school's progressive philosophy and its practices." The curriculum takes the project approach to its highest levels.

Influenced by Dewey's progressive education movement, the philosophies and practices of Reggio Emilia owe a great deal as well to Piaget's constructivist theory, Vygotsky's belief in social discourse as a method of learning, and Gardner's theory of multiple intelligences (see Chapters 1, 4, and 13). Children are actively engaged in long-term projects that they initiate, design, and carry out with the support of the teacher. Art is the primary medium for learning.

Some of the key components of the Reggio Emilia approach are: a materials-rich environment that is aesthetically appealing; a community-based attitude involving the entire city; a family support system; and a commitment to process.

These elements are manifested in the program through astonishingly beautiful school settings, replete with the work of children and evidence of their projects elegantly displayed throughout; by support realized through a large portion of the city's budget; through small groups of children who stay together for a three-year period with the same teacher; and through intentionally bringing the children's culture into school life.

Play, in the Reggio Emilia classroom, is focused on children's ability to represent their experiences through the arts. As such, play is more collaborative with several children working on one project while another group is working elsewhere. "Working" in this context is playing; art is the form that play often takes in this model. The

The Reggio approach: order and beauty.

Reggio Emilia: a materials-rich environment.

teacher's role is more involved than in other models because the philosophy of Reggio Emilia is to work with children and assist them with their activities.

Cadwell (1997) identifies eight fundamentals of the Reggio Emilia approach. Each has implications for creating a curriculum that is fully integrated and one that emerges from children's interests and ideas. These eight essential points are:

1. *The child as protagonist.* All children are strong and capable and have the potential and preparation to construct their learning. They are protagonists (i.e., central characters) with teachers and parents in the educational process.
2. *The child as collaborator.* There is an emphasis on working in small groups. This stems from the belief that we are social beings and form ourselves through interactions with people and things.
3. *The child as communicator.* Symbolic representation, through dance, art, painting, sculpting, building, dramatic play, music, and words help children discover and communicate what they know and what they question. Teachers support the use of these "many languages" to help children make their thinking visible.
4. *The environment as third teacher.* Every corner of the environment has an identity and purpose and encourages encounters, communication, and relationships. There is order and beauty in the design of the equipment, the space, and the materials.
5. *The teacher as partner, nurturer, and guide.* Teachers listen and observe children closely in order to facilitate and guide their process of open-ended discovery. They ask questions to find out about children's

ideas and theories and then provide the opportunities for their learning.

6. *The teacher as researcher.* Teachers work in pairs and collaborate with other members of the staff, engaging in continuous discussion and interpretation of their work and the work of the children. This provides ongoing staff development and deeper exploration of theoretical foundations. Teachers see themselves as researchers who prepare and document their work. They consider children researchers as well.
7. *The documentation as communication.* Thoughtful care is given to ways in which the thinking of children is presented. Teachers make transcripts of children's dialogue, take series of photographs of their projects, and arrange them in panels that hang throughout the school or in books. This documentation is a way to communicate to the rest of the school what the children's work is about, to help parents become aware of their children's work, to assist teachers in evaluating children's work, and to show children that their work is valued.
8. *The parents as partner.* Parent participation is considered essential, and parents discuss their ideas and skills with the teachers. This underscores the collegiality and collaboration between home and school and ensures a curriculum that represents the diversity of the children and their families.

The teacher's role is unique: Two coequal teachers work with a class of 25 children. There is no head teacher or director of the school. The teachers are supported by a pedigogista, a person trained in early childhood education who meets with the teachers weekly. Also on the staff of every school is an atelierista, a person trained in the arts who teaches techniques and skills the children learn for their projects.

The process of the activity is highly respected as the way to plan and work together. Teachers and children—collaborators—listen to one another, and many points of view are encouraged. Debate and discussion are key elements in the process of deciding what project to do and how to go about it. The attitude that a child is a natural researcher as well as an able learner and communicator has molded the organization and structure of the schools.

The schools of Reggio Emilia are worth knowing about just for the strong and powerful view they hold of the child and the concept of teacher and student learning from one another. There are a growing number of American models as well.

Cadwell (1997), who has assisted two schools in St. Louis, Missouri, to adopt the Reggio Emilia approach

TeachSource Video

Watch the TeachSource Video entitled "The Reggio Emilia Approach and Purpose-Built Schools." After you view the clip, reflect on the following questions:

1. How does the Reggio Emilia philosophy promote the community's responsibility to work together for quality child care and education?

2. What do you think is the most important aspect of the Reggio Emilia approach to care and educating young children?

described on these pages, offers a hopeful challenge: "We can learn from the Reggio educators to look at children differently, to expect more of them and of ourselves, and to offer them many more possibilities for full development."

Waldorf Schools

The Waldorf curriculum, shaped by Rudolf Steiner in 1919 (see Chapter 1), emphasizes the development of the whole child through "the head, heart, and hands." Based on the belief that young children learn primarily through observation, imitation, and experience, the curriculum provides a rich environment for children to explore and role models who provide appealing activities. Waldorf schools are play-based: A hallmark of the curriculum is learning through play, and large periods of time are devoted to creative play. Steiner agreed with Froebel and others that education should begin where the learner is: Whatever the child brings to the educational experience is to be worked with, not against. Academics are de-emphasized in the early years of schooling. Looping is common in the elementary school years as the teacher stays with the class for up to eight years. Other defining features (WECAN, 2005) of a Waldorf curriculum include:

- *Strong rhythmic elements based on the cycles of life and nature*: A daily rhythm of play, work, circletime, and outdoor play, ending with a nature or folk tale creates a consistent pattern for each session. The weekly rhythm evolves from activities, with one day for baking, another for crafts, and another for painting, and so on. Seasonal activities, such as planting bulbs, harvesting produce, or gathering leaves, stress nature's impact on our lives.

- *Environments that nourish the senses*: The walls of the classrooms are usually painted with soft watercolors, curtains may be made from plant-dyed fabrics, and tables and chairs are made of solid wood. The materials used are natural and real; the surroundings are simple and calming.

- *Extensive use of natural materials*: Wood, cotton, and wool are used throughout the classroom. Most of the toys are handcrafted from these natural materials, encouraging children to use their imagination. A piece of wood becomes a ticket to ride the train, which is made from chairs and pieces of wood. It may also become a telephone, a piece of food, or animal in a barn made of similar materials. The Waldorf philosophy suggests that other, more "finished" toys limit the power of fantasy, imagination, and creativity that is natural in a young child.

- *Play as an imitation of life*: The curriculum fosters skills that imitate the work of adults. Children participate in activities focused on the home—cooking and baking, cleaning, washing and sewing, and gardening and building. Engaging in meaningful life activities are seen as preparation for later academic challenges.

- *Enhancement of a sense of reverence and wonder*: Children's natural sense of awe and wonder is fostered and deepened, primarily through activities, stories and festivals that celebrate the cycles of the seasons. In the fall, the classroom may be decorated with corn stalks and sheaves of grain; the seasonal table is draped with beautiful fabrics in fall colors and hold gourds, pumpkins, acorns, and leaves. When parents join them for a harvest festival, songs of thankfulness and praise are sung before the feast begins. Each season this is repeated in order to expand the child's sense of reverence for life.

A Waldorf curriculum has much to offer, especially to those who put a premium on the use of imagination and an appreciation for the natural world. Learning is noncompetitive with no grades or set textbooks. There are many elements in the Waldorf method that are common to the Montessori method and to the Reggio Emilia schools.

Montessori Schools

In Chapter 1, Maria Montessori was discussed in relation to the history of early childhood education. What follows here is an explanation of the Montessori Method as a curriculum model for young children.

Montessori's approach to learning has had a continuing influence in education since those early years. Of her work, three features stand out: 1) adapting school work to the individual rather than molding the child to fit the curriculum; 2) insisting on freedom for children in selection of materials and choice of activities; and 3) training of the senses and on practical life issues.

Montessori programs may not be play-based in the way the four previous models are, but they are certainly child-centered and child-based in philosophy and practice. Montessori held that the choices children make during free activity time is work that others might rightly identify as play. Montessori programs have art activities as well as music, movement, and some group games. Fantasy play, a staple in other early childhood settings, is not part of the Montessori curriculum. Instead, the Practical Life area, where children learn personal care and care of the environment, is the closest Montessori comes to dramatic play. In the Practical Life area, children imitate adult activities, such as pouring and food preparation, but with real glasses, pitchers, and utensils readily available to them.

The Program

A common misunderstanding is that all schools with the Montessori name are the same. They are not. There are many variations and types of Montessori schools throughout the United States, reflecting an infinite variety of interpretations of the Montessori Method. Within the Montessori movement itself, there are at least two factions claiming to be the voice of the true Montessori approach to education.

Although the most common form of Montessori program is one in which 3- to 5-year-olds are grouped together, there are a growing number of schools for 6- to 9-year-olds and even 9- to 12-year-olds. Teacher education programs now prepare Montessori teachers to work with infants and toddlers as well as high school students.

The most striking feature of the Montessori classroom is its materials. Many are made of wood and designed to stress the philosophy of learning through the senses. Color, texture, and quality of craftsmanship of the materials appeal to the hand as well as the eye; they demand to be touched. "Smooth" and "oval" take on new meaning as a child runs a finger around Montessori-designed puzzle shapes.

Montessori materials have other unique characteristics besides their tactile appeal. They are self-correcting; that is, they fit together or work in only one way so that children know immediately whether they are successful. The Montessori curriculum presents the materials in a sequence, from simplest to most difficult. Many of the learning tasks have a series of steps and must be learned in a prescribed order. Whether sponging a table clean or using the number rods, the child is taught the precise order in which to use the materials. Montessori developed curriculum materials and tasks that are related to real life. Practical Life activities range from cleaning tasks (hands, tables) to dressing tasks (lacing, buttoning, or tying garment closures).

In a Montessori classroom, children work by themselves at their own pace. They are free to choose the materials with which they want to "work"—the word used to describe their activity. Children must accomplish one task before starting another one, including the replacing of the materials on the shelf for someone else to use.

The prepared environment in a Montessori program has child-sized furniture and equipment—one of Froebel's ideas that Montessori used. Materials are set out on low shelves, in an orderly fashion, to encourage children's independent use. Only one set of any materials—their shape, form, and the way they are presented for children to use—are the vehicles for learning.

The teacher in the Montessori setting has a prescribed role, one of observing the children. Teachers become familiar with skills and developmental levels, and then match the children to the appropriate material or task. There is little teacher intervention beyond giving clear directions for how to use the materials. Group instruction is not common; learning is an individual experience.

Program Changes

Many changes have taken place in Montessori practices over the years, and today's best Montessori programs are those that are true to philosophical traditions of the Montessori method but constantly make small changes and adjustments. Many Montessori schools are adding curriculum areas of art, dramatic play, gross motor development, and computers. There is also greater teacher flexibility to promote social interaction.

For years, Montessori was separated from the mainstream of American education. Today that has changed, with more than 100 public school districts offering Montessori programs in their elementary schools and with the increased interaction between Montessorians and other early childhood professionals.

Maria Montessori has found her way into nearly every early education program in existence today. Whether labeled so or not, much of the material and equipment, as well as many of the teaching techniques, in use today originated with this dynamic woman nearly 100 years ago. She is firmly established in early childhood history and its future. The Montessori method should be weighed in light of contemporary knowledge and should be tailored to meet the needs of vigorous, eager, often needy children of the 21st century.

Summary

LO 1 Developmentally appropriate curriculum is age-appropriate, individually appropriate, and framed in the context of a child's culture. Culturally appropriate curriculum reflects the children, their families, and their community and enhances children's ability to view events and situations from a different perspective. Integrated curriculum provides opportunities for children of diverse skills and abilities to learn through the same experience. Inclusive curriculum ensures that all children are able to participate fully in all aspects of the program. Integrated curriculum fosters learning concepts through many curriculum subjects and activities. Emergent curriculum takes its cues from the children's interests, and the teacher helps them to explore their ideas in more depth. Multiples Intelligences and learning styles help teachers create a curriculum that covers a broad range of interests and abilities.

LO 2 Play-based curriculum is the foundation for learning in early childhood settings. Skills, knowledge, and learning take place in a setting where teachers support play by their interest, involvement, and setting the stage for children's experiences. Play is recognized as the curriculum of the child through activity centers and hands-on activities where discovery and experiment are the basis for learning.

LO 3 Planning curriculum includes setting goals, establishing priorities, knowing what resources are available, and evaluating the process. As teachers develop their curriculum plans, they may focus on the classroom activity or learning centers and the skills of the children. All three lend themselves to a basis for curriculum planning, and all are important vehicles for creative and effective curriculum for young children. State mandated learning standards influence curriculum development in the early childhood and elementary years. Although standards have the potential to improve teaching and learning, they carry the risk that inappropriate teaching and testing take the place of developmentally appropriate practices.

LO 4 Various curriculum models, such as High/Scope, Bank Street, the schools of Reggio Emilia, Waldorf schools, and Montessori schools are unique yet they have some common characteristics. They all model developmentally appropriate practices, and the development of skills and knowledge through play-based learning.

Key Terms

curriculum
developmentally appropriate
   practice (DAP)
culturally appropriate curriculum
transformative curriculum
holistically
inclusive curriculum
emergent curriculum

learning styles
dramatic play
activity centers
prerequisite
linchpin
standards
webbing
brainstorming

project approach
interactive media
non-interactive media
screen time
pedigogista
atelierista
tactile

Review Questions

1. Define developmentally and culturally appropriate curriculum for early childhood programs. What three core considerations determine whether a curriculum is DAP?
2. What are the most compelling arguments that play-based curriculum is the foundation for learning?
3. What elements do you include when you plan curriculum to meet the needs of all students? What is the importance of written plans, and how do they support teaching and learning?
4. Describe five play-based curriculum models that are developmentally appropriate, including the elements that foster development through play. How do these five models differ? How are they similar?

Observe and Apply

1. Observe an infant/toddler program, a preschool program, and an early elementary grade program. How do these programs exemplify developmentally and culturally appropriate curriculum? What is missing? What would you suggest they do to improve their program(s) to meet the DAP criteria?

2. Observe teachers as children play. What is the difference in the play when 1) a teacher interacts with children in their play and 2) a teacher intervenes? What happens to the play immediately after teacher contact is made? How long does the play last? What is your conclusion?

3. Develop a written plan for a week for 1) a 3-year-old class; 2) a family child care home; and 3) an after-school program for 6, 7, and 8 year olds. Use a nonholiday theme.

4. Use Gardner's Multiple Intelligences to determine your own ways of knowing. How has this style affected your abilities as a student? How do you think it affects your abilities as a teacher? What did you learn from this activity?

5. Observe a teacher-directed activity in an early childhood setting. What was the focus and what strategies did the teacher use to communicate the concept? Do you think this activity was a success or failure? Why?

Helpful Websites

High/Scope   www.highscope.org
NAEYC   www.naeyc.org

The Creative Curriculum®
   www.TeachingStrategies.com
Reggio Emilia   www.reggiochildren.org

The Education CourseMate website for this text offers many helpful resources and interactive study tools. Go to CengageBrain.com to access the TeachSource Videos, flashcards, tutorial quizzes, direct links to all of the websites mentioned in the chapter, downloadable forms, and more.

References

Armstrong, T. (2000). *Multiple intelligences in the classroom.* Alexandria, VA: Association for Supervision and Curriculum Development.

Banks, J. (2006). *Cultural diversity and education: Foundations, curriculum and teaching.* Boston: Allyn & Bacon.

Cadwell, L. (1997). *Bringing Reggio Emilia home.* New York: Teachers College Press.

Copple, C., & Bredekamp, S. (Eds.) (2009). *Developmentally appropriate practice in early childhood programs serving children from birth through age 8.* Washington, D.C.: National Association for the Education of Young Children.

Derman-Sparks, L., & Edwards, J. O., (2010). *Anti-bias education for young children and ourselves.* Washington, DC: National Association for the Education of Young Children.

Edwards, C., Gandini, L., & Forman, G. (1993). *The hundred languages of children: The Reggio Emilia approach to early childhood education.* Norwood, NJ: Ablex.

Epstein, A.S. (2007). *The intentional teacher: Choosing the best strategies for young children's learning.* Washington, D.C.: National Association for the Education of Young Children.

Erikson, E. H. (1972). Play and actuality. In M. W. Piers (Ed.) *Play and development* (pp. 127–168). New York: Norton.

Frost, J. L., Wortham, S. C., & Refifel, S. (2008). *Play and child development.* Upper Saddle River, NJ: Pearson Education, Inc.

Gestwicki, C. (2007). *Developmentally appropriate practice: Curriculum and development in early education.* Clifton Park, NY: Thomson Delmar Learning.

Gronlund, G. (2006). *Making early learning standards come alive: Connecting your practice and curriculum to state guidelines.* St. Paul, MN: Redleaf Press.

Helm, J. H., & Katz, L. (2001). *Young investigators: The project approach in the early years.* New York: Teachers College Press.

Jensen, E. (2005). *Teaching with the brain in mind.* Alexandria, VA: Association for Supervision and Curriculum Development.

Jones, E. (1994). An emergent curriculum expert offers this afterthought. *Young Children,* 54, p. 16.

Jones, E., & Nimmo, J. (1994). *Emergent curriculum.* Washington, D.C.: National Association for the Education of Young Children.

Katz, L. G. (1994). *The project approach.* Champaign, IL: ERIC Clearinghouse on Elementary and Early Childhood Education.

Katz, L., & Chard, S. (2000). *Engaging children's minds: The project approach.* Norwood, NJ: Ablex.

McNeely, S. L. (1997). *Observing students and teachers through objective strategies.* Boston: Allyn & Bacon.

National Association for the Education of Young Children (NAEYC) & National Association of Early Childhood Specialists in State Departments of Education (NAECS/SDE). (2002). Position Paper: Early Learning Standards: Creating the Conditions for Success. http://www.naeyc.org. Retrieved March 2009.

National Association for the Education of Young Children (NAEYC) & the Fred Rogers Center for Early Learning and Children's Media (2012). Position Paper: Technology and Interactive media as Tools in Early Childhood Programs Serving Children from Birth through Age 8. http://www.naeyc.org. Retrieved May 31, 2012.

New City School. (1994). *Celebrating multiple intelligences: Teaching for success.* St. Louis, MO: The New City School.

Poldrack, R. A., Clark, J., Pare-Blagoev, E. J., Shohamy, D., Creso Moyano, J., Myers, C., & Gluck, M. A. (2001, November 29). Interactive memory systems in the human brain. *Nature,* 414, pp. 546–550.

Ramirez, M., & Casteñada, A. (1974). *Cultural democracy, bicognitive development, and education.* New York: Academic Press.

WECAN (Waldorf Early Childhood Association of North America). (2005). *The Waldorf kindergarten: The world of the young child.* Retrieved from www.waldorfearlychildhood.org, March, 2012.

Woolfolk, A. (2001). *Educational psychology.* Boston: Allyn & Bacon.

York, S. (2003). *Roots and wings: Affirming culture in early childhood programs.* St. Paul, MN: Redleaf Press.

Appendix

Code of Ethical Conduct and Statement of Commitment

A position statement of the *National Association for the Education of Young Children*

Revised April 2005. Reaffirmed and Updated May 2011.

Preamble

NAEYC recognizes that those who work with young children face many daily decisions that have moral and ethical implications. The NAEYC Code of Ethical Conduct offers guidelines for responsible behavior and sets forth a common basis for resolving the principal ethical dilemmas encountered in early childhood care and education. The Statement of Commitment is not part of the Code but is a personal acknowledgement of an individual's willingness to embrace the distinctive values and moral obligations of the field of early childhood care and education.

The primary focus of the Code is on daily practice with children and their families in programs for children from birth through 8 years of age, such as infant/toddler programs, preschool and prekindergarten programs, child care centers, hospital and child life settings, family child care homes, kindergartens, and primary classrooms. When the issues involve young children, then these provisions also apply to specialists who do not work directly with children, including program administrators, parent educators, early childhood adult educators, and officials with responsibility for program monitoring and licensing. (Note: See also the "Code of Ethical Conduct: Supplement for Early Childhood Adult Educators," online at www.naeyc.org/about/positions/pdf/ethics04.pdf and the "Code of Ethical Conduct: Supplement for Early Childhood Program Administrators," online at http://www.naeyc.org/files/naeyc/file/positions/PSETH05_supp.pdf.)

Core Values

Standards of ethical behavior in early childhood care and education are based on commitment to the following core values that are deeply rooted in the history of the field of early childhood care and education. We have made a commitment to

- Appreciate childhood as a unique and valuable stage of the human life cycle.
- Base our work on knowledge of how children develop and learn.
- Appreciate and support the bond between the child and family.
- Recognize that children are best understood and supported in the context of family, culture,* community, and society.
- Respect the dignity, worth, and uniqueness of each individual (child, family member, and colleague).
- Respect diversity in children, families, and colleagues.
- Recognize that children and adults achieve their full potential in the context of relationships that are based on trust and respect.

Conceptual Framework

The Code sets forth a framework of professional responsibilities in four sections. Each section addresses an area of professional relationships: (1) with chil-

---

*The term *culture* includes ethnicity, racial identity, economic level, family structure, language, and religious and political beliefs, which profoundly influence each child's development and relationship to the world.

dren, (2) with families, (3) among colleagues, and (4) with the community and society. Each section includes an introduction to the primary responsibilities of the early childhood practitioner in that context. The introduction is followed by a set of ideals (I) that reflect exemplary professional practice and by a set of principles (P) describing practices that are required, prohibited, or permitted.

The **ideals** reflect the aspirations of practitioners. The **principles** guide conduct and assist practitioners in resolving ethical dilemmas.[†] Both ideals and principles are intended to direct practitioners to those questions which, when responsibly answered, can provide the basis for conscientious decision making. While the Code provides specific direction for addressing some ethical dilemmas, many others will require the practitioner to combine the guidance of the Code with professional judgment.

The ideals and principles in this Code present a shared framework of professional responsibility that affirms our commitment to the core values of our field. The Code publicly acknowledges the responsibilities that we in the field have assumed, and in so doing supports ethical behavior in our work. Practitioners who face situations with ethical dimensions are urged to seek guidance in the applicable parts of this Code and in the spirit that informs the whole.

Often "the right answer"—the best ethical course of action to take—is not obvious. There may be no readily apparent, positive way to handle a situation. When one important value contradicts another, we face an ethical dilemma. When we face a dilemma, it is our professional responsibility to consult the Code and all relevant parties to find the most ethical resolution.

Section I: Ethical Responsibilities to Children

Childhood is a unique and valuable stage in the human life cycle. Our paramount responsibility is to provide care and education in settings that are safe,

healthy, nurturing, and responsive for each child. We are committed to supporting children's development and learning; respecting individual differences; and helping children learn to live, play, and work cooperatively. We are also committed to promoting children's self-awareness, competence, self-worth, resiliency, and physical well-being.

Ideals

I-1.1—To be familiar with the knowledge base of early childhood care and education and to stay informed through continuing education and training.

I-1.2—To base program practices upon current knowledge and research in the field of early childhood education, child development, and related disciplines, as well as on particular knowledge of each child.

I-1.3—To recognize and respect the unique qualities, abilities, and potential of each child.

I-1.4—To appreciate the vulnerability of children and their dependence on adults.

I-1.5—To create and maintain safe and healthy settings that foster children's social, emotional, cognitive, and physical development and that respect their dignity and their contributions.

I-1.6—To use assessment instruments and strategies that are appropriate for the children to be assessed, that are used only for the purposes for which they were designed, and that have the potential to benefit children.

I-1.7—To use assessment information to understand and support children's development and learning, to support instruction, and to identify children who may need additional services.

I-1.8—To support the right of each child to play and learn in an inclusive environment that meets the needs of children with and without disabilities.

I-1.9—To advocate for and ensure that all children, including those with special needs, have access to the support services needed to be successful.

I-1.10—To ensure that each child's culture, language, ethnicity, and family structure are recognized and valued in the program.

I-1.11—To provide all children with experiences in a language that they know, as well as support children in maintaining the use of their home language and in learning English.

[†]There is not necessarily a corresponding principle for each ideal.

I-1.12—To work with families to provide a safe and smooth transition as children and families move from one program to the next.

Principles

P-1.1—**Above all, we shall not harm children. We shall not participate in practices that are emotionally damaging, physically harmful, disrespectful, degrading, dangerous, exploitative, or intimidating to children. *This principle has precedence over all others in this Code.***

P-1.2—We shall care for and educate children in positive emotional and social environments that are cognitively stimulating and that support each child's culture, language, ethnicity, and family structure.

P-1.3—We shall not participate in practices that discriminate against children by denying benefits, giving special advantages, or excluding them from programs or activities on the basis of their sex, race, national origin, immigration status, preferred home language, religious beliefs, medical condition, disability, or the marital status/ family structure, sexual orientation, or religious beliefs or other affiliations of their families. (Aspects of this principle do not apply in programs that have a lawful mandate to provide services to a particular population of children.)

P-1.4—We shall use two-way communications to involve all those with relevant knowledge (including families and staff) in decisions concerning a child, as appropriate, ensuring confidentiality of sensitive information. (See also P-2.4.)

P-1.5—We shall use appropriate assessment systems, which include multiple sources of information, to provide information on children's learning and development.

P-1.6—We shall strive to ensure that decisions such as those related to enrollment, retention, or assignment to special education services, will be based on multiple sources of information and will never be based on a single assessment, such as a test score or a single observation.

P-1.7—We shall strive to build individual relationships with each child; make individualized adaptations in teaching strategies, learning environments, and curricula; and consult with the family so that each child benefits from the program. If after such efforts have been exhausted, the current placement does not meet a child's needs, or the child is seriously jeopardizing the ability of other children to benefit from the program, we shall collaborate with the child's family and appropriate specialists to determine the additional services needed and/or the placement option(s) most likely to ensure the child's success. (Aspects of this principle may not apply in programs that have a lawful mandate to provide services to a particular population of children.)

P-1.8—We shall be familiar with the risk factors for and symptoms of child abuse and neglect, including physical, sexual, verbal, and emotional abuse and physical, emotional, educational, and medical neglect. We shall know and follow state laws and community procedures that protect children against abuse and neglect.

P-1.9—When we have reasonable cause to suspect child abuse or neglect, we shall report it to the appropriate community agency and follow up to ensure that appropriate action has been taken. When appropriate, parents or guardians will be informed that the referral will be or has been made.

P-1.10—When another person tells us of his or her suspicion that a child is being abused or neglected, we shall assist that person in taking appropriate action in order to protect the child.

P-1.11—When we become aware of a practice or situation that endangers the health, safety, or well-being of children, we have an ethical responsibility to protect children or inform parents and/or others who can.

Section II: Ethical Responsibilities to Families

Families* are of primary importance in children's development. Because the family and the early childhood practitioner have a common interest in the child's

---

*The term *family* may include those adults, besides parents, with the responsibility of being involved in educating, nurturing, and advocating for the child.

wellbeing, we acknowledge a primary responsibility to bring about communication, cooperation, and collaboration between the home and early childhood program in ways that enhance the child's development.

Ideals

I-2.1—To be familiar with the knowledge base related to working effectively with families and to stay informed through continuing education and training.

I-2.2—To develop relationships of mutual trust and create partnerships with the families we serve.

I-2.3—To welcome all family members and encourage them to participate in the program, including involvement in shared decision making.

I-2.4—To listen to families, acknowledge and build upon their strengths and competencies, and learn from families as we support them in their task of nurturing children.

I-2.5—To respect the dignity and preferences of each family and to make an effort to learn about its structure, culture, language, customs, and beliefs to ensure a culturally consistent environment for all children and families.

I-2.6—To acknowledge families' childrearing values and their right to make decisions for their children.

I-2.7—To share information about each child's education and development with families and to help them understand and appreciate the current knowledge base of the early childhood profession.

I-2.8—To help family members enhance their understanding of their children, as staff are enhancing their understanding of each child through communications with families, and support family members in the continuing development of their skills as parents.

I-2.9—To foster families' efforts to build support networks and, when needed, participate in building networks for families by providing them with opportunities to interact with program staff, other families, community resources, and professional services.

Principles

P-2.1—We shall not deny family members access to their child's classroom or program setting unless access is denied by court order or other legal restriction.

P-2.2—We shall inform families of program philosophy, policies, curriculum, assessment system, cultural practices, and personnel qualifications, and explain why we teach as we do—which should be in accordance with our ethical responsibilities to children (see Section I).

P-2.3—We shall inform families of and, when appropriate, involve them in policy decisions. (See also I-2.3.)

P-2.4—We shall ensure that the family is involved in significant decisions affecting their child. (See also P-1.4.)

P-2.5—We shall make every effort to communicate effectively with all families in a language that they understand. We shall use community resources for translation and interpretation when we do not have sufficient resources in our own programs.

P-2.6—As families share information with us about their children and families, we shall ensure that families' input is an important contribution to the planning and implementation of the program.

P-2.7—We shall inform families about the nature and purpose of the program's child assessments and how data about their child will be used.

P-2.8—We shall treat child assessment information confidentially and share this information only when there is a legitimate need for it.

P-2.9—We shall inform the family of injuries and incidents involving their child, of risks such as exposures to communicable diseases that might result in infection, and of occurrences that might result in emotional stress.

P-2.10—Families shall be fully informed of any proposed research projects involving their children and shall have the opportunity to give or withhold consent without penalty. We shall not permit or participate in research that could in any way hinder the education, development, or wellbeing of children.

P-2.11—We shall not engage in or support exploitation of families. We shall not use our relationship with a family for private advantage or personal gain, or enter into relationships with family members that might impair our effectiveness working with their children.

P-2.12—We shall develop written policies for the protection of confidentiality and the disclosure of children's records. These policy documents shall be made available to all program personnel and families. Disclosure of children's records beyond family members, program personnel, and consultants having an obligation of confidentiality shall require familial consent (except in cases of abuse or neglect).

P-2.13—We shall maintain confidentiality and shall respect the family's right to privacy, refraining from disclosure of confidential information and intrusion into family life. However, when we have reason to believe that a child's welfare is at risk, it is permissible to share confidential information with agencies, as well as with individuals who have legal responsibility for intervening in the child's interest.

P-2.14—In cases where family members are in conflict with one another, we shall work openly, sharing our observations of the child, to help all parties involved make informed decisions. We shall refrain from becoming an advocate for one party.

P-2.15—We shall be familiar with and appropriately refer families to community resources and professional support services. After a referral has been made, we shall follow up to ensure that services have been appropriately provided.

Section III: Ethical Responsibilities to Colleagues

In a caring, cooperative workplace, human dignity is respected, professional satisfaction is promoted, and positive relationships are developed and sustained. Based upon our core values, our primary responsibility to colleagues is to establish and maintain settings and relationships that support productive work and meet professional needs. The same ideals that apply to children also apply as we interact with adults in the workplace. (Note: Section III includes responsibilities to co-workers and to employers. See the "Code of Ethical Conduct: Supplement for Early Childhood Program Administrators" for responsibilities to personnel (*employees* in the original 2005 Code revision), online at http://www.naeyc.org/files/naeyc/file/positions/PSETH05_supp.pdf).

A—Responsibilities to co-workers

Ideals

I-3A.1—To establish and maintain relationships of respect, trust, confidentiality, collaboration, and cooperation with co-workers.

I-3A.2—To share resources with co-workers, collaborating to ensure that the best possible early childhood care and education program is provided.

I-3A.3—To support co-workers in meeting their professional needs and in their professional development.

I-3A.4—To accord co-workers due recognition of professional achievement.

Principles

P-3A.1—We shall recognize the contributions of colleagues to our program and not participate in practices that diminish their reputations or impair their effectiveness in working with children and families.

P-3A.2—When we have concerns about the professional behavior of a co-worker, we shall first let that person know of our concern in a way that shows respect for personal dignity and for the diversity to be found among staff members, and then attempt to resolve the matter collegially and in a confidential manner.

P-3A.3—We shall exercise care in expressing views regarding the personal attributes or professional conduct of co-workers. Statements should be based on firsthand knowledge, not hearsay, and relevant to the interests of children and programs.

P-3A.4—We shall not participate in practices that discriminate against a co-worker because of sex, race, national origin, religious beliefs or other affiliations, age, marital status/family structure, disability, or sexual orientation.

B—Responsibilities to employers

Ideals

I-3B.1—To assist the program in providing the highest quality of service.

I-3B.2—To do nothing that diminishes the reputation of the program in which we work unless it is violating laws and regulations designed to protect children or is violating the provisions of this Code.

Principles

P-3B.1—We shall follow all program policies. When we do not agree with program policies, we shall attempt to effect change through constructive action within the organization.

P-3B.2—We shall speak or act on behalf of an organization only when authorized. We shall take care to acknowledge when we are speaking for the organization and when we are expressing a personal judgment.

P-3B.3—We shall not violate laws or regulations designed to protect children and shall take appropriate action consistent with this Code when aware of such violations.

P-3B.4—If we have concerns about a colleague's behavior, and children's well-being is not at risk, we may address the concern with that individual. If children are at risk or the situation does not improve after it has been brought to the colleague's attention, we shall report the colleague's unethical or incompetent behavior to an appropriate authority.

P-3B.5—When we have a concern about circumstances or conditions that impact the quality of care and education within the program, we shall inform the program's administration or, when necessary, other appropriate authorities.

Section IV: Ethical Responsibilities to Community and Society

Early childhood programs operate within the context of their immediate community made up of families and other institutions concerned with children's welfare. Our responsibilities to the community are to provide programs that meet the diverse needs of families, to cooperate with agencies and professions that share the responsibility for children, to assist families in gaining access to those agencies and allied professionals, and to assist in the development of community programs that are needed but not currently available.

As individuals, we acknowledge our responsibility to provide the best possible programs of care and education for children and to conduct ourselves with honesty and integrity. Because of our specialized expertise in early childhood development and education and because the larger society shares responsibility for the welfare and protection of young children, we acknowledge a collective obligation to advocate for the best interests of children within early childhood programs and in the larger community and to serve as a voice for young children everywhere.

The ideals and principles in this section are presented to distinguish between those that pertain to the work of the individual early childhood educator and those that more typically are engaged in collectively on behalf of the best interests of children—with the understanding that individual early childhood educators have a shared responsibility for addressing the ideals and principles that are identified as "collective."

Ideal (Individual)

1-4.1—To provide the community with high-quality early childhood care and education programs and services.

Ideals (Collective)

I-4.2—To promote cooperation among professionals and agencies and interdisciplinary collaboration among professions concerned with addressing issues in the health, education, and well-being of young children, their families, and their early childhood educators.

I-4.3—To work through education, research, and advocacy toward an environmentally safe world in which all children receive health care, food, and shelter; are nurtured; and live free from violence in their home and their communities.

I-4.4—To work through education, research, and advocacy toward a society in which all young children have access to high-quality early care and education programs.

I-4.5—To work to ensure that appropriate assessment systems, which include multiple sources of information, are used for purposes that benefit children.

I-4.6—To promote knowledge and understanding of young children and their needs. To work toward greater societal acknowledgment of children's rights and greater social acceptance of responsibility for the well-being of all children.

I-4.7—To support policies and laws that promote the well-being of children and families, and to work to change those that impair their well-being. To participate in developing policies and laws that are needed, and to cooperate with families and other individuals and groups in these efforts.

I-4.8—To further the professional development of the field of early childhood care and education and to strengthen its commitment to realizing its core values as reflected in this Code.

Principles (Individual)

P-4.1—We shall communicate openly and truthfully about the nature and extent of services that we provide.

P-4.2—We shall apply for, accept, and work in positions for which we are personally well-suited and professionally qualified. We shall not offer services that we do not have the competence, qualifications, or resources to provide.

P-4.3—We shall carefully check references and shall not hire or recommend for employment any person whose competence, qualifications, or character makes him or her unsuited for the position.

P-4.4—We shall be objective and accurate in reporting the knowledge upon which we base our program practices.

P-4.5—We shall be knowledgeable about the appropriate use of assessment strategies and instruments and interpret results accurately to families.

P-4.6—We shall be familiar with laws and regulations that serve to protect the children in our programs and be vigilant in ensuring that these laws and regulations are followed.

P-4.7—When we become aware of a practice or situation that endangers the health, safety, or well-being of children, we have an ethical responsibility to protect children or inform parents and/or others who can.

P-4.8—We shall not participate in practices that are in violation of laws and regulations that protect the children in our programs.

P-4.9—When we have evidence that an early childhood program is violating laws or regulations protecting children, we shall report the violation to appropriate authorities who can be expected to remedy the situation.

P-4.10—When a program violates or requires its employees to violate this Code, it is permissible, after fair assessment of the evidence, to disclose the identity of that program.

Principles (Collective)

P-4.11—When policies are enacted for purposes that do not benefit children, we have a collective responsibility to work to change these policies.

P-4.12—When we have evidence that an agency that provides services intended to ensure children's wellbeing is failing to meet its obligations, we acknowledge a collective ethical responsibility to report the problem to appropriate authorities or to the public. We shall be vigilant in our follow-up until the situation is resolved.

P-4.13—When a child protection agency fails to provide adequate protection for abused or neglected children, we acknowledge a collective ethical responsibility to work toward the improvement of these services.

Statement of Commitment*

As an individual who works with young children, I commit myself to furthering the values of early childhood education as they are reflected in the ideals and principles of the NAEYC Code of Ethical Conduct. To the best of my ability I will

- Never harm children.
- Ensure that programs for young children are based on current knowledge and research of child development and early childhood education.
- Respect and support families in their task of nurturing children.
- Respect colleagues in early childhood care and education and support them in maintaining the NAEYC Code of Ethical Conduct.

---

*This Statement of Commitment is not part of the Code but is a personal acknowledgment of the individual's willingness to embrace the distinctive values and moral obligations of the field of early childhood care and education. It is recognition of the moral obligations that lead to an individual becoming part of the profession.

- Serve as an advocate for children, their families, and their teachers in community and society.
- Stay informed of and maintain high standards of professional conduct.
- Engage in an ongoing process of self-reflection, realizing that personal characteristics, biases, and beliefs have an impact on children and families.
- Be open to new ideas and be willing to learn from the suggestions of others.
- Continue to learn, grow, and contribute as a professional.
- Honor the ideals and principles of the NAEYC Code of Ethical Conduct.

Reprinted by permission of the National Association for the Education of Young Children. Copyright © 2011 by the National Association for the Education of Young Children.